# Dante In America

## *The First Two Centuries*

medieval & renaissance texts & studies

Volume 23

# Dante In America

## *The First Two Centuries*

EDITED BY

A. Bartlett Giamatti

medieval & renaissance texts & studies
Binghamton, New York
1983

*This volume has been published in collaboration with the Dante Society of America*



**Library of Congress Cataloging in Publication Data**
Main entry under title:

Dante in America.

(Medieval & Renaissance texts & studies ; 23)
1. Dante Alighieri, 1265–1321—Criticism and interpretation —Addresses, essays, lectures. 2. Dante Alighieri, 1265–1321—Appreciation—United States—Addresses, essays, lectures.
I. Giamatti, A. Bartlett. II. Series.
PQ4385.U5D36 1983 851'.1 83-2350
ISBN 0-86698-059-8

Printed in the United States of America

# Contents

# *Acknowledgement*

I wish to thank my colleagues R. W. B. Lewis, Edmund S. Morgan and John E. Smith for advice during the early stages of this project. I am also grateful to the Officers of the Dante Society who assisted me at the outset and to the current president, Robert Hollander, who has been unfailingly supportive and interested and generous with his counsel. My warm thanks also to Michele Margetts, Katherine Gardiner, and Jo Lynn Bennett for their proofreading assistance.

# Preface

In October 1974, the Council of the Dante Society of America voted to sponsor, as a Bicentennial offering, an anthology of significant essays on Dante written by Americans or by other nationals in an American context. The volume, tentatively entitled "Dante and American Intellectual Life," was intended to demonstrate the impact Dante has had on American letters and thought, broadly conceived, and was not meant to confine itself solely to literary criticism. The Council wanted representative essays from people either born in America, or born abroad but educated here, from as early as possible in America's history to the present, and from a variety of perspectives.

I undertook, at the Council's request, to edit this volume, always mindful of the general guidelines established by the Council. Using the leads furnished by a number of printed sources, chief among them the excellent study by Angelina La Piana, *Dante's American Pilgrimage,* and the advice of various colleagues, I canvassed a good deal of material and made the following selections for the following reasons.

The review by Gray was among the earliest extended pieces of writing in America on Dante that I could find; for this reason I thought it a good opening essay. Two other reasons recommended it to me: the piece established Cambridge as the seat of Dante studies in America—a tradition perpetuated not only by the distinguished Dantists who would ornament Harvard but also by the fact that the Dante Society was founded in Cambridge in 1881—and the review was also an American reaction to a translation made by an Englishman. American reactions to Dante, as to so much else, would often be shaped by English mediators. As the last essay in the volume testifies, this constant adjustment between English and American still continues, and Dante continues to engage us as we search for our language.

Da Ponte was chosen because he was not a Bostonian but an Italian who proselytized for Dante in New York. Although he does not strictly conform to the guidelines concerning American birth or training, Mozart's librettist is intrinsically interesting, he wrote in English, and a chair was founded in his name at Columbia University.

Longfellow, Norton and Lowell need little justification. Among the most distinguished devotees of Dante in American letters, each has made unique contributions to Dante studies and American writing. From Longfellow, I have chosen an excerpt from a long review to show the range of the professorial Longfellow, and, from *Poets and Poetry of Europe*, I have chosen passages of his own translations of the *Commedia*; from Norton, I chose a part of an essay on *La Vita Nuova* that struck me as interesting and that is not reprinted in *On "The Vita Nuova"* (1859); and from Lowell's very influential essay—much too long to be reprinted in its entirety—I have chosen an excerpt from the middle.

William Torrey Harris, founder and leading exponent of the "St. Louis Hegelians," wrote voluminously on Dante. From the *Journal of Speculative Philosophy*, which he founded and edited, I have chosen excerpts that seem to speak to, if they do not anticipate, more modern concerns.

The next four selections take us back again to Cambridge, specifically to Harvard, and again need little justification. Santayana continues the interest shown by professional philosophers in Dante, and here I have taken an excerpt that includes the ending of his famous essay on Dante. The next three complete essays come from the *Dante Society of America Annual Reports* and have all endured superbly. Rand was a distinguished classicist who wrote also on medieval subjects, Wilkins would become famous for, among other achievements, his studies on Petrarch, and Grandgent is among the greatest *dantisti* to have been produced by America or to have lived here.

The next selection picks up the Anglo-American conversation about Dante begun by Gray on Cary. Here, Pound reviews Binyon's *Inferno*. One might ask—why nothing from *The Spirit of Romance*? The answer is that here, as elsewhere, I have tried to provide complete selections, excerpting only when the original is too long to reprint, and that I have tried to reprint less well known selections from well known authors. *The Spirit of Romance* would require extensive cutting, and is (justifiably) widely known.

Silverstein brings us to the outbreak of World War II. I have chosen this essay from among the possible selections by this important scholar because, among other aims, I have tried to find essays not only on the *Commedia* but on other works of Dante as well. T. S. Eliot, born in St. Louis, educated at Harvard, resident of England, seems to pick up a number of the strands we have been observing. As a poet, Eliot is not simply part of the Anglo-American conversation on Dante; he embodies that conversation. As with Pound, so with Eliot I have avoided the better known writing on Dante—in Eliot's case, his immensely influential essay of 1929—and have chosen a shorter, less well known but engrossing talk he gave in 1950.

With Bigongiari, who taught at Columbia for 50 years beginning in 1904, we return to the milieu first established by Da Ponte. Indeed, Bigongiari held the Da Ponte Chair at Columbia. An exacting textual scholar and profoundly influential teacher, Bigongiari is represented by his essay on the *canzone.*

The last essays may be perceived in an order not strictly chronological. Singleton and Bergin, both scholars, editors and translators of remarkable range, are the most prominent American Dantists since the War. Singleton's widely influential views on Dante's allegory and fourfold interpretation result from historical scholarship and close textual analysis. He is represented here by a fine early essay. Bergin has always been equally concerned, though in different ways, with moral and structural issues in Dante; he is also the leading scholar of Provençal in the country. His essay on "Dante's Provençal Gallery" shows him combining these interests. Mazzeo, a noted literary scholar and expert in the history of ideas, brings erudition and clarity to some of the most difficult passages in the *Commedia*. Freccero and Hollander are our best younger Dantists. Student of Singleton at Johns Hopkins, successor of Bergin at Yale, Freccero's perspective on Dante is powerfully and persuasively his own. Hollander, noted for his comparative perspective and interest in the complexity of the transmission of poetic themes, examines the earliest and most complex of Dante's literary relationships.

Tate's and Fergusson's extraordinary essays from the 1950s testify to Dante's continuing impact on American men of letters. Tate's essay is a dense meditation on Dante's poetics; Fergusson's is a cogent appreciation of Dante's method. Translation is the matter of the last essay. Here, Fitzgerald, the greatest translator into our language of our century, examines the correspondence of Pound and Binyon about Binyon's translation of Dante. Fitzgerald also comments on other translations, notably Sayers'. It is fitting to end the volume as we began it, by listening to American comments on the efforts of Englishmen to render Dante anew. It has been a constant theme—beneath the literary, cultural and philosophical commentary—this conversation between our speech and Dante: from Gray on Cary, through Longfellow, to

Pound on Binyon, to Eliot, to Fitzgerald on the whole effort and art of translating. American culture has itself been an effort in translation; through its reaction to Dante we can see a culture grappling with a concern crucial to itself, as it was to Dante, the timeless and deeply human problem of fashioning the "parlar materno."

A. BARTLETT GIAMATTI

*July 1982*

# Dante In America

## *The First Two Centuries*

# John Chipman Gray

## [Review of *La Divina Commedia*]

1. *La Divina Commedia di Dante Alighieri.* Firenze, 1813.

2. *The Vision, or Hell, Purgatory and Paradise of Dante Alighieri, translated by the Rev. H. F. Cary, A. M. in three volumes,* 1814.

IT IS THE FATE of many of the Italian writers, to enjoy a reputation equally just and splendid in their own country, and to be comparatively little known to the rest of the world. Such has been more peculiarly the lot of Dante, one of the earliest, and if Italians are to judge, by far the greatest of them all. He has received for five centuries the title of Divine, is revered as the father of Tuscan poetry, and many of the most celebrated writers of that school have passed much of their lives in explaining his difficulties and extolling his beauties. Faults, if we may believe the greater part of them, he has none; and the more candid maintain the opinion, expressed by Alfieri in one of his manuscripts, that more is learned from the defects of Dante, than from the beauties of others. With foreign nations, these high claims are not only unacknowledged, but derided. The inscription over the gate of hell, and the stories of Francesca of Rimini and Count Ugolino, are the only parts which have been generally admired; the rest of the Divine Comedy is considered as owing the high character which it has acquired at home, to its obscurity only. Dante has been almost wholly neglected by the French, and though read by several of the English, is mentioned by none as he deserves, and by many with the most general and contemptuous censure. Lord Chesterfield has the candour or the assurance to state, that as he could not understand Dante, by great exertion, he did not believe him to be worth understanding. This we cannot but think is the real opinion of many foreigners;

while many more are deterred from the attempt by the bare reputation of the difficulty. This idea of the extreme obscurity of Dante is indeed founded, in some measure, in truth, but principally on the representations of the Italians themselves. The Divine Comedy, as Dante informs us more than once, is an allegory, and his commentators, as might be expected from the nature of the subject, have busied themselves partly in explaining, and partly in creating mysteries. After reading through some of the easier parts, and supposing ourselves in full possession of their meaning, we are told that the larger and better portion remains undiscovered, that the obscurity is greater because we do not perceive that it exists, because there is not light enough to render the darkness visible. When the commentators have agreed that an explanation is necessary, each proceeds to give his own, and overthrow those of others. We were well acquainted with one now engaged in publishing his lucubrations, who has employed sixteen years solely on this subject, and possesses great natural abilities, and he has declared repeatedly that no person but himself ever completely understood Dante, — Petrarch and Boccacio perhaps excepted. — It is indeed true, that the meaning of the allegory is too faintly disclosed to be discovered with certainty; but why should this deter us from perusing the poem? If we consider its interest heightened by looking beyond the literal meaning, the simplest, most concise, and most obvious interpretation seems in all respects to be the best. But the story itself is more easy and more interesting, and in this, as in many other fables, it is rather a concern of commentators, than of readers, what mystical meaning we should affix, or whether any, to the simple narration. We read through Homer, and scarcely look at the expositions of the moral said to be involved in his machinery; and are fully satisfied with the pleasure derived from Virgil's description of Hell, without tracing with Warburton its relation to the Eleusinian mysteries, or perplexing ourselves with the insurmountable question respecting the gates of horn and ivory.

Our language possesses a production of a humbler kind, which bears in the character of its general allegory a strong resemblance to Dante's vision; — the Pilgrim's Progress. The complete interpretation of Bunyan's dream is a task, that has baffled the efforts of mature and cultivated minds, while the narrative is the delight of children, in the humblest classes of society. To understand Dante's work, as far as we understand these, requires no uncommon strength of intellect. If the difficulties, arising both from the vocabulary and construction of the Italian language, are greater in him than in the rest of his countrymen, they are so far removed by numerous and valuable annotations, as to exact only an ordinary degree of assiduity. It is surprising that this has not been devoted to him oftener.

Another reason why Dante is so little known to the English especially, is the want of a popular translator. Hoole's versions of Ariosto and Tasso, dissimilar as they are to their simple and concise originals, have contributed in no slight degree to render them objects of general attention, and consequently general admiration. It would be more difficult and more desirable to present Dante in a translation, which should be at once accurate, spirited and harmonious, and we find little that deserves this high praise in the only two we know, —those of Boyd and Cary. Boyd has been peculiarly unfortunate in the choice of his measure. We shall select one of his most successful efforts, both to prove our remark, and to represent, even in a humble imitation, the gloomy sublimity of the inscription over the gate of Hell, —a passage which in the original is equally unexampled and inimitable.

"Through me the newly-damned forever fleet
In ceaseless shoals to Pain's eternal seat:
  Through me they march, and join the tortured crew;
The mighty gulph offended Justice made,
Unbounded Power the strong foundation laid,
  And Love, by Wisdom led, the limits drew.

  Long ere the infant world arose to light
I found a being in the womb of night
  Eldest of all—but things that ever last!
And I forever last!—Ye heirs of Hell,
Here bid at once your ling'ring hope farewell,
  And mourn the moment of repentance past."

A poem so long, and yet so concise (we trust our meaning is evident) as the Divine Comedy, requires a style of verse, which can both awaken and support our interest, by its union of sententiousness, majesty and liveliness.

Our heroic rhyme seems adapted to this purpose, far better than any other kind of English measure, for one more rapid would be too gay, and one more grave would be fatiguing. The selection of so unwieldy a species of verse is one of the slightest defects of Boyd. He has failed to give it the harmony of which it is susceptible, and by a profusion of unmeaning epithets and useless circumlocutions, he has often obscured, and generally weakened the meaning of his author. Yet Dante is deeply interesting even in Boyd's version, though we should rather refer those, who are satisfied with reading him in English, to that of Cary. This we can pronounce with confidence, to be the most literal translation in poetry in our language. Not satisfied, however, with rendering the sense, he has copied in a great degree the construction of the original. He has forced our language into Italian idioms, with a license which outrages taste, and almost violates grammar. So close is his fidelity, as he probably thought it, that while he evinces a complete knowledge of his author, he occasionally transfuses into his version the difficulties as well as the beauties of the original; and a few of the more obscure parts of the poem exact almost an equal degree of attention in the English and Italian. But if he has failed to explain with sufficient perspicuity some of the perplexing passages of Dante, he has succeeded in many more. As a mere assistant to the English reader, he deserves the greatest praise, and in doing justice to all the striking merits of the original, far excels Boyd. Cary's translation has a very short preface and a few notes. Boyd's is preceded by some just but incomplete observations on the Inferno, but the merits of the Purgatory and Paradise are not formally noticed by either. As Dante's claims to our attention have been so inadequately represented and so hastily disallowed, we shall endeavour to state them faithfully, though imperfectly, in a few remarks; an attempt rendered excusable, if not necessary, by the neglect of English writers.

Dante Alighieri was born at Florence, of noble parents, in the year 1265. We learn from the poet himself, that he was inspired, at a very early period of life (in his ninth year say his commentators) with a passion for a lady named Beatrice, and both poet and commentators assert, that his affection was purely Platonic; a supposition much more probable at that age, than at one more advanced. This passion, however, continued several years without changing its character, and so great was the influence of the lady, the docility of the poet, and the genius of both, that he derived from his acquaintance with her the wisest and purest principles. His interesting guardian was removed by death, in the twenty-sixth year of her age. Notwithstanding the purely intellectual nature of Dante's affections, their vigour soon declined, when he was deprived of her visible and corporeal presence, and as he no longer felt her influence, he ceased to regard her lessons. His unsustained inclinations soon descended to objects of a sensual nature, and led him so far in vice as to endanger imminently his eternal happiness. Beatrice, now a heavenly spirit, still watched over the destinies of her wayward pupil, and admonished him of his increasing danger by mysterious suggestions, dreams and visions. Perceiving that these means were all ineffectual, she obtained permission, as a last resort, to exhibit to him the condition of disembodied spirits, the tortures of hell, the chastisements of purgatory, and the happiness of paradise. Such are the circumstances disclosed by Beatrice, in the thirtieth canto of Purgatory; for Dante commences, like most epic poets, in the midst of events, at the period to which we have just brought our readers. The vision is supposed to have happened in the thirty-fifth year of the poet's age, A.D. 1300, and to have occupied three days. The poem opens as follows.

> In the midway of this our mortal life,
> I found me in a gloomy wood astray
> Gone from the path direct and e'en to tell
> It were no easy task, how savage wild
> That forest, how robust and rough its growth,
> Which to remember only my dismay
> Renews, in bitterness not far from death.
> How first I entered it I scarce can say,
> Such sleepy dulness in that instant weighed
> My senses down, when the true path I left;—
> But when a mountain's foot I reached, where closed
> The valley, that had pierced my heart with dread,
> I looked aloft, and saw his shoulders broad
> Already vested with that planet's beam
> Who leads all wanderers safe through every way.

On endeavouring to climb this eminence, his course is arrested by three wild beasts, a panther, a lion, and a wolf,—said by all his commentators to be images of sensuality, ambition and avarice,—who not only prevent his ascent, but pursue him into the valley. Here while flying breathless before them, he encounters a majestic figure and implores his aid. This personage announces himself to be Virgil, and after according his protection, discloses a divine commission, lately communicated to him by Beatrice, to exhibit to Dante the two inferior departments of the world of spirits,—hell and purgatory. In conformity with this command, he promises his guidance through those regions, adding that his own want of Christian faith had excluded him from Paradise, and that Beatrice herself would conduct her pupil there. Dante, after expressing a very natural diffidence, which is quickly relieved, consents to follow Virgil with implicit submission. After reading the sublime inscription already quoted, they immediately enter the gate of the infernal regions. Dante's hell, like Virgil's, is subterraneous. Its form is that of a hollow cone, the base placed at the surface of the earth, and the point at the centre; the interior is divided into circular ledges, and in these the damned are tortured by punishments of different kinds and degrees.

The indolent are not suffered to cross the river Styx, which here, as in the Eneid, forms a sort of interior boundary to the regions of woe. Dante assigns as a reason for this singular exclusion, that their lives were so inactive, so perfectly negative, that even a seat in hell would be too high an honour. They are not however permitted to wander, like Virgil's souls of the unburied, in undisturbed sadness, but are driven along in a perpetual circuit, by the stings of wasps and hornets. Immediately beyond the river is the Limbo, which bears a strong resemblance in its scenery and inhabitants, to Virgil's Elysian fields. Here are the shades of the virtuous Pagans; for Dante, with all Catholics, maintains that the want of the true faith, though resulting from blameless ignorance, is an insurmountable exclusion from eternal happiness. Virgil informs him, that here also were once confined the souls of the pious Antediluvians and Jews, but that our Saviour at his death entered this region in person and bore them off in triumph. The inhabitants of this part of the infernal world are exempted from all material tortures, and subjected to no other punishment than that of experiencing perpetual and unsatisfied desire. Dante proceeds to view, in the following circles, the pains inflicted on positive and premeditated offences. Here he has displayed his exhaustless invention, in the great number and strongly marked variety of his tortures, but more especially in the peculiar conformity of the punishments to the crimes. A distinct species of both is presented in almost every canto, but we shall illustrate our remark by slightly noticing a very few instances. The souls of incontinent lovers are hurried along in darkness, by an irresistible whirlwind, and those of suicides condemned to animate trees, and tortured by harpies who prey upon the foliage. Murderers are immersed in a torrent of boiling blood, and the heads of hypocrites concealed and weighed down by gilded cowls of lead. We find the degrees of guilt and punishment increasing as we descend, and the lowest circle is appropriated to traitors, who are inclosed in ice. At the bottom of hell, and in the centre of the earth, stands Lucifer.

After passing this point, the two poets ascend rapidly to the surface of the southern hemisphere, where they emerge into day. The Inferno is not merely a description of an ingenious variety of sufferers, tortures, and executioners. The poet seldom descends into a circle, without selecting and addressing some individual, generally of great celebrity, often one of his own countrymen; and our thoughts are frequently called off from the sombre spectacle before us, by curious and interesting narrations, vehement invectives, and apt and novel similes. Sismondi has translated his story of Francesca of Rimini, and that of Ugolino has been made known to the world by Sir Joshua Reynolds. We shall only mention in addition, the narrative of Ulysses, who informs Dante that he sailed through the pillars of Hercules, and discovered land beyond the Western ocean.[1]

On their return to the regions of light, Dante and Virgil find themselves, at early dawn, on a pyramidal island, and are immediately accosted by the shade of Cato Uticensis, who is removed, we know not why, from his Pagan brethren, and appointed governor of Purgatory.

The first canto contains a description equally remarkable for its intrinsic merits and its apt position. Nothing can be more soothing, than, after descending through the continually increasing horrors of the eternal prison, to revisit with the poets our native sphere, to breath the vital air, to contemplate again the dawn and the morning star, and gaze for the first time at the cross of the southern heavens and the majestic countenance of Cato, on which its beams are playing. With respect to its shape, Dante's Purgatory is best described by calling it his Hell reversed. It is a conical mountain;—transgressors are disposed in different circles round its sides, and its summit is crowned with the garden of Eden. Into this region those are admitted, who escaped eternal perdition by repentance previous to death. Through this the poet proceeds, and is no longer a mere spectator, as in the Inferno, but an actor in the scenes he describes. The seven deadly sins are inscribed on his forehead by an angel, and disappear one by one, as he rises through the different degrees of punishment, till he reaches the terrestrial paradise.

Here he sees a band of celestial personages, and these, after performing several solemn rites, are joined by Beatrice, who descends from heaven, like Thomson's spring, in a shower of roses. At the sight of her his passion revives in its greatest activity, and he turns round to ask the long tried assistance of Virgil, but finds that he has vanished. Beatrice orders Dante to direct his regret from the loss of a guide to his own offences; and after relating in his hearing to her heavenly companions, the history of his errours and her efforts, concludes by a direct and severe reproof, which extorts from the poet a heartfelt confession. His repentance is accepted, all remembrance of his remitted offences washed away in Lethe, and his mind, like 'a plant clothed with new foliage,' is thoroughly renovated and prepared for paradise.

The Purgatory and Paradise of Dante are either wholly neglected by foreign commentators, or styled in general terms, fallings off from his Inferno. With respect to the Purgatory, this remark, if founded in truth, is much too unqualified. Though it may seem at first less novel and striking than the Inferno, it is, in our opinion, the part of all the three, which most invites, and best rewards a repeated perusal. There is something wearying and revolting in descriptions of the hopeless tortures of our fellow-creatures, which depends on our feelings of natural humanity,—feelings too deep to be suspended by all the art of the poet. Our attention can seldom dwell on such images long, and never with unmingled pleasure. It is one of the clearest and noblest proofs of Dante's merit, that in travelling through the Inferno, we feel this disadvantage no more; but though it would be difficult to leave our journey unfinished, it would be unnatural to wish it longer. We contemplate, with far more calmness, the sufferings of the souls in Purgatory, because we can dwell on their sure prospects of future relief, because their punishments are of a milder and less degrading nature, and because the design is more evidently beneficent. The scenery, too, is more interesting than that of the Inferno, since it is more like our own, and the pathetic passages are introduced much less sparingly. There is indeed a spirit of tenderness running through every part of the Purgatory, which is deeply affecting, and shows that Dante's excellence by no means consisted solely in gloomy grandeur. So pleasing is it as a whole, that it is alike difficult to notice its defects, and select its beauties. We shall make no remarks in this place on the few faults it contains, as they are equally displayed in the two other divisions of the Divine Comedy. To beauties of the same kind with those of the Inferno, it adds many different in their nature, and equal if not superior in excellence. We have noticed already those of the first canto. The eighth opens with a description of Evening, equally natural and novel, and, in our opinion, unrivalled in simplicity and pathos by that of any writer whatever. In the tenth and twelfth he describes the figures carved on the rock, for the reproof of the proud, with a spirit and exactness as wonderful as that which he attributes to the artist. In the thirtieth are collected many of the most important and interesting parts of the poem, the descent of Beatrice, the departure of Virgil, her affecting history of the poet's life previous to the commencement of his supernatural journey, and his holy veneration and sincere remorse are all displayed with such an union of simplicity and ornament, as to render this one of the most striking portions of the whole Divine Comedy.

In his Paradise, Dante has introduced the bold and unexampled idea of peopling the spheres of the solar system, with the spirits of the blest. He ascends to them with Beatrice, in the succession in which they are placed by the Ptolemaic theory. Each planet is filled with those, whose lives were peculiarly distinguished by the virtues over which it was supposed to preside; the Moon, for instance, with holy virgins,—Mars with warriours for the

Christian faith,—Jupiter with upright judges,—Saturn with men of devout and lonely contemplation. After visiting all these, and passing through the 'Primum Mobile,' Dante ascends to the Empyrean, and there concludes his poem. In the Paradise, taken as a whole, it must be acknowledged that the reader's expectations are greatly disappointed. It is the most difficult, and happily least interesting part of the Divine Comedy. The poet is perpetually stopping to ask questions in natural philosophy and metaphysics, which after all are solved much more to his satisfaction than that of his readers. He meets with all the saints of the old and new Testaments, and with many of the most distinguished worthies of the early ages, but seems more intent on rendering his dialogues profitable than interesting, and as scholastic theology was the favourite topic of his age, it is on this he mainly dwells. Dante's Paradise would probably have been far more pleasing, had his astronomy been more enlightened. The real nature of the heavenly bodies was then scarcely suspected. We can hardly conceive the description which one of Dante's powers would have given, had he been acquainted with their similarity, as habitable spheres, to our planet, and with the variety of their magnitudes, seasons, and satellites. That even he should have failed under these circumstances is not so surprising, as that succeeding poets should have made so little use of the interesting discoveries of modern astronomy. There are however parts of the Paradise distinguished by poetical merits of every kind, in which the author displays his unincumbered genius, and more than rewards us for his perplexing and fruitless disputations. Such is the description of the triumph of the blest in the twenty-third canto, of which we shall select as many lines as our limits permit.

As in the calm full moon, when Trivia smiles
In peerless beauty, 'mid th' eternal nymphs
That deck through all its gulphs the blue profound,
In bright pre-eminence, so saw I there
O'er million lamps a sun, from whom all drew
Their radiance, as from ours the starry train

. . . Prompt I heard
Her bidding, and encountered once again
The strife of aching vision. As erewhile
Through glance of sunlight, streamed through broken cloud,
Mine eyes a flower-besprinkled mead have seen,

Though veiled themselves in shade, so saw I there
Legions of splendours, on whom burning rays
Shed lightnings from above, yet saw I not
The fountain whence they flowed.

Previous to any remark on Dante's claims to our attention, we shall devote ourselves to a task more unpleasant, but more easy,—that of stating his principal defects. There is sometimes, though rarely, the same strange mixture of truth and fable, Pagan and Christian theology, with which the whole of the Lusiad is so deeply tinctured. The early part of the poem presents us with one of the most glaring instances, in the doubt entertained of the truth of Virgil's communications, because the high privilege which they announced had never been conferred on any, but Eneas and St. Paul. We have touched upon his fondness for the metaphysics of the schools, in our remarks on his Paradise, because it is displayed principally though not exclusively there.

His work is sometimes rendered obscure by the profusion and variety of his learning, and the concise phraseology into which it is crowded. We are told in reply by his admirers, that it is not he who is obscure, but we who are stupid and ignorant, that it is only a proof of the superiority of his talents and information over ours; but we consider this as a repetition of the objection, in different terms. Authors are bound to display their knowledge intelligibly, or not at all. We look to them for information, and must be permitted to complain, when we are told that if we were as wise as our masters, their lessons would be perfectly intelligible. We would ask how far in that case their instructions would be necessary or useful? For most of these general defects we may offer a brief and weighty apology,—that they were those of his time, and that they have been imitated by the most celebrated poets in more enlightened days. There are in the Inferno two short passages for which this excuse, were it true, would be insufficient. The punishment appropriated to flatterers, seducers, and parasites, at the end of the eighteenth canto, is too offensive to be described in any way whatever. This passage is indeed countenanced by translators and praised by commentators, but it is in vain to tell us, that it is as well expressed as the subject admits, that no punishment could be too degrading for such characters, and that no class of offenders deserved it better. Allowing these reasons all possible weight, we still maintain that Dante, in his detail of sufferings, should have considered not only what could be justly inflicted, but what could be decently told. We may object also to the vulgar incident related at the end of the twenty-first canto, and the jocular comment upon it with which the next commences; for the humour, which the lines really contain, is too low to render them tolerable, in a poem of much less solemnity and majesty. These passages excepted, the Divine Comedy, long and varied as it is, contains nothing offensive to the most refined ears. There is one well known habit of Dante, which we think an errour merely because he has followed it too constantly,—the lightness, we may say the negligence, with which he introduces many of his most beautiful figures. He just points to their principal features, leaves the rest to our imagination and hurries onward. We complain, we think with reason, that he has so very unfrequently endeavoured to amplify his allusions; the more so because those rare attempts are always successful. Poets, as observed by Lucan, should present by turns the close and the open flower. The same genius which selected the figure, may sometimes be necessary to develop its latent beauties; and if it is a merit to be able to condense, it is a charm to be willing to display.

In attempting to do justice to the merits of Dante's poem, we should consider for a moment the age when it was composed. It was in the beginning of the fourteenth century,—before any of the present languages of Europe were established, before our own poetry commenced with the rude and now obsolete strains of Chaucer,—that Dante presented the world with the first specimen of Tuscan, we may say of modern literature. It was then that he formed by his Divine Comedy a language, which his succeeding countrymen have gloried in preserving unaltered, to which foreign nations have united in resigning the palm for flexibility and harmony, and which divides with our own the claim to the highest reputation in European poetry. But if it is little considered that he was the earliest writer of any celebrity in the living languages, it is scarcely known, to strangers at least, how rich a source of ideas and expressions his work has proved to others. Many of the most admired passages in those Italian poets, whose celebrity is more general than his, are closely imitated, if not exactly transcribed from the Divine Comedy. Ariosto's idea of sending Astolpho to the moon is a natural and easy improvement of part of Dante's Paradise. No portion of the Jerusalem Delivered excites more interest than Tancred's adventures in the wood, which was peopled by the incantations of Armida; and yet after reading the account of that, in which Dante has lodged the souls of his suicides, we must allow that Tasso has little of his own except the style. It would be endless to repeat the many passages, which (though unacknowledged and unhonoured) he has furnished to the celebrated English writers, who had read him, and the many more derived from him indirectly by those who had not. For a large number of the most beautiful flowers of modern poetry, the credit is due to him as the first if not the only discoverer. As there are few from whom so much has been drawn, so there are few who have borrowed less.

The first and highest merit of a poet, originality, is apparent in every feature of his production, in its general plan, its narrative and didactic portions, its machinery and its allusions. But novelty, though the universal characteristic, is far from being the sole recommendation of the various efforts of his genius. Of his sublimity foreign critics have formed high but limited ideas. They have seen it principally in the Inferno, and finding it there, as it should be, dark and terrific, have concluded that Dante's genius, like Young's, was distinguished only by sombre energy. The study of his Purgatory and Paradise would convince them he could display a sublimity milder and more serene, that he could vary it with the nature of his subjects, dissimilar as they are. The dryest and most hopeless are never without it long. Even in all the chaos of his most perplexed scholastic disputations, we are occasionally relieved and illuminated, by an idea equally true, novel and sublime.

The sacred influence
Of light appears, and from the walls of heaven
Shoots far into the bosom of dim night
A glimmering dawn.

Dante's tenderness, though, like his sublimity, all his own, sometimes reminds us of that of his adored Virgil. We perceive it in his narratives, his reflections and his discourses; but in nothing more than in his figures. This is the merit, by which, if by any one more than another, his similes and allusions are distinguished. He was, like all the greatest poets, a close observer, warm admirer and lively describer of nature. No object was too latent or too insignificant for his notice. But he drew from this universal source with the originality of an elevated mind. He presents no cold and trite images of the daily operations and ordinary beauties of the material world; his figures are either wholly original, or if he ever selects the more commonly observed objects, he develops some charm unknown before; he gives them some striking personification, he annexes some circumstance calculated to touch the feelings, as well as enliven the fancy. A few examples will illustrate our meaning more concisely and completely than any thing else we can add. The following is so much more copious than most of his comparisons, that no previous explanation is necesssary.

In the year's early nonage, when the Sun
Tempers his tresses in Aquarius' urn,
And now towards equal day the night recedes;
When as the frost upon the earth puts on
Her dazzling sister's image, but not long
Her milder sway endures, then riseth up
The village hind, whom fails his wint'ry store,
And looking out beholds the plain around
All whitened, then impatiently he smites
His thighs, and to his hut returning in
There paces to and fro, and wails his lot
As a discomfited and helpless man.
Then comes he forth again and feels new hope
Spring in his bosom, finding e'en thus soon
The world hath changed its countenance, grasps his crook
And forth to pasture drives his little flock.
So me my guide disheartened when I saw
His troubled countenance, and so speedily
That ill was cured.

Cary, *Inf.*, C. 25.

With what an appropriate and impressive aspect has he invested the morning star by a single line!

About the hour,
As I believe, when Venus from the east
First lightened on the mountain, she whose orb
Seems always glowing with the fire of love.

Cary, *Purg.*, C. 27.

We may observe his power of giving an unexpected interest to the most ordinary operations of nature, in his description of the reflection of the rays of heaven from earth;

They "upward rise
E'en as a pilgrim bent on his return."

Cary, *Par.*, C. 1.

How is the mind refreshed, after an incessant contemplation of supernatural objects, by the following rural images.

> . . . As the goats
> That late have skipped and wantoned rapidly
> Upon the craggy cliffs, ere they had ta'en
> Their supper on the herbs, now silent lie
> And ruminate beneath the umbrage brown,
> While noonday rages and the goatherd leans
> Upon his staff, and leaning watches them.
>
> Cary, *Purg.*, C. 27.

> E'en as the bird, who midst the leafy bower
> Has in her nest sat darkling through the night
> With her sweet brood, impatient to descry
> Their wished looks and to bring home their food,
> In the fond quest unconscious of her toil,
> She of the time prevenient, on the spray
> That overhangs their couch, with wakeful gaze
> Expects the sun; nor ever till the dawn
> Removeth from the east her eager ken;—
> So stood the dame erect and bent her glance
> Wistfully on that region.
>
> Cary, *Purg.*, C. 23.,

But it is his own species which furnishes to Dante his most animated and interesting figures. Their daily occupations, their domestic life, their very manners, amusements and dress, have all been made subservient to his ever wakeful genius. We shall commence our selections with two comparisons drawn from the latter sources, as most strongly illustrative of his comprehensive yet exact observation. The poet likens his own situation, when thronged in purgatory by a crowd of eager spirits, to that of a gambler when rising from the table.

> When from the game of dice men separate,
> He, who hath lost, remains in sadness fixed,
> Revolving in his mind what luckless throws
> He cast; but meanwhile all the company

Go with the other; one before him runs
And one behind his mantle twitches, one
Fast by his side bids him remember him.
He stops not, and each one to whom his hand
Is stretched well knows he bids him stand aside,
And thus he from the press defends himself;
E'en such was I in that close-crowding throng,
And turning so my face around to all
And promising, I 'scaped from it with pains.

Cary, *Purg.*, C. 6.

The following figures are introduced to illustrate the indistinctness of some of the airy phantoms of paradise.

As from translucent and smooth glass or wave
Clear and unruffled, flowing not so deep
As that its bed is dark, the shape returns
So faint of our impictured lineaments,
That on white forehead set a pearl as strong
Comes to the eye,—such saw I many a face
All stretched to speak.

Cary, *Par.*, C. 3.

If he has the power of giving a new dignity to the most ordinary subjects, he has no less that of doing justice to the more important and interesting. With what accuracy and delicacy has he represented the finest feelings of the female heart!

. . . My view
Reverted to those lofty things, which came
So slowly moving towards us, that the bride
Would have outstripped them on her bridal day.

Cary, *Purg.*, C. 29.

And as the unblemished dame, who in herself
Secure from censure, yet at bare report
Of other's failing, shrinks with maiden fear
So Beatricé in her semblance changed.

Id, *Par.* C. 27.

To these descriptions of female modesty we may add the following of maternal tenderness.

> . . . Suddenly my guide
> Caught me, e'en as a mother that from sleep
> Is by the noise aroused and near her sees
> The climbing fires, who snatches up her babe
> And flies, ne'er pausing, careful more of him
> Than of herself, though but a single vest
> Clings round her limbs
>
> Id. *Inf.*, C. 23.

> After utterance of a piteous sigh, She towards me bent her eyes with such a look As on a frenzied child a mother casts.
>
> Cary, *Par.*, C. 1.

But Dante's favourite subjects of allusion are the simplicity, helplessness, and playfulness of infancy. Every one has admired in Goldsmith a figure of which the application only is original.

> . . . Towards Virgil I
> Turned me to leftward, panting like a babe
> That flies for refuge to his mother's breast
> If aught have terrified or done him harm.
>
> Id. *Purg.*, C. 30.

In the twenty-seventh Purg. Virgil conquers Dante's unwillingness to proceed, by presenting to his mind the idea of his approaching meeting with Beatrice. Dante hesitates no longer on overcoming his transient waywardness, and Virgil

> . . . Smiles as one would smile
> Upon a child that eyes the fruit and yields.

In the twenty-seventh Par. a portion of the heavenly host are represented under the form of celestial flames;

And like to babe that stretches forth its arms
For very eagerness toward the breast
After the milk is taken, so outstretched
Their wavy summits all the fervent band
Through zealous love to Mary.

The last figure we shall quote not only serves to illustrate the tenderness of many of his images, but evinces his skill in comparing together objects of the most remote and opposite nature.

. . . Heaven's sphere that ever whirls
As restless as an infant in his play.

Cary, *Par.*, C. 15.

These extracts are, we think, sufficient to show that Dante's reflections on nature are not those of one who studies her only in retirement and observes only her simplest forms.

But his knowledge of the human heart was not confined to the tenderer feelings. His remarks on sentiments of every species, whether made in his own person or those of the spirits to whom he listens, are so acute and profound as to prove that he had studied human life in its most refined, complicated and disguised state, and what is more, are so lively and confident as to shew that he spoke from experience as well as reason. As few possessed a mind like his, so few have enjoyed so largely the double advantage of contemplating mankind in solitude and society, or united in so eminent a degree the active and contemplative life. The nature of his work precludes him in a great measure from drawing particular human characters; but we may find proofs of his power in this respect, in the peculiar propriety of the speeches uttered by some of the most remarkable of his departed spirits. We refer as striking examples to those of Capaneus and Vanni Fucci in the fourteenth and twenty-fifth Cantos of the Inferno. We would rely still more on his occasional reflections, but above all, on his vehement and eloquent invectives, as proofs of his knowledge of the hearts of men and his power of communicating it to others. He possessed all that acute and discriminating satire so necessary to give effect to the observations of the most profound genius on the endless variety of human errour. Where shall we find it exercised with a greater union of ingenuity and earnestness than in his address to the

Popes in the nineteenth Inferno, the observations on Italy and more particularly on Florence in the sixth Purgatory (so highly extolled by Sismondi) and the contrast between the apostles and cardinals in the twenty-first Paradise?

To Dante is eminently due the credit, which Hayley gives so justly to Cowper, of the rare union of sublimity, pathos and wit. We know indeed that he possessed the latter, by a few humorous passages in the Inferno; but as we consider them misplaced in a poem like his, we had rather have remained ignorant of the fact, than have learned it from those sources only. But we are not obliged to resort to these. We find his wit elsewhere displayed as it should be, sometimes in direct reproof, but more frequently in that contemptuous and bitter irony, which adds new dignity to the most solemn and majestic eloquence. To natural powers, so great in number, so various in kind, so eminent in degree, to the highest proficiency in "the proper study of mankind," Dante united an extraordinary share of classical learning, and a freedom in that age no less extraordinary from classical pedantry. His work often displays his obligations to his predecessors, but always in a manner which diminishes nothing of his own credit; sometimes by beautiful allusions, sometimes by improvements on their ideas, which show a genius equal at least to theirs;—but never by tediously quoting or servilely imitating. He acknowledges in express terms the advantages he has derived from the perusal of their works. To Virgil, in particular, he attributes the style on which he rests his own reputation.

> Glory and light of all the tuneful train,
> May it avail me that I long with zeal
> Have sought thy volume and with love immense
> Have conned it o'er. My master thou and guide,
> Thou he, from whom alone I have derived
> That style which for its beauty into fame
> Exalts me.
>
> Cary, *Inf.*, C. 1.

Yet his work is so little a copy of the Eneid, that the merits of his thoughts and language, even when of the same general nature as those of his master, are varied from them by strong and original characteristics; and his defects are precisely those, from which Virgil is of all poets most exempt. Does not the example of Dante serve to show that the deep study and warm admiration of the classics produces a servile imitation of them only in men of inferior understanding or perverted taste,—that an author of a great and properly cultivated mind will and must be original,—that they will assist and not encumber his genius, and that he will read them rather to avoid than repeat what has been said before? The purity of Dante's language is sufficiently proved by the circumstance, that in a poem of 13000 lines there are not more than two or three hundred obsolete words. For clear and majestic conciseness of style he was probably the model, and we believe his own countrymen think an unequalled one, to all the distinguished poets of Italy. We could speak highly from experience of the effect produced by the harmony of his work, notwithstanding its foreign language and novel measure, but will not dwell on points so obvious to the senses of every reader. Dante's production exhibits that union of mental and moral excellence too rare in the works of poets. Others have said that if their writings are licentious, their lives were chaste. We think that as far as respects society the offence would be much lighter, and the apology much more sufficient, could they say, as Dante might do, that if their lives were faulty, their verses are pure. In the Divine Comedy, as in the Jerusalem Delivered, there is not a single licentious passage. Its moral tendency is evident in every line. Its pictures of rewarded virtue are of the most animating nature, and it exhibits vice in the most discouraging situations, detected and punished, tortured in hopeless misery, or forgiven only after rigorous chastisement and bitter remorse. Yet his morality was pure without austerity, for how severely does he censure those who give way to causeless melancholy;—

> . . . Man can do violence
> To himself and his own blessings, and for this,
> He in the infernal world must aye deplore
> With unavailing penitence his crime,
> Whoe'er deprives himself of life and light,
> In reckless lavishment his talent wastes,
> Or sorrows there, where he should dwell in joy.
>
> Cary, *Inf.*, C. 11.

Not satisfied with pursuing his end merely by directing our attention to the offences of others, he does not scruple to unveil his own. We not only accompany him in his travels and listen to his precepts, but are the confidents of his errors. Few authors have excited an interest so deep for the characters of their heroes, as that with which Dante has inspired us for his own. He possesses a power, partly resulting from the varied excellencies which we have attempted to point out, and partly from a certain something, which we confess ourselves unable to describe, of producing in his readers the most undivided and unwearied attention. Even in the dryest passages we are impelled to hurry on, but never induced to desist. We need say but little of a poem possessing a merit like this; and instead of enforcing any longer Dante's claims to our attention, we have only to advise our readers to overcome the difficulty at first presented by the language, and they will enforce themselves.

Those of our own poets whom Dante most resembles are Shakspeare, Milton, and Cowper. With Shakspeare he was the poet of nature, with Milton that of the invisible world, with Cowper that of Christian morality. He reminds us sometimes of Shakspeare, by his insight into the human heart in the highest and humblest situations, by his beautiful allusions to the works of nature, and his power of presenting a crowd of ideas in a single word. His similarity to Cowper appears more frequently in the strain of his moral sentiment, now lofty and now tender, in the indignant satire of his reflections and harangues, and the uniform direction of it where it is best deserved. Milton resembles him so much more generally and strongly than any other English poet, that we shall conclude by a slight sketch of some of their principal points of likeness and contrast. Were other evidence wanting, the bare perusal of the two poems proves that Milton has largely imitated Dante. It is to Dante that the credit is due for the bold and novel sublimity of the general plan of both works, for which English critics, from a want either of knowledge or of candour, have combined in extolling their own countryman. It was Dante that first drew aside the starry curtain which surrounds us, and created definite regions worthy the sublime but mysterious ideas which Christianity had given us of the invisible world. In the description of the beings who people those realms, Milton has varied from all preceding poets by committing a capital error. We allude to that, so well developed by Johnson, of "perplexing his poetry with his philosophy, of making his infernal and celestial powers sometimes pure spirit and sometimes animated matter." With the exception of one or two instances of trifling inadvertence, Dante has avoided this difficulty by not attempting impossibilities. He has been satisfied with giving to the inhabitants of his triple kingdom, the qualities of airy phantoms, sufficiently material to possess a definite and unvarying form, and yet so unsubstantial as to elude the grasp of earthly objects.—

> . . . On shadows vain,
> Except in outward semblance! thrice my hands
> I clasped behind it, they as oft returned
> Empty into my breast again.

Cary, *Purg.*, C. 2.

By the time in which Milton has chosen to place the action of Paradise Lost, he has precluded himself from an advantage of which Dante well knew how to estimate the value. Milton has selected a period when the pages of history were a blank, and the realms of death a void, and his scenes of happiness and woe are destitute of the spirits so interesting above all others to mankind, — those of their departed fathers. The Paradise Lost, like the Divine Comedy, opens with a view of Hell, but Milton's description of punishments consists altogether in a few general, though beautiful passages, and its effects on the mind and heart are far feebler than those of Dante's narration. This possesses all the merits of Milton's, and adds to them a degree of copiousness and distinctness, which produces an impression both more violent and lasting. Of all the ingenious variety of Dante's punishments, Milton scarcely employs any, but those of darkness and fire; but his fire is less intense, and his darkness less deep. Dante's hell is a terrific dungeon; every thing within it is made subservient solely to the purposes of torture; — Milton's, a world diversified by many of the features, and stored with all the treasures of our own. Hence, instead of the shuddering horror which overpowers the whole soul at the view of Dante's representations, we contemplate the situation of Milton's demons with an undisturbed and not unpleasing pensiveness. When we see them sitting in quiet consultation on the jewelled thrones of Pandemonium, repeating like the heroes in Virgil's Elysium their military exercises, employing themselves in retirement on those metaphysical perplexities so pleasing to some of the best of our own race, or listening to music of celestial origin, we feel little inclined to dispute the opinion of Belial, that their situation might be altered greatly for the worse, or ridicule the hope of Mammon, that time and custom might render it more than tolerable. Dante's description of the prince of hell, as well as his kingdom, short as it is, is far more appropriate than Milton's. The Lucifer of the Inferno evinces his torture by speechless anguish, and his disposition by the most fiend-like actions. The poet has divested him of all that could excite even a doubtful admiration; and if he has left him any thing of his former grandeur, it is only to increase our terror. He recalls to us his ancient splendour only to render him still more detestable. —

> . . . If he were beautiful
> As he is hideous now, and yet did dare
> To scowl upon his maker, well from him
> Might all our misery flow.

How often and how justly has Milton been censured for giving so frequently to Satan's character the semblance at least of heroism. If there is all that we abhor, there is much that we admire. Such is human nature that we cannot but respect the dignity with which he fills the throne even of hell, the readiness he constantly displays to be foremost to act and suffer for the advantage of his community, the lofty spirit which enables him to feel or to feign a hope in the most desperate circumstances. When he verifies his promises to his subjects by his journey to the newly created world, we contemplate with admiration his bold and novel enterprise, detestable as was its object and ruinous as were its effects. We are willing to excuse him from any imputation of meanness in the various disguises he assumes after reaching the sphere of day, for we look upon them as stratagems allowed by the customs of every species of warfare. When they are detected and exposed, we are strongly inclined to praise the courage worthy a better cause, with which he singly confronts Gabriel at the head of legions of Angels. Scarcely any part of Paradise Lost exceeds in poetical merit his account of his motives, condition and designs, contained in his address to the Sun; but does its perusal inspire us with the unmingled detestation due to the great adversary of our race and our Maker? This speech has been praised as containing no ideas derogatory to the Deity. His perfections are indeed stated justly, but this very circumstance greatly disarms our indignation against an adversary who could acknowledge them so fairly. How are we inclined to forget Satan's malignity, when we find him displaying, with the most unsparing justice, his own ingratitude, disclosing the real feelings excited by the mistaken admiration of his associates, half resolved to seek pardon by submission, and deterred from it by a prevailing frailty of our own,—the dread of shame, and by a rational belief that his repentance could be but transient. It is only after being obliged to bid farewell to hope, that he forms the resolution of divesting himself of remorse, of placing his sole good in evil, and of achieving the destruction of unoffending man. He preserves every where the same gloomy greatness; he always elicits our pity and commands our respect in the character of an "Arch Angel ruined." He may well be compared to the Sun in a partial eclipse, shedding every where around him a light faded and solemn, but by no means terrific or baleful.

If we follow Milton to the celestial regions, we shall find that he was largely indebted to Dante for particular passages, as well as for the general plan of his heaven. In his account of the celestial hosts, he has followed him much less closely. Dante has not attempted in his Paradise the delineation of any particular angelic characters. His seraphs are not like Milton's,—images of men,—they are presented to us in a thousand varieties of form and degrees of distinctness. If his Paradise is destitute of any thing similar to the lively and well discriminated characters of Michael, Abdiel and Raphael, it is also free from the celestial battles and their concomitant absurdities, which fill the sixth book of Paradise Lost. Milton's descriptions of the Deity have a radical defect, which we think places them far below Dante's. An equal proportion of both poems is occupied by tedious metaphysical subtilties, but those of Dante are limited to inferior spirits, while those of Milton are appropriated to their sovereign. The Creator in Paradise Lost, explains his designs, justifies his proceedings and expresses his feelings, not always in the most dignified language. We grant that a part of these difficulties necessarily resulted from Milton's idea of giving us clearer and more definite conceptions of the Divinity; but we think the main error lies in the project itself. He has committed a fault similar to that of those Italian painters, who have represented the Eternal Father under a visible image. Every one who has seen such pictures, will bear witness to their tendency to narrow and lower our ideas. To give to the Deity an earthly language, is an attempt nearly as perilous as to invest him with an earthly form. When he is made a definite object of perception to any of our senses, our thoughts lose in sublimity more than they gain in distinctness. The Supreme Being of Dante is rather a Power than a person; he is represented as pervading the 'whole ocean of existence;' he is described in no other manner than by the most distant allusion; we see his attributes only in his works, and hear his commands only through his ministers; he every where impresses us with that mysterious sublimity so appropriate to our most natural and noble ideas of an infinite being. If we except a few fine passages, Milton's peculiar excellence lies in his descriptions of the scenery and inhabitants of Eden. Every touch of his native earth seems to renew his vigour; it is here that he excels not only Dante, but every other poet. Dante's Eden,—*Paradiso Terrestre*,—has little terrestrial except the name. All things in it are allegorical, and we cannot but perceive that they are so. The soil is watered by rivers of a magic virtue, the atmosphere filled with supernatural splendor, we are surrounded by airy visions, and find the whole uninteresting in proportion as it is unearthly. Above all, it is destitute of the latest and highest charm of the Eden we have been accustomed to contemplate,—human love. Hence, Dante's description excites sensations far less lively and touching than those resulting from the perusal of Milton's, and as there is nothing to recall them in the world around us, their hold on the memory is comparatively transient.

Thus in the sun-thaw is the snow unsealed,

Thus in the winds on flitting leaves was lost
The Sybil's sentence.

Cary, *Par.*, 33.

We find in Milton's Paradise all the natural beauties of our own earthly regions, in their highest excellence and most boundless variety; we breathe an atmosphere as pure as Dante's, but more substantial, and feel that we are roaming through a portion of our native home. Instead of the refined, vague and unintelligible affection of Dante for Beatrice, Milton presents us with the union of the hearts of our first parents in their orisons, labours and relaxations, developing with equal simplicity and acuteness the mixed nature of that passion, which can be imagined and may be felt by every one,—displaying all that is intellectual, without obscurity, and all that is sensual, without grossness. Dante is the poet of our hours of sober contemplation. When we would escape for a season from the vexations of life, when we would relinquish awhile its pleasures and labours that we may resume them with renovated interest and unclouded judgment, we may accompany Dante through regions far beyond the sphere of all earthly objects and feelings. Milton's description merely of the inanimate and irrational charms of Paradise will render his memory as lasting as the beauty of rural scenery; and his name could scarcely be better known, or more certainly transmitted, were it engraved on every rock and inscribed on every flower. But he has fixed it far more deeply in human hearts, by his description of the passion which so generally sways them; and his Eden must interest all but the few, who can contemplate with insensibility, not only the charms of nature, but the happiness of domestic life.

## Notes

1. Our readers will recollect that this poem was written nearly two hundred years before the discoveries of Columbus.

# Lorenzo Da Ponte

## Critique on Certain Passages in Dante

*To the Editors of the Atheneum Magazine.*

GENTLEMEN,—In the course of my investigations of the difficulties which the language and manner of Dante occasionally present, I have been led to believe, that in ten or twelve instances at least, in the Inferno alone, modes of interpretation might be offered, which would reconcile the objections of the critics, and remove all doubts of the meaning of the author. Of these, I now subjoin the first, reserving the others for another opportunity.

INF. CANT. I. V. 29, 30.
Ripresi via per la piaggia deserta
Sicchè il piè fermo sempre era il più basso.

In order to ascertain the actual situation, position, and movement of Dante, we ought to go back to verse 13.

Ma poi ch'io fui appiè del colle giunto
Là ove terminava quella valle—

and give to the expression *appiè del colle*, a signification, similar to that conveyed by the following line from one of Petrarch's sonnets:

Appiè de' colli ove la bella vesta.

Here every one will admit that the poet does not speak of a place *actually adjoining*, but merely of a place *very near* the foot of the hills, in which place Laura was born, and where too the five *pernici*, supposed to be referred to by the poet, ranged while they lived "unhindered and unhurt."

There appear to me to be two good reasons for this interpretation. First, Dante in order to express perfect contact, makes use, elsewhere, of a much stronger expression. I refer to the 134th verse, of the 17th canto of the Inferno:

Appiè appiè della stagliata rocca

Secondly, if Dante had been actually at the foot of the hill, in the strict sense of the word, he could not possibly have seen its summit,[1] "clad in the sun's bright rays." Let us now examine how this construction agrees with the context.

Dante, "in the middle of the way of life," finds himself in the forest of Error. He cannot tell how he came there, but merely recollects, that a moment previous, he was "oppressed with sleep," that is, in a state of intellectual unconsciousness, arising from the violence of his passions. In this "rugged, wild, and gloomy" forest, he loses his way, and soon after, finds himself (he either will not or cannot tell how) at the foot of a hill, bounding this valley or forest. Alarmed at this, he raises his eyes to the summit of the hill, and there sees the rays of the sun. *Allor fu la paura un poco queta*, and he turns round to look upon the pass *che non lasciò giammai persona viva*, that is, *lasciò passar*, or in other words—the pass which no living soul ever omitted, or was exempted from passing. Then—

Riprese via per la piaggia deserta—

and this brings us to the difficulty.

It would be difficult to persuade me, that this *piaggia deserta* means the beginning of the *ascent*. Dante says expressly, that he resumed his previous way, or walked again along the *piaggia*,

Sicchè il piè fermo sempre era il più basso,

and then began to ascend. This ascent is moreover announced by an emphatic *Ed ecco*, denoting that then, and not till then, did the rise begin.

To conclude—

Ripresi via per la piaggia deserta,

I resumed my way along the solitary *plain*, (where alone *il piè fermo* sempre *è il più basso*,) and walked toward the hill, — that is, toward the seat of truth; but in such a way, that my firm foot was always lower than the other. This I take to mean, I still continued in the path of error, not daring to ascend the hill of truth. After going a short distance, and just as I had reached the beginning of the rise, my further progress is opposed by Pleasure, Pride, and Avarice, so much so that, (to repeat Dante's *jeu de mots*,)

Back to return, at every turn I turned.

In this way, the literal sense is abundantly perspicuous, and the allegorical extremely apt and beautiful.

*L. Da Ponte*
*[July, 1825]*

GENTLEMEN,

Among the arguments I offered, in my last communication, to support the interpretation I proposed, of the thirtieth line of the first canto of Dante's Inferno, I omitted to call your attention to the thirty-first line:

And lo! not far from the hill's first ascent —[2]

which not only points out the place of the first appearance of the panther, but shows conclusively that Dante had *not yet* reached the "cominciar dell' erta" — the beginning or foot of the ascent; because the interjection *ecco* is almost always used to denote the time and place of the first appearance of a new object, or the first occurrence of a new event. If Dante was prevented from going further by the "panther," when this panther was only "*quasi* al cominciar dell' erta," it follows of course that Dante had not yet arrived at the foot of the hill, his progress towards it being intercepted by the panther. — I now pass on to another passage, which appears to me to have been always strangely misunderstood.

INF. CANT. III. v. 109, 111.
Caron dimonio, con occhi di bragia
Loro accennando tutte le raccoglie,
Batte col remo qualunque s' adagia.

The commentators have uniformly made *batte* an active verb, and have agreed to consider this last line as meaning—that Charon, impatient at the delay,

> Beats soundly with his oar the loitering shades!

Let us see how this strange commentary is supported by the context. At verse 71, Dante seeing a great number of souls collecting on the bank of a river, turns to his conductor, saying,

> Master, give me to know what souls are these,
> And what is that which makes them seem, (for so
> Even through this feeble light to me they seem)
> In *such swift haste* to pass from shore to shore.

At verse 111, 117, these souls, which according to the commentators, require the stimulus of Charon's oar, (a long oar by the way, he must have had,) are described in the beautiful similitudes of Dante, as hastening to the boat

> Like autumn foliage dropping to the ground,
> Or falcons stooping to the fowler's call.[3]

Again, at verse 124, Virgil says that these 'lazy' souls, who, like asses at a ferry, must, it seems, be beaten with an oar to make them move, are always eager to get over; because, to use the poet's own strong language,

> The justice of their Judge so pricks them on,
> That fear is lost in longing.

Surely, such a commentary has no need of comment. The following is the explanation I would offer. Charon, says the poet,

> With eyes of fire, and guiding glance and sign
> Gathers them all together.

With what *sign*?—The answer, one would think was obvious enough: the 'grim ferryman' *batte col remo*;—strikes with his oar,—and then—*qualunque s' adagia*—each one takes his seat in Charon's barque,[4] and that willingly, and even eagerly; because in the words of Dante, above translated,

La divina giustizia gli sprona
Sì che la tema si volge in disio.

*L. Da Ponte.*
*[August 1825]*

INF. CANT. V. 77, 78.

Vedrai quando saranno
Più presso a noi: e tu allor gli prega
Per quell' amor ch' *ei* mena; e quei verranno.

Thou shalt see,
When they are nearer; then, adjure them by
That love which is their lord, and they will come.

Venturi tells us, that *ei* is here taken in the sense of *eglino*; but yet, he adds with great gravity, you cannot say *eino* instead of *eglino*; whereupon he utters maledictions against the absurdities of grammar. Volpi, I believe, has closed his eyes upon this passage, as well as the Avignon editor, who on more occasions than one, shows himself marvellously clever in getting round a difficulty. Lombardi has recourse to a ridiculous paraphrasis, and Biagioli thinks *ch' ei mena* means *ch' ei mena insieme*, which might answer, if we make *ei* the nominative case singular, referring to *amore*. It is certainly very singular, that amidst such a variety of explanation, not a commentator among them all appears to have suspected the interpretation which I take to be undoubtedly the true one, and which one would think is almost as obvious as it is completely satisfactory. To have the right reading, it is not necessary to alter a letter or a stop; in the word *ei* detach the *i* from the *e*, and every thing is clear.

E tu gli prega
Per quell' amor che i mena, e quei verranno.

The pronoun *i* is then in the objective case plural, for *li* or *gli*, and this is so far from being a harsh construction, that we have the authority of Dante himself for this identical license.

La sconoscente vita *che i* fe sozzi.

INF. CANT. VII. V. 53.

In the same way, another sentence which has been considered an obscure one, is made perfectly intelligible. Let the eighteenth verse of the eighteenth canto of the Inferno be printed thus;

Infino al pozzo che i tronca e raccogli;

and all the forced and far-fetched explanations of the commentators fall to the ground as useless or absurd.

INF. CANT. IX v. 7, 8.
Pure a noi converrà vincer la pugna,
Cominciò ei—se non—tal ne s' offerse.

The commentators, without exception, consider the pronoun *tal* as referring here to Beatrice. With all due respect to that "donna gentile," I cannot help thinking that the angel is the person here alluded to, and that for these three reasons: First, because the lady Beatrice did not offer any personal assistance to Dante, but merely solicited in his behalf the services of Virgil; and after having thus addressed him,

Or muovi, e con la tua parola ornata,
E con ciò ch'è mestieri al suo campare
L'ajuta sì ch'io ne sia consolata;

she then told him her name, and her desire to return to the place she had left, and concluded, by assuring him that she would not forget to speak well of him when she went back to Heaven.

Quando sarò d'avanti al Signor mio
Di te mi loderò sovente a lui.

Secondly, because *ne s' offerse* does not so much signify, "offered her assistance," as "made her appearance to us," and seems to have reference to the passage,

E già di quà da lei discende l' erta
Passando per li cerchi senza scorta
*Tal* che per lui ci fia la terra aperta.

And thirdly, because *tal ne s' offerse*, with *ne* in the plural number, is scarcely compatible with the interpretation hitherto received, but peculiarly appropriate to the one I have proposed. Beatrice appeared only to Virgil, but the Angel was then descending to present himself before Virgil while Dante was with him, as appears by the verses we have quoted above.

How the aposiopesis, *se non*—, is to be supplied, it is perhaps not very easy to determine. But it is probable that Virgil was on the point of saying something which was either disagreeable to Dante, or at least calculated to increase his apprehensions; for instance, "if Beatrice has not deceived us," "if Heaven has not altered its decrees," or something similar; and then suddenly correcting himself, or recollecting the promises of the Angel, finished his sentence in the tone and language of encouragement.

I add a short remark on the third line of the first Canto.

> Che la diritta via era smarrita.

To say that *che* has in this place, the meaning of *talmente chè*, or *perocchè*, or *perchè*, which is the explanation almost universally given, is certainly a mistake. Biagioli is the only annotator who has pointed out the error and inconsistency of this interpretation. He agrees with Volpi, that there is here an ellipsis of the preposition *in*, but neither he, nor Volpi, adduces any classical authority for the use of *che* in the sense of *in che*. There exists, however, a remarkable and conclusive instance of this kind in Petrarch, Part I. Son. II v. 1.

> Era il giorno *che* al Sol si scoloraro.

Dante himself furnishes another example, INF. CANT. I. V. 11.

> Tanto era pien di sonno in su quel punto
> *Che* la verace via abbandonai.

*L. Da Ponte.*

# Notes

1. *Spalle* certainly means the summit of the hill, and not the *quasi sommità*, as Biagioli wishes us to believe; because if the sun's rays had reached the side of the hill, the forest would not have been dark, nor would the poet have been obliged to raise his eyes to see the light.

2. Ed ecco, quasi al cominciar dell' erta.

3. Come d'autunno si levan le foglie
L'una appresso dell' altra, infin che 'l ramo
Rende alla terra tutte le sue spoglie;
Similemente il mal seme d' Adamo
*Gittansi* di quel lito ad una ad una
Per cenni, com' augel per suo richiamo.

4. This is certainly one of the significations of *adagiarsi*, which means not only to walk *adagio* or slowly, but to sit *a suo agio*—at one's ease—in a convenient or reclining posture. This is, in all probability, the meaning of the word as it occurs in Petrarch. Part I. CANZON. V. St. iii. vers. 10.

Il Pastor &c.—
Ivi senza pensier s' adagia e dorme.

# Henry Wadsworth Longfellow

## [Dante's Language]

### A Review of *A History of the Italian Language and Dialects*

We hold, then, to the generally received opinion, that like the French and Spanish, the Italian is a branch of that wide-spread and not very uniform *Romana Rustica*, which was formed by the intermingling of Barbaric words and idioms with the lower latinity of Italy, France and Spain, and which prevailed in the earlier part of the middle ages, with many local forms and peculiarities, through a large portion of the South of Europe. But, in the language of a polished Italian writer,[1] '*who* was the first author that wrote, *what* the first work composed in this tongue? It would be curious to inquire, but impossible to ascertain. The origin of this, like the origin of most things else, is uncertain, confused, and undetermined; for all things spring from insensible beginnings, and we cannot say of any, *here* it commenced.'—All that literary historians can do is to preserve the earliest existing monuments of the language and literature of a nation. All beyond must remain a subject of vague conjecture, till patient research or fortunate accident removes the boundaries of our knowledge farther and farther back into the shadowy regions of the past.

The earliest well-authenticated specimen of the Italian language belongs to the close of the twelfth century.[2] It is the *Canzone* of Ciullo d'Alcamo, by birth a Sicilian, and the earliest Italian poet, whose name is on record. He wrote about the year 1197. The song consists of thirty-two stanzas, some of which are not entire, and is written in the form of a colloquy between the poet and a lady. The language is a rude Sicilian dialect, and in many places unintelligible. We give two stanzas, the first and the fifteenth.

Proposta.

Rosa Fresca aulentissima ca pari in ver l'estate
Le Donne te desiano pulcelle maritate

Traheme deste focora se teste a bolontate
Per te non aio abento nocte e dia
Pensando pur di voi Madonna mia. . . .

Risposta.

Poi tanto trabagliastiti faccioti meo pregheri
Che tu vadi addomannimi a mia mare e a mon peri.
Se dare mi ti degnano menami a lo mosteri
E sposami davanti de la jente
E poi farò lo tuo comannamento.

Fresh and most fragrant rose, that appearest towards summer, the ladies desire thee, virgins and wedded dames. Take me from this flame, if such be thy will. For thee I have no rest night nor day, thinking always of thee, my Lady.

Since thou hast so much suffered, listen to my prayer; go, ask me of my mother and of my father; if they deign to give me to thee, lead me to the altar, and wed me before the world, and then I will do what thou commandest.

The whole of this canzone may be found in the sixth volume of Nardini's collection, p. 217.

The names of several Italian poets, who lived at the commencement of the thirteenth century, and portions at least of their writings, are still preserved. The first specimen which we shall offer of the language as it then existed is drawn from the *Lamento d' Amore*, a canzone of Folcachiero de' Folcachieri, of Siena, a poet who flourished about the year 1200. The reader will be struck with the great purity of language and ease of versification of the Sienese poet, when compared with the rude melody of the Sicilian who flourished but a few years before him. It seems evident from this and other extracts of a little later date, which we shall presently bring forward, that the Italian language was much more cultivated in the northern provinces, than in the southern; and if Sicily claims the honor of having been the cradle of the Italian language and literature, the cities of the north can boast of having given them the severe discipline of education. We extract the first two stanzas of the *lamento* of the Sienese poet.

Tutto lo mondo vive senza guerra,
Ed eo pace non posso haver niente.

O Deo come faraggio,
O Deo come sostienemi la terra.
E par ch' eo viva en noia della gente;
Ogni uomo m' è selvaggio;
Non paiono li fiori
Per me com' già soleano,
E gli augei per amori
Doci versi aceano agli albori.
E quando eo veggio gli altri cavalieri
Arme portare, e d'amore parlando,
Ed eo tutto mi doglio;
Sollazzo m' è tornato in pensieri.
La gente mi riguardano parlando
S' eo sono quello che essere soglio;
Non so ciò ch' eo mi sia,
Nè so perchè m' avvene
Forte la vita mia;
Tornato m' è lo bene in dolori.

The whole world lives without war, and I alone can have no peace. O heaven, what shall I do?—how can this earth sustain me?—It seems that I live at war with all mankind, and every man is strange and savage to me. The flowers do not look to me as they were wont, when the birds in their woodland loves sang sweet songs to the trees.

And when I see the other cavaliers bearing their arms, and speaking still of love, and I in sorrow mute, all consolation turns to musing care. The crowd gazes at me, asking if I am he whom they were wont to know;—I know not what I am, nor know I wherefore this life has grown so weary to me, nor why my joys are changed to sorrows.

It is evident from this specimen, that the cultivated language of the north of Italy, at the commencement of the thirteenth century, was far form being rude and unpolished. Still, it will be observed, there are forms then used which a few years afterwards had become obsolete, and which are not found in the extract which follows.

Nearly a quarter of a century later, in 1220, flourished Guido Guinizelli of Bologna, to whom by acclamation is given the honor of being the first among the Italian poets, who embodied in verse the subtleties of philosophy, and gave terseness, force and elevation to poetic style. Dante has recorded his fame in Canto XXVI of the Purgatory, where he speaks of his *dolci detti*, and calls him

———il padre mio e degli altri miei miglior, che
mai Rime d' amore usar dolci e leggiadre.

The praise of sweet-flowing language is certainly merited by this ancient poet, as may be seen from the following extract. It is the commencement of the most beautiful of the author's canzoni; its subject is the Nature of Love. This poem is given entire in Nardini, Vol. VI p. 212.

Al cor gentil ripara sempre Amore
Sì com' augello in selva a la verdura;
Non fe Amore anzi che gentil core,
Nè gentil core, anzi ch' Amor Natura;
Ch' adesso com' fu 'l sole,
Sì tosto lo splendore suo lucente;
Nè fue davante al sole,
E prende Amore in gentilezza loco,
Così propiamente
Com' il calore in clarità del fuoco.

Fuoco d' Amore in gentil cor s'apprende,
Come vertute in pietra preziosa,
Chè dalla stella valor non discende,
Anzi che 'l sol la faccia gentil cosa;
Poichè n' ha tratto fuore
Per la sua forza il sol ciò che gli è vile,
La stella i dà valore;
Cosi lo cor che fatto è da Natura
Alsetto, pur, gentile,
Donna, a guisa di stella lo 'nnamora.

To noble heart love doth for shelter fly,
As seeks the bird the forest's leafy shade;
Love was not felt till noble heart beat high,
Nor before love the noble heart was made;
Soon as the sun's broad flame

Was formed, so soon the clear light filled the air;
Yet was not till he came;
So love springs up in noble breasts, and there
Has its appointed space,
As heat in the bright flame finds its allotted place.

Kindles in noble heart the fire of love,
As hidden virtue in the precious stone;
This virtue comes not from the stars above,
Till round it the ennobling sun has shone;
But when his powerful blaze
Has drawn forth what was vile, the stars impart
Strange virtue in their rays;
And thus when nature doth create the heart
Noble, and pure, and high,
Like virtue from the star, love comes from woman's eye.

Setting aside the poetic merit of this canzone, of which we have extracted about one third, the language in which it is composed clearly bears away the palm from all other writings of an earlier date. Something had been gained in softness and flexibility, even in the short interval which had elapsed between the date of this extract and that of the preceding: and probably the writings of Guido Guinizelli exhibit the Italian language under the best form it wore during the first half of the thirteenth century. Otherwise they would not have been so highly extolled by Dante, who never loses an opportunity of setting forth their merit, and who still more plainly shows the esteem, in which he held the quaint language of his poetic father, by appropriating one of his lines.

Amor, ch' al cor gentil ratto s' apprende,

in the description of Francesco da Rimini, in the fifth Canto of the Inferno, was doubtless taken from Guinizelli's

Fuoco d' Amore in gentil cor s' apprende.

We will now step forward a half-century to the days of Brunetto Latini, the celebrated poet, philosopher and rhetorician, and the still more celebrated master of Dante. He was born about 1220, and died in 1294.

The following extract will show to what degree of perfection the language had advanced in his day. It is a description of the Creation, taken from the *Tesoretto*, the Little Treasure, Cap.VI.

| | |
|---|---|
| Dio fece lo giorno, | God created the day, |
| E la luce joconda, | And the jocund light, |
| E ciela e terra, e onda. | And heaven, and earth, and sea. |
| E l' aere creao, | And the air he created, |
| E li angeli formao, | And formed the angels, |
| Ciascun partitamente; | Each one separately; |
| E tutto di neente. | And all out of nothing. |
| Poi la seconda dia, | Then on the second day |
| Per la sua gran balía, | By his great power, |
| Stabilì 'l firmamento, | He established the firmament, |
| E 'l suo ordinamento. | And the order thereof. |
| Il terzo, ciò mi pare, | The third, so seemeth it to me, |
| Specificò lo mare, | He gave the ocean bounds, |
| E la terra divise: | And divided the dry land; |
| E 'n ella fece e mise | And created and placed therein |
| Onne cosa barbata, | All vegetable life |
| Ch' è 'n terra radicata. | That in the earth taketh root. |
| Al quarto die presente | And on the fourth day |
| Fece compitamente | He created wholly |
| Tutte le luminarie; | The lights in the firmament; |
| Stelle diverse e varie. | The stars of various glory. |
| Nella quinta giornata | On the fifth day |
| Si fue da lui creata | By him was created |
| Ciascuna creatura, | Every living creature |
| Che nuota in acqua pura. | That swimmeth in the pure water. |
| Lo sesto die fu tale, | And the sixth day was such, |
| Che fece ogne anemale, | That in it he created all animals, |
| E fece Adam et Eva | He created Adam and Eve, |
| Che poi rupper la tregua | Who afterwards broke the law |
| Del suo comandamento. | Of his commandment. |
| Per quel trapassamento | For which transgression |
| Mantenente fu miso | Straightway they were driven |
| Fora del Paradiso. | Forth out of Paradise. |

These lines are remarkably simple, and in their structure and language so easy to be understood, that they render comment and annotation entirely useless, and hardly require a translation. But this was the polished Tuscan of the age. The same pen that indited it was skilful in a ruder dialect. Brunetto Latini was the author of a satirical poem, entitled *Il Pataffio*, written in a low Florentine jargon, which is for the most part quite unintelligible, even to Italians. The editor of the *Saggi di Prose e Poesie* says, that it is written *in un gergo, che neppure col comento si può intendere.*[3]

Such was the state of the Italian language during the thirteenth century. One step farther ushers us into the august presence of the three *gran maestri del bel parlar Toscano*, Dante, Petrarca and Boccaccio. Their praise is on every lip; their eulogy flows from every pen. They were giants of an early age, when gigantic strength was wanted to fix the uncertain foundations of their national language and literature broad, deep and massive. This glorious work was theirs. They did not wholly create, but they advanced, and developed and rendered permanent. They did not strike the first spade into the soil, but they drew the stone from the quarry, set the landmarks, polished the rough marble, and piled and cemented the mis-shapen blocks, till beneath their hands the noble structure rose, majestic, towering, beautiful. It is the high prerogative of genius to give transcendant value to whatever it touches. It copies from the world around, it works with the same instruments and upon the same material with other minds, but from its hand material forms come forth, breathing, moving, instinct with life, like the marble of the Cyprian statue. It dips in the fountains of Castaly, and their cold depths flash and sparkle like the golden sands of Pactolus. It was by the power of such a spell, that from the rude and diversified dialects of the thirteenth century, issued forth the *idioma gentil sonante e puro*.

Before proceeding farther with this part of our subject, it will be necessary to throw a passing glance upon the various dialects, which divide the Italian language. These are all of greater antiquity than the classic Italian, the *parlare Illustre, Cardinale, Aulico e Cortigiano*; and many of them dispute the honor of having given it birth, with an obstinacy, which reminds one of Lessing's *nichtswürdige Rangstreit der Thiere*, wherein the ape and the ass were the last to leave the contest. Dante enumerates fifteen dialects existing in his day, and gives their names. He then observes farther: 'From this it appears, that the Italian language alone is divided into at least fourteen dialects, each of which is again subdivided into underdialects, as the Tuscan into the Sienese and Aretine, the Lombard into the dialects of Ferrara and Piacenza; and even in the same city some varieties of language may be found. Hence if we include the leading dialects of the Italian *Volgare* with the under-dialects and their subdivisions, the varieties of language common in this little corner of the world will amount to a thousand, and even more.'[4] This diversity of the Italian dialects is doubtless to be attributed in a great measure to the varieties of dialect existing in the vulgar Latin at the time of the northern invasions, and to similar varieties in the original dialects of the invaders themselves, who, it will be recollected, were of different tribes of the vast family of the Gotho-Germans, among which were the Ostrogoths, the Visigoths, the Lombards, the Gepidi, the Bulgari, the Sarmati, the Pannonii, the Suevi, and the Norici. Much, too, must be attributed to the accidental but inevitable changes, wrought in a language by the gradual progress of its history and the contingencies of time and place; and something to the new development of national character produced by the admixture of the Roman and Teutonic races.[5]

After enumerating the dialects, which prevailed in his day, Dante goes into a discussion of the beauties and defects of some of the more prominent. He disposes of all these by observing that neither of them is the *Volgare Illustre*, to discover which he had instituted the inquiry; and hence draws the conclusion 'that the *Volgare Illustre, Cardinale, Aulico, e Cortigiano* of Italy is the language common to all the Italian cities, but peculiar to none.' In other words, it exists everywhere in parts, but no where as a whole, save in the pages of the classic writer. This opinion, however, has been warmly contested, and the champions of four or five parties have taken the field. The first, with Machiavelli and the host of the Florentine Academy at their head, have asserted the supremacy of the language of the city of Florence; and, actuated it would seem more by the zeal of local prejudice, than any generous feeling of national pride, have contended, that the classic language of that literature, in whose ample field the name of their whole country was already so proudly emblazoned, was the dialect of Florence, and should be called, not Italian, not even Tuscan,—but *Florentine*. In the bitterness of dispute, Machiavelli exclaims against the author of the *Divina Commedia*; 'In every thing he has brought infamy upon his country, and now even in her language he would tear from her that reputation, which he imagines his own writings have conferred upon her.'[6] There spake the politician, not the scholar. Machiavelli's own writings are the best refutation of his theory. Bembo,[7] though a Venetian, and Varchi,[8] the historian of the wars of the Florentine Republic, were also advocates of the same opinion. In humble imitation of these, some members of the Academy of the *Intronati* in Siena put in their claims in favor of their native *Sanese*; and one writer at least of Bologna asserted the supremacy of the *Bolognese*.[9] Their pretensions however seem neither to have caused alarm, nor even to have excited attention. The champions of the name and glory of the Tuscan show a more liberal spirit, inasmuch as they extend to a whole province, what the Florentine and Sienese Academicians would have shut up within the walls of a single city. Among those who have enlisted beneath this banner, are Dolce[10] and Tolomei.[11] But far more of the high and liberal spirit of the scholar is shown by those writers who do not arrogate to their own native city or province, that glory which rightly belongs to their whole country. Among those who assert the common right of all the provinces of Italy to share in the honor of having contributed something to the classic Italian, and, consequently, say that it should bear the name of Italian rather than that of Florentine, Sienese, or Tuscan, after Dante, are Castelvetro[12], Muzio[13], and Cesarotti[14]. Now, as is pretty universally the case in literary warfare, an exclusive and uncompromising spirit has urged the combatants onward, and they have contended for victory rather than for truth, which seems to lie prostrate in the field midway between the contending parties, unseen and trampled upon by all. The facts which we can gather from the contending arguments, lead us to embrace the opinion that the classic Italian is based upon the Tuscan, but adorned and enriched by words and idioms from all the provinces of Italy. In other words, each of the Italian dialects has contributed something to its formation, but most of all the Tuscan; and the language thus formed belongs not to a single city, nor a single province, but is the common possession of the whole of

Il bel paese là dove il sì suona

Such was the language, which in the fourteenth century was carried to its highest state of perfection in the writings of Dante, Petrarch and Boccaccio. Beneath their culture, the tree, whose far-spreading roots drew nourishment from the soil of every province, reared aloft its leafy branches to the sky, vocal with song, and proffered shelter to all who deigned to sit beneath its shadow and listen to the laughing tale, the amorous lay, or the fearful mysteries of another life. Dante Alighieri was born at Florence in 1265, and died at Ravenna in 1321. As an author, he belongs to the fourteenth century. Boccaccio says, that he wrote in his native dialect; but it is conceded on all hands, and all his writings prove the fact, that he did not confine himself exclusively to any one dialect, but drew from all whatever they contained of force and beauty.[15] In the words of Cesarotti, in his Essay on the Philosophy of Language, 'the genius of Dante was not the slave of his native idiom. His zeal was rather national than simply patriotic. The creator of a philosophic language, he sacrifices all conventional elegance to expressiveness and force;

and far from flattering a particular dialect, lords it over the whole language, which he seems at times to rule with despotic sway.' In this way, Dante advanced the Italian to a high rank among the living languages of his age. Posterity has not withheld the honor, then bestowed upon him, of being the most perfect master of the vulgar tongue, that had appeared:[16] and this seems to strengthen and establish the argument, that the Italian language consists of the gems of various dialects enchased in the pure gold of the Tuscan.

# Notes

1. Saverio Bettinelli: *Il Risorgimento d'Italia*.

2. The literary historians of Italy have preserved two inscriptions of a more ancient date; but strong doubts are entertained of their authenticity. The first bears the date of 1135. It was an inscription in mosaic over the high altar of the Cathedral of Ferrara, which is now demolished. As the original no longer exists, there seems to be some doubt in regard to the reading of the last three lines. We give the generally received version,and for the other refer our readers to *Nardini*. Vol. VI. p. 228.

Il mille cento trentacinque nato
Fo questo tempio a Zorzi consecrato
Fo Nicolao scolptore
E Glielmo fo l' auctore.

Quadrio. T.I. p. 43.—*Tiraboschi*.
T.III. Lib. IV. p. 365

The second was written in the year 1184. It was placed in the castle of the Ubaldim near Florence, in commemoration of a stag-hunt in the neighborhood, wherein Ubaldino degli Ubaldini seized the stag by the horns, and held him until the Emperor Frederick I. coming up, despatched the weary animal. The inscription thus commences:

DE FAVORE ISTO
GRATIAS REFERO CHRISTO.
FACTUS IN FESTO SERENAE
SANCTAE MARIAE MAGDALENAE.
IPSA PECULIARITER ADORI
AD DEUM PRO ME PECCATORI.
CON LO MEO CANTARE
DALLO VERO VERO NARRARE
NULLO NE DIPARTO.
ANNO MILESIMO

CHRISTI SALUTE CENTESIMO
OCTUAGESIMO QUARTO.

The entire inscription may be found in *Quadrio*. T. II. p. 150.— *Tiraboschi*. T. III. Lib. IV. p. 366.—*Crescimbeni*, Istoria della Volgar Poesia. T. I, p. 100.—*Nardini*, Vol. VI. p. 226.

3. We subjoin a few lines of this curious and unintelligible poem, in order to show how great a difference already existed between the cultivated Italian and one at least of the popular dialects.

Squasimodeo, introcque e a fusone
  Ne hai ne hai, pilorcio, e con mattana:
  Al can la tigna; egli è un mazzamarrone.
La difalta perecchi adana adana
  A cafisso, e a busso, e a ramata:
  Tutto codesto è della petronciana,
Bituschio, Scraffo, e ben l' abbiam filata
  A chiedere a balante, e gignignacca.
  Punzone, e sergozzone, e la recchiata.
Bindo mio no, chè l' è una zambracca:
  In pozzanghera cadde il muscia cheto;
  E pur di palo in frasco, e bulinacca, etc.

*Nardini*, Vol. VI. p. 194.

Would the disciples of Bruni or Maffei attempt to trace back all these words to a Latin origin?

4. *De Vulgari Eloquio*. Cap. X.

5. Each of the Italian cities is marked by peculiar traits of character in its inhabitants, which bear in the mouths of the populace some epithet of praise, or are the subject of gibe and ribadry. For example, the Milanese have the *sobriquet* of *buoni buzziconi*; and in the following lines, which we find quoted in Howell's '*Signorie of Venice*,' p. 55, numerous epithets are applied.

Fama tra noi; Roma *pomposa* e *santa*;
Venetia *saggia, rica signorile*;
Napoli *odorifera* e *gentile*;
Fiorenza *bella*, tutto il mondo canta;
*Grande* Milano in Italia si vanta;
Bologna *grassa*; Ferrara *civile*;
Padoua *dotta*, e Bergamo *sottile*;
Genoa di *superbia* altiera pianta;
Verona *degna*; e Perugia *sanguigna*;
Brescia l' *armata*; et Mantoa *gloriosa*;
Rimini *buona*; e Pistoia *ferrigna*;
Cremona *antica*, e Luca *industriosa*;
Furli *bizarro*, e Ravenna *benigna*; etc.

6. *Discorso in cui si esamina se la lingua in cui scrissero Dante, il Boccaccio, e il Petrarca si debba chiamare Italiana, Toscana, o Fiorentina.* Machiavelli: Opere. T.x. p. 371.

7. Pietro Bembo: Opere, Vol. X. Della Volgar Lingua.

8. Benedetto Varchi: *L'Ercolano, nel qual si ragiona delle lingue, e in particolare della toscana e della fiorentina.*

9. Gian Filoteo Achillini: *Annotazioni della Volgar Lingua.*

10. Lodovico Dolce: *Osservazioni della Volgar Lingua.*

11. Claudio Tolomei; *Il Cesano, nel quale si dispula del nome con cui si dee chiamare la Volgar Lingua.*

12. Lodovico Castelvetro: *Correzione di alcune cose nel dialogo delle lingue* (Varchi's Ercolano.)

13. Gerolamo Muzio; *Battaglie per difesa dell' Italica lingua.*

14. Melchior Cesarotti: *Saggio sulla filosofia delle lingue.*

15. Gianvicenzo Gravina, in a work entitled *Della Ragion Poetica*, has the following passage upon this point: 'Dante, abbracciando la lingua comunemente intesa ed usata in iscritto per tutta l' Italia, che volgare appelliamo, accrebbe a quella parole e locuzione trasportate da' Lombardi, Romagnuoli e Toscani, il di cui dialletto fe' prevalere: onde Boccaccio disse aver Dante scritto in idioma, cioè idiotismo fiorentino . . . E sparse alle volte anche delle voci da lui inventate, ed altre derivate dall' antica, cioè dalla latina.'

16. 'Lo stile, [di Dante] che sente ora alcun poco del rancido, era a quel tempo per certissima testimonianza del Villani e del Boccacio, il più vago stile e il più polito, che si fosse veduto mai più per innanzi in alcuna scrittura volgare.' Denina, *Saggio sopra la Letteratura Italiana.*

# Henry Wadsworth Longfellow

## Selected Translations

### The Celestial Pilot.

FROM DANTE. PURGATORIO, II.

AND now, behold! as at the approach of morning,
Through the gross vapors, Mars grows fiery red
Down in the west upon the ocean floor,

Appeared to me, — may I again behold it! —
A light along the sea, so swiftly coming,
Its motion by no flight of wing is equalled.

And when therefrom I had withdrawn a little
Mine eyes, that I might question my conductor,
Again I saw it brighter grown and larger.

Thereafter, on all sides of it, appeared
I knew not what of white, and underneath,
Little by little, there came forth another.

My master yet had uttered not a word,
While the first brightness into wings unfolded;
But, when he clearly recognised the pilot,

He cried aloud; "Quick, quick, and bow the knee!
Behold the Angel of God! fold up thy hands!
Henceforward shalt thou see such officers!

"See, how he scorns all human arguments,
So that no oar he wants, nor other sail
Than his own wings, between so distant shores!

"See, how he holds them, pointed straight to heaven,
Fanning the air with the eternal pinions,
That do not moult themselves like mortal hair!"

And then, as nearer and more near us came
The Bird of Heaven, more glorious he appeared,
So that the eye could not sustain his presence,

But down I cast it; and he came to shore
With a small vessel, gliding swift and light,
So that the water swallowed nought thereof.

Upon the stern stood the Celestial Pilot!
Beatitude seemed written in his face!
And more than a hundred spirits sat within.

"*In exitu Israel* out of Egypt!"
Thus sang they all together in one voice,
With whatso in that Psalm is after written.

Then made he sign of holy rood upon them,
Whereat all cast themselves upon the shore,
And he departed swiftly as he came.

## The Terrestrial Paradise.

FROM DANTE. PURGATORIO, XXVIII.

LONGING already to search in and round
The heavenly forest, dense and living-green,
Which to the eyes tempered the new-born day,

Withouten more delay I left the bank,
Crossing the level country slowly, slowly,
Over the soil, that everywhere breathed fragrance.

A gently-breathing air, that no mutation
Had in itself, smote me upon the forehead,
No heavier blow, than of a pleasant breeze,

Whereat the tremulous branches readily
Did all of them bow downward towards that side
Where its first shadow casts the Holy Mountain;

Yet not from their upright direction bent
So that the little birds upon their tops
Should cease the practice of their tuneful art;

But, with full-throated joy, the hours of prime
Singing received they in the midst of foliage
That made monotonous burden to their rhymes,

Even as from branch to branch it gathering swells,
Through the pine forests on the shore of Chiassi,
When Æolus unlooses the Sirocco.

Already my slow steps had led me on
Into the ancient wood so far, that I
Could see no more the place where I had entered.

And lo! my farther course cut off a river,
Which, towards the left hand, with its little waves,
Bent down the grass, that on its margin sprang.

All waters that on earth most limpid are,
Would seem to have within themselves some mixture,
Compared with that, which nothing doth conceal,

Although it moves on with a brown, brown current,
Under the shade perpetual, that never
Ray of the sun lets in, nor of the moon.

# Beatrice.

FROM DANTE. PURGATORIO, XXX., XXXI.

EVEN as the Blessed, in the new covenant,
Shall rise up quickened, each one from his grave,
Wearing again the garments of the flesh,

So, upon that celestial chariot,
A hundred rose *ad vocem tanti senis*,
Ministers and messengers of life eternal.

They all were saying; "*Benedictus qui venis*,"
And scattering flowers above and round about,
"*Manibus o date lilia plenis*."

I once beheld, at the approach of day,
The orient sky all stained with roseate hues,
And the other heaven with light serene adorned,

And the sun's face uprising, overshadowed,
So that, by temperate influence of vapors,
The eye sustained his aspect for long while;

Thus in the bosom of a cloud of flowers,
Which from those hands angelic were thrown up,
And down descended inside and without,

With crown of olive o'er a snow-white veil,
Appeared a lady, under a green mantle,
Vested in colors of the living flame.

. . . . . . . . . . . . . . . . . . . . . . . . .

Even as the snow, among the living rafters
Upon the back of Italy, congeals,
Blown on and beaten by Sclavonian winds,

And then, dissolving, filters through itself,
Whene'er the land, that loses shadow, breathes,
Like as a taper melts before a fire,

Even such I was, without a sigh or tear,
Before the song of those who chime for ever
After the chiming of the eternal spheres;

But, when I heard in those sweet melodies
Compassion for me, more than had they said,
"O wherefore, lady, dost thou thus consume him?"

The ice, that was about my heart congealed,
To air and water changed, and, in my anguish,
Through lips and eyes came gushing from my breast.

. . . . . . . . . . . . . . . . . . . . . . . .

Confusion and dismay, together mingled,
Forced such a feeble "Yes!" out of my mouth,
To understand it one had need of sight.

Even as a cross-bow breaks, when 't is discharged,
Too tensely drawn the bow-string and the bow,
And with less force the arrow hits the mark;

So I gave way under this heavy burden,
Gushing forth into bitter tears and sighs,
And the voice, fainting, flagged upon its passage.

# Charles Eliot Norton

## "The New Life" of Dante

### [Concluded.]

### III.

THE YEAR 1289 WAS one marked in the annals of Florence and of Italy by events which are still famous, scored by the genius of Dante upon the memory of the world. It was in this year that Count Ugolino and his sons and grandsons were starved by the Pisans in their tower prison. A few months later, Francesca da Rimini was murdered by her husband. Between the dates of these two terrible events the Florentines had won the great victory of Campaldino; and thus, in this short space, the materials had been given to the poet for the two best-known and most powerful stories and for one of the most striking episodes of the "Divina Commedia."

In the great and hard-fought battle of Campaldino Dante himself took part. "I was at first greatly afraid," he says, in a letter of which but a few sentences have been preserved,[1]—"but at the end I felt the greatest joy,—according to the various chances of the battle." When the victorious army returned to Florence, a splendid procession, with the clergy at its head, with the arts of the city each under its banner, and with all manner of pomp, went out to meet it. There were long-continued feasts and rejoicings. The battle had been fought on the 11th of June, the day of St. Barnabas, and the Republic, though already engaged in magnificent works of church-building, decreed that a new church should be erected in honor of the Saint on whose day the victory had been won.

A little later in that summer, Dante was one of a troop of Florentines who joined the forces of Lucca in levying war upon the Pisan territory. The stronghold of Caprona was taken, and Dante was present at its capture; for he says, (*Inferno,* XXI, 94–96,) "I saw the foot-soldiers, who, having made terms, came out from Caprona, afraid when they beheld themselves among so many enemies."[2]

Thus, during a great part of the summer of 1289, Dante was in active service as a soldier. He was no lovesick idler, no mere home-keeping writer of verses, but was already taking his part in the affairs of the state which he was afterwards to be called on for a time to assist in governing, and he was laying up those stores of experience which were to serve as the material out of which his vivifying imagination was to form the great national poem of Italy. But of this active life, of these personal engagements, of these terrible events which took such strong possession of his soul, there is no word, no suggestion even, in the book of his "New Life." In it there is no echo, however faint, of those storms of public violence and private passion which broke dark over Italy. In the midst of the tumults which sprang from the jealousies of rival states, from the internal discords of cities, from the divisions of parties, from the bitterness of domestic quarrels,—this little book is full of tenderness and peace, and tells its story of love as if the world were the abode of tranquility. No external excitements could break into the inner chambers of Dante's heart to displace the love that dwelt within them. The contrast between the purity and the serenity of the "Vita Nuova" and the coarseness and cruelty of the deeds that were going on while it was being written is complete. Every man in some sort leads a double life,—one real and his own, the other seeming and the world's,—but with few is the separation so entire as it was with Dante.

But in these troubled times the "New Life" was drawing to its close. The spring of 1290 had come, and the poet, now twenty-five years old, sixteen years having passed since he first beheld Beatrice, was engaged in writing a poem to tell what effect the virtue of his lady wrought upon him. He had written but the following portion when it was broken off, never to be resumed:—

"So long hath Love retained me at his hest,
And to his sway hath so accustomed me,
That as at first he cruel used to be,
So in my heart he now doth sweetly rest.
Thus when by him my strength is dispossessed,
So that the spirits seem away to flee,
My frail soul feels such sweetness verily,
That with it pallor doth my face invest.
Then Love o'er me such mastery doth seize,
He makes my sighs in words to take their way,

And they unto my lady go to pray
That she to give me further grace would please
Where'er she sees me, this to me occurs,
Nor can it be believed what humbleness is hers."

"Quomodo sedet sola civitas plena populo! facta est quasi vidua domina gentium!"

[How doth the city sit solitary that was full of people! how is she become as a widow, she that was great among the nations!][3]

"I was yet engaged upon this Canzone, and had finished the above stanza, when the Lord of justice called this most gentle one unto glory under the banner of that holy Queen Mary whose name was ever spoken with greatest reverence by this blessed Beatrice.[4]

"And although it might give pleasure, were I now to tell somewhat of her departure from us, it is not my intention to treat of it here for three reasons. The first is, that it is no part of the present design, as may be seen in the proem of this little book. The second is, that, supposing it were so, my pen would not be sufficient to treat of it in a fitting manner. The third is, that, supposing both the one and the other, it would not be becoming in me to treat of it, since, in doing so, I should be obliged to praise myself,—a thing altogether blameworthy in whosoever does it,—and therefore I leave this subject to some other narrator.

"Nevertheless, since in what precedes there has been occasion to make frequent mention of the number nine,[5] and apparently not without reason, and since in her departure this number appeared to have a large place, it is fitting to say something on this point, seeing that it seems to belong to our design. Wherefore I will first tell how it had place in her departure, and then I will assign some reason why this number was so friendly to her. I say, that, according to the mode of reckoning in Italy, her most noble soul departed in the first hour of the ninth day of the month; and according to the reckoning, in Syria, she departed in the ninth month of the year, since the first month there is Tismim, which with us is October; and according to our reckoning, she departed in that year of our indiction, that is, of the years of the Lord, in which the perfect number[6] was completed for the ninth time in that century in which she had been set in the world; and she was of the Christians of the thirteenth century.[7]

"One reason why this number was so friendly to her may be this: since, according to Ptolemy and the Christian truth, there are nine heavens which move, and, according to the common astrological opinion, these heavens work effects here below according to their relative positions, this number was her friend, to the end that it might be understood that at her generation all the nine movable heavens were in most perfect conjunction.[8] This is one reason; but considering more subtilely and according to infallible truth, this number was she herself,—I speak in a similitude, and I mean as follows. The number three is the root of nine, since, without any other number, multiplied by itself, it makes nine,—as we see plainly that three times three are nine. Then, if three is the factor by itself of nine, and the Author of Miracles[9] by himself is three,—Father, Son, and Holy Spirit, who are three and one,—this lady was accompanied by the number nine that it might be understood that she was a nine, that is, a miracle, whose only root is the marvellous Trinity. Perhaps a more subtle person might discover some more subtile reason for this; but this is the one that I see for it, and which pleases me the best."

After thus treating of the number nine in its connection with Beatrice, Dante goes on to say, that, when this most gentle lady had gone from this world, the city appeared widowed and despoiled of every dignity; whereupon he wrote to the princes of the earth an account of its condition, beginning with the words of Jeremiah which he quoted at the entrance of this new matter. The remainder of this letter he does not give, because it was in Latin, and in this work it was his intention, from the beginning, to write only in the vulgar tongue; and such was the understanding of the friend for whom he writes,—that friend being, as we may suppose, Guido Cavalcanti, whom Dante, it may be remembered, has already spoken of as the chief among his friends. Then succeeds a Canzone lamenting the death of Beatrice, which, instead of being followed by a verbal exposition, as is the case with all that have gone before, is preceded by one, in order that it may seem, as it were, desolate and like a widow at its end. And this arrangement is preserved in regard to all the remaining poems in the little volume. In this poem he says that the Eternal Sire called Beatrice to himself, because he saw that this world was not worthy of such a gentle thing; and he says of his own life, that no tongue could tell what it has been since his lady went away to heaven.

Among the sonnets ascribed to Dante is one which, if it be his, must have been written about this time, and which, although not included in the "Vita Nuova," seems not unworthy to find a place here. Its imagery, at least, connects it with some of the sonnets in the earlier portion of the book.

"One day came Melancholy unto me,
And said, 'With thee I will awhile abide';
And, as it seemed, attending at her side,
Anger and Grief did bear her company.
" 'Depart! Away!' I cried out eagerly.
Then like a Greek she unto me replied;
And while she stood discoursing in her pride,
I looked, and Love approaching us I see.
"In cloth of black full strangely was he clad,
A little hood he wore upon his head,
And down his face tears flowing fast he had.
" 'Poor little wretch! what ails thee?' then I said.
And he replied, 'I woful am, and sad,
Sweet brother, for our lady who is dead.' "

About this time, Dante tells us, a person who stood to him in friendship next to his first friend, and who was of the closest relationship to his glorious lady, so that we may believe it was her brother, came to him and prayed him to write something on a lady who was dead. Dante, believing that he meant the blessed Beatrice, accordingly wrote for him a sonnet; and then, reflecting that so short a poem appeared but a poor and bare service for one who was so nearly connected with her, added to it a Canzone, and gave both to him.

As the months passed on, his grief still continued fresh, and the memory of his lady dwelt continually with him. It happened, that, "on that day which completed a year since this lady was made one of the citizens of eternal life, I was seated in a place where, remembering her, I drew an Angel upon certain tablets. And while I was drawing it, I turned my eyes, and saw at my side certain men to whom it was becoming to do honor, and who were looking at what I did; and, as was afterward told me, they had been there now some time before I perceived them. When I saw them, I rose, and, saluting them, said, 'Another was just now with me, and on that account I was in thought.' When these persons had gone, I returned to my work, that is, to drawing figures of Angels; and while doing this, a thought came to me of saying words in rhyme, as for an anniversary poem for her, and of addressing them to those who had come to me. Then I said this sonnet, which has two beginnings:

FIRST BEGINNING.

"Unto my mind remembering had come
The gentle lady, with such pure worth graced,
That by the Lord Most High she had been placed
Within the heaven of peace, where Mary hath her home."

SECOND BEGINNING.

"Unto my mind had come, indeed, in thought,
That gentle one for whom Love's tears are shed,
Just at the time when, by his power led,
To see what I was doing you were brought.
"Love, who within my mind did her perceive,
Was roused awake within my wasted heart,
And said unto my sighs, 'Go forth! depart!'
Whereon each one in grief did take its leave.
"Lamenting they from out my breast did go,
And uttering a voice that often led
The grievous tears unto my saddened eyes.
"But those which issued with the greatest woe,
'O noble soul,' they in departing said,
'To-day makes up the year since thou to heaven didst rise.' "

The preceding passage is one of the many in the "Vita Nuova" which are of peculiar interest, as illustrating the personal tastes of Dante, and the common modes of his life. "I was drawing," he says, "the figure of an Angel"; and this statement is the more noticeable, because Giotto, the man who set painting on its modern course, was not yet old enough to have exercised any influence upon Dante.[10] The friendship which afterwards existed between them had its beginning at a later period. At this time Cimabue still held the field. He often painted angels around the figures of the Virgin and her Child; and in his most famous picture, in the Church of Sta. Maria Novella, there are certain angels of which Vasari says, with truth, that, though painted in the Greek manner, they show an approach toward the modern style of drawing. These angels may well have seemed beautiful to eyes accustomed to the hard unnaturalness of earlier works. The love of Art pervaded Florence, and a nature so sensitive and so sympathetic as Dante's could not but partake of it in the fullest measure. Art was then no adjunct of sentimentalism, no encourager of idleness. It was connected with all that was most serious and all that was most delightful in life. It is difficult, indeed, to realize the delight which it gave, and the earnestness with which it was followed at this period, when it seemed, as by a miracle, to fling off the winding-sheet which had long wrapped its stiffened limbs, and to come forth with new and unexampled life.

The strength and the intelligence of Dante's love of Art are shown in many beautiful passages and allusions in the "Divina Commedia." There was something of universality, not only in his imagination, but also in his acquisitions. Of the sources of learning which were then open, there was not one which he had not visited; of the fountains of inspiration, not one out of which he had not drunk. All the arts—poetry, painting, sculpture, and music—were alike dear to him. His Canzoni were written to be sung; and one of the most charming scenes in the great poem is that in which is described his meeting with his friend Casella, the musician, who sang to him one of his own Canzoni so sweetly, that "the sweetness still within me sounds."[11]

"Dante took great delight in music, and was an excellent draughtsman," says Aretino, his second biographer; and Boccaccio reports, that in his youth he took great pleasure in music, and was the friend of all the best musicians and singers of his time. There is, perhaps, in the whole range of literature, no nobler homage to Art than that which is contained in the tenth and twelfth cantos of the "Purgatory," in which Dante represents the Creator himself as using its means to impress the lessons of truth upon those whose souls were being purified for the final attainment of heaven. The passages are too long for extract, and though their wonderful beauty tempts us to linger over them, we must return to the course of the story of Dante's life as it appears in the concluding pages of the "New Life."

Many months had passed since Beatrice's death, when Dante happened to be in a place which recalled the past time to him, and filled him with grief.

While standing here, he raised his eyes and saw a young and beautiful lady looking out from a window compassionately upon his sad aspect. The tenderness of her look touched his heart and moved his tears. Many times afterwards he saw her, and her face was always full of compassion, and pale, so that it reminded him of the look of his own most noble lady. But at length his eyes began to delight too much in seeing her; wherefore he often cursed their vanity, and esteemed himself as vile, and there was a hard battle within himself between the remembrance of his lady and the new desire of his eyes.

At length, he says, "The sight of this lady brought me into so new a condition, that I often thought of her as of one who pleased me exceedingly,—and I thought of her thus: 'This is a gentle, beautiful, young, and discreet lady, and she has perhaps appeared by will of Love, in order that my life may find repose.' And often I thought more amorously, so that my heart consented in it, that is, approved my reasoning. And after it had thus consented, I, moved as if by reason, reflected, and said to myself, 'Ah, what thought is this that in so vile a way seeks to console me, and leaves me scarcely any other thought?' Then another thought rose up and said, 'Now that thou hast been in so great tribulation of Love, why wilt thou not withdraw thyself from such bitterness? Thou seest that this is an inspiration that sets the desires of Love before thee, and proceeds from a place no less gentle than the eyes of the lady who has shown herself so pitiful toward thee.' Wherefore, I, having often thus combated with myself, wished to say some words of it. And as, in this battle of thoughts, those which spoke for her won the victory, it seemed to me becoming to address her, and I said this sonnet, which begins, 'A gentle thought'; and I called it *gentle* because I was speaking to a gentle lady,—but otherwise it was most vile.

"A gentle thought that of you holds discourse
Cometh now frequently with me to dwell,
And in so sweet a way of Love doth tell,
My heart to yield unto him he doth force.
" 'Who, then, is this,' the soul says to the heart,
'Who cometh to bring comfort to our mind?
And is his virtue of so potent kind,
That other thoughts he maketh to depart?'
" 'O saddened soul,' the heart to her replies;
'This is a little spirit fresh from Love,

Whose own desires he before me brings;
" 'His very life and all his power doth move
Forth from the sweet compassionating eyes
Of her so grieved by our sufferings.' "

"One day, about the ninth hour, there arose within me a strong imagination opposed to this adversary of reason. For I seemed to see the glorified Beatrice in that crimson garment in which she had first appeared to my eyes, and she seemed to me young, of the same age as when I first saw her. Then I began to think of her, and, calling to mind the past time in its order, my heart began to repent bitterly of the desire by which it had so vilely allowed itself for some days to be possessed, contrary to the constancy of reason. And this so wicked desire being expelled, all my thoughts returned to their most gentle Beatrice, and I say that thenceforth I began to think of her with my heart possessed utterly by shame, so that it was often manifested by my sighs; for almost all of them, as they went forth, told what was discoursed of in my heart,—the name of that gentlest one, and how she had gone from us. . . . And I wished that my wicked desire and vain temptation might be known to be at an end; and that the rhymed words which I had before written might induce no doubt, I proposed to make a sonnet in which I would include what I have now told."

With this sonnet Dante ends the story in the "Vita Nuova" of the wandering of his eyes, and the short faithlessness of his heart; but it is retold with some additions in the "Convito" or "Banquet," a work written many years afterward; and in this later version there are some details which serve to fill out and illustrate the earlier narrative.[12] The same tender and refined feeling which inspires the "Vita Nuova" gives its tone to all the passages in which the poet recalls his youthful days and the memory of Beatrice in this work of his sorrowful manhood. In the midst of its serious and philosophic discourse this little story winds in and out its thread of personal recollection and of sweet romantic sentiment. It affords new insight into the recesses of Dante's heart, and exhibits the permanence of the gracious qualities of his youth.

Its opening sentence is full of the imagery of love. "Since the death of that blessed Beatrice who lives in heaven with the angels, and on earth with my soul, the star of Venus had twice shone in the different seasons, as the star of morning and of evening, when that gentle lady, of whom I have made mention near the close of the "New Life," first appeared before my eyes accompanied by Love, and gained some place in my mind.

. . . And before this love could become perfect, there arose a great battle between the thought that sprang from it and that which was opposed to it, and which still held the fortress of my mind for the glorified Beatrice."[13]

And so hard was this struggle, and so painful, that Dante took refuge from it in the composition of a poem addressed to the Angelic Intelligences who move the third heaven, that is, the heaven of Venus; and it is to the exposition of the true meaning of this Canzone that the second book or treatise of the "Convito" is directed. In one of the later chapters he says, (and the passage is a most striking one, from its own declaration, as well as from its relation to the vision of the "Divina Commedia,")—"The life of my heart was wont to be a sweet and delightful thought, which often went to the feet of the Lord of those to whom I speak, that is, to God,—for, thinking, I contemplated the kingdom of the Blessed. And I tell [in my poem! the final cause of my mounting thither in thought, when I say, 'There I beheld a lady in glory'; [and I say this! in order that it may be understood that I was certain, and am certain, through her gracious revelation, that she was in heaven, whither I in my thoughts oftentimes went,—as it were, seized up. And this made me desirous of death, that I might go there where she was."[14] Following upon the chapter in which this remarkable passage occurs is one which is chiefly occupied with a digression upon the immortality of the soul,—and with discourse upon this matter, says Dante, "it will be beautiful to finish speaking of that living and blessed Beatrice, of whom I intend to say no more in this book. . . . . . And I believe and affirm and am certain that I shall pass after this to another and better life, in which that glorious lady lives of whom my soul was enamored."[15]

But it is not from the "Convito" alone that this portion of the "Vita Nuova" receives illustration. In that passage of the "Purgatory" in which Beatrice is described as appearing in person to her lover the first time since her death, she addresses him in words of stern rebuke of his fickleness and his infidelity to her memory. The whole scene is, perhaps, unsurpassed in imaginative reality; the vision appears to have an actual existence, and the poet himself is subdued by the power of his own imagination. He tells the words of Beatrice with the same feeling with which he would have repeated them, had they fallen on his mortal ear. His grief and shame are real, and there is no element of feigning in them. That in truth he had seemed to himself to listen to and to behold what he tells, it is scarcely possible to doubt. Beatrice says,—

"Some while at heart my presence kept him sound;

My girlish eyes to his observance lending,
I led him with me on the right way bound.
When of my second age the steps ascending,
I bore my life into another sphere,
Then stole he from me, after others bending.
When I arose from flesh to spirit clear,
When beauty, worthiness, upon me grew,
I was to him less pleasing and less dear."[16]

But although Beatrice only gives utterance to the self-reproaches of Dante, we have seen already how fully he had atoned for this first and transient unfaithfulness of his heart. The remainder of the "Vita Nuova" shows how little she had lost of her power over him, how reverently he honored her memory, how constant was his love of her whom he should see never again with his earthly eyes. Returning to the "New Life,"—

"After this tribulation," he says, "at that time when many people were going to see the blessed image which Jesus Christ left to us as the likeness of his most beautiful countenance,[17] which my lady now beholds in glory, it happened that certain pilgrims passed through a street which is almost in the middle of that city where the gentlest lady was born, lived, and died,—and they went along, as it seemed to me, very pensive. And thinking about them, I said to myself, 'These appear to me to be pilgrims from a far-off region, and I do not believe that they have even heard speak of this lady, and they know nothing of her; their thoughts are rather of other things than of her; for, perhaps, they are thinking of their distant friends, whom we do not know.' Then I said to myself, 'I know, that, if these persons were from a neighboring country, they would show some sign of trouble as they pass through the midst of this grieving city.' Then again I said, 'If I could hold them awhile, I would indeed make them weep before they went out from this city; for I would say words to them which would make whoever should hear them weep.' Then, when they had passed out of sight, I proposed to make a sonnet in which I would set forth that which I had said to myself; and in order that it might appear more pity-moving, I proposed to say it as if I had spoken to them, and I said this sonnet, which begins, 'O pilgrims.'

"I called them *pilgrims* in the wide sense of that word; for pilgrims may be understood in two ways,—one wide, and one narrow. In the wide, whoever is out of his own country is so far a pilgrim; in the narrow use, by pilgrim is meant he only who goes to or returns from the house of St. James.[18] Moreover, it is to be known that those who travel in the service of the Most High are called by three distinct terms. Those who go beyond the sea, whence often they bring back the palm, are called *palmers*. Those who go to the house of Galicia are called *pilgrims*, because the burial-place of St. James was more distant from his country than that of any other of the Apostles. And those are called *romei* who go to Rome, where these whom I call pilgrims were going.

"O pilgrims, who in pensive mood move slow,
Thinking perchance of those who absent are,
Say, do ye come from land away so far
As your appearance seems to us to show?
"For ye weep not, the while ye forward go
Along the middle of the mourning town,
Seeming as persons who have nothing known
Concerning the sad burden of her woe.
"If, through your will to hear, your steps ye stay,
Truly my sighing heart declares to me
That ye shall afterwards depart in tears.
"For she[19] her Beatrice hath lost: and ye
Shall know, the words that man of her may say
Have power to make weep whoever hears."

Some time after this sonnet was written, two ladies sent to Dante, asking him for some of his rhymes. That he might honor their request, he wrote a new sonnet and sent it to them with two that he had previously composed. In his new sonnet, he told how his thought mounted to heaven, as a pilgrim, and beheld his lady in such condition of glory as could not be comprehended by his intellect; for our intellect, in regard to the souls of the blessed, is as weak as our eyes are to the sun. But though he could not clearly see where his thought led him, at least he understood that his thought told of his lady in glory.

"Beyond the sphere that widest orbit hath
Passeth the sigh that issues from my heart,
While weeping Love doth unto him impart
Intelligence which leads him on his path.
"When at the wished-for place his flight he stays,
A lady he beholds, in honor dight,
And shining so, that, through her splendid light,
The pilgrim spirit upon her doth gaze.
"He sees her such that his reporting words
I understand not, for he speaketh low
And strange to the sad heart which makes him tell;
"He speaketh of that gentle one, I know,
Since oft he Beatrice's name records;
So, ladies dear, I understand him well."

This was the last of the poems which Dante composed in immediate honor and memory of Beatrice, and is the last of those which he inserted in the "Vita Nuova." It was not that his love grew cold, or that her image became faint in his remembrance; but, as he tells us in a few concluding and memorable words, from this time forward he devoted himself to preparation for a work in which the earthly Beatrice should have less part, while the heavenly and blessed spirit of her whom he had loved should receive more becoming honors. The lover's grief was to find no more expression; the lamentations for the loss which could never be made good to him were to cease; the exhibition of a personal sorrow was at an end. Love and grief, in their double ministry, had refined, enlarged, and exalted his spirit to the conception of a design unparalleled in its nature, and of which no intellectual genius, unpurged by suffering, and unpenetrated in its deepest recesses by the spiritualizing heats of emotion, would have been capable of conceiving. Moreover, as time wore on, its natural result was gradually to withdraw the poet from the influence of temporary excitements of feeling, resulting from his experience of love and death, and to bring him to the contemplation of life as affected by the presence and the memory of Beatrice in its eternal and universal relations.

He tells us in the "Convito," that, "after some time, my mind, which neither such consolation as I could give it, nor that offered to it by others, availed to comfort, determined to turn to that method by which others in grief had consoled themselves. And I set myself to read that book, but little known, of Boethius, in which in prison and exile he had consoled himself. And hearing, likewise, that Tully had written a book, in which, treating of friendship, he had offered some words of comfort to Laelius, a most excellent man, on the death of Scipio, his friend, I read this also. And although at first it was hard for me to enter into their meaning, I at length entered into it so far as my knowledge of language, and such little capacity as I had, enabled me; by means of which capacity, I had already, like one dreaming, seen many things, as may be seen in the 'New Life.' And as it might happen that a man seeking silver should, beyond his expectation, find gold, which a hidden chance presents to him, not, perhaps, without Divine direction, so I, who sought for consolation, found not only a remedy for my tears, but also acquaintance with authors, with knowledge, and with books.

Nor did these serious and solitary studies withdraw him from the pursuit of wisdom among men and in the active world. Year by year, he entered more fully into the affairs of state, and took a larger portion of their conduct upon himself.

His heart kept fresh by abiding recollections of love, his faith quickened by and intermingled with the tenderest hopes, his imagination uplifted by the affection which overleaped the boundaries of the invisible world, and his intellect disciplined by study of books and of men, his experience enlarged by constant occupation in affairs, his judgment matured by the quick succession of important events in which he was involved,—every part of his nature was thus prepared for the successful accomplishment of that great and sacred design which he set before himself now in his youth. Heaven had called and selected him for a work which even in his own eyes partook somewhat of the nature of a prophetic charge. His strength was to be tested and his capacity to be approved. Life was ordered for the fulfilment of his commission. The men to whom God intrusts a message for the world find the service to which they are appointed one in which they must be ready to sacrifice everything. Dante looked forward, even at the beginning, to the end, and saw what lay between.

The pages of the "New Life" fitly close with words of that life in which all things shall be made new, "and there shall be no more death, neither sorrow, nor crying, neither shall there be any more pain; for the former things are passed away." The little book ends thus:—

"Soon after this, a wonderful vision appeared to me, in which I saw things which made me purpose to speak no more of this blessed one until I could more worthily treat of her. And to attain to this, I study to the utmost of my power, as she truly knoweth. So that, if it shall please Him through whom all things live, that my life be prolonged for some years, I hope to speak of her as never was spoken of any woman. And then may it please Him who is the Lord of Grace, that my soul may go to behold the glory of its lady, the blessed Beatrice, who in glory looks upon the face of Him, *qui est per omnia saecula benedictus* [who is Blessed forever]!"

In 1320, or perhaps not till 1321, the "Paradiso" was finished; in 1321, Dante died.

# Notes

1. See Lionardo Aretino's *Vita di Dante*.

2. Landino, and most of the commentators after him, state that Dante refers in this passage to the fear of the garrison taken in the place when it was recaptured the next year by the Pisans. But as Florence and Pisa continued at desperate enmity, Dante could hardly have witnessed this latter scene.

3. *Lamentations,* I, 1.

4. There is among the Canzoni of Dante one beginning, "Morte poich' io non truovo a cui mi doglia," which seems to have been written during the illness of Beatrice, in view of her approaching death. It is a beautiful and touching poem. Death is besought to spare that lady, "who of every good is the true gate."—"If thou extinguishest the light of those beautiful eyes, which were wont to be so sweet a guide to mine, I see that thou desirest my death."

"O Death, delay not mercy, if 'tis thine!
For now I seem to see the heavens ope,
And Angels of the Lord descending here,
Intent to bear away the holy soul
Of her whose honor there above is sung."

5. In the earlier part of the *Vita Nuova* there are many references to this number. We translate in full the passage given above, as one of the most striking illustrations of Dante's youthful fondness for seeking for the mystical relations and inner meanings of things. The attributing such importance to the properties of the number nine, though it might at first view seem puerile and an indication of poverty of feeling, was a portion

of the superstitious belief of the age, in which Dante naturally shared. The mysterious properties of numbers were a subject of serious study, and were connected with various branches of science and of life.

"Themistius vero, et Boethius, et Averrois Babylonius, cum Platone, sic numeros extollunt, ut neminem absque illis posse recte philosophari putent. Loquuntur autem de numero rationali et formali, non de materiali, sensibili, sive vocali numero mercatorum. . . . Sed intendunt ad proportionem ex illo resultantem, quem numerum naturalem et formalem et rationalem vocant; ex quo magna sacramenta emanant, tam in naturalibus quam divinis atque coelestibus. . . . In numeris itaque magnam latere efficaciam et virtutem tam ad bonum quam ad malum, non modo splendidissimi philosophi unanimiter docent, sed etiam doctores Catholici."—Cornelii Agrippae *De Occultâ Philosophiâ*, Liber Secundus, cc. 2, 3.

6. The perfect number is ten.

7. Thus it appears that Beatrice died on the 9th of June, 1290. She was a little more than twenty-four years old.

8. Compare with this passage Ballata v., "Io mi son pargoletta bella e nova," and Sonnet xlv., "Da quella luce che 'l suo corso gira"; the latter probably in praise of Philosophy.

9. The point is here lost in a translation—*factor* and *author* being expressed in the original by one word, *fattore*.

10. In this year, 1291, Giotto was but fifteen years old, and probably a student with Cimabue. Benvenuto da Imola, who lectured publicly at Bologna on the *Divina Commedia* in the year 1378, reports, that, while Giotto, still a young man, was painting at Padua, Dante visited him. And Vasari says, that it was a tradition, that Giotto had painted, in a chapel at Naples, scenes out of the *Apocalypse*, from designs furnished him by the poet. If we may believe another tradition, which there seems indeed little reason to doubt, Giotto went to Ravenna during the last years of Dante's life, that he might spend there some time in company with his exiled friend.

11. This Canzone, to the exposition of which the third Trattato of the *Convito* is devoted, has been inimitably translated by the Reverend Charles T. Brooks. We believe it to be the happiest version of one of Dante's minor poems that exists in our language,—and every student of the poet will recognize the success with which very great difficulties have been overcome. It appeared in the *Crayon*, for February, 1858.

12. The differences in the two accounts of this period of Dante's experience, and the view of Beatrice presented in the *Convito*, suggest curious and interesting questions, the solution of which has been obscured by the dulness of commentators. We must, however, leave the discussion of these points till some other opportunity.

13. *Convito*, Tratt. ii. c. 3.

14. *Convito*, Tratt. ii. c. 8.

15. Id. c. 9.

16. *Purgatory*, c. xxx. vv. 118–126.—Cayley's Translation.

17. The most precious relic at Rome, and the one which chiefly attracted pilgrims, during a long period of the Middle Ages, was the Veronica, or representation of the Saviour's face, supposed to have been miraculously impressed upon the handkerchief with which he wiped his face on his way to Calvary. It was preserved at St. Peter's and shown

only on special occasions. Compare with this passage the lines in the *Paradiso*, c. XXXI. 103–8:—

"As one that haply from Croatia came
    To see our Veronica, and no whit
Could be contented with its olden fame,
    Who in his heart saith, when they're showing it,
'O Jesu Christ! O very Lord God mine!
    Does truly this thy feature counterfeit?' "

Cayley

G. Villani says, that in 1300, the year of jubilee, for the consolation of Christian pilgrims, the Veronica was shown in St. Peter's every Friday, and on other solemn festivals." viii. 36.

18. The shrine of St. James, at Compostella, (contracted from *Giacomo Apostolo*,) in Galicia, was a great resort of pilgrims during the Middle Ages,—and Santiago, the military patron of Spain, was one of the most popular saints of Christendom. Chaucer says, the Wif of Bathe

"Had passed many a straunge streem;
At Rome sche hadde ben, and at Boloyne,
In Galice at Seynt Jame, and at Coloyne."

And Shakspeare, in *All's Well that Ends Well*, makes Helena represent herself as "St. Jacques's pilgrim."

19. The city.

# James Russell Lowell

## Dante

We shall barely allude to the minor poems, full of grace and depth of mystic sentiment, and which would have given Dante a high place in the history of Italian literature, even had he written nothing else. They are so abstract, however, that without the extrinsic interest of having been written by the author of the *Commedia*, they would probably find few readers. All that is certainly known in regard to the *Commedia* is that it was composed during the nineteen years which intervened between Dante's banishment and death. Attempts have been made to fix precisely the dates of the different parts, but without success, and the differences of opinion are bewildering. Foscolo has constructed an ingenious and forcible argument to show that no part of the poem was published before the author's death. The question depends somewhat on the meaning we attach to the word "published." In an age of manuscript the wide dispersion of a poem so long even as a single one of the three divisions of the *Commedia* would be accomplished very slowly. But it is difficult to account for the great fame which Dante enjoyed during the latter years of his life, unless we suppose that parts, at least, of his greatest work had been read or heard by a large number of persons. This need not, however, imply publication, and Witte, whose opinion is entitled to great consideration, supposes even the *Inferno* not to have been finished before 1314 or 1315. In a matter where certainty would be impossible, it is of little consequence to reproduce conjectural dates. In the letter to Can Grande, before alluded to, Dante himself has stated the theme of his song. He says that "the literal subject of the whole work is the state of the soul after death simply considered. But if the work be taken allegorically, the subject is man, as by merit or demerit, through freedom of the will, he renders himself liable to the reward or punishment of justice." He tells us that the work is to be interpreted in a literal, allegorical, moral, and anagogical sense, a mode then commonly employed with the Scriptures,[1] and of which he gives the following example: "To make which mode of treatment more clear, it may be applied in the following verses: *In exitu Israel de Aegypto, domus Jacob de populo barbaro, facta est Judaea sanctificatio ejus, Israel potestas ejus.*[2] For if we look only at the literal sense, it signifies the going out of the children of israel from Egypt in the time of Moses; if at the allegorical, it signifies our redemption through Christ; if at the moral, it signifies the conversion of the soul from the grief and misery of sin to a state of grace; and if at the anagogical, it signifies the passage of the blessed soul from the bondage of this corruption to the freedom of eternal glory." A Latin couplet, cited by one of the old commentators, puts the matter compactly together for us:

> "*Litera* gesta refert; quid credas *allegoria*;
> *Moralis* quid agas; quid speres *anagogia*.

Dante tells us that he calls his poem a comedy because it has a fortunate ending, and gives its title thus: " Here begins the comedy of Dante Alighieri, a Florentine by birth, but not in morals."[3] The poem consists of three parts, Hell, Purgatory, and Paradise. Each part is divided into thirty-three cantos, in allusion to the years of the Savior's life; for though the Hell contains thirty-four, the first canto is merely introductory. In the form of the verse (triple rhyme) we may find an emblem of the Trinity, and in the three divisions, of the threefold state of man, sin, grace, and beatitude. Symbolic meanings reveal themselves, or make themselves suspected, everywhere, as in the architecture of the Middle Ages. An analysis of the poem would be out of place here, but we must say a few words of Dante's position as respects modern literature. If we except Wolfram von Eschenbach, he is the first Christian poet, the first (indeed, we might say the only) one whose whole system of thought is colored in every finest fibre by a purely Christian theology. Lapse through sin, mediation, and redemption, these are the subjects of the three parts of the poem: or, otherwise stated, intellectual conviction of the result of sin, typified in Virgil (symbol also of that imperialism whose origin he sang); moral conversion after repentance, by divine grace, typified in Beatrice: reconciliation with God, and actual blinding vision of him,—"The pure in heart shall see God." Here are general truths which any Christian may accept and find comfort in. But the poem comes nearer to us than this. It is the real history of a brother man, of a tempted, purified, and at last triumphant human soul; it teaches the benign ministry of sorrow, and that the ladder of that faith by which man climbs to the actual fruition of things not seen *ex quovis ligno non fit*, but only of the cross manfully borne. The poem is also, in a very intimate sense, an apotheosis of woman. Indeed, as Marvell's drop of dew mirrored the whole firmament, so we find in the *Commedia* the image of the Middle Ages, and the sentimental gyniolatry of chivalry, which was at best but skin-deep, is lifted in Beatrice to an ideal and universal plane. It is the same with Catholicism, with imperialism, with the scholastic philosophy; and nothing is more wonderful than the power of absorption and assimilation in this man, who could take up into himself the world that then was, and reproduce it with such cosmopolitan truth to human nature and to his own individuality, as to reduce all contemporary history to a mere comment on his vision. We protest, therefore, against the parochial criticism which would degrade Dante to a mere partisan, which sees in him a Luther before his time, and would clap the *bonnet rouge* upon his heavenly muse.

Like all great artistic minds, Dante was essentially conservative, and, arriving precisely in that period of transition when Church and Empire were entering upon the modern epoch of thought, he strove to preserve both by presenting the theory of both in a pristine and ideal perfection. The whole nature of Dante was one of intense belief. There is proof upon proof that he believed himself invested with a divine mission. Like the Hebrew prophets, with whose writings his whole soul was imbued, it was back to the old worship and the God of the fathers that he called his people; and not Isaiah himself was more destitute of that humor, that sense of ludicrous contrast, which is an essential in the composition of a sceptic. In Dante's time, learning had something of a sacred character; the line was hardly yet drawn between the clerk and the possessor of supernatural powers; it was with the next generation, with the elegant Petrarch, even more truly than with the kindly Boccaccio, that the purely literary life, and that dilettanteism, which is the twin sister of scepticism, began. As a merely literary figure, the position of Dante is remarkable. Not only as respects thought, but as respects aesthetics also, his great poem stands as a monument on the boundary line between the ancient and modern. He not only marks, but is in himself, the transition. *Arma virumque cano*, that is the motto of classic song; the things of this world and great men. Dante says, *subjectum est homo*, not *vir*; my theme is man, not a man. The scene of the old epic and drama was in this world, and its catastrophe here; Dante lays his scene in the human soul, and his fifth act in the other world. He makes himself the protagonist of his own drama. In the *Commedia* for the first time Christianity wholly revolutionizes

Art, and becomes its seminal principle. But aesthetically also, as well as morally, Dante stands between the old and the new, and reconciles them. The theme of his poem is purely subjective, modern, what is called romantic; but its treatment is objective (almost to realism, here and there), and it is limited by a form of classic severity. In the same way he sums up in himself the two schools of modern poetry which had preceded him, and, while essentially lyrical in his subject, is epic in the handling of it. So also he combines the deeper and more abstract religious sentiment of the Teutonic races with the scientific precision and absolute systematism of the Romanic. In one respect Dante stands alone. While we can in some sort account for such representative men as Voltaire and Goethe (nay, even Shakespeare) by the intellectual and moral fermentation of the age in which they lived, Dante seems morally isolated and to have drawn his inspiration almost wholly from his own internal reserves. Of his mastery in style we need say little here. Of his mere language, nothing could be better than the expression of Rivarol: "His verse holds itself erect by the mere force of the substantive and verb, without the help of a single epithet." We will only add a word on what seems to us an extraordinary misapprehension of Coleridge, who disparages Dante by comparing his Lucifer wih Milton's Satan. He seems to have forgotten that the precise measurements of Dante were not prosaic, but absolutely demanded by the nature of his poem. He is describing an actual journey, and his exactness makes a part of the verisimilitude. We read the "Paradise Lost" as a poem, the *Commedia* as a record of fact; and no one can read Dante without believing his story, for it is plain that he believed it himself. It is false aesthetics to confound the grandiose with the imaginative. Milton's angels are not to be compared with Dante's, at once real and supernatural; and the Deity of Milton is a Calvinistic Zeus, while nothing in all poetry approaches the imaginative grandeur of Dante's vision of God at the conclusion of the *Paradiso*. In all literary history there is no such figure as Dante, no such homogeneousness of life and works, such loyalty to ideas, such sublime irrecognition of the unessential; and there is no moral more touching than that the contemporary recognition of such a nature, so endowed and so faithful to its endowment, should be summed up in the sentence of Florence: *Igne comburatur sic quod moriatur.*[4]

The range of Dante's influence is not less remarkable than its intensity. Minds, the antipodes of each other in temper and endowment, alike feel the force of his attraction, the pervasive comfort of his light and warmth. Boccaccio and Lamennais are touched with the same reverential enthusiasm. The imaginative Ruskin is rapt by him, as we have seen, perhaps beyond the limit where critical appreciation merges in enthusiasm; and the matter-of-fact Schlosser tells us that "he, who was wont to contemplate earthly life wholly in an earthly light, has made use of Dante, Landino, and Vellutello in his solitude to bring a heavenly light into his inward life." Almost all other poets have their seasons, but Dante penetrates to the moral core of those who once fairly come within his sphere, and possesses them wholly. His readers turn students, his students zealots, and what was a taste becomes a religion. The homeless exile finds a home in thousands of grateful hearts. *E venne da esilio in questa pace!*

Every kind of objection, aesthetic and other, may be, and has been, made to the *Divina Commedia*, especially by critics who have but a superficial acquaintance with it, or rather with the *Inferno*, which is as far as most English critics go. Coleridge himself, who had a way of divining what was in books, may be justly suspected of not going further, though with Carey to help him. Mr. Carlyle, who has said admirable things of Dante the man, was very imperfectly read in Dante the author, or he would never have put Sordello in hell and the meeting with Beatrice in paradise. In France it was not much better (though Rivarol has said the best thing hitherto of Dante's parsimony of epithet[5]) before Ozanam, who, if with decided ultramontane leanings, has written excellently well of our poet, and after careful study. Voltaire, though not without relentings toward a poet who had put popes heels upward in hell, regards him on the whole as a stupid monster and barbarian. It was no better in Italy, if we may trust Foscolo, who affirms that "neither Pelli nor others deservedly more celebrated than he ever read attentively the poem of Dante, perhaps never ran through it from the first verse to the last."[6] Accordingly we have heard that the *Commedia* was a sermon, a political pamphlet, the revengeful satire of a disappointed Ghibelline, nay, worse, of a turncoat Guelph. It is narrow, it is bigoted, it is savage, it is theological, it is mediaeval, it is heretical, it is scholastic, it is obscure, it is pedantic, its Italian is not that of *la Crusca*, its ideas are not those of an enlightened eighteenth century, it is everything, in short, that a poem should not be; and yet, singularly enough, the circle of its charm has widened in proportion as men have receded from the theories of Church and State which are supposed to be its foundation, and as the modes of thought of its author have become more alien to those of his readers. In spite of all objections, some of which are well founded, the *Commedia* remains one of the three or four universal books that have ever been written.

We may admit, with proper limitations, the modern distinction between the Artist and the Moralist. With the one Form is all in all, with the other

Tendency. The aim of the one is to delight, of the other to convince. The one is master of his purpose, the other mastered by it. The whole range of perception and thought is valuable to the one as it will minister to imagination, to the other only as it is available for argument. With the moralist use is beauty, good only as it serves an ulterior purpose; with the artist beauty is use, good in and for itself. In the fine arts the vehicle makes part of the thought, coalesces with it. The living conception shapes itself a body in marble, color, or modulated sound, and henceforth the two are inseparable. The results of the moralist pass into the intellectual atmosphere of mankind, it matters little by what mode of conveyance. But where, as in Dante, the religious sentiment and the imagination are both organic, something interfused with the whole being of the man, so that they work in kindly sympathy, the moral will insensibly suffuse itself with beauty as a cloud with light. Then that fine sense of remote analogies, awake to the assonance between facts seemingly remote and unrelated, between the outward and inward worlds, though convinced that the things of this life are shadows, will be persuaded also that they are not fantastic merely, but imply a substance somewhere, and will love to set forth the beauty of the visible image because it suggests the ineffably higher charm of the unseen original. Dante's ideal of life, the enlightening and strengthening of that native instinct of the soul which leads it to strive backward toward its divine source, may sublimate the senses till each becomes a window for the light of truth and the splendor of God to shine through. In him as in Calderon the perpetual presence of imagination not only glorifies the philosophy of life and the science of theology, but idealizes both in symbols of material beauty. Though Dante's conception of the highest end of man was that he should climb through every phase of human experience to that transcendental and supersensual region where the true, the good, and the beautiful blend in the white light of God, yet the prism of his imagination forever resolved the ray into color again, and he loved to show it also where, entangled and obstructed in matter, it became beautiful once more to the eye of sense. Speculation, he tells us, is the use, without any mixture, of our noblest part (the reason). And this part cannot in this life have its perfect use, which is to behold God (who is the highest object of the intellect), except inasmuch as the intellect considers and beholds him in his effects.[7] Underlying Dante the metaphysician, statesman, and theologian, was always Dante the poet,[8] irradiating and vivifying, gleaming through in a picturesque phrase, or touching things unexpectedly with that ideal light which softens and subdues like distance in the landscape. The stern outline of his system wavers and melts away before the eye of the reader in a mirage of imagination that lifts from beyond the sphere of vision and hangs in serener air images of infinite suggestion projected from worlds not realized, but substantial to faith, hope, and aspiration. Beyond the horizon of speculation floats, in the passionless splendor of the empyrean, the city of our God, the Rome whereof Christ is a Roman,[9] the citadel of refuge, even in this life, for souls purified by sorrow and self-denial, transhumanized[10] to the divine abstraction of pure contemplation. "And it is called Empyrean," he says in his letter to Can Grande, "which is the same as a heaven blazing with fire or ardor, not because there is in it a material fire or burning, but a spiritual one, which is blessed love or charity." But this splendor he bodies forth, if sometimes quaintly, yet always vividly and most often in types of winning grace.

Dante was a mystic with a very practical turn of mind. A Platonist by nature, an Aristotelian by training, his feet keep closely to the narrow path of dialectics, because he believed it the safest, while his eyes are fixed on the stars and his brain is busy with things not demonstrable, save by that grace of God which passeth all understanding, nor capable of being told unless by far-off hints and adumbrations. Though he himself has directly explained the scope, the method, and the larger meaning of his greatest work,[11] though he has indirectly pointed out the way to its interpretation in the *Convito*, and though everything he wrote is but an explanatory comment on his own character and opinions, unmistakably clear and precise, yet both man and poem continue not only to be misunderstood popularly, but also by such as should know better.[12] That those who confined their studies to the *Commedia* should have interpreted it variously is not wonderful, for out of the first or literal meaning others open, one out of another, each of wider circuit and purer abstraction, like Dante's own heavens, giving and receiving light.[13] Indeed, Dante himself is partly to blame for this. "The form or mode of treatment," he says, "is poetic, fictive, descriptive, digressive, transumptive, and withal definitive, divisive, probative, improbative and positive of examples." Here are conundrums enough, to be sure! To Italians at home, for whom the great arenas of political and religious speculation were closed, the temptation to find a subtler meaning than the real one was irresistible. Italians in exile, on the other hand, made Dante the stalking-horse from behind which they could take a long shot at Church and State, or at obscurer foes.[14] Infinitely touching and sacred to us is the instinct of intense sympathy which draws these latter toward their great forerunner, *exul immeritus* like themselves.[15] But they have too often wrung a meaning from Dante which is injurious to the man and out of keeping with the ideas of his age. The aim in expounding a great poem should be, not to discover an endless variety of meanings often contradictory, but whatever it has of great and perennial significance; for such it must have, or it would long ago have ceased to be living and operative, would long ago have taken refuge in the Chartreuse of great libraries, dumb thenceforth to all mankind. We do not mean to say that this minute exegesis is useless or unpraiseworthy, but only that it should be subsidiary to the larger way. It serves to bring out more clearly what is very wonderful in Dante, namely, the omnipresence of his memory throughout the work, so that its intimate coherence does not exist in spite of the reconditeness and complexity of allusion, but is woven out of them. The poem has many senses, he tells us, and there can be no doubt of it; but it has also, and this alone will account for its fascination, a living soul behind them all and informing all, an intense singleness of purpose, a core of doctrine simple, human, and wholesome, though it be also, to use his own phrase, the bread of angels.

Nor is this unity characteristic only of the *Divina Commedia*. All the works of Dante, with the possible exception of the *De vulgari Eloquio* (which is unfinished), are component parts of a Whole Duty of Man mutually completing and interpreting one another. They are also, as truly as Wordsworth's "Prelude," a history of the growth of a poet's mind. Like the English poet he valued himself at a high rate, the higher no doubt after Fortune had made him outwardly cheap. *Sempre il magnanimo si magnifica in suo cuore; e così lo pusillanimo per contrario sempre si tiene meno che non è.*[16] As in the prose of Milton, whose striking likeness to Dante in certain prominent features of character has been remarked by Foscolo, there are in Dante's minor works continual allusions to himself of great value as material for his biographer. Those who read attentively will discover that the tenderness he shows toward Francesca and her lover did not spring from any friendship for her family, but was a constant quality of his nature, and that what is called his revengeful ferocity is truly the implacable resentment of a lofty mind and a lover of good against evil, whether showing itself in private or public life; perhaps hating the former manifestation of it the most because he believed it to be the root of the latter,—a faith which those who have watched the course of politics in a democracy, as he had, will be inclined to share. His gentleness is all the more striking by contrast, like that silken compensation which blooms out of the thorny stem of the cactus. His moroseness,[17] his party spirit, and his personal vindictiveness are all predicated upon the *Inferno*, and upon a misapprehension or careless reading even of that. Dante's zeal was not of that sentimental kind, quickly kindled and as soon quenched, that hovers on the surface of shallow minds,

"Even as the flame of unctuous things is wont
To move upon the outer surface only";[18]

it was the steady heat of an inward fire kindling the whole character of the man through and through, like the minarets of his own city of Dis.[19] He was, as seems distinctive in some degree of the Latinized races, an unflinching *à priori* logician, not unwilling to "syllogize invidious verities,"[20] wherever they might lead him, like Sigier, whom he has put in paradise, though more than suspected of heterodoxy. But at the same time, as we shall see, he had something of the practical good sense of that Teutonic stock whence he drew a part of his blood, which prefers a malleable syllogism that can yield without breaking to the inevitable, but incalculable pressure of human nature and the stiffer logic of events. His theory of Church and State was not merely a fantastic one, but intended for the use and benefit of men as they were; and he allowed accordingly for aberrations, to which even the law of gravitation is forced to give place; how much more, then, any scheme whose very starting-point is the freedom of the will!

We are thankful for a commentator at last who passes dry-shod over the *turbide onde* of inappreciative criticism, and, quietly waving aside the thick atmosphere which has gathered about the character of Dante both as man and poet, opens for us his City of Doom with the divining rod of reverential study. Miss Rossetti comes commended to our interest, not only as one of a family which seems to hold genius by the tenure of gavelkind, but as having a special claim by inheritance to a love and understanding of Dante. She writes English with a purity that has in it something of feminine softness with no lack of vigor or precision. Her lithe mind winds itself with surprising grace through the metaphysical and other intricacies of her subject. She brings to her work the refined enthusiasm of a cultivated woman and the penetration of sympathy. She has chosen the better way (in which Germany took the lead) of interpreting Dante out of himself, the pure spring from which, and from which alone, he drew his inspiration, and not from muddy Fra Alberico or Abbate Giovacchino, from stupid visions of Saint Paul or voyages of Saint Brandan. She has written by far the best comment that has appeared in English, and we should say the best that has been done in England, were it not for her father's *Comento analitico*, for excepting which her filial piety will thank us. Students of Dante in the original will be grateful to her for many suggestive hints, and those who read him in English will find in her volume a travelling map in which the principal points and their connections are clearly set down. In what we shall say of Dante we shall endeavor only to supplement her interpretation with such side-lights as may have been furnished us by twenty years of assiduous study. Dante's thought is multiform, and, like certain street signs, once common, presents a different image according to the point of view. Let us consider briefly what was the plan of the *Divina Commedia* and Dante's aim in writing it, which, if not to justify, was at least to illustrate, for warning and example, the ways of God to man. The higher intention of the poem was to set forth the results of sin, or unwisdom, and of virtue, or wisdom, in this life, and consequently in the life to come, which is but the continuation and fulfilment of this. The scene accordingly is the spiritual world, of which we are as truly denizens now as hereafter. The poem is a diary of the human soul in its journey upwards from error through repentance to atonement with God. To make it apprehensible by those whom it was meant to teach, nay, from its very nature as a poem, and not a treatise of abstract morality, it must set forth everything by means of sensible types and images.

> "To speak thus is adapted to your mind,
> Since only from the sensible it learns
> What makes it worthy of intellect thereafter.
> On this account the Scripture condescends
> Unto your faculties, and feet and hands
> To God attributes, and means something else."[21]

Whoever has studied mediaeval art in any of its branches need not be told that Dante's age was one that demanded very palpable and even revolting types. As in the old legend, a drop of scalding sweat from the damned soul must shrivel the very skin of those for whom he wrote, to make them wince if not to turn them away from evil-doing. To consider his hell a place of physical torture is to take Circe's herd for real swine. Its mouth yawns not only under Florence, but before the feet of every man everywhere who goeth about to do evil. His hell is a condition of the soul, and he could not find images loathsome enough to express the moral deformity which is wrought by sin on its victims, or his own abhorrence of it. Its inmates meet you in the street every day.

> "Hell hath no limits, nor is circumscribed
> In one self place; for where we are is hell,
> And where hell is there we must ever be."[22]

It is our own sensual eye that gives evil the appearance of good, and out of a crooked hag makes a bewitching siren. The reason enlightened by the grace of God sees it as it truly is, full of stench and corruption.[23] It is this office of reason which Dante undertakes to perform, by divine commission, in the *Inferno*. There can be no doubt that he looked upon himself as invested with the prophetic function, and the Hebrew forerunners, in whose society his soul sought consolation and sustainment, certainly set him no example of observing the conventions of good society in dealing with the enemies of God. Indeed, his notions of good society were not altogether those of this world in any generation. He would have defined it as meaning "the peers" of Philosophy, "souls free from wretched and vile delights and from vulgar habits, endowed with genius and memory."[24] Dante himself had precisely this endowment, and in a very surprising degree. His genius enabled him to see and to show what he saw to others; his memory neither forgot nor forgave. Very hateful to his fervid heart and sincere mind would have been the modern theory which deals with sin as involuntary error, and by shifting off the fault to the shoulders of Atavism or those of Society, personified for purposes of excuse, but escaping into impersonality again from the grasp of retribution, weakens that sense of personal responsibility which is the root of self-respect and the safeguard of character. Dante indeed saw clearly enough that the Divine justice did at length overtake Society in the ruin of states caused by the corruption of private, and thence of civic, morals; but a personality so intense as his could not be satisfied with such a tardy and generalized penalty as this. "It is Thou," he says sternly, "who hast done this thing, and Thou, not Society, shalt be damned for it; nay, damned all the worse for this paltry subterfuge. This is not my judgment, but that of universal Nature[25] from before the beginning of the world."[26] Accordingly the highest reason, typified in his guide Virgil, rebukes him for bringing compassion to the judgments of God,[27] and again embraces him and calls the mother that bore him blessed, when he bids Filippo Argenti begone among the other dogs.[28] This latter case shocks our modern feelings the more rudely for the simple pathos with which Dante makes Argenti answer when asked who he was, "Thou seest I am one that weeps." It is also the one that makes most strongly for the theory of Dante's personal vindictiveness,[29] and it may count for what it is worth. We are not greatly concerned to defend him on that score, for he believed in the righteous use of anger, and that baseness was its legitimate quarry. He did not think the Tweeds and Fisks, the political wire-pullers and convention-packers, of his day merely amusing, and he certainly did think it the duty of an upright and thoroughly trained citizen to speak out severely and unmistakably. He believed firmly, almost fiercely, in a divine order of the universe, a conception whereof had been vouchsafed him, and that whatever and whoever hindered or jostled it, whether wilfully or blindly it mattered not, was to be got out of the way at all hazards; because obedience to God's law, and not making things generally comfortable, was the highest duty of man, as it was also his only way to true felicity. It has been commonly assumed that Dante was a man soured by undeserved misfortune, that he took up a wholly new outfit of political opinions with his fallen fortunes, and that his theory of life and of man's relations to it was altogether reshaped for him by the bitter musings of his exile. This would be singular, to say the least, in a man who tells us that he "felt himself indeed four-square against the strokes of chance," and whose convictions were so intimate that they were not merely intellectual conclusions, but parts of his moral being. Fortunately we are called on to believe nothing of the kind. Dante himself has supplied us with hints and dates which enable us to watch the germination and trace the growth of his double theory of government, applicable to man as he is a citizen of this world, and as he hopes to become hereafter a freeman of the celestial city. It would be of little consequence to show in which of two equally selfish and short-sighted parties a man enrolled himself six hundred years ago, but it is worth something to know that a man of ambitious temper and violent passions, aspiring to office in a city of factions, could rise to a level of principle so far above them all. Dante's opinions have life in them still, because they were drawn from living sources of reflection and experience, because they were reasoned out from the astronomic laws of history and ethics, and were not weather-guesses snatched in a glance at the doubtful political sky of the hour.

> Swiftly the politic goes: is it dark? he borrows a lantern;
> Slowly the statesman and sure, guiding his feet by the stars.

It will be well, then, to clear up the chronology of Dante's thought. When his ancestor Cacciaguida prophesies to him the life which is to be his after 1300,[30] he says, speaking of his exile:

> "And that which most shall weigh upon thy shoulders
> Will be the bad and foolish company
> With which into this valley thou shalt fall;
> . . . . . . . . . . . . . . . . . . . . . . . . . . . . . . . . . . . .
> Of their bestiality their own proceedings

> Of their bestiality their own proceedings
> Shall furnish proof; *so 't will be well for thee*
> *A party to have made thee by thyself.*"

Here both context and grammatical construction (infallible guides in a writer so scrupulous and exact) imply irresistibly that Dante had become a party by himself before his exile. The measure adopted by the Priors of Florence while he was one of them (with his assent and probably by his counsel), of sending to the frontier the leading men of both factions, confirms this implication. Among the persons thus removed from the opportunity of doing mischief was his dearest friend Guido Cavalcanti, to whom he had not long before addressed the *Vita Nuova*.[31] Dante evidently looked back with satisfaction on his conduct at this time, and thought it both honest and patriotic, as it certainly was disinterested. "We whose country is the world, as the ocean to the fish," he tells us, "though we drank of the Arno in infancy, and love Florence so much that, *because we loved her, we suffer exile unjustly,* support the shoulders of our judgment rather upon reason than the sen ses."[32] And again, speaking of old age, he says: "And the noble soul at this age blesses also the times past, and well may bless them, because, revolving them in memory, she recalls her righteous conduct, without which she could not enter the port to which she draws nigh, with so much riches and so great gain." This language is not that of a man who regrets some former action as mistaken, still less of one who repented it for any disastrous consequences to himself. So, in justifying a man for speaking of himself, he alleges two examples,—that of Boethius, who did so to "clear himself of the perpetual infamy of his exile"; and that of Augustine, "for, by the process of his life, which was from bad to good, from good to better, and from better to best, he gave us example and teaching."[33] After middle life, at least, Dante had that wisdom "whose use brings with it marvellous beauties, that is, contentment with every condition of time, and contempt of those things which others make their masters."[34] If Dante, moreover, wrote his treatise *De Monarchiâ* before 1302, and we think Witte's inference,[35] from its style and from the fact that he nowhere alludes to his banishment in it, conclusive on this point, then he was already a Ghibelline in the same larger and unpartisan sense which ever after distinguished him from his Italian contemporaries.

> "Let, let the Ghibllines ply their handicraft
> Beneath some other standard; for this ever
> Ill follows he who it and justice parts,"

he makes Justinian say, speaking of the Roman eagle.[36] His Ghibellinism, though undoubtedly the result of what he had seen of Italian misgovernment, embraced in its theoretical application the civilized world. His political system was one which his reason adopted, not for any temporary expediency, but because it conduced to justice, peace, and civilization, — the three conditions on which alone freedom was possible in any sense which made it worth having. Dante was intensely Italian, nay, intensely Florentine, but on all great questions he was, by the logical structure of his mind and its philosophic impartiality, incapable of intellectual provincialism.[37] If the circle of his affections, as with persistent natures commonly, was narrow, his thought swept a broad horizon from that tower of absolute self which he had reared for its speculation. Even upon the principles of poetry, mechanical and other,[38] he had reflected more profoundly than most of those who criticise his work, and it was not by chance that he discovered the secret of that magical word too few, which not only distinguishes his verse from all other, but so strikingly from his own prose. He never took the bit of art[39] between his teeth where only poetry, and not doctrine, was concerned.

If Dante's philosophy, on the one hand, was practical, a guide for the conduct of life, it was, on the other, a much more transcendent thing, whose body was wisdom, her soul love, and her efficient cause truth. It is a practice of wisdom from the mere love of it, for so we must interpret his *amoroso uso di sapienzia,* when we remember how he has said before[40] that "the love of wisdom for its delight or profit is not true love of wisdom." And this love must embrace knowledge in all its branches, for Dante is content with nothing less than a pancratic training, and has a scorn of *dilettanti*, specialists, and quacks. "Wherefore none ought to be called a true philosopher who for any delight loves any part of knowledge, as there are many who delight in composing *Canzoni*, and delight to be studious in them, and who delight to be studious in rhetoric and in music, and flee and abandon the other sciences which are all members of wisdom.[41] "Many love better to be held masters than to be so." With him wisdom is the generalization from many several knowledges of small account by themselves; it results therefore from breadth of culture and would be impossible without it. Philosophy is a noble lady (*donna gentil*)[42], partaking of the divine essence by a kind of eternal marriage, while with other intelligences she is united in a less measure "as a mistress of whom no lover takes complete joy."[43] The eyes of this lady are her demonstrations, and her smile is her persuasion. "The eyes of wisdom are her demonstrations by which truth is behold most certainly; and her smile is her persuasions in which the interior light of wisdom is shown under a certain veil, and in these two is felt that highest pleasure of beatitude which is the greatest good in paradise."[44] "It is to be known that the beholding this lady was so largely ordained for us, not merely to look upon the face which she shows us, but that we may desire to attain the things which she keeps concealed. And as through her much thereof is seen by reason, so by her we believe that every miracle may have its reason in a higher intellect, and consequently may be. Whence our good faith has its origin, whence comes the hope of those unseen things which we desire, and through that the operation of charity, by the which three virtues we rise to philosophize in that celestial Athens where the Stoics, Peripatetics, and Epicureans through the art of eternal truth accordingly concur in one will."[45]

# Notes

1. As by Dante himself in the Convito.
2. Psalm cxiv. 1, 2.
3. He commonly prefaced his letters with some such phrase as *exul immeritus*.
4. In order to fix more precisely in the mind the place of Dante in relation to the history of thought, literature, and events, we subjoin a few dates: Dante born, 1265; end of Crusades, death of St. Louis, 1270; Aquinas died, 1274; Bonaventura died, 1274; Giotto born, 1276; Albertus Magnus died, 1280; Sicilian vespers, 1282; death of Ugolino and Francesca da Rimini, 1282; death of Beatrice, 1290; Roger Bacon died, 1292; death of Cimabue, 1302; Dante's banishment, 1302; Petrarch born, 1304; Fra Dolcino burned, 1307; Pope Clement v at Avignon, 1309; Templars suppressed, 1312; Boccaccio born, 1313; Dante died, 1321; Wycliffe born, 1324; Chaucer born, 1328.
5. Rivarol characterized only a single quality of Dante's style, who knew how to spend as well as spare. Even the Inferno, on which he based his remark, might have put him on his guard. Dante understood very well the use of ornament in its fitting place. *Est enim exornatio alicujus convenientis additio*, he tells us in his De Vulgari Eloquio (Lib. II. C. II.). His simile of the doves (Inferno, v. 82 et seq.), perhaps the most exquisite in all poetry, quite oversteps Rivarol's narrow limit of "substantive and verb."
6. Discorso sul testo, ec., XVIII.
7. Convito, B. IV. C. XXII.
8. It is remarkable that when Dante, in 1297, as a preliminary condition to active politics, enrolled himself in the guild of physicians and apothecaries, he is qualified only with the title *poeta*. The arms of the Alighieri (curiously suitable to him who *sovra gli altri come aquila vola*) were a wing of gold in a field of azure. His vivid sense of beauty even hovers sometimes like a *corposant* over the somewhat stiff lines of his Latin prose. For example, in his letter to the kings and princes of Italy on the coming of Henry

VII.: "A new day brightens, revealing the dawn which already scatters the shades of long calamity; already the breezes of morning gather; *the lips of heaven are reddening!*"

9. Purgatorio, XXXII. 100.

10. Paradiso, I. 70.

11. In a letter to Can Grande (XI. of the Epistolae).

12. Witte, Wegele, and Ruth in German, and Ozanam in French, have rendered ignorance of Dante inexcusable among men of culture.

13. Inferno, VII. 75. "Nay, his style," says Miss Rossetti, "is more than concise: it is elliptical, it is recondite. A first thought often lies coiled up and hidden under a second; the words which state the conclusion involve the premises and develop the subject." (p. 3.)

14. A complete vocabulary of Italian billingsgate might be selected from Biagioli. Or see the concluding pages of Nannucci's excellent tract "Intorno alle voci usate da Dante," Corfù, 1840. Even Foscolo could not always refrain. Dante should have taught them to shun such vulgarities. See Inferno, XXX. 131–148.

15. "My Italy, my sweetest Italy, for having loved thee too much I have lost thee, and, perhaps, . . . . ah, may God avert the omen! But more proud than sorrowful, for an evil endured for thee alone, I continue to consecrate my vigils to thee alone. . . . An exile full of anguish, perchance, availed to sublime the more in thy Alighieri that lofty soul which was a beautiful gift of thy smiling sky; and an exile equally wearisome and undeserved now avails, perhaps, to sharpen my small genius so that it may penetrate into what he left written for thy instruction and for his glory." (Rossetti, Disamina, ec., p. 405.) Rossetti is himself a proof that a noble mind need not be narrowed by misfortune. His "Comment" (unhappily incomplete) is one of the most valuable and suggestive.

16. The great-minded man ever magnifies himself in his heart, and in like manner the pusillanimous holds himself less than he is. (Convito, Tr. I. c. 11.)

17. Dante's notion of virtue was not that of an ascetic, nor has any one ever painted her in colors more soft and splendid than he in the Convito. She is "sweeter than the lids of Juno's eyes," and he dwells on the delights of her love with a rapture which kindles and purifies. So far from making her an inquisitor, he says expressly that she "should be gladsome and not sullen in all her works." (Convito, Tr. I. c. 8.) "Not harsh and crabbed as dull fools suppose"!

18. Inferno, XIX. 28, 29.

19. Inferno, VIII. 70–75.

20. Paradiso, X. 138.

21. Paradiso, IV. 40–45 (Longfellow's version).

22. Marlowe's "Faustus." "Which way I fly is hell; myself am hell." (Paradise Lost, IV. 75.) In the same way, *ogni dove in cielo e Paradiso*. (Paradiso, III. 88, 89.)

23. Purgatorio, XIX. 7–33.

24. Convito, Tr. II. c. 16.

25. *La natura universale, cioè Iddio*. (Convito, Tr. III c. 4.)

26. Inferno, III. 7, 8.

27. Inferno, XX. 30. Mr. W. M. Rossetti strangely enough renders this verse "Who hath a passion for God's judgeship." *Compassion porta*, is the reading of the best texts, and Witte adopts it. Buti's comment is "*cioè porta pena e dolore di colui che giustamente*

è condannato da Dio che e sempre giusto." There is an analogous passage in "The Revelation of the Apostle Paul," printed in the "Proceedings of the American Oriental Society" (Vol. VIII. pp. 213, 214): "And the angel answered and said, 'Wherefore dost thou weep? Why! art thou more merciful than God?' And I said, 'God forbid, O my lord; for God is good and long-suffering unto the sons of men, and he leaves every one of them to his own will, and he walks as he pleases.' " This is precisely Dante's view.

28. Inferno, VIII. 40.

29. "I following her (Moral Philosophy) in the work as well as the passion, so far as I could, abominated and disparaged the errors of men, not to the infamy and shame of the erring, but of the errors." (Convito, Tr. IV. c. 1.) "Wherefore in my judgment as he who defames a worthy man ought to be avoided by people and not listened to, so a vile man descended of worthy ancestors ought to be hunted out by all." (Convito, Tr. IV. c. 29.)

30. Paradiso, XVII. 61–69.

31. It is worth mentioning that the sufferers in his Inferno are in like manner pretty exactly divided between the two parties. This is answer enough to the charge of partiality. He even puts persons there for whom he felt affection (as Brunetto Latini) and respect (as Farinata degli Uberti and Frederick II.). Till the French looked up their MSS., it was taken for granted that the *beccajo di Parigi* (Purgatorio, XX. 52) was a drop of Dante's gall. "Ce fu Huez Capez c' on apelle bouchier." Hugues Capet, p. 1.

32. De Vulgari Eloquio, Lib. I. Cap. VI. Cf. Inferno, XV. 61–64.

33. Convito, Tr. IV. c. 23. Ib. Tr. I. c. 2.

34. Convito, Tr. III. c. 13.

35. Opp. Min., ed. Fraticelli, Vol. II. pp. 281 and 283. Witte is inclined to put it even earlier than 1300, and we believe he is right.

36. Paradiso, VI. 103–105.

37. Some Florentines have amusingly enough doubted the genuineness of the De vulgari Eloquio, because Dante therein denies the pre-eminence of the Tuscan dialect.

38. See particularly the second book of the De vulgari Eloquio.

39. Purgatorio, XXXIII. 141. "That thing one calls beautiful whose parts answer to each other, because pleasure results from their harmony." (Convito, Tr. I. c. 5.) Carlyle says that "he knew too, partly, that his work was great, the greatest a man could do." He knew it fully. Telling us how Giotto's fame as a painter had eclipsed that of Cimabue, he takes an example from poetry also, and selecting two Italian poets,—one the most famous of his predecessors, the other of his contemporaries,—calmly sets himself above them both (Purgatorio, XI. 97–99), and gives the reason for his supremacy (Purgatorio, XXIV. 49–62). It is to be remembered that *Amore* in the latter passage does not mean love in the ordinary sense, but in that transcendental one set forth in the Convito,—that state of the soul which opens it for the descent of God's spirit, to make it over into his own image. "Therefore it is manifest that in this love the Divine virtue descends into men in the guise of an angel, . . . . and it is to be noted that the descending of the virtue of one thing into another is nothing else than reducing it to its own likeness." (Convito, Tr. III. c. 14.)

40. Convito, Tr. III. c. 11. Ib. Tr. I. c. 11.

41. Convito, Tr. III. c. 12–15.

42. Inferno, II. 94. The *donna gentil* is Lucia, the prevenient Grace, the *light* of God

which shows the right path and guides the feet in it. With Dante God is always the sun, "which leadeth others right by every road." (Inferno, I. 18.) "The spiritual and unintelligible Sun, which is God." (Convito. Tr. III. c. 12) His light "enlighteneth every man that cometh into the world," but his dwelling is in the heavens. He who wilfully deprives himself of this light is spiritually dead in sin. So when in Mars he beholds the glorified spirits of the martyrs he exclaims, "O Elios, who so arrayest them!" (Paradiso, XIV. 96.) Blanc (Vocabolario, *sub voce*) rejects this interpretation. But Dante, entering the abode of the Blessed, invokes the "good Apollo," and shortly after calls him *divina virtù*. We shall have more to say of this hereafter.

43. Convito, Tr. III. c. 12.

44. Convito, Tr. III. c. 15. Recalling how the eyes of Beatrice lift her servant through the heavenly spheres, and that smile of hers so often dwelt on with rapture, we see how Dante was in the habit of commenting and illustrating his own works. We must remember always that with him the allegorical exposition is the true one (Convito, Tr. IV. c. 1), the allegory being a truth which is hidden under a beautiful falsehood (Convito, Tr. II. c. 1), and that Dante thought his poems without this expostion "under some shade of obscurity, so that to many their beauty was more grateful than their goodness" (Convito, Tr. I. c. 1), "because the goodness is in the meaning, and the beauty in the ornament of the words" (Convito, Tr. II. c. 12).

45. Convito, Tr. III. c. 14.

# W. T. Harris

## The Spiritual Sense of Dante's "Divina Commedia."

### PREFACE

TO THIS ESSAY on the spiritual significance of the "Divina Commedia" I prefix a few words, interesting only to the few who study works of literature for spiritual insight. Such insight is of very slow growth, and though I cannot be permitted to claim anything more than a very feeble approach to it in the reflections which I bring forward here, yet I know that the theme dignifies the writer, and that the circumstances of a struggle to attain a high object are worthy of mention, even if the success of the struggle is not great.

My first reading in Dante began as early as 1858, and continued at intervals for four years, by which time I had completed only the "Inferno," studying it superficially in the original and using Carlyle's translation as a sort of dictionary and general guide to its meaning—perhaps better described in college slang as a "pony" or "crib." I read also the translations of Wright and Cary of the "Purgatorio" and "Paradiso" at this time.

The poem had attractive poetic passages for me at the time, but as a vision of the future state of any portion of mankind I could not accept it. Its horrors repelled me. After this I began to look for some point of view whence I could see a permanent truth in the poem. The possibility of an inner meaning that would reconcile me to the outer form of a work of art I had already learned in 1861 by studying landscape painting and afterward by a like study of Beethoven's masterpieces and, more especially, of Schumann's "Pilgrimage of the Rose" and Mendelssohn's "Song of Praise."

The "Last Judgment," by Michel Angelo, I had begun to study as early as 1863 in an outline engraving, and by 1865 a permanent meaning had begun to dawn upon me. I saw that the picture presented symbolically the present condition of the saints and sinners, not as they seem to themselves and others, but as they are in very truth. It placed them under the form of eternity, to use the expressive phrase of Spinoza, "*Sub specie* aeternitatis." At once Dante's "Inferno" also became clear, as having substantially the same meaning. I saw that the great sculptor and painter had derived his ideas from the poet. The ideas of Thomas Carlyle, in his chapter on "Natural Supernaturalism" in the "Sartor Resartus," seemed to me to offer a parallel thought to the "Last Judgment." Remove the illusion of time, and thus bring together the deed and its consequence, and you see it under the form of eternity. So, too, paint the deed with colors derived from all its consequences, and you will picture its final or ultimate judgment. This interpretation I wrote out in 1868 and read to a circle of friends, sometimes called "The St. Louis Art Society," and it was published in the April number of the "Journal of Speculative Philosophy" for 1869, under the title "Michel Angelo's Last Judgment." I quote below the passage in which I connected the view of the sculptor and the poet.

It was about this time (1869) that it occurred to me that there is a threefold view of human deeds. First, there is the deed taken with the total compass of its effects and consequences—this is the picture of the "Inferno."

Secondly, there is the evil deed seen in its secondary effects by way of reaction on the doer—a process of gradual revelation to the doer that his deed is not salutary either for himself or for others. The evil doer at first does not see that his being is so closely connected with the being of society that if he does injury to his fellows, thinking to derive selfish benefit at the expense of others, he always works evil to himself sooner or later. He thinks that his cunning is sufficient to secure the good to himself, and at the same time to avoid the reaction of evil on himself. But the real process of reaction which comes with time teaches him the lesson of the impossibility of divorcing the individual doer from the consequences of his deeds. This secondary process of reaction is a purifying process in so far as it teaches this lesson to the evil doer. He cannot escape purification to the extent that he becomes enlightened by the wisdom of this experience.

If he sees that he has to receive the consequences of his deeds, he must needs acquire the habit on considering the ultimate effects of actions; he will renounce deeds that can end only in pain and repression of normal growth.

Hence a third aspect of human deeds becomes manifest—the purified action which emits only such deeds as build up the social whole affirmatively, and consequently return upon the doer to bless him continually. The purified human will dwells in the "Paradiso," while during the process of purification it is in the "Purgatorio." It is in purgatory so long as it is in the state of being surprised by the discovery that its selfish deeds invariably bring their punishment upon the doer, and so long as the individual still hesitates to renounce utterly and entirely the selfish deed. This renunciation, of course, takes place when the soul has thoroughly accustomed itself to seeing the selfish deed and its consequences in one unity; then its loveliness has entirely departed. The taste of a poison may be sweet to the mouth of a child, but it soon produces painful gripes. The child learns to associate the sweet taste and the gripes with the mental picture of the poison, and now the very sight of it becomes loathsome. When temptation is no longer possible, the child is purified as regards this danger.

From 1870 to 1880 every year brought me seemingly valuable thoughts on some part of Dante's great work. I presented these views in lectures to audiences from time to time. In the summer and fall of 1883 I made new studies on the whole poem, and gave a course of ten lectures to a St. Louis audience in 1884 (January to March). The present paper, which was written in 1886 for the Concord School of Philosophy, is a summary of the St. Louis course, with marginal notes added at this time.

In 1886 I came into possession of a copy of Scartazzini's essay, "Ueber die Congruenz der Sünden in Dante's Hölle," and discovered that many of the conjectures as to the relation between sins and punishments in the "Inferno" which I had set forward in these lectures were already the property of the Dante public through that distinguished scholar's paper in the Annual of the German Dante Society ("Jahrb. d. deutschen Dante Gesellschaft," vol. iv, 1877). In this very valuable article Scartazzini frequently quotes with approval the interpretations of Karl Graul, who seems to have suggested many happy explanations of the symbolism.[1] One would wish to see this work of Graul reproduced in English. Meanwhile I expect to publish in the next number of this Journal the essay of Scartazzini, which has been translated by Miss Thekla Bernays, of St. Louis, for the purpose.

Had I met with Graul's work twenty-five years ago, when I first began to see the inner meaning of the poem, I should have adopted it as my guide. Graul's volume bears the imprint of 1843; but Scartazzini's essay did not appear until 1877, or after my views had taken shape.

In matters of interpreting myths and symbols there is so wide a margin for arbitrary exercise of fancy that it must be regarded as a strong evidence of the probable truthfulness of a theory when two entirely independent readers arrive at the same results in detail. At least I have been much strengthened in my own views, and have gained in respect for my own way of studying the poem on reading the thoughts of the greatest of living Dante scholars and finding so many coincidences.

(From an Essay on Michel Angelo's "Last Judgment" in the "Journal of Speculative Philosophy" for April, 1869.)

"Michel Angelo passes by all subordinate scenes and seizes at once the supreme moment of all History—of the very world itself and all that it contains. This is the vastest attempt that the Artist can make, and is the same that Dante has ventured in the 'Divina Commedia.'

"In Religion we seize the absolute truth as a process going on in Time: the deeds of humanity are judged 'after the end of the world.' After death Dives goes to torments, and Lazarus to the realm of the blest.

"The immense significance of the Christian idea of Hell as compared with the Hades of Greek and Roman Mythology we cannot dwell upon. This idea has changed the hearts of mankind. That man by will determines his destiny, and that "between right and wrong doing there is a difference eternally fixed"—this dogma has tamed the fierce barbarian blood of Europe and is the producer of what we have of civilization and freedom in the present time. In the so-called heathen civilizations there is a substratum of fate presupposed under all individual character which prevents the complete return of the consequences of individual acts upon their author. Thus the citizen was not made completely universal by the laws of the state as in modern times. The Christian doctrine of Hell is the first appearance in a conceptive form of this deepest of all comprehensions of Personality; and out of it have grown our modern humanitarian doctrines, however paradoxical this may seem.

"In this supreme moment all worldly distinctions fall away, and the naked soul stands before Eternity with naught save the pure essence of its deeds to rely upon. All souls are equal before God so far as mere worldly eminence is concerned. Their inequality rest solely upon the degree that they have realized the Eternal will by their own choice.

"But this dogma as it is held in the Christian Religion is not merely a dogma; it is the deepest of speculative truths. As such it is seized by Dante and Michel Angelo, and in this universal form every one must recognize it if he would free it from all narrowness and sectarianism. The point of view is this: The whole world is seized at once under the form of Eternity; all things are reduced to their lowest terms. Every deed is seen through the perspective of its own consequences. Hence every human being under the influence of any one of the deadly sins—Anger, Lust, Avarice, Intemperance, Pride, Envy, and Indolence—is being dragged down into the Inferno just as Michel Angelo has depicted. On the other hand, any one who practises the cardinal virtues— Prudence, Justice, Temperance, and Fortitude—is elevating himself toward celestial clearness.

"If any one will study Dante carefully he will find that the punishments of the 'Inferno' are emblematical of the very states of mind one experiences when under the influence of the passions there punished.

"To find the punishment for any given sin, Dante looks at the state of mind which it causes in the sinner, and gives it its appropriate emblem.

"The angry and sullen are plunged underneath deep putrid mud, thus corresponding to the state of mind produced by anger. If we try to understand a profound truth, or to get into a spiritual frame of mind, when terribly enraged, we shall see ourselves in putrid mud, and breathing its thick, suffocating exhalations. So, too, those who yield to the lusts of the flesh are blown about in thick darkness by violent winds. The avaricious carry heavy weights; the intemperate suffer the eternal rain of foul water, hail, and snow (dropsy, dyspepsia, delirium tremens, gout, apoplexy, etc.).

"So Michel Angelo in this picture has seized things in their essential nature: he has pierced through the shadows of time, and exhibited to us at one view the world of humanity as it is in the sight of God, or as it is in its ultimate analysis. Mortals are there, not as they seem to themselves or to their companions, but as they are when measured by the absolute standard—the final destiny of spirit. This must recommend the work to all men of all times, whether one holds to this or that theological creed, for it is the Last Judgment in the sense that it is the ultimate or absolute estimate to be pronounced upon each deed, and the question of the eternal punishment of any individual is not necessarily brought into account. Everlasting punishment is the true state of all who persist in the commission of those sins. The sins are indissolubly bound up in pain. Through all time anger shall bring with it the 'putrid-mud' condition of the soul; the indulgence of lustful passions, the stormy tempest and spiritual night; intemperance, the pitiless rain of hail and snow and foul water. The wicked sinner —so far forth and so long as he is a sinner—shall be tormented forever, for we are now and always in Eternity. 'Every one of us,' as Carlyle says, 'is a Ghost. Sweep away the Illusion of Time; glance from the near moving cause to its far-distant mover; compress the threescore years into three minutes—are we not spirits that are shaped into a body, into an Appearance, and that fade away again into air and invisibility? We start out of Nothingness, take figure, and are apparitions; 'round us, as 'round the veriest spectre, is Eternity; and to Eternity minutes are as years and aeons.'

"Thus by the Divine Purpose of the Universe—by the Absolute—every deed is seen in its true light, in the entire compass of its effects. Just as we strive in our human laws to establish justice by turning back upon the criminal the effects of his deeds, so, in fact, when placed 'under the form of Eternity,' all deeds do return to the doer, and this is the final adjustment, the 'end of all things'—it is the Last Judgment. And this judgment is now and is always the only actual Fact in the world."

(From an article on "The Relation of Religion to Art,"
"Journal of Speculative Philosophy," April, 1876.)

'This first great Christian poem (Dante's 'Divina Commedia') is regarded by Schelling as the archetype of all Christian poetry. . . . The poem embodies the Catholic view of life, and for this reason is all the more wholesome for study by modern Protestants. The threefold future world—Inferno, Purgatorio, Paradiso—presents us the exhaustive picture of man's relation to his deeds. The Protestant 'hereafter' omits the purgatory but includes the Inferno and Paradiso. What has become of this missing link in modern Protestant Art? we may inquire, and our inquiry is a pertinent one, for there is no subject connected with the relation of Religion to Art which is so fertile in suggestive insights to the investigator. . . .

"One must reduce life to its lowest terms, and drop away all consideration of its adventitious surroundings. The deeds of man in their threefold aspect are judged in this 'mystic, unfathomable poem.' The great fact of human responsibility is the key-note. Whatever man does he does to himself. If he does violence, he injures himself. If he works righteousness, he creates a paradise for himself.

"Now, a deed has two aspects: First, its immediate relation to the doer. The mental atmosphere in which one does a deed is of first consideration. If a wrong or wicked deed, then is the atmosphere of the criminal close and stifling to the doer. The angry man is rolling about suffocating in putrid mud. The incontinent is driven about by violent winds of passion. Whatever deed a man shall do must be seen in the entire perspective of its effects to exhibit its relation to the doer. The Inferno is filled with those whose acts and habits of life surround them with an atmosphere of torture.

"One does not predict that such punishment of each individual is eternal; but one thing is certain: that with the sins there punished, there is such special torture eternally connected. . . .

"Wherever the sin shall be, there shall be connected with it the atmosphere of the Inferno, which is its punishment. The doer of the sinful deed plunges into the Inferno on its commission.

"But Dante wrote the 'Purgatorio,' and in this portrays the secondary effect of sin. The inevitable punishment bound up with sin burns with purifying flames each sinner. The immediate effect of the deed is the Inferno, but the secondary effect is purification. Struggling up the steep side of purgatory under their painful burdens go sinners punished for incontinence—lust, gluttony, avarice, anger, and other sins that find their place of punishment also in the Inferno.

"Each evil doer shall plunge into the Inferno, and shall scorch over the flames of his own deeds until he repents and struggles up the mountain of purgatory.

"In the 'Paradiso' we have doers of those deeds, which, being thoroughly positive in their nature, do not come back as punishment upon their authors.

"The correspondence of sin and punishment is noteworthy. Even our jurisprudence discovers a similar adaptation. If one steals and deprives his neighbor of property, we manage by our laws to make his deed glide off from society and come back on the criminal, and thus he steals his own freedom and gets a cell in jail. If a murderer takes life, his deed is brought back to him, and he takes his own.

"The depth of Dante's insight discovers to him all human life stripped of its wrappings, and every deed coming straight back upon the doer, inevitably fixing his place in the scale of happiness and misery. It is not so much a 'last judgment' of individual men as it is of deeds in the abstract, for the brave man who sacrifices his life for another dwells in paradise so far as he contemplates his participation in that deed, but writhes in the Inferno in so far as he has allowed himself to slip, through some act of incontinence.

"If we return now to our question, What has become of the purgatory in modern literature? a glance will show us that the fundamental idea of Dante's purgatory has formed the chief thought of Protestant, 'humanitarian,' works of art.

"The thought that the sinful and wretched live a life of reaction against the effects of their deeds is the basis of most of our novels. Most notable are the works of Nathaniel Hawthorne in this respect. His whole art is devoted to the portrayal of the purgatorial effects of sin or crime upon its authors. The consciousness of the deed and the consciousness of the verdict of one's fellow-men continually burn at the heart, and with slow, eating fires, consume the shreds of selfishness quite away. In the 'Marble Faun' we have the spectacle of an animal nature betrayed by sudden impulse into a crime; and the torture of this consciousness gradually purifies and elevates the semi-spiritual being into a refined humanity.

"The use of suffering, even if brought on by sin and error, is the burden of our best class of novels. George Eliot's 'Middle-march,' 'Adam Bede,' 'Mill on the Floss,' and 'Romola'—with what intensity these portray the spiritual growth through error and pain!

"Thus, if Protestantism has omitted Purgatory from its Religion, certainly Protestant literature has taken it up and absorbed it entire."

## § 1. Introduction

That a poem should possess a spiritual sense does not seem to the common view to be at all necessary to it. It must have a poetic structure; but does a poetic structure involve a spiritual sense? It is essential that a poem should be built out of tropes and personification. Its real poetic substance, in fact, is an insight into the correspondence that exists between external events and situations on the one hand and internal ideas and movements of the soul on the other. Rhyme and rhythm are less essential than this. The true poet is a creator in a high sense, because he turns hitherto opaque facts into transparent metaphors, or because he endows dead things with souls and thus personifies them. The poet uses material forms, so that there glows a sort of morning redness through them.

There is something symbolic in a poem, but there is quite as much danger from symbolism and allegory in a work of art as from philosophy. If the poet can think philosophic ideas in a philosophic form he will be apt to spoil his poem by attempting to introduce them into its texture. An allegory is repellent to the true poetic taste. The music of a verse is spoiled by the evidence of a forced rhyme. So the glad surprise of a newly discovered correspondence between the visible and invisible is unpleasantly suppressed by an intimation that it is a logical consequence of a previously assumed comparison or metaphor. To force a symbol into an allegory necessarily demands the sacrifice of the native individuality of the facts and events which follow in the train of the primary event or situation. They must all wear its livery, whereas fresh poetic insight is fain to turn each one into a new and original revelation of eternal beauty.

Neither philosophy as such nor allegory can be the best feature of a genuine poem. Nevertheless, there are certain great poems which owe their supreme pre-eminence to the circumstance that they treat themes of such universal significance that they reflect the operation of a supreme principle and its consequences in the affairs of a world, and hence exhibit a philosophy realized, or incarnated, as it were. Their events and situations, too, being universal types, may be interpreted into many series of events within the world order, and hence stand for so many allegories. Such poems may be said to have a spiritual sense. Homer's "Iliad," and more especially his "Odyssey," contain a philosophy and many allegories. Goethe's "Faust" contains likewise a philosophy, and its poetic types are all allegoric, without detriment to their genuine poetic value.

But of all the great world-poems, unquestionably Dante's "Divina Commedia" may be justly claimed to have a spiritual sense, for it possesses a philosophic system and admits of allegorical interpretation. It is *par excellence* the religious poem of the world. And religion, like philosophy, deals directly with a first principle of the universe, while, like poetry, it clothes its universal ideas in the garb of special events and situations, making them types, and hence symbols, of the kind which may become allegories.

Homer, too, shows us the religion of the Greeks, but it is an art-religion, having only the same aim as essential poetry—to turn the natural into a symbol of the spiritual. Dante's theme is the Christian religion, which goes beyond the problem of transfiguring nature and deals with the far deeper problem of the salvation of man. For man, as the summit of nature, transfigures nature at the same time that he attains the divine. The insight into the divine-human nature of the highest principle of the universe, and the consequent necessity of human immortality and possibility of human growth into divine perfection, includes the Greek principle as a subordinate phase.

It is proper, therefore, to study the spiritual sense of the great poem of Dante, and to inquire into its philosophy and its allegory. What is Dante's theory of the world and what manner of world-order results from it? Not that we should expect that the philosophic thought of a poet would be of a conscious and systematic order; that would not promise us so much. It is rather his deep underlying view of the world—so deep a conviction that he knows of no other adequate statement for it than the structure of his poem. If an artist does not feel that his work of art utters more completely his thought than some prosaic statement may do it, he is not an artist.

In fact, a poet may introduce a theory of the world into his poem which is not so deep and comprehensive as that implied in the spiritual sense of his poem. This, we shall see, is often true in the case of Dante—that his poetic vision has glimpses of a higher world-view than is contained in his interpretation of the philosophy of the school men; and his poetic discrimination of the states of the soul under mortal sin is deeper and truer than the ethical scheme which he borrowed from that philosophy.

Moreover, although allegory is the favorite vehicle for religious revelation, and we have in this, the most religious of poems, a predominating tendency toward it, yet his allegory does not cover (or discover) so deep a spiritual sense as the genuine art-structure of his poem reveals.

In the beginning, let us call to mind the fundamental distinction between Christianity and Eastern religions. In the latter the Absolute or Supreme Principle is conceived as utterly without form and void. It is conceived as entirely lacking in particularity, utterly devoid of attributes, properties, qualities, modes, and distinctions of any kind whatever. Such is the Brahm of the Hindoo or the subjective state of Nirvana of the Buddhists. Such is the western reflection of this thought at Alexandria and elsewhere in the doctrines of Gnosticism and Neo-Platonism. Basilides and Valentinus, Proclus and Jamblichus, all hold to an utterly indeterminate, formless first principle. As a result, it follows that they are obliged to resort to arbitrary and fanciful constructions in order to explain the origin of a world of finite creatures.

Quite different is the Christian view of the Absolute. It holds that the Absolute is not formless, but the very essence of all form— pure form, pure self-distinction, or self-consciousness, or reason. For conscious personality is form in the highest sense, because its energy is creative of form; it is self-distinction, subject and object, and hence in its very essence an activity; an unconditioned energy— unconditioned from without but self-conditioned from within.

In this great idea, so radically differing from the Oriental thought, Christianity has a twofold support—the intuition of the Jewish prophets and the philosophy of the Greeks.

The survey of the entire realm of thought by Plato and Aristotle has settled the question as to the possibilities of existence. There can be no absolute which is utterly formless. Any absolute whatsoever must be thought of as self-determining; as a pure sef-active energy, of the nature of thinking reason, although in degree more comprehensive than human reason and entirely without its intermittencies and eclipses.

An Absolute which is absolute form—and this means self-formative, self-distinguishing, and hence self-particularizing, living, or, what is the same, conscious personal being—is essentially a Creator. Moreover, its creation is its own self-revelation, and, according to this, God is essentially a self-revealing God. Hence Christianity is in a very deep sense a "revealed religion," for it is the religion not of a hidden God who is a formless absolute, but of a God whose essence it is to reveal Himself, and not remain hidden in Himself.

In the first canto of the "Paradiso" Dante reports Beatrice as laying down this doctrine of form:

> "All things collectively have an order among themselves, and this is form, which makes the universe resemble God."[2]

Christianity has united in its views the Jewish intuition of holy personality with the Greek philosophic conception of absolute Reason. It has not *put these ideas together*—so to speak—but has reached a new idea which includes and transcends them. Moreover, the deepest thought of Roman national life is in like manner subsumed and taken up. While the Greek has theoretically reached this highest principle of *essential form* and the Hebrew has discovered it through his heart, the Roman has experienced it through his will or volition. He has discovered that the highest form in the universe is pure will. And this again is only a new way of naming pure self-determination, pure reason, or pure personality. It sees the absolute form from the standpoint of the will. According to this, all activity of the will returns to the doer. Whatever man as free will does, he does to himself. Here is the root of Dante's Divine Comedy.

Dante is a Roman, although he has Teutonic blood in his veins. The Roman world-view preponderates in Italy to this day. According to the view of the absolute first principle as Will, each being in acting acts upon itself and thereby becomes its own fate. It creates its environment. The responsibility of the free agent is infinite. If it acts so as to make for itself an environment of deeds that are in harmony with its freedom, it lives in the "Paradiso." If it acts so as to contradict its nature, it makes for itself the "Inferno." All acts of a free will that do not tend to create an external environment of *freedom* will, of course, result in limiting the original free will and in building up around it walls of *hostile fate*. Fate is only a "maya" or illusion produced by not recognizing the self-contradiction involved in willing in particular what is contrary to the nature of will in general.

Since the Absolute is free will, it energizes creatively to form a universe of free wills. But it cannot constrain wills to be free. A created being's will is free to contradict its own essence and to defy the absolute Free Will of God.

Here is the problem which exercised Paul and St. Augustine—and Calvin. What is the mediation between the free will of the Creator and the free will of the creature? There can be no constraint of the free will except through itself. It makes for itself its own fate. But can it relieve itself from its fate also by its own act? Here is the all-important question.

The creature is a part of creation—each man is only a member of humanity. His will utters deeds that affect for good or ill his fellow-men. He in turn is affected in like manner by the deeds of his fellows. Here is the secret of the method of the return of the deed upon the doer. The individual acts upon his fellow-men, and they react upon him according to the quality of his deeds.

Hence the individual man by his will creates his environment through and by means of society, so that his fate or his freedom is the reflection of what he does to his fellow-men. Only it is not returned upon him by his own might, but by the freedom of his fellow-members of society.

Here is the clew to the question of salvation. The circle of a man's freedom includes not only his own deeds, but also the reaction of society. Inasmuch as the whole of society stands to the individual in the relation of infinite to finite (for he cannot measure its power), the return of his deed to him is the work of a higher power, and his freedom is the work of grace and not the result of his own strength. This is the conception of GRACE as it occurs in the Christian thought of the world. Man is free through grace, and he perfects himself through grace, or indeed suffers evil through grace; for this conception of Grace includes Justice as one of its elements.

Deeds, then, are to be judged by their effect upon society, whether they re-enforce the freedom of others or curtail that freedom. Man as individual combines with his fellows, so as to reap the results of the united effort of the whole. The individual thus avails himself of the entire species, and heals his imperfections.

Looking at human life in this way, Dante forms his views of the deeds of men, and slowly constructs the framework of his three worlds and fills them with their people. His classification and gradation of sins in accordance with their effect on society furnishes the structure of the first and second parts of the poem. His insight into the subjective effects of these sins—both their *immediate effect* in producing a mental atmosphere in which the individual breathes and lives his spiritual life, and their *mediate effect*, which comes to the individual after the social whole reacts upon him by reason of his deed—his insight into these two effects on the individual gives him the poetic material for painting the sufferings of the wicked and the struggles of the penitent.

There is in many respects an excess of philosophic structure in the "Divine Comedy." That there should be three parts to the poem does not suggest itself as a formalism. But that there should be exactly thirty-three cantos in each part and, adding the introductory canto, exactly one hundred cantos in the whole, seems an excess in this respect. So, too, when we are told that the triple rhyme suggests the Trinity, we find that the suggestion is a vague and trivial one, approaching a vulgar superstition. So, too, the fact that thirty-three years suggests the years of Christ's earthly life. In the second Treatise (Chapter I) of his "Convito" Dante tells us that it is possible to understand a book in four different ways. There is in a poem a literal, an allegorical, a moral and a mystical sense (*litterale, allegorico, morale, anagogico cioè sovra senso*). As the leading of Israel out of Egypt should signify, besides its literal meaning, mystically (anagogically) or spiritually the soul's liberation from sin—the exodus of the soul, as it were. He says the literal must go first, because you cannot come to the allegorical except through the literal; it is impossible to come to that which is within except through the without. "The allegorical is a truth concealed under a beautiful untruth." The moral sense of a book is its practical wisdom—what it contains useful for practical guidance (*a utilità di loro*). But, in spite of all his ingenuity, we must all, I think, confess that Dante's elaborate syntactical analyses of his love poems in the "Vita Nuova," as well as his disquisitions in the "Convito," seem much too artificial, and that they become soon repugnant to us. They seem a sort of trifling in comparison with the grim earnest which the "Divine Comedy" shows. And yet they furnish, after a sort, a key to be kept in hand while we accompany our poet on his journey.

* * * * *

## § 39. *The Poetic Mythos—What it Embodies*

It may be said that the supreme object of a great poetic work of art is the production of a myth. A myth furnishes a poetic explanation for a class of phenomena observed in the world. The mind that can see tropes in natural objects sees his way lighted by their converging rays to an underlying unity. Under tropes of small compass lie more extensive tropes, which unite the former into a consistent whole. And, as the poet's fundamental insight into the world is this, that the things and events of the world are means of spiritual expression, themselves moved and shaped by spiritual being, which they both hide and reveal, it follows that his combination of these poetic elements produces a whole structure that is spiritual throughout and a revelation of human nature such as the poet has conceived and fitted to the world he has created.

Most beloved among mortal men is the poet. He is eyes to the blind and ears to the deaf. He is intuition and reflection for all. He furnishes his people a view of the world in which they can all unite. Hence he is the inspired

Orpheus who builds cities and civilizations. His inspired mythos is recognized as the highest possession of the race, and implicit faith in it is demanded of all men. While it is permitted to deny the reality of existing facts and events, it is never permitted to deny the truth of the poetic mythos which unites a people in one civilization.

It is worth while, therefore, to study with all care the workings of a great poet's mind, and to note also what phases of nature he finds most available as vehicles for his myths. It has already been observed that the poet sees in the inanimate things and events of nature a revelation of rational will—that is to say, of spiritual being like himself and humanity. Conscious being is the key to the universe in the poet's hands.

Not only in poetic art, but in all art—sculpture, poetry, music, and architecture—there is a seeking after rhythm or after regularity, symmetry, and harmony, and a delight in them simply as such as though they constituted indubitable evidence of a rational cause identical in nature with the human mind that beholds it. What is consciousness but the rhythm of subject and object continually distinguishing and continually recognizing and identifying? In this is regularity and symmetry and also harmony. There is the repetition involved in self-knowing—the self being subject and likewise object—hence regularity. The shallowest mind, the child or the savage, delights in monotonous repetition, not possessing, however, the slightest insight into the cause of his delight. To us the phenomenon is intelligible. We see that his perception is like a spark under a heap of smoking flax. There is little fire of conscious insight, but much smoke of pleasurable feeling. He feels rather than perceives the fact of the identity which exists in form between the rhythm of his internal soul-activity and the sense-perception by which he perceives regularity.

* * * * *

## § 45. *Metempsychosis versus Eternal Punishment in Hell*

Metempsychosis—the doctrine of the transmigration of souls, or the return to earth of the soul after death and its reincarnation—we see is held by Plato and Virgil. This, too, although Plato makes the soul responsible for its choice of the lot in life that it shall lead.

It was necessary that Christianity should recognize the perfect responsibility of the human soul as well as its immortal destination. The mythos which should contain the idea of complete freedom of the will, or, what is the same thing, perfected individuality, would be forced to express this insight by laying infinite stress on the determining power of the individual in this life. Nothing else could bring men to realize the true dignity of the human soul and its exalted destiny. The individual soul is strictly responsible to God and to the visible body of the Divine Spirit here on earth—the Church—for his choice of his career and for his deeds.

The only form in which the due emphasis could be given to this doctrine of responsibility was that chosen by the mythos of Hell—"bitter, remorseless, endless Hell"—as the future lot of all who reject the proffered eternal life and refuse to enter the body of the Holy Spirit through union with the visible Church. In translating the philosophical idea of essential or substantial into the poetic form of a mythos, it is always necessary to represent it by infinite time. The will, in determining itself, affects itself for all time. It determines itself completely in this life, and there is no probation in the next. This dogma alone could bring man to a consciousness of his independent personality—his "substantia separata." In this way the mythos expressed the true and profound doctrine of the determinability of human destiny by the actual exertion of volition on the part of the soul itself, and of the utter non-effectiveness of vague postponement and reliance on external influences. External influences cannot initiate one's salvation either here or hereafter, is the doctrine of responsibility. The initiation lies always in free choice.

There is found no hope on the line of mortal sin—only alienation more and more profound. It is not a progress; sin is not a necessary stage on the way to growth, but a retrogradation. Nevertheless, it is not extinction—one can never reach that. Once immortality is reached, the individual remains a responsible being to all eternity. The negative will of the sinner builds up a wall of fate about him, it is true, but within this wall he ever holds his free volition, his absolute individuality.

Dante's poetic treatment of this mythos forms one of the few great works of all time.

## § 46. *Dante's Mythos of the Formation of the Inferno and the Purgatorial Mount*

Dante conceives that certain of the angels fell immediately after creation ("Paradiso," xxix, 49). Before one could so much as count twenty, Lucifer fell. He struck the earth under Jerusalem and hollowed it out to the very centre, thus making the tunnel-shaped Inferno and raising on the opposite side in the southern Atlantic Ocean the mountain of Purgatory.

"On this side fell he down from heaven; and here the land, which erst stood out, through fear of him veiled itself with sea and came to our hemisphere; and perhaps, in order to escape from him, that which on this side appears, left here the empty space, and upward rushed." (J. C., Tr.), Inf., xxx, 121.

The Mountain of Purgatory arises in the southern Atlantic Ocean; for the earth, according to his view, is not 8,000 miles in diameter, but only 6,500. (See for some of the passages in which Dante gives this item, "Convito," ii, 7; iii, 5.) In the Southern Hemisphere Dante knows the most remarkable constellation of stars there. He probably had travelled far enough south to see them with his own eyes. He knows, too, the Precession of Equinoxes by which the pole of the heavens changes so as to bring up the Southern Cross to the view of Europeans: "Seen only by the primitive peoples," says he.

The streams of sorrow, wrath, malice, fraud, and treachery that flow down into this region Dante explains as flowing from the tears of the human race, which he figures as a gigantic Man standing within the Idaen mountain of Crete and looking toward Rome. He borrows the eternal form of the figure from the vision of the Great Image in Daniel, which there prefigured the fate of the Babylonian Empire and the world-movement of nations that followed it—the rise of the Persian Empire under Cyrus, and possibly the final supremacy of Rome.

Daniel describes the King's Dream: "This image's head was of fine gold, his breast and his arms of silver, his belly and his thighs of brass, his legs of iron, his feet part of iron and part of clay. . . . This head of gold is Nebuchadnezzar.

"And after thee shall arise *another kingdom* inferior to thee, and another *third kingdom* of brass, which shall bear rule over all the earth.

"And the *fourth kingdom* shall be as strong as iron; forasmuch as iron breaketh in pieces and subdueth all things, and as iron that breaketh all these, shall it break in pieces and bruise.

"And whereas thou sawest the feet and toes, part of potter's clay and part of iron, the kingdom shall be divided; but there shall be in it of the strength of the iron, forasmuch as thou sawest the iron mixed with miry clay. . . .

"And in the days of these kings shall the God of Heaven set up a kingdom, which shall never be destroyed; and the kingdom shall not be left to other people, but it shall break in pieces and consume all these kingdoms, and it shall stand forever. . . ."

Dante would think of the Roman Empire and the Christian Church as signified by this kingdom, which shall break in pieces all other kingdoms, but which shall itself stand forever. The Holy Roman Empire is, as we know, to Dante this kingdom. It was a stone carved out of a mountain, and it came to fill the whole earth, which clearly enough the Persian Empire never did, for it failed to conquer Europe.

## § 47. *Dante's Mythos of the Roman Empire*

Under the guidance of Virgil's mythos of the Roman Empire, Dante had been in the habit of looking upon Troy and the Trojans as the ancestors of the Romans. Crete, too, was a still more remote ancestor—the nursery of Zeus, the god of civil order and the father of Minos, the first king who made just laws and secured peace and harmony by their rigid execution.

Hence, too, Dante, in the "Inferno," shows so much bitterness toward the Greek heroes and statesmen, punishing, for example, Alexânder and Pyrrhus in the seething purple flood of Phlegethon; Diomede and the great Ulysses in the *bolge* of evil counsellors in the circle of fraud.

In the fourteenth canto of the "Inferno" Dante explains the origin of the rivers by this mythos of Crete and the Image of the Human Race, or perhaps, more accurately, the Image of Human Civil Government (as the reference to Daniel's vision seems to indicate):

> " 'In the middle of the sea lies a waste country,' he then said, 'which is named Crete,'[3] under whose King the world once was chaste. A mountain is there, called Ida, which once was glad with waters and foliage; now it is deserted like an antiquated thing. Rhea of old chose it for the faithful cradle of her son; and the better to conceal him, when he wept, caused cries to be made on it.
>
> "Within the mountain stands erect a great Old Man, who keeps his shoulders turned toward Damietta, and looks at Rome as if it were his mirror. His head is shapen of fine gold, his arms and his breast are

pure silver; then he is of brass to the cleft; from thence downward he is all of chosen iron, save that the right foot is of baked clay; and he rests more on this than on the other. Every part, except the gold, is broken with a fissure that drops tears, which collected perforate that grotto. Their course descends from rock to rock into this valley. They form Acheron, Styx, and Phlegethon; then, by this narrow conduit, go down to where there is no more descent. They form Cocytus; and thou shalt see what kind of lake that is; here, therefore, I describe it not." (J. C. Tr.), Inf., XIV, 94–120.

In Virgil ("Aeneid," III, 104) we find the suggestion which reveals to us the idea in Dante's mind in its entirety: "Crete, the island of great Jove, lies in the middle of the sea, where is Mount Ida and the nursery of our race; they inhabit a hundred great cities, most fertile realms, whence Teucer, our first ancestor, if rightly I remember the things I have heard, was first carried to the Rhoetian coasts [promontory of Troas], and there selected the place for his kingdom. Ilium stood not yet," etc.

According to Apollodorus (III, 1, § 1), Teutamus, the son of Dorus and a descendant of Deucalion, mythic founder of the Dorian race, came to Crete with a Greek colony. In the time of his son Asterion, Zeus came to Crete with Europa and became father of Minos, Sarpedon, and Rhadamanthus, who were adopted by Asterion upon his marriage with Europa.

Zeus, according to the Greek mythos, is the divine founder of civil order, and to be son of Zeus is to be a hero of civilization. Minos became the greatest king of the mythic heroic period, being the inventor of wonderful laws for the securing of justice. He freed the seas of pirates.

The circumstances of his obtaining his kingdom gave rise to feuds symbolized by the story of the wild bull of Crete—probably an independent freebooter who sought alliance with Minos. The Minotaur is the symbol of blood violence which Minos repressed by shutting up the monster in a labyrinth wonderfully constructed.

## § 48. *The Minotaur and the Labyrinth in the Light of this Mythos*

In the myth of the labyrinth we have a symbolic description of the nature of feuds and blood violence and of the manner in which they are suppressed by a Jove-nurtured king. Within a labyrinth the avenues continually lead from one into the other without making any progress toward a final goal. One goes foward and forward, but after weary labors finds himself at length where he started, or even farther off from his goal.

So long as there was no kingly authority and no just laws, feuds arose; violence on the part of one led to retaliation on the part of another, and this to counter-retaliation. Each avenging of a deed was taken as a new case of violence to be avenged again.

Thus the island of Crete and the surrounding nations were in a labyrinth of blood revenge. The Minotaur is used by Dante as symbol of blood revenge, and the labyrinth, which is not named in the "Divina Commedia," signifies the endless nature of feuds thus avenged.

But the labyrinth has also the meaning of a code of justice which imprisons the Minotaur; for when this system of blood revenge is throttled by just laws, the State steps in and, apprehending the first aggressor, makes a labyrinth of him by making his deed return upon him at once, and thus rendering unnecessary the blood revenge on the part of the injured one; hence the labyrinth in this sense is a device by which the endless progress of private revenge is stopped in its first steps—it is shut up and the labyrinth is reduced to a jail or prison conducted according to just criminal laws. Formerly all Crete was a labyrinth and all the neighboring islands of the Aegean seas and the main-land were infested by pirates and robber States continually at feud with each other. Minos, it is said, not only checked piracy about Crete, but made himself master of the Greek islands, and was able, it seems, to punish the blood violence and treachery even of a colony like Athens. His son Androgeus was assassinated at Athens on account of some jealousy or feud. Minos subdued Megara and compelled the Athenians to send every nine years or oftener a tribute of fourteen youths and maidens to be devoured by the Minotaur— that is to say, confined in the labyrinth as hostages, or perhaps executed for new deeds of violence done against Cretans.

It was the national hero of Athens, Theseus, also a law-giver, who slew this Minotaur, at least so far as the Athenian tribute was concerned—probably entering into a treaty by which he suppressed the blood violence of his own subjects and assisted Minos in his endeavors to suppress such violence everywhere, and thus put an end to the Minotaur altogether.

Wonderful insight, therefore, Dante displays in making the Minotaur or blood violence stand as guardian at the entrance of the circles of violence.

From this good law-maker, Minos, descends the Trojan Aeneas, as Virgil asserts and Dante believes, and hence by direct descent the Roman Empire appointed by divine right to give laws to the whole world and suppress the complex of private revenge and feuds—a complex in the fact that each avenging deed is a new crime and thus forms a labyrinth out of which it is impossible to extricate the state. Dante knew—bitterly knew—how this labyrinth of blood revenge extended over his native Italy; cities divided by factions and continually at war with each other.

## §49. *Minos as Judge in the Light of this Mythos*

The island of Crete has great significance to Dante for these reasons: He accordingly selects Minos, as the typical dispenser of justice, to preside over the court of the Inferno, following Homer and Virgil in this choice. Minos invented a code which secured the return of his own deed, or at least its symbol, upon the criminal. The sinners, on entering the presence of Minos, lay open their secret lives to him. His judgment is indicated by coiling about him his tail, "making as many circles round himself as the number of grades or circles that the sinner will have to descend." Minos symbolically indicates that the sinner's own beastiality has made its coil about him and that the sinner's own deed makes his circle of hell.

## §50. *Other Mythologic Figures used by Dante*

It is noteworthy that Virgil places in the gates of his Inferno Centaurs, Briareus, the Chimaera, the Lernaean Hydra, Harpies, and the three-bodied Geryon—all indicating the instrumentalities that send men to their death. Dante uses most of these figures in his own way, always showing a profound insight into the capacity of the symbol for spiritual expression.

THE CENTAURS were nomadic peoples, without organized laws of justice, who marauded on the Greek civil communities and escaped punishment on their swift horses; hence also they are symbols of violence of a special kind. Dante employs them to guard the banks of Phlegethon and punish the violent. It is the fitting punishment of the violent that they make for themselves an environment of violence. The Centaurs were also teachers of the Greek heroes in the arts of single combat, medicine, and music— means useful to a life of roving adventure—but they were not teachers of laws; of the art of commanding armies or organized bodies; of anything specially useful to cities. Like the Cyclops, they symbolize man as individual apart from man as social whole—the little self over against the greater self.

THE HARPIES are placed by Dante in the doleful woods of the suicides as symbolic of their hypochondria. The gloomy presage of coming evil causes suicide. These are birds, airy creatures, symbolic therefore of fancy and the future. They defile the feast of the present with forebodings of evil.

THE FURIES and THE GORGONS guard the sixth circle, from of old the symbols of all that is destructive in violence against civil order—discord, slander, mistrust, suspicion, and deadly revenge. MEDUSA the Gorgon paralyzes the beholder—is it hardened rebellion against God (as Carlyle thinks), is it atheism or petrifying scepticism regarding immortality (as Philalethes thinks), or is it simply panic terror which deprives one of all control of his limbs?—a significance which the Greeks may have given to the Medusa face. One may see the reflection of such panic fear—*i.e.*., hear of it at a distance, but he must not look upon it directly if he would escape its paralyzing effects.

GERYON is the well-described image of fraud in Dante's portraiture. The ancients did not thus specially characterize him. He was simply the three-bodied king of Hesperia, who owned the famous herd of oxen that Hercules obtained. Perhaps Dante confounded him with Cacus, the wily thief of those oxen in Virgil's story. He is represented with the face of the just man, mild of aspect. The fraudulent purpose is covered with a special appearance of conformity to law and justice—submission of the individual will to the general will of the community. But he has a reptile's body covered with knots and circlets like a lizard or a toad, the paws of a beast, and an envenomed scorpion tail. He seeks not, like the violent, to rob his fellow-men directly and attack the civil order with his individual might. But he seeks to use the civil order against itself, under a semblance of obedience to it to gain the faith of men and then abuse their confidence. This, of course, will weaken their confidence in civil order. While direct violence forces every one to trust civil order all the more and draw close to the protecting shelter of the state, Fraud, on the other hand, weakens the faith of the citizen in the power of the State to protect him. For, see, have not I been wronged under the semblance of mild-faced justice?

THE GIANTS in the lowest round have already been mentioned as typical of the entirely savage state of society, utterly isolated human life. The individual by himself must do all for himself. He cannot share with others the conquest of nature. It is his own individual might against the world. The subduing of wild beasts, the cultivation of the soil, the arts of manufacture—in all these he is unaided. Worse than all, he is deprived of human intercourse and does not inherit the accumulated wisdom and experience of the human race. Homer, as we saw, has painted this state of savagery in the Cyclops.

CERBERUS furnishes a familiar type of greed in general. Dante, after Virgil, makes him the type of intemperance and gluttony.

PLUTUS, the ancient god of wealth, presides over the fourth circle of the "Inferno." The avaricious make property their god; it should be their means for achieving earthly freedom and leisure for divine works such as tend to the spiritual good of one's fellow-men and one's own growth in wisdom. The prodigal misuse their property and are always in want, or "hard up," as the slang phrase has it. Hence they are always trying to come at a little money to help them over a "tight place." Hence, too, they are always giving their minds to getting property, and are in the same hell with the avaricious. Both long for property in the same degree.

CHARON, the infernal ferryman, is likewise borrowed from Virgil, and is not found in the early Greek poets. His fiery eyes and wheels of flame—typical of the red-weeping eyes of mourners for the dead, or possibly a symbol of his keen watchfulness required to separate (in Virgil's "Inferno") the souls whose bodies are buried with due ceremony from those unsepultured; or in Dante's "Inferno," to exclude the souls of the pusillanimous from his boat—this circumstance of the flaming eyes is also borrowed from Virgil.

## §51. *The Mythos of Dante's "Purgatorio"*

The finest portion of the "Divina Commedia" is unquestionably the Purgatory, but it needs the "Inferno" to precede it for the sake of effect. It is filled with the light of the stars, the verdure of spring, growth of character, and the aspiration for perfection. In it the human will shows its true power to make the years reenforce the days, while in the "Inferno" there is constant self-contradiction of the will and constant building up of Fate between man and society.

The mythos of Purgatory is more entirely Dante's work than that of the "Inferno." He found it a shadowy middle state of the soul, and built it up into a systematic structure, definitely outlined in all its phases. It is *the* true state of man as a condition of perpetual education in holiness here and hereafter. All men who are struggling here in the world with an earnest aspiration for spiritual growth can find no book to compare with the second part of Dante's Poem. In climbing the steep sides of this mountain the air continually grows purer and the view wider and less obstructed. On the summit is the terrestrial paradise of the Church symbolizing the invisible Church of all sincere laborers for good on earth. The Church on earth holds humanity in so far as it lives in the contemplation of the divine and in the process of realizing the divine nature in the will and in the heart. Dante collects in a complex symbol the various ceremonial devices of the Church—almost mechanically, in fact. It is an allegory rather than a poetic symbol. But he adds dramatic action to it first by introducing the scene between Dante and Beatrice, secondly by the dumb show of the history of the Church—the tragedy of its corruption, its seizure by France, and its transfer from Rome to Avignon.

## §52. *The Mythos of Dante's "Paradiso"—Gnosticism*

The mythos of the "Paradiso" is constructed on a wholly new plan. There is no hint of it elsewhere except in the Platonic myth in the "Phaedo" (the allusion to the complete disembodiment of the soul). The Mysticism of sixteen hundred years enters it as material.

Gnosticism represented the first attempt to reconcile Christianity with philosophy, as Neoplatonism represented a later attempt on the part of Greek Philosophy to reach the Oriental unity by transcending the first principle of Plato and Aristotle.

Gnosticism and Neoplatonism, accordingly, have substantially the same problem before them. Both systems agree in adopting the doctrine of Philo that God is exalted above virtue and knowledge, and even above good and evil altogether. Plato had identified God with the Absolute Good, while Aristotle had made him absolute reason.

From God, according to Gnosticism and Neoplatonism, there emanates Nous as His image, and then directly or after some interval the Psyche or Soul, from which emanates finally matter or body from the soul as the soul's object, created result, or achievement.

These four cardinal points are common to all Gnostic and Neoplatonist systems; but great diversity exists in regard to intermediate steps and in regard to names and definitions. Gnosticism likes to use the word "aeon" (αἰών) where Platonism likes the word "idea." By aeon it means individual or complete cycle of activity—a self-determined being (*substantia separata*), in short. There may be many ideas or aeons, or complete cycles of process, between the Nous or Reason and the Soul. There are, in fact, twenty-eight of these in the system of Valentinus (who came to Rome from Alexandria about the year 140 A.D.). He made thirty aeons in all—wishing to symbolize the thirty years of Christ's life, as is said, somewhat as Dante wished to do this by the number thirty-three (the number of the cantos in each part of the "Divina Commedia"). These aeons were yoked together in pairs, each pair being called a syzigy, such a syzigy being, for example: 1. Truth (ἀλήθεια). * 2. Reason (Νοῦς). These beget the second syzigy. 3. The creative word (λόγος). * 4. Life (ζωή) The Word and Life beget the third syzigy. 5. Man (ἀνθρώπος). * 6. Church (ἐκκλησία), and so on until one comes to Sophia (Σοφία) or wisdom, which is the youngest of the third division of aeons and (we are curious to learn) is conscious of her remoteness from God, and hence flies toward God, the source of emanation. Wisdom proceeds to imitate the other aeons by creating, but begets only chaos and confusion. In her grief at this dreadful result the other aeons take pity and conspire with God to produce two new aeons—Christ and the Holy Spirit, who redeem the world of chaos and confusion, acting as the Demiurgos or world-builder. Here we have a mythos of the fall into finitude—the lapse from the One to the Many, from the Perfect to the Imperfect, and the redemption from the latter.

In Proclus's system there are many unities issuing from the primal essence—all above life and reason and the power of comprehension. Then there are many triads corresponding to aeons between reason and matter. Marcion of Pontus had no aeons in his system of Gnosticism, but retained the Demiurgos or world-maker (as Jehovah of the Old Testament who is opposed to Christ as Savior).

The emanation theories of both Gnosticism and Neoplatonism have the principle of Lapse as the principle of their philosophic method, and not the principle of self-determination, which is the true principle of philosophic method. The principle of Lapse finds only a descending scale and is obliged to introduce an arbitrary and miraculous interference into its world-order, in order to explain progressive development and redemption. The principle of self-determination shows us an ascending scale, all of whose steps are miraculous and yet none of them arbitrary.

In the later forms of Neoplatonism there is a slight trace of return toward the pure doctrines of Aristotle and Plato. The pupils of Plutarch of Athens seem to have learned from him that Plato and Aristotle substantially agree in their world-view. Syrianus and Hierocles, of Alexandria, the former the teacher of Proclus, both recognize this fact, and Hierocles insists that Ammonius Saccas, the founder of Neoplatonism, proved once for all the substantial agreement of the two great Greek philosophers. Proclus in his great work on the theology of Plato, treating chiefly of the dialogue of "Parmenides," has undertaken, however, to show that Plato himself holds the doctrine of a primal essence above reason in several of his works; such an essence would, of course, be unrevealed and unrevealable, and thus could not be the God of Christianity. Proclus lived a century and a half after Christianity had become the state religion, and the Neoplatonic school at Athens was closed in 529 by Justinian, forty-four years after the death of Proclus. The influence of the school continued into Christian philosophy and mysticism for many centuries, the chief channel through which this influence flowed being the writings of the Pseudo-Dionysius, about whom Dante readers hear so much.

## §53. *The Mythos of the "Paradiso" developed in the Doctrine of the Celestial Hierarchies*

The chief work of Dionysius, according to historians, must have been written after the year 450, because it contains expressions used in the Council of Chalcedon in 451.[4] Purporting to be written by the first bishop of Athens, a convert of St. Paul, the work exercised great authority. Its chief doctrine is that of the fourfold division of natures into (1) that which is created and does not create—matter; (2) that which is created but creates again, as, for example, souls; (3) that which creates but is not created, as Christ, the Logos; and (4) that which neither creates nor is created, as the Absolute One or the Father. Here is Neoplatonism in its most heretical form.

The highest cannot be called by a name, according to Dionysius. It may be spoken of symbolically only. It is above truth and above goodness; nor does it create.

Through the thinking of the Gnostics and Neoplatonists, using the results of Plato and Aristotle and endeavoring to solve the problems of Christianity by them, arose a new *mythos*—a mythos of symbolic thinking which came over into Christian Theology as the doctrine of the Celestial Hierarchy. On this mythos Dante has constructed his "Paradiso." It is modified to meet the wants of Christian doctrine in such a manner that what were emanating Aeons or Ideas become one hierarchy of Angels, consisting of nine separate orders, divided, according to office and participation in divine gifts, into three triads.

The highest triad behold God's judgments directly and are called THRONES; but there are two grades of excellence above the common rank of these—to wit, CHERUBIM, who are filled perfectly with divine light, and hence *comprehend* most. The SERAPHS are filled more especially with divine charity and excel in *will power*. The common angels of this class are called THRONES.

The second triad are distinguished for announcing things divine, and are called POWERS, the common principle of all being this. But elevated to an extraordinary degree are DOMINIONS, who are supreme in ability to distinguish the proper order and fitness of what is to be done. Then, secondly, the VIRTUES, who are eminent in providing the faculty of fulfilling or in planning the means.

The lowest triad has the common function of arranging and executing the duties of the angelic ministry so far as it deals directly with men. ANGELS are the common principle, ARCHANGELS the superior, and PRINCIPALITIES the highest directors of this function of angelic ministry.

These bizarre expressions used to name the different degrees of celestial perfection arose in the interpretation of obscure passages in St. Paul's writings. In "Romans" we have a passage speaking of "death, life, angels, principalities, powers, things present and things to come," and a still more remarkable passage in Colossians (i, 16, 17): "By him were all things created that are in heaven or that are in earth, visible and invisible, whether they be thrones or dominions or principalities or powers. All things were created by him and for him. He is before all things, and by him all things consist."

This passage is otherwise famous as the most important place in which St. Paul gives his version of St. John's doctrine of the Word or Logos, which was in the beginning and which made all created things.

## §54. *The Heretical Tendency in this Mythos*

It is essential to note that the hierarchy may be interpreted to mean that the highest, or the THRONES (Seraphim, Cherubim, Thrones), are of an angelic ministry more removed from mediation with what is below—more immediate in their contemplation of the divine. This is heretical when the mediation is denied—*i.e.*, when it is thought to be more divine to be above and apart from the world of humanity—but not heresy when it is held that "Thrones" *complete* their mediation perfectly, and come to use their power to elevate fallen humanity, and are not held aloof as through fear of contamination by contact with sinners. The Highest Logos goes down into the manger of Space and Time, and raises all up—as contemplative Cherub, the Logos pierces clear through the mediation of time and space intellectually and philosophically and sees the face of God. As Seraph it loves God through loving all creation, down to the lowest insect or plant or clod.

Seraph and Cherub are of the highest triad, because they make the deepest and completest mediation and see clearest the divine shining through creation. They can see the praise of God even in sin and evil. But the danger of heresy lurks in this doctrine. If it is held that the Cherubim see God directly face to face *without* the mediation of creation, then mere quietism is reached. Buddhism holds that the highest states of perfection for its saints are most aloof from the world of man and nature.

"From the lowest to the highest stations of human activity, to serve as a servant who does menial work is everywhere necessary. For the lowest class of laborers, whatever they do is only a trade; for the next higher it is an art; and for the highest, whatever they do is to them the image of the totality."—(Paraphrase of one of Goethe's sayings.)

Hence it is not the angels, archangels, and principalities that make the human mediation most perfectly. It is to them a "trade." But the powers, virtues, and dominions are higher toward a perfect mediation and can go down lower into the depths safely to bring up the lowest. But the thrones can make the complete mediation from the lowest to highest.

Dante has connected this artificial system (which refuses, even in the expositions of its greatest disciples, to take on a perfectly rational and logical form) to the heavens of the Ptolemaic system, and thereby fastened his degrees of spiritual perfection to astronomical distinctions observable by all men. In the "Convito" second treatise, Chapter XIV, he has stated in detail his astronomical theory.

That there remained a sediment of Neoplatonism, and hence of Oriental thinking, in Dante's mind, even after the chidings of Beatrice in the Terrestrial Paradise, and perhaps, too, even in the teachings of Beatrice herself in the twenty-eighth canto of the "Paradiso," may well be believed. But the main great points of his theology, founded on Aristotle as interpreted by the Schoolmen, will stand the scrutiny of all time.

The doctrine of the Divine form or the self-activity of the absolute involves the common nature of man and God—or God as divine-human. This is the great central truth (of which the doctrine of the Trinity is the symbol) on which all modern civilization is built as its open secret.

## §55. *The Symbol of the Trinity embodies the Highest Philosophic Truth*

God the absolute reason is perfect knowing and willing in one—what he knows he creates; for his knowing causes to be, that which he intellectually perceives. His intuition of himself then contemplates the eternal Word—the Second Person—equal in all respects to himself. The Second Person, the Logos, knows and wills likewise himself, and thus arises a Third Person. But a difference makes its appearance here; the Second Person knows himself as having been begotten, in the timeless past of "The Beginning," as having arisen through all stages of imperfection up to the highest. This knowledge is also creation, and the Word creates a world of imperfect beings in the form of evolution from pure space and time up to the highest and holiest on earth—the "New Jerusalem"—the "City of God," the "Invisible Church" whose spirit is the Holy Spirit or the Third Person. The world of man and nature thus belongs to the *processio*—to the hypostasis of derivation or the genesis of the Eternal Word. The Logos, contemplating its own derivation, logically implied, causes it to be, as an actual creation in Time and Space. As the Holy Spirit proceeds from all eternity, it is not a generation, but a procession always complete, but always continuing. Here is the highest view possible of human nature; it is part of the procession of the Holy Spirit.

Man reaches perfection in the infinite, eternal, immortal, and invisible Church.

This is the river and the Great White Rose of Paradise.

The symbol of philosophy as the knowledge of the highest truth is Beatrice, and Dante has recorded his conviction that this highest truth is revealed and can be known in the following words:

> I see well that our intellect is never sated if the truth does not illuminate it, beyond whose circuit no truth exists. In that truth it reposes as a wild animal in its lair, as soon as it has reached it. And it can reach it, for were this not so all desire would be created in vain. (*Paradiso,* IV, 124–129)

# Notes

1. In the "Harvard University Bulletin," "Biographical Contributions, Edited by Justin Windsor, No. 7, the Dante Collections in Harvard College and Boston Public Libraries, Part I, by William Coolidge Lane, 1885," I find the work of Graul named under No. 208: "Göttliche Komoedie in's Deutsche uebertragen, und historisch, aesthetisch, und vornehmlich theologisch erläutert von Karl Graul, Leipzig, 1843." Only the "Inferno" published.

2. Le cose tutte quante Hann' ordine tra loro; e questo è forma Che l'universo a Dio fa simigliante.

3. Virgil, *"Aeneid,"* iii, 104:

"Creta Jovis magni medio jacet insula ponto
Mons Idaeus ubi, et gentis cunabula nostrae;
Centum urbes habitant magnas, uberrima regna
Maximus unde pater, si rite audita recordor
Teucrus Rhoeteas primum est advectus in oras."

4. The following is condensed from Ueberweg's account: "The writings that purport to be the works of Dionysius the Areopagite of Athens (Acts, xvii, 34), first Bishop of Athens, are mentioned first in the year A.D. 532. They were accepted as genuine and of high authority on account of the connection of their supposed author with Paul. They gained credit in the Church in the eighth and ninth centuries and after a commentary had been written on them by Maximus Confessor early in the seventh century. Laurentius Valla, about the middle of the fifteenth century, asserted their spuriousness, which was demonstrated afterward by Morinus, Dallaeus, and others."

# George Santayana

## Dante

IN A LETTER WHICH TRADITION assigns to Dante, addressed to his protector, Cangrande della Scala, lord of Verona and Vicenza, are these words about the *Divine Comedy*: "The subject of the whole work, taken merely in its literal sense, is the state of souls after death, considered simply as a fact. But if the work is understood in its allegorical intention, the subject of it is man, according as, by his deserts and demerits in the use of his free will, he is justly open to rewards and punishments." This by no means exhausts, however, the significations which we may look for in a work of Dante's. How many these may be is pointed out to us in the same letter, and illustrated by the beginning of the one hundred and fourteenth Psalm: "When Israel went out of Egypt, the house of Jacob from a people of strange language; Judah was his sanctuary, and Israel his dominion." Here, Dante tells us, "if we look to the *letter* only, what is conveyed to us is the deliverance of the children of Israel out of Egypt in the time of Moses; if we look to the *allegory* of it, what is signified is our redemption accomplished through Christ; if we consider the *moral sense*, what is signified is the conversion of the soul from her present grief and wretchedness to a state of grace; and if we consider the *anagogical sense* [that is, the revelation contained concerning our highest destiny], what is signified is the passing of the sanctified soul from the bondage of earthly corruption to the freedom of everlasting glory."

When people brooded so much over a simple text as to find all these meanings in it, we may expect that their own works, when meant to be profound, should have stage above stage of allegorical application. So in the first canto of the *Inferno* we find a lion that keeps Dante from approaching a delectable mountain; and this lion, besides what he is in the landscape of the poem, is a symbol for pride or power in general, for the king of France in particular, and for whatever political ambitions in Dante's personal life may have robbed him of happiness or distracted him from faith and from piety. Thus, throughout the *Divine Comedy*, meaning and meaning lurk beneath the luminous pictures; and the poem, besides being a description of the other world, and of the rewards and punishment meted out to souls, is a dramatic view of human passions in this life; a history of Italy and of the world; a theory of Church and State; the autobiography of an exile; and the confessions of a Christian, and of a lover, conscious of his sins and of the miracle of divine grace that intervenes to save him.

The subject-matter of the *Divine Comedy* is accordingly the moral universe in all its levels, —romantic, political, religious. To present these moral facts in a graphic way, the poet performed a double work of imagination. First he chose some historical personage that might plausibly illustrate each condition of the soul. Then he pictured this person in some characteristic and symbolic attitude of mind and of body, and in an appropriate, symbolic environment. To give material embodiment to moral ideas by such a method would nowadays be very artificial, and perhaps impossible; but in Dante's time everything was favourable to the attempt. We are accustomed to think of goods and evils as functions of a natural life, sparks struck out in the chance shock of men with things or with one another. For Dante, it was a matter of course that moral distinctions might be discerned, not merely as they arise incidentally in human experience, but also, and more genuinely, as they are displayed in the order of creation. The Creator himself was a poet producing allegories. The material world was a parable which he had built out in space, and ordered to be enacted. History was a great charade. The symbols of earthly poets are words or images; the symbols of the divine poet were natural things and the fortunes of men. They had been devised for a purpose; and this purpose, as the Koran, too, declares, had been precisely to show forth the great difference there is in God's sight between good and evil.

In Platonic cosmology, the concentric spheres were bodies formed and animated by intelligences of various orders. The nobler an intelligence, the more swift and outward, or higher, was the sphere it moved; whence the identification of "higher" with better, which survives, absurdly, to this day. And while Dante could not attribute literal truth to his fancies about hell, purgatory, and heaven, he believed that an actual heaven, purgatory, and hell had been fashioned by God on purpose to receive souls of varying deserts and complexion; so that while the poet's imagination, unless it reëchoed divine revelation, was only human and not prophetic, yet it was a genuine and plausible imagination, moving on the lines of nature, and anticipating such things as experience might very well realize. Dante's objectification of morality, his art of giving visible forms and local habitations to ideal virtues and vices, was for him a thoroughly serious and philosophical exercise. God had created nature and life on that very principle. The poet's method repeated the magic of Genesis. His symbolical imagination mirrored this symbolical world; it was a sincere anticipation of fact, no mere laboured and wilful allegory.

This situation has a curious consequence. Probably for the first and last time in the history of the world a classification worked out by a systematic moralist guided the vision of a great poet. Aristotle had distinguished, named, and classified the various virtues, with their opposites. But observe: if the other world was made on purpose—as it was—to express and render palpable those moral distinctions which were eternal, and to express and render them palpable in great detail, with all their possible tints and varieties; and if Aristotle had correctly classified moral qualities, as he had—then it follows that Aristotle (without knowing it) must have supplied the ground-plan, as it were, of hell and of heaven. Such was Dante's thought. With Aristotle's *Ethics* open before him, with a supplementary hint, here and there, drawn from the catechism, and with an ingrained preference (pious and almost philosophic) for the number three and its multiples, he needed not to voyage without a chart. The most visionary of subjects, life after death, could be treated with scientific soberness and deep sincerity. This vision was to be no wanton dream. It was to be a sober meditation, a philosophical prophecy, a probable drama,—the most poignant, terrible, and consoling of all possible truths.

The good—this was the fundamental thought of Aristotle and of all Greek ethics,—the good is the end at which nature aims. The demands of life cannot be radically perverse, since they are the judges of every excellence. No man, as Dante says, could hate his own soul; he could not at once be, and contradict, the voice of his instincts and emotions. Nor could a man hate God; for if that man knew himself, he would see that God was, by definition, his natural good, the ultimate goal of his actual aspirations.[1] Since it was impossible, according to this insight, that our faculties should be intrinsically evil, all evil had to arise from the disorder into which these faculties fall, their too great weakness or strength in relation to one another. If the animal part of man was too strong for his reason, he fell into incontinence,—that is, into lust, gluttony, avarice, wrath, or pride. Incontinence came from an excessive or ill-timed pursuit of something good, of a part of what nature aims at; for food, children, property, and character are natural goods. These sins are accordingly the most excusable and the least odious. Dante puts those who have sinned through love in the first circle of hell, nearest to the sunlight, or in the topmost round of purgatory, nearest to the earthly paradise. Below the lovers, in each case, are the gluttons,—where a northern poet would have been obliged to place his drunkards. Beneath these again are the misers,—worse because less open to the excuse of a merely childish lack of self-control.

The disorder of the faculties may arise, however, in another way. The combative or spirited element, rather than the senses, may get out of hand, and lead to crimes of violence. Violence, like incontinence, is spontaneous enough in its personal origin, and would not be odious if it did not inflict, and intend to inflict, harm on others; so that besides incontinence, there is malice in it. Ill-will to others may arise from pride, because one loves to be superior to them, or from envy, because one abhors that they should seem superior to oneself; or through desire for vengeance, because one smarts under some injury. Sins of these kinds are more serious than those of foolish incontinence; they complicate the moral world more; they introduce endless opposition of interests, and perpetual, self-propagating crimes. They are hateful. Dante feels less pity for those who suffer by them: he remembers the sufferings these malefactors have themselves caused, and he feels a sort of joy in joining the divine justice, and would gladly lash them himself.

Worse still than violence, however, is guile: the sin of those who in the service of their intemperance or their malice have abused the gift of reason. *Corruptio optimi pessima*; and to turn reason, the faculty that establishes order, into a means of organizing disorder, is a perversity truly satanic: it turns evil into an art. But even this perversity has stages; and Dante distinguishes ten sorts of dishonesty or simple fraud, as well as three sorts of treachery.

Besides these positive transgressions there is a possibility of general moral sluggishness and indifference. This Dante, with his fervid nature, particularly hates. He puts the Laodiceans in the fringe of his hell; within the gate, that they may be without hope, but outside of limbo, that they may have torments to endure, and be stung by wasps and hornets into a belated activity.[2]

To these vices, known to Aristotle, the Catholic moralist was obliged to add two others: original sin, of which spontaneous disbelief is one consequence, and heresy, or misbelief, after a revelation has been given and accepted. Original sin, and the paganism that goes with it, if they lead to nothing worse, are a mere privation of excellence and involve in eternity merely a privation of joy: they are punished in limbo. There sighs are heard, but no lamentation, and the only sorrow is to live in desire without hope. This fate is most appropriately imputed to the noble and clear-sighted in the hereafter, since it is so often their experience here. Dante was never juster than in this stroke.[3] Heresy, on the other hand, is a kind of passion when honest, or a kind of fraud when politic; and it is punished as pride in fiery tombs,[4] or as faction by perpetual gaping wounds and horrible mutilations.[5]

So far, with these slight additions, Dante is following Aristotle; but here a great divergence sets in. If a pagan poet had conceived the idea of illustrating the catalogue of vices and virtues in poetic scenes, he would have chosen suitable episodes in human life, and painted the typical characters that figured in them in their earthly environment; for pagan morality is a plant of earth. Not so with Dante. His poem describes this world merely in retrospect; the foreground is occupied by the eternal consequences of what time had brought forth. These consequences are new facts, not merely, as for the rationalist, the old facts conceived in their truth; they often reverse, in their emotional quality, the events they represent. Such a reversal is made possible by the theory that justice is partly retributive; that virtue is not its own sufficient reward, nor vice its own sufficient punishment. According to this theory, this life contains a part of our experience only, yet determines the rest. The other life is a second experience, yet it does not contain any novel adventures. It is determined altogether by what we have done on earth; as the tree falleth so it lieth, and souls after death have no further initiative.

The theory Dante adopts mediates between two earlier views; in so far as it is Greek, it conceives immortality ideally, as something timeless; but in so far as it is Hebraic, it conceives of a new existence and a second, different taste of life. Dante thinks of a second experience, but of one that is wholly retrospective and changeless. It is an epilogue which sums up the play, and is the last episode in it. The purpose of this epilogue is not to carry on the play indefinitely: such a romantic notion of immortality never entered Dante's mind. The purpose of the epilogue is merely to vindicate (in a more unmistakable fashion than the play, being ill acted, itself could do) the excellence of goodness and the misery of vice. Were this life all, he thinks the wicked might laugh. If not wholly happy, at least they might boast that their lot was no worse than that of many good men. Nothing would make an overwhelming difference. Moral distinctions would be largely impertinent and remarkably jumbled. If I am a simple lover of goodness, I may perhaps put up with this situation. I may say of the excellences I prize what Wordsworth says of his Lucy: there may be none to praise and few to love them, but they make all the difference to me.

Dante, however, was not merely a simple lover of excellence: he was also a keen hater of wickedness, one that took the moral world tragically and wished to heighten the distinctions he felt into something absolute and infinite. Now any man who is *enragé* in his preferences will probably say, with

Mohammed, Tertullian, and Calvin, that good is dishonoured if those who contemn it can go scot-free, and never repent of their negligence; that the more horrible the consequences of evil-doing, the more tolerable the presence of evil-doing is in the world; and that the everlasting shrieks and contortions of the damned alone will make it possible for the saints to sit quiet, and be convinced that there is perfect harmony in the universe. On this principle in the famous inscription which Dante places over the gate of hell, we read that primal love, as well as justice and power, established that torture-house; primal love, that is, of that good which, by the extreme punishment of those who scorn it, is honoured, vindicated, and made to shine like the sun. The damned are damned for the glory of God.

This doctrine, I cannot help thinking, is a great disgrace to human nature. It shows how desperate, at heart, is the folly of an egotistic or anthropocentric philosophy. This philosophy begins by assuring us that everything is obviously created to serve our needs; it then maintains that everything serves our ideals; and in the end, it reveals that everything serves our blind hatreds and superstitious qualms. Because my instinct taboos something, the whole universe, with insane intensity, shall taboo it for ever. This infatuation was inherited by Dante, and it was not uncongenial to his bitter and intemperate spleen. Nevertheless, he saw beyond it at times. Like many other Christian seers, he betrays here and there an esoteric view of rewards and punishments, which makes them simply symbols for the intrinsic quality of good and evil ways. The punishment, he then seems to say, is nothing added; it is what the passion itself pursues; it is a fulfilment, horrifying the soul that desired it.

For instance, spirits newly arrived in hell require no devil with his prong to drive them to their punishment. They flit towards it eagerly, of their own accord.[6] Similarly, the souls in purgatory are kept by their own will at the penance they are doing. No external force retains them, but until they are quite purged they are not able, because they are not willing, to absolve themselves.[7] The whole mountain, we are told, trembles and bursts into psalmody when any one frees himself and reaches heaven. Is it too much of a gloss to say that these souls change their prison when they change their ideal, and that an inferior state of soul is its own purgatory, and determines its own duration? In one place, at any rate, Dante proclaims the intrinsic nature of punishment in express terms. Among the blasphemers is a certain king of Thebes, who defied the thunderbolts of Jupiter. He shows himself indifferent to his punishment and says: "Such as I was alive, such I am dead." Whereupon Virgil exclaims, with a force Dante had never found in his voice before: "In that thy pride is not mortified, thou art punished the more. No torture, other than thy own rage, would be woe enough to match thy fury."[8] And indeed, Dante's imagination cannot outdo, it cannot even equal, the horrors which men have brought upon themselves in this world. If we were to choose the most fearful of the scenes in the *Inferno*, we should have to choose the story of Ugolino, but this is only a pale recital of what Pisa had actually witnessed.

A more subtle and interesting instance, if a less obvious one, may be found in the punishment of Paolo and Francesca di Rimini. What makes these lovers so wretched in the Inferno? They are still together. Can an eternity of floating on the wind, in each other's arms, be a punishment for lovers? That is just what their passion, if left to speak for itself, would have chosen. It is what passion stops at, and would gladly prolong for ever. Divine judgement has only taken it at its word. This fate is precisely what Aucassin, in the well-known tale, wishes for himself and his sweetheart Nicolette,—not a heaven to be won by renunciation, but the possession, even if it be in hell, of what he loves and fancies. And a great romantic poet, Alfred de Musset, actually upbraids Dante for not seeing that such an eternal destiny as he has assigned to Paolo and Francesca would be not the ruin of their love,[9] but the perfect fulfilment of it. This last seems to be very true; but did Dante overlook the truth of it? If so, what instinct guided him to choose just the fate for these lovers that they would have chosen for themselves?

There is a great difference between the apprentices in life, and the masters,—Aucassin and Alfred de Musset were among the apprentices; Dante was one of the masters. He could feel the fresh promptings of life as keenly as any youngster, or any romanticist; but he had lived these things through, he knew the possible and the impossible issue of them; he saw their relation to the rest of human nature, and to the ideal of an ultimate happiness and peace. He had discovered the necessity of saying continually to oneself: Thou shalt renounce. And for this reason he needed no other furniture for hell than the literal ideals and fulfilments of our absolute little passions. The soul that is possessed by any one of these passions nevertheless has other hopes in abeyance. Love itself dreams of more than mere possession; to conceive happiness, it must conceive a life to be shared in a varied world, full of events and activities, which shall be new and ideal bonds between the lovers. But unlawful love cannot pass out into this public fulfilment. It is condemned to be mere possession—possession in the dark, without an environment, without a future. It is love among the ruins. And it is precisely this that is the torment of Paolo and Francesca—love among the ruins of themselves and of all else they might have had to give to one another. Abandon yourself,

Dante would say to us,—abandon yourself altogether to a love that is nothing but love, and you are in hell already. Only an inspired poet could be so subtle a moralist. Only a sound moralist could be so tragic a poet.

The same tact and fine feeling that appear in these little moral dramas appear also in the sympathetic landscape in which each episode is set. The poet actually accomplishes the feat which he attributes to the Creator; he evokes a material world to be the fit theatre for moral attitudes. Popular imagination and the precedents of Homer and Virgil had indeed carried him halfway in this symbolic labour, as tradition almost always carries a poet who is successful. Mankind, from remotest antiquity, had conceived a dark subterranean hell, inhabited by unhappy ghosts. In Christian times, these shades had become lost souls, tormented by hideous demons. But Dante, with the Aristotelian chart of the vices before him, turned those vague windy caverns into a symmetrical labyrinth. Seven concentric terraces descended, step by step, towards the waters of the Styx, which in turn encircled the brazen walls of the City of Dis, or Pluto. Within these walls, two more terraces led down to the edge of a prodigious precipice—perhaps a thousand miles deep—which formed the pit of hell. At the bottom of this, still sinking gently towards the centre, were ten concentric furrows or ditches, to hold ten sorts of rogues; and finally a last sheer precipice fell to the frozen lake of Cocytus, at the very centre of the earth, in the midst of which Lucifer was congealed amongst lesser traitors.

Precision and horror, graphic and moral truth, were never so wonderfully combined as in the description of this hell. Yet the conception of purgatory is more original, and perhaps more poetical. The very approach to the place is enchanting. We hear of it first in the fatal adventure ascribed to Ulysses by Dante. Restless at Ithaca after his return from Troy, the hero had summoned his surviving companions for a last voyage of discovery. He had sailed with them past the Pillars of Hercules, skirting the African shore; until after three months of open sea, he saw a colossal mountain, a great truncated cone, looming before him. This was the island and hill of purgatory, at the very antipodes of Jerusalem. Yet before Ulysses could land there, a squall overtook him; and his galley sank, prow foremost, in that untraversed sea, within sight of a new world. So must the heathen fail of salvation, though some oracular impulse bring them near the goal.

How easy is success, on the other hand, to the ministers of grace! From the mouth of the Tiber, where the souls of Christians congregate after death, a light skiff, piloted by an angel, and propelled only by his white wings, skims the sea swiftly towards the mountain of purgatory, there deposits the spirits it carries, and is back at the mouth of the Tiber again on the same day. So much for the approach to purgatory. When a spirit lands it finds the skirts of the mountain broad and spreading, but the slope soon becomes hard and precipitous. When he has passed the narrow gate of repentance, he must stay upon each of the ledges that encircle the mountain at various heights, until one of his sins is purged, and then upon the next ledge above, if he has been guilty also of the sin that is atoned for there. The mountain is so high as to lift its head into the sphere of the moon, above the reach of terrestrial tempests. The top, which is a broad circular plain, contains the Garden of Eden, watered by the rivers Lethe and Eunoe, one to heal all painful memories, and the other to bring all good thoughts to clearness. From this place, which literally touches the lowest heaven, the upward flight is easy from sphere to sphere.

The astronomy of Dante's day fell in beautifully with his poetic task. It described and measured a firmament that would still be identified with the posthumous heaven of the saints. The whirling invisible spheres of that astronomy had the earth for their centre. The sublime complexities of this Ptolemaic system were day and night before Dante's mind. He loves to tell us in what constellation the sun is rising or setting, and what portion of the sky is then over the antipodes; he carries in his mind an orrery that shows him, at any given moment, the position of every star.

Such a constant dragging in of astronomical lore may seem to us puerile or pedantic; but for Dante the astronomical situation had the charm of a landscape, literally full of the most wonderful lights and shadows; and it also had the charm of a hard-won discovery that unveiled the secrets of nature. To think straight, to see things as they are, or as they might naturally be, interested him more than to fancy things impossible; and in this he shows, not want of imagination, but true imaginative power and imaginative maturity. It is those of us who are too feeble to conceive and master the real world, or too cowardly to face it, that run away from it to those cheap fictions that alone seem to us fine enough for poetry or for religion. In Dante the fancy is not empty or arbitrary; it is serious, fed on the study of real things. It adopts their tendency and divines their true destiny. His art is, in the original Greek sense, an imitation or rehearsal of nature, an anticipation of fate. For this reason curious details of science or theology enter as a matter of course into his verse. With the straightforward faith and simplicity of his age he devours these interesting images, which help him to clarify the mysteries of this world.

There is a kind of sensualism or aestheticism that has decreed in our day that theory is not poetical; as if all the images and emotions that enter a cultivated mind were not saturated with theory. The prevalence of such a sensualism or aestheticism would alone suffice to explain the impotence of the arts. The life of theory is not less human or less emotional than the life of sense; it is more typically human and more keenly emotional. Philosophy is a more intense sort of experience than common life is, just as pure and subtle music, heard in retirement, is something keener and more intense than the howling of storms or the rumble of cities. For this reason philosophy, when a poet is not mindless, enters inevitably into his poetry, since it has entered into his life; or rather, the detail of things and the detail of ideas pass equally into his verse, when both alike lie in the path that has led him to his ideal. To object to theory in poetry would be like objecting to words there; for words, too, are symbols without the sensuous character of the things they stand for; and yet it is only by the net of new connections which words throw over things, in recalling them, that poetry arises at all. Poetry is an attenuation, a rehandling, an echo of crude experience; it is itself a theoretic vision of things at arm's length.

Never before or since has a poet lived in so large a landscape as Dante; for our infinite times and distances are of little poetic value while we have no graphic image of what may fill them. Dante's spaces were filled; they enlarged, to the limits of human imagination, the habitations and destinies of mankind. Although the saints did not literally inhabit the spheres, but the empyrean beyond, yet each spirit could be manifested in that sphere the genius of which was most akin to his own. In Dante's vision spirits appear as points of light, from which voices also flow sometimes, as well as radiance. Further than reporting their words (which are usually about the things of earth) Dante tells us little about them. He has indeed, at the end, a vision of a celestial rose; tier upon tier of saints are seated as in an amphitheatre, and the Deity overarches them in the form of a triple rainbow, with a semblance of man in the midst. But this is avowedly a mere symbol, a somewhat conventional picture to which Dante has recourse unwillingly, for want of a better image to render his mystical intention. What may perhaps help us to divine this intention is the fact, just mentioned, that according to him the celestial spheres are not the real seat of any human soul; that the pure rise through them with increasing ease and velocity, the nearer they come to God; and that the eyes of Beatrice—the revelation of God to man—are only mirrors, shedding merely reflected beauty and light.

These hints suggest the doctrine that the goal of life is the very bosom of God; not any finite form of existence, however excellent, but a complete absorption and disappearance in the Godhead. So the Neoplatonists had thought, from whom all this heavenly landscape is borrowed; and the reservations that Christian orthodoxy requires have not always remained present to the minds of Christian mystics and poets. Dante broaches this very point in the memorable interview he has with the spirit of Piccarda, in the third canto of the *Paradiso*. She is in the lowest sphere of heaven, that of the inconstant moon, because after she had been stolen from her convent and forcibly married, she felt no prompting to renew her earlier vows. Dante asks her if she never longs for a higher station in paradise, one nearer to God, the natural goal of all aspiration. She answers that to share the will of God, who has established many different mansions in his house, is to be truly one with him. The wish to be nearer God would actually carry the soul farther away, since it would oppose the order he has established.[10]

Even in heaven, therefore, the Christian saint was to keep his essential fidelity, separation, and lowliness. He was to feel still helpless and lost in himself, like Tobias, and happy only in that the angel of the Lord was holding him by the hand. For Piccarda to say that she accepts the will of God means not that she shares it, but that she submits to it. She would fain go higher, for her moral nature demands it, as Dante—incorrigible Platonist—perfectly perceived; but she dare not mention it, for she knows that God, whose thoughts are not her thoughts, has forbidden it. The inconstant sphere of the moon does not afford her a perfect happiness; but, chastened as she is, she says it brings her happiness enough; all that a broken and a contrite heart has the courage to hope for.

Such are the conflicting inspirations beneath the lovely harmonies of the *Paradiso*. It was not the poet's soul that was in conflict here; it was only his traditions. The conflicts of his own spirit had been left behind in other regions; on that threshing-floor of earth which, from the height of heaven, he looked back upon with wonder,[11] surprised that men should take so passionately this trouble of ants, which he judges best, says Dante, who thinks least of it.

In this saying the poet is perhaps conscious of a personal fault; for Dante was far from perfect, even as a poet. He was too much a man of his own time, and often wrote with a passion not clarified into judgement. So much does the purely personal and dramatic interest dominate us as we read of a Boniface or an Ugolino that we forget that these historical figures are supposed to have been transmuted into the eternal, and to have become bits in the mosaic of Platonic essences. Dante himself almost forgets it. The modern reader, accustomed to insignificant, wayward fictions, and expecting to be entertained by images without thoughts, may not notice this lack of perspective, or may rejoice in it. But, if he is judicious, he will not rejoice in it long. The Bonifaces and the Ugolinos are not the truly deep, the truly lovely figures of the *Divine Comedy*. They are, in a relative sense, the vulgarities in it. We feel too much, in these cases, the heat of the poet's prejudice or indignation. He is not just, as he usually is; he does not stop to think, as he almost always does. He forgets that he is in the eternal world, and dips for the moment into a brawl in some Italian market-place, or into the council-chamber of some factious *condottiere*. The passages—such as those about Boniface and Ugolino—which Dante writes in this mood are powerful and vehement, but they are not beautiful. They brand the object of their invective more than they reveal it; they shock more than they move the reader.

This lower kind of success—for it is still a success in rhetoric—falls to the poet because he has abandoned the Platonic half of his inspiration and has become for the moment wholly historical, wholly Hebraic or Roman. He would have been a far inferior mind if he had always moved on this level. With the Platonic spheres and the Aristotelian ethics taken out, his *Comedy* would not have been divine. Persons and incidents, to be truly memorable, have to be rendered significant; they have to be seen in their place in the moral world; they have to be judged, and judged rightly, in their dignity and value. A casual personal sentiment towards them, however passionate, cannot take the place of the sympathetic insight that comprehends and the wide experience that judges.

Again (what is fundamental with Dante) love, as he feels and renders it, is not normal or healthy love. It was doubtless real enough, but too much restrained and expressed too much in fancy; so that when it is extended Platonically and identified so easily with the grace of God and with revealed wisdom, we feel the suspicion that if the love in question had been natural and manly it would have offered more resistance to so mystical a transformation. The poet who wishes to pass convincingly from love to philosophy (and that seems a natural progress for a poet) should accordingly be a hearty and complete lover—a lover like Goethe and his Faust—rather than like Plato and Dante. Faust, too, passes from Gretchen to Helen, and partly back again; and Goethe made even more passages. Had any of them led to something which not only was loved, but deserved to be loved, which not only could inspire a whole life, but which ought to inspire it—then we should have had a genuine progress.

In the next place, Dante talks too much about himself. There is a sense in which this egotism is a merit, or at least a ground of interest for us moderns;

for egotism is the distinctive attitude of modern philosophy and of romantic sentiment. In being egotistical Dante was ahead of his time. His philosophy would have lost an element of depth, and his poetry an element of pathos, had he not placed himself in the centre of the stage, and described everything as his experience, or as a revelation made to himself and made for the sake of his personal salvation. But Dante's egotism goes rather further than was requisite, so that the transcendental insight might not fail in his philosophy. It extended so far that he cast the shadow of his person not only over the terraces of purgatory (as he is careful to tell us repeatedly), but over the whole of Italy and of Europe, which he saw and judged under the evident influence of private passions and resentments.

Moreover, the personality thrust forward so obtrusively is not in every respect worthy of contemplation. Dante is very proud and very bitter; at the same time, he is curiously timid; and one may tire sometimes of his perpetual tremblings and tears, of his fainting fits and his intricate doubts. A man who knows he is under the special protection of God, and of three celestial ladies, and who has such a sage and magician as Virgil for a guide, might have looked even upon hell with a little more confidence. How far is this shivering and swooning philosopher from the laughing courage of Faust, who sees his poodle swell into a monster, then into a cloud, and finally change into Mephistopheles, and says at once: *Das also war des Pudels Kern!* Doubtless Dante was mediaeval, and contrition, humility, and fear of the devil were great virtues in those days; but the conclusion we must come to is precisely that the virtues of those days were not the best virtues, and that a poet who represents that time cannot be a fair nor an ultimate spokesman for humanity.

Perhaps we have now reviewed the chief objects that peopled Dante's imagination, the chief objects into the midst of which his poetry transports us; and if a poet's genius avails to transport us into his enchanted world, the character of that world will determine the quality and dignity of his poetry. Dante transports us, with unmistakable power, first into the atmosphere of a visionary love; then into the history of his conversion, affected by this love, or by the divine grace identified with it. The supreme ideal to which his conversion brought him back is expressed for him by universal nature, and is embodied among men in the double institution of a revealed religion and a providential empire. To trace the fortunes of these institutions, we are transported next into the panorama of history, in its great crises and its great men; and particularly into the panorama of Italy in the poet's time, where we survey the crimes, the virtues, and the sorrows of those prominent in furthering or thwarting the ideal of Christendom. These numerous persons are set before us with the sympathy and brevity of a dramatist; yet it is no mere carnival, no *danse macabre*: for throughout, above the confused strife of parties and passions, we hear the steady voice, the implacable sentence, of the prophet that judges them.

Thus Dante, gifted with the tenderest sense of colour, and the firmest art of design, has put his whole world into his canvas. Seen there, that world becomes complete, clear, beautiful, and tragic. It is vivid and truthful in its detail, sublime in its march and in its harmony. This is not poetry where the parts are better than the whole. Here, as in some great symphony, everything is cumulative: the movements conspire, the tension grows, the volume redoubles, the keen melody soars higher and higher; and it all ends, not with a bang, not with some casual incident, but in sustained reflection, in the sense that it has not ended, but remains by us in its totality, a revelation and a resource for ever. It has taught us to love and to renounce, to judge and to worship. What more could a poet do? Dante poetized all life and nature as he found them. His imagination dominated and focused the whole world. He thereby touched the ultimate goal to which a poet can aspire; he set the standard for all possible performance, and became the type of a supreme poet. This is not to say that he is the "greatest" of poets. The relative merit of poets is a barren thing to wrangle about. The question can always be opened anew, when a critic appears with a fresh temperament or a new criterion. Even less need we say that no greater poet can ever arise; we may be confident of the opposite. But Dante gives a successful example of the *highest species* of poetry. His poetry covers the whole field from which poetry may be fetched, and to which poetry may be applied, from the inmost recesses of the heart to the uttermost bounds of nature and of destiny. If to give imaginative value to something is the minimum task of a poet, to give imaginative value to all things, and to the system which things compose, is evidently his greatest task.

Dante fulfilled this task, of course under special conditions and limitations, personal and social; but he fulfilled it, and he thereby fulfilled the conditions of supreme poetry. Even Homer, as we are beginning to perceive nowadays, suffered from a certain conventionality and one-sidedness. There was much in the life and religion of his time that his art ignored. It was a flattering, a euphemistic art; it had a sort of pervasive blandness, like that which we now associate with a fashionable sermon. It was poetry addressed to the ruling caste in the state, to the conquerors; and it spread an intentional glamour over their past brutalities and present self-deceptions. No such partiality in

Dante; he paints what he hates as frankly as what he loves, and in all things he is complete and sincere. If any similar adequacy is attained again by any poet, it will not be, presumably, by a poet of the supernatural. Henceforth, for any wide and honest imagination, the supernatural must figure as an idea in the human mind,—a part of the natural. To conceive it otherwise would be to fall short of the insight of this age, not to express or to complete it. Dante, however, for this very reason, may be expected to remain the supreme poet of the supernatural, the unrivalled exponent, after Plato, of that phase of thought and feeling in which the supernatural seems to be the key to nature and to happiness. This is the hypothesis on which, as yet, moral unity has been best attained in this world. Here, then, we have the most complete idealization and comprehension of things achieved by mankind hitherto. Dante is the type of a consummate poet.

# Notes

1. *Purgatorio,* XVII. 106–11:

> Or perchè mai non può dalla salute
> Amor del suo suggetto volger viso,
> Dall' odio proprio son le cose tute:
> E perchè intender non si può diviso,
> E per sè stante, alcuno esser dal primo,
> Da quello odiare ogni affetto è deciso.

2. *Inferno,* III. 64–66:

> Questi sciaurati, che mai non fur vivi,
> Erano ignudi e stimolati molto
> Da mosconi e da vespe ch' erano ivi.

3. *Ibid.,* IV. 41, 42:

> Semo perduti, e sol di tanto offesi
> Che senza speme vivemo in disio.

Cf. *Purgatorio,* III. 37–45, where Virgil says:

> "State contenti, umana gente, al *quia*;

Chè se potuto aveste veder tutto,
Mestier non era partorir Maria;
E disiar vedeste senza frutto
Tai, che sarebbe lor disio quetato,
Ch' eternalmente è dato lor per lutto.
Io dico d'Aristotele e di Plato,
E di molti altri." E qui chinò la fronte;
E più non disse, e rimase turbato.

4. *Inferno,* IX. 106–33, and X.
5. *Ibid.,* XXVIII.
6. *Inferno,* III. 124–26:

E pronti sono a trapassar lo rio,
Chè la divina giustizia gli sprona
Sì che la tema si volge in disio.

7. *Purgatorio,* XXI. 61–69:

Della mondizia sol voler fa prova,
Che, tutta libera a mutar convento,
L'alma sorprende, e di voler le giova. . . .
Ed io che son giaciuto a questa doglia
Cinquecento anni e più, pur mo sentii
Libera volontà di miglior soglia.

8. *Inferno,* XIV. 63–66:

"O Capaneo, in ciò che non s' ammorza
La tua superbia, se' tu più punito:
Nullo martiro, fuor che la tua rabbia,
Sarebbe al tuo furor dolor compito."

9. Alfred de Musset, *Poésies Nouvelles, Souvenir*:

Dante, pourquoi dis-tu qu'il n'est pire misère
Qu'un souvenir heureux dans les jours de douleur?
Quel chagrin t'a dicté cette parole amère,
Cette offense au malheur?

. . . Ce blasphème vanté ne vient pas de ton coeur.
Un souvenir heureux est peut-être sur terre
Plus vrai que le bonheur. . . .

Et c'est à ta Françoise, à ton ange de gloire,
Que tu pouvais donner ces mots à prononcer,

Elle qui s'interrompt, pour conter son histoire,
  D'un éternel baiser!

10. *Paradiso*, III. 73–90:

"Se disiassimo esser più superne,
  Foran discordi li nostri disiri
  Dal voler di colui che qui ne cerne, . . .
E la sua volontate è nostra pace;
  Ella è quel mare al qual tutto si move
  Ciò ch'ella crea, e che natura face."
Chiaro mi fu allor com' ogni dove
  In cielo è Paradiso, e sì la grazia
  Del sommo ben d'un modo non vi piove.

11. *Paradiso*, XXII. 133–39:

Col viso ritornai per tutte e quante
  Le sette spere, evidi questo globo
  Tal, ch'io sorrisi del suo vil sembiante;
E quel consiglio per migliore approbo
  Che l'ha per meno; e chi ad altro pensa
  Chiamar si puote veramente probo.

# Edward Kennard Rand

## Dante and Servius

How did Dante study his *buon maestro* Virgil? Directly, of course, and with a penetrating vision denied to many a humanist of the Renaissance and many a philologian of our own day. But Dante doubtless did not despise the assistance offered by commentators of the ancient poet. The commentator was a distinctly exalted person in the Middle Ages. The Latin authors entered the Carolingian period accompanied by their faithful interpreters—Horace with Porphyrius, Statius with "Lactantius Placidus," Virgil with Servius; if an author had no ancient commentary, as was true of Ovid and at first of Terence, some gallant scholar, not infrequently an Irishman, came to the rescue, and equipped his work with glosses. A writer without this retinue of respectful comment was somehow lacking in dignity. Hence, perhaps, arose in the early Middle Ages the practice of an author's commenting on his own work in case nobody appeared to perform the task for him. Hence, also, a fresh impulse was given to allegory; for if a work was to receive the honor of a commentary, it should contain matter that needed explanation. The tradition thus started prevailed through the mediaeval period, and is illustrated by Dante himself in his observations on his own poems in the *Vita Nuova* and the *Convivio*. In another way he may have paid tribute to the literary customs of his age. His elaborate system of allegory, described in the *Convivio*[1] and the letter to Can Grande della Scala,[2] may have been inspired not only by the currrent theory on the matter, as expounded by St. Thomas Aquinas,[3] but by a special study of some allegorical exposition of Virgil's *Aeneid*. Dante very probably knew Fulgentius, or possibly some mediaeval affair of like temper, such as the commentary written on Virgil by Bernard Silvester of Tours.[4] Thus infused with esoteric meanings, the Aeneid became a human document of somewhat alarming proportions; one could say of it most emphatically, as of Dante's poem, "*subiectum est homo*." This *Aeneis moralizata*, no less than the true *Aeneid* that Dante well understood, may have served as a pattern for the *Commedia*.

The present paper is concerned not with the abstruse divinations of the allegorists, but with the humbler interpretation of Servius. It is almost a foregone conclusion that Dante should have at least consulted Servius occasionally, and students of Dante to-day have found helpful clues to the poet's meaning in the ancient commentator's remarks. Having chanced on several such passages which, so far as I know, have not been adequately noticed, I have set them forth in the hope that some more competent hand may carry the investigation further.

## I

The casual reader of Virgil's epic may not observe that the revelation made to Aeneas in the world below is, like that in Dante's vision, divided between two mediators. Virgil at least adumbrates the idea, so plainly set forth in the *Commedia*, of a preliminary and partial revelation succeeded by fuller and loftier truth. Aeneas and the Sibyl cross the Styx, pass through the Limbo and the Mournful Fields, which are reserved for those whose lives on earth were for various reasons incomplete, stop by the walls of Tartarus, where the Sibyl describes the punishments of the mighty sinners confined within, and then make their way to Anchises in the Elysian Fields. Thus far the Sibyl has given all the explanations. From that moment on she has nothing to say, but remains by the hero's side, πρόσωπον κωφόν, while Anchises expounds the mystic philosophy which the poet, for dramatic as well as temperamental reasons, chooses as a setting for his panorama of Roman history and his exalted panegyric of the Roman state. Perhaps Dante caught from Virgil's text alone a suggestion for the twofold revelation of the *Commedia*. Perhaps he devised his scheme on the promptings of his own imagination. But also, perhaps, his imagination may have been spurred by the following note in Servius on the Sibyl's words to the bard Musaeus, who meets her and the hero at the entrance to Elysium:

> Tuque optime vates (*Aen.* VI, 669): quia (i.e. Musaeus) theologus fuit. Et sciendum hoc loco Sibyllam iam a numine derelictam; unde et interrogat, quod alias non faceret.

In matters of theology, the Sibyl has to ask questions; before long she will be dumb in the presence of a greater prophet who, like Beatrice in the *Com-*

*media*, has power to explain the innermost mysteries of creation and human history.

## II

Why is Dante's Inferno partitioned into nine circles? Perhaps to make a pendant to a Paradise of nine circles, which owes its design to the ancient astronomy handed down to the Middle Ages first and foremost, it would appear, in Cicero's *Somnium Scipionis* and Macrobius's commentary thereon. Dante loved the number nine, and starting with a ninefold Paradise might well without prompting have contrived an Inferno to match. Certainly Virgil's text gives no hint of such a picture. There is a *facilis descensus* from earth to Hades, but no succcession of descents when Hades is once reached. There are undulating valleys in Elysium, and Tartarus, like a huge well, has its own depths; but Virgil's Hell is constructed, vaguely and mysteriously, on a generally uniform level. One searches in vain for anything like nine descending circles. The Styx, to be sure, winds nine times about the dolorous country; that is to imprison its inmates the more securely:

> fas obstat, tristisque palus inamabilis undae
> alligat et novies Styx interfusa coercet (vv. 438 f.).

But Servius cannot let the definite numeral *novies* go by without elucidation. According to him, the poet declares "*novem esse circulos Stygis quae inferos cingit*," and in his note on another passage, the commentator describes them.

> In limine primo (v.427): novem circulis inferi cincti esse dicuntur, quos nunc exsequitur. Nam primum dicit animas infantum tenere, secundum eorum qui sibi per simplicitatem adesse nequiverunt, tertium eorum qui evitantes aerumnas se necarunt, quartum eorum qui amarunt, quintum virorum fortium dicit, sextum nocentes tenent qui puniuntur a iudicibus, in septimo animae purgantur, in octavo sunt animae ita purgatae ut redeunt in corpora, in nono ut iam non redeant, scilicet campus Elysius.

Now of course such a topography, which incidentally reveals in Servius an abysmal ignorance of Virgil's meaning, has no relation to the divisions of the Inferno, with a Limbo and subsequent circles of Lust, Gluttony, Avarice and Prodigality, Anger, Heresy, Violence, Fraud and Deceit, and Treachery; Servius's plan has to include not only Hell, but Purgatory and Paradise. But the idea of nine separate compartments or circles was accessible to Dante in Servius. Servius has other passages, which I cannot discuss here, on the divisions of Hades. He makes the curious attempt (on vv. 127 and 439) to impress Ptolemaic astronomy into the service of Epicurean theology, which has dispensed with the *Tartareae sedes* altogether and located Hell on this earth; but as this idea is assigned to the subtler philosophers (*qui altius de mundi ratione quaesiverunt*), Servius perhaps thought his simpler explanation truer to the poet's intention.

One question remains: Are the circles, as in Dante, arranged on a downward grade? We should imagine that even Servius would not put Elysium at the bottom of the well; he doubtless did not intend to do so. There is reason to believe, however, that at least part of Virgil's underworld was thought by Servius to have a downward incline, as appears in his comments on the rivers of Hell.

## III

The Virgilian Hades is nine times belted by the river Styx (v. 439). But this bounding stream seems also to be called Acheron,[5] or Cocytus.[6] The situation is more distinct, though not much more, when Aeneas and the Sibyl come through the portal of Orcus to the bank of the river (vv. 295 ff.):

> Hinc via Tartarei quae fert Acherontis ad undas.
> Turbidus hic caeno vastaque voragine gurges
> aestuat atque omnem Cocyto eructat harenam.

The bounding river here, then, is Acheron, a dirty brawling stream, which belches all its sand into the Cocytus. As they stand on the banks, the Sibyl informs Aeneas that he beholds the pools of Cocytus and the Stygian marsh—

> Cocyti stagna alta vides Stygiamque paludem (v. 323).

Then Charon appears and ferries them over—it were rash to say what river. Virgil leaves the picture in the blur of impressionism of which he is fond. The *nützliche Wandkarte* of the lower regions prepared for the schoolroom by a German savant gives us no help here. Virgil has a penchant for coloring rather than topography. He locates Phlegethon, however, more definitely it is a river of fire surrounding the walls of Tartarus.

Servius, as ever, constructs a formal scheme for the rivers, finding one cluin the etymology, or his etymology, of their names. Acheron (v. 107), coming from ἄνευ Χαρᾶς, means *sine gaudio*; Styx (v. 134), ἀπὸ τοῦ στυγεροῦ, is *maeror* or *tristitia*; Cocytus (v. 132), ἀπὸ τοῦ χωκύειν, is *luctus*; and Phlegethon (v. 265), from φλόξ, is *ignis*—the last two explanations fairly hit the mark. On v. 295 (*Hinc via Tartarei,* etc.) Servius remarks that Aeneas and his guide come *"post errorem silvarum"* (Dante's *selva oscura*), to the streams of Hades. Taking *Tartarei* as an exact topographical term, the commentator infers that Acheron rises in the depths of Hell, flows upwards, and eventually belches its sand into the Cocytus; the Styx, for no very good reason that we can see, serves as a connecting link between the two.

> Acheronta vult quasi di imo nasci Tartaro, huius aestuaria Stygem creare, de Styge autem nasci Cocyton.

This order of the streams, however, Acheron, Styx, Cocytus, is due merely to the poet's fancy. Calling etymology into play, Servius finds that the real or "physiological" order—psychological we should say—is different:

> Et haec est mythologia: nam physiologia hoc habet, quia qui caret gaudio sine dubio tristis est. Tristitia autem vicina luctui est, qui procreatur ex morte: unde haec esse apud inferos dicit.

The ultimate begetter at the bottom of the pit is thus Mors, whence spring in succession, Cocytus, Styx, and Acheron. This order is repeated in the note on v. 385, where Servius adds that there are various tributaries:

> De his autem nascuntur alia unde est (v. 439) *et novies Styx interfusa coercet.*

Dante may well have read Servius's account of the Infernal rivers, and preferred, for matters of fact, the testimony of the commentator to that of the poet. Mythology was not Dante's concern; his order is the real and "physiological." Acheron is his outermost and uppermost stream. Styx is reached at the fifth circle, that of the Wrathful and Sullen. With the sixth circle, we come to the City of Dis, about which we might expect Phlegethon to flow, as in Virgil; it appears instead after the sudden drop to the seventh circle. Cocytus is at the bottom of the lowest and coldest circle of all. May we venture a further step and suppose that Dante saw in Servius's phrase *luctui . . . qui procreatur ex morte* a hint of the personified Mors who accompanies Satan in the mediaeval mysteries on the Harrowing of Hell? Dante's grim imagination and his sense of climax are cause enough for his setting Satan at the bottom of Hell; but as the Devil stands in the midst of the frozen pools of Cocytus, we may suspect some connection between Dante's picture and the remark of Servius that the Cocytus is derived from Mors. We must admit, of course, that though Dante started with Servius, as I think reasonable to assume, he readapted his material in the twenty-fourth Canto of the *Inferno*. Here the rivers do not spring from the depths of Hell; they accumulate from the tears of sin and suffering shed by the huge statue that symbolizes mankind. Dante has moulded bits from Servius and Nebuchadnezzar's dream in Daniel (ii, 31–33) into splendid imagery of his own.[7]

## IV

We turn from topographical to ethical considerations. The sin of sloth (*accidia*) seems a characteristically mediaeval, or at least Christian, affair—not the state of mind, which has probably existed from the beginning of the world, but the exaltation of the vice into one of the principal categories. Aristotle's discussion of πραότης broaches the matter,[8] but Cassian seems to have been the first to draw up a formal list of the sins, among which the sin of sloth is numbered; his book *De Institutione Coenobiorum et de Octo Principalium Vitiorum Remediis* was written down to 426 A.D., and describes monastic theory and practice as Cassian had learned them in the East. His scheme of the vices does not differ essentially from that of Dante in the *Purgatorio*; both have a place for *accidia* (ἀκηδία). Perhaps Servius can point us to another origin for the Christian classification which, however novel in its outcome, may have been based on older conceptions than those of monasticism. In his note on Lethe (v. 714), Servius has the following:

> Docent autem philosophi, anima descendens quid per singulos circulos perdat: unde etiam mathematici fingunt, quod singulorum numinum potestatibus corpus et anima nostra conexa sunt ea ratione, quia cum descendunt animae trahunt secum torporem Saturni, Martis iracundiam, libidinem Veneris, Mercurii lucri cupiditatem, Iovis regni desiderium: quae res faciunt perturbationem animabus, ne possint uti vigore suo et viribus propriis.

According, then, to the philosophers, who here seem like Neoplatonists, the soul, after leaving the ideal world, descends through the different spheres, losing some virtues in every circle; incidentally it would interest us to know what these virtues are. Similarly, the astrologers have a fable (*fingunt* is not a complimentary word) that the soul acquires a vice from every planet; thus the poor soul, dropping a virtue and picking up a vice at every station, is adequately attempered to human conditions by the time it reaches the earth. Now among the five examples given by Servius, not only is *accidia* represented (*torpor*), but *ira, libido,* and *lucri cupiditas* have their equivalents in the lists of Cassian and Dante. Does not the formal classification of the sins derive in part, at least, from astronomical fancies? The bit of Neoplatonic speculation in Servius's note is also tantalizing. Eduard Norden, in his magnificent edition of the *Sixth Aeneid,*[9] suggests that certain of the philosophical remarks in Servius, Macrobius, and St. Augustine are taken from a set of Neoplatonic *quaestiones* on the sixth *Aeneid*; the author, Norden thinks, may have been Marius Victorinus, the eminent Neoplatonic philosopher who became a Christian and who both before and after his conversion enjoyed the friendship of St. Augustine and St. Jerome. A pupil of Norden's, F. Bitzch, has written a dissertation on the subject,[10] and it is ripe for still further investigation. As a preliminary, I would here express the belief, which will be more fully set forth elsewhere,[11] that the genuine commentary of Servius is hardly more than an extract from the longer version first published by Pierre Daniel in 1600, and that this longer version is substantially the supposedly lost commentary of Donatus. If this theory is correct, the Neoplatonistic and astronomical matter in the Servian commentary is pushed back in date, with the commentary as a whole, about half a century before the time of Servius. In this case it seems a little doubtful if Marius Victorinus, who was certainly not active as a teacher before Donatus, would have supplied the latter with material for his commentary; it is possible, of course, but Donatus's purpose, expounded in the introductory letter that accompanies his work, is to gather the opinions of the ancients. The bearing of all this on Dante is not immediate, except as it shows the pagan coloring of some of the traditional philosophy, and suggests a further examination of Dante's astronomy in the light of Servius.

## V

My last example is a vexed point in literary history. In the twentieth Canto of the *Inferno*, Virgil is made to discourse on the founding of his native Mantua. The town, he declares, commemorates Manto, daughter of the seer Tiresias, who, leaving her Theban home for Italy, came down Lake Benaco and the river Mincio to a flat plain, marshy and pestilential. In this abandoned spot,

> *per fuggire ogni consorzio umano* (v. 85),

she settled. On her death men built the city over her dead bones. This, Virgil protests, is the true story of the founding of Mantua (vv. 97 ff.):

> "Però t'assenno, che se tu mai odi
> Originar la mia terra altrimenti,
> La verità nulla menzogna frodi."

Curiously, the version which by implication Dante's Virgil denies, is that of the real Virgil, who names the founder as Ocnus (*Aen.* x, 198 ff.):

> Ille etiam patriis agmen ciet Ocnus ab oris,
> fatidicae Mantus et Tusci filius amnis,
> qui muros matrisque dedit tibi, Mantua, nomen.

The Manto here mentioned is generally assumed to be an entirely different person from the Theban prophetess; she is called a river-nymph, and thought to figure in some native Italian tradition that Virgil knew.[12] It is also suggested that Dante knew of the Greek Manto from Statius or from the brief statement in St. Isidore (*Origines* xv, i, 59):

> Manto Tiresiae filia post interitum Thebanorum dicitur delata in Italiam Mantuam condidisse: est autem in Venetia, quae Gallia Cisalpina dicitur: et dicta Mantua, quod manes tuetur.

But, why, the reader wonders, should Dante be so concerned with refuting his revered Virgil? Did he consider Statius or St. Isidore better authorities? It is Servius again, I believe, who helps us solve the question. On *Aen.* x, 198, he remarks:

> Ocnus. Iste est Ocnus, quem in *Bucolicis* Bianorem dicit (*Ecl.* ix, 60). Hic Mantuam dicitur condidisse, quam a matris nomine appellavit: nam fuit filius Tiberis et Mantus, Tiresiae Thebani vatis, quae post patris interitum ad Italiam venit.

St. Isidore was not the first, then, to identify Virgil's Manto with the

Theban. Virgil's commentator Servius has this tradition too. Servius, if I am right, is really Donatus; both Donatus and Isidore drew copiously from Suetonius. There is no evidence for tracking the present comment back to Suetonius, but whether he had it or not, it may well interpret Virgil's meaning correctly. What proof is there that his Manto was a river-nymph? The daughter of Tiresias might have become the mother of Ocnus by Father Tiber; river-gods, as the stories of Rea Silvia and Anna Perenna show, did not confine their attentions to nymphs. It is this part of the legend in which Dante does contradict his master. He may have felt so authorized on observing the uncertainty of Virgil himself; for in the ninth *Eclogue* the founder of Mantua is called Bianor. We may now add the rest of the note in Servius.

> Alii Manto filiam Herculis vatem fuisse dicunt. Hunc Ocnum alii Aulestis filium, alii fratrem, qui Perusiam condidit, referunt: et, ne cum fratre contenderet, in agro Gallico Felsinam, quae nunc Bononia dicitur, condidisse: permisisse etiam exercitui suo, ut castella muniret, in quorum numero Mantua fuit. Alii a Tarchone Tyrrheni fratre conditam dicunt: Mantuam autem ideo nominatam, quod Etrusca lingua Mantum, Ditem patrem appellant, cui etiam cum ceteris urbibus et hanc consecravit.

Here are contrarieties enough to puzzle any reader and justify him in making his own selection. Servius, as he tells us several times,[13] relates the *historia* at which Virgil often glances, but which, according to the law of poetry, he need not report exactly. Dante, with the help of Servius, can go back to *historia* and, finding it a tangle, draw his own inferences and even instruct his master. His main prompting to do so is doubtless artistic; he would adjust the old material to the needs of his own creation. Manto is the chief figure in the fourth part of the eighth circle, where the soothsayers are confined. Amphiaraus, Tiresias, Aruns, Manto, and Eurypylus are taken from the ancient authors, Michael Scott and Asdente are modern. Dante chose to develop Manto, out of regard for Virgil's Mantua, and fashion for her an impressively repulsive character. For this, Statius gave a model in his account[14] of the gloomy rites in honor of the Powers of Darkness performed in a dismal wood by Tiresias with the assistance of Manto, who sips a libation from a bowl of blood. It has been remarked[15] that the present Canto was written after *Purgatorio* XXII, since the poet there implies (v. 113) that Manto was in the Limbo, not in one of the lower circles of Hell. Manto has had a development in the poet's imagination. His chief purpose was not to contradict Virgil in the light of later authorities; he would doubtless infer from Servius that

Virgil's Manto was Tiresias's daughter. But not to clutter his picture with irrelevant details, he omitted the uncertain story of Ocnus, and in a few lines, with the help of Statius, gave to the *vergine cruda* a distinct and most unpleasant personality, appropriate for a sinner confined in the lower Hell. He then makes Virgil swear that this is the truth and the only truth.[16]

In these various instances, I believe, it is Servius that gives a not unimportant clue to the workings of Dante's imagination. Servius himself is in many ways a plodder and a bungler, but he has preserved after all an intensely valuable assortment of information and misinformation. He offers a good point of departure for the imaginative. If it be conceded that Dante read him and to some extent borrowed from him in the passages discussed, a more systematic search in the old commentator might further serve to illuminate, in a humble way, the art of the *Divine Comedy*.

## Notes

1. *Conviv.* II, 1.

2. *Epist.* x, 7.

3. *Summa Theol.*, Pars I, Quaest. I, Art. ix–x.

4. Only excerpts have been published. See Cousin, *Ouvrages inédits d'Abélard* 1836, pp. 639 ff.

5. V. 106f.: quando hic inferni ianua regis / dicitur et tenebrosa palus Acheronte refuso, etc.

6. Vv. 131 f.: tenent media omnia silvae, / Cocytusque sinu labens circumvenit atro.

7. Possibly some form of Plato's account of Tartarus and its rivers had also reached Dante. See *Phaedo*, 112 A: ὃ καὶ ἄλλοθι καὶ ἐκεῖνος καὶ ἄλλοι πολλοὶ τῶν ποιητῶν Τάρταρον κεκλήκασιν. εἰς γὰρ τοθτο τὸ χάσμα συρρέουσί τε πάντες οἱ ποταμοὶ καὶ ἐκ τούτου πάλιν ἐκρέουσιν.

8. *Eth. Nic.* IV, 11. See on the whole subject Dr. Moore's admirable essay in his *Studies in Dante*, Second Series, pp. 175 ff.

9. Leipzig, 1903, p. 29.

10. *De Platonicorum quaestionibus quibusdam Vergilianis*. Berlin, 1911.

11. The subject will also be treated in a dissertation by Mr. H. T. Smith, candidate for the degree of Doctor of Philosophy in Harvard University.

12. See, for example, Conington on *Aen.* x, 198, and Grandgent, *Inferno* (ed. 1909), p. 161.

13. For example, on *Aen.* I, 382: hoc loco per transitum tangit historiam, quam per legem artis poeticae aperte non potest ponere. There follows a quotation from Varro to show what the facts are.

14. *Thebaid,* IV, 406 ff., esp. 463 ff. Another passage descriptive of Manto is X, 678 ff.

15. See Grandgent, *loc. cit.*

16. Dr. Edward Moore, *Studies in Dante,* I, 173, refers to Servius's account of Manto, without drawing the conclusions that I have presented here. His special section on Servius contains several matters that I have not discussed.

Ernest Hatch Wilkins

# Dante and the Mosaics of His *Bel San Giovanni*

## I

In May of the year 1225, forty years before the birth of Dante, a Franciscan friar by the name of Jacobus began the mosaic of the *tribuna* of the Florentine Baptistery (Plate I, centre). The work was probably completed in 1228 or soon thereafter.[1]

Within the same century the Baptistery was further decorated by the mosaics of the octagonal cupola (Plate II). Those on the three faces to the west, above the *tribuna*, represent the Last Judgment; those on the other five faces narrate, in four bands, each containing fifteen scenes, the story of Genesis up to the Deluge, the life of Joseph, the life of Christ, and the life of John the Baptist. Above all these the topmost band represents the nine orders of the angels.[2]

There are two opinions with regard to the dates of these mosaics. Van Marle regards the Last Judgment and the angels as earlier than the narrative scenes; Venturi regards them as contemporary. Van Marle thinks that the Last Judgment and the angels may have been begun at the same time as the mosaic of the *tribuna*; and that the narrative scenes were begun in 1271 or soon thereafter and not finished until after 1300. Venturi assigns them all to the period 1271–1300.

The general appearance of the mosaics representing the Last Judgment and the angels is certainly more archaic than that of the narrative scenes. Venturi is, I think, misled by his belief that the lack of narrative scenes for the lives of Abraham, Isaac, Jacob, and Esau indicates that the plan of including the Last Judgment in the decorative scheme was an afterthought which prevented the carrying out of the previous plan. This belief, however, does not appear to be valid. The Last Judgment is the dominating feature of the decoration and holds the position of honor over the high altar; the narrative scenes are subsidiary to it. Surely it is probable that the Last Judgment was from the beginning the dominating element of the decorative plan. Each of the four narrative bands is complete in itself, and each begins to the right of the Last Judgment.

In any case, we may be confident that the mosaics of the *tribuna* and the upper mosaics representing the Last Judgment and the angels were known to Dante.

It is inherently probable that Dante, as boy and young man, was very greatly interested in all the mosaics of the Baptistery visible to him. There is no need of stressing his love for his *bel san Giovanni*; there is no need of stressing his sensitiveness to art. And the mosaics of the Baptistery, instead of being, as they are now, very minor items in the extraordinary artistic wealth of Florence, were in Dante's boyhood and youth the most notable works of modern art in Florence. There was, indeed, nothing to rival them, so far as I can ascertain, except the small mosaic of the façade of San Miniato, and at the very end of the century the mosaic of the apse of San Miniato and possibly the mosaic of the coronation of the Virgin, now in the cathedral.[3] We have no record of any Florentine fresco sequence prior to 1300; and even the altarpieces were few.[4]

It is further to be borne in mind that this representation of the Last Judgment was presumably better known to Dante than any other representation of the same theme, and that it is indeed the only representation of the Last Judgment which we know him to have seen;[5] also that there must have been a natural psychological tendency for him to form or modify his youthful concept of Heaven by what he saw when he looked upward in his church.

It would seem to be worth while, therefore, to consider whether there be a relation between the mosaics of the Baptistery and any of the visual imaginings of the *Commedia*.

## II

Let us examine first the mosaic of the *tribuna* (Plate III). To the right Mary sits enthroned; opposite her, to the left, John the Baptist sits enthroned; between them is a round design, floreate in decoration, containing curiously shaped compartments occupied by individual figures. This round design, with its compartments, suggests a flower with its petals—even more strongly when seen from an angle (see Plate I) than when seen from directly below.

The visible semblance of Dante's Empyrean consists of a great Rose containing a petal-seat for each of the redeemed. At one point of the upper rim is the throne of Mary, and directly opposite is that of John the Baptist (*Par.* XXXII, 28–31):

E come quinci il glorioso scanno
de la donna del cielo e li altri scanni
di sotto lui cotanta cerna fanno,
così di contra quel del gran Giovanni.[6]

The figures in the round design of the mosaic fall historically into an earlier and a later group. The four to the left are patriarchs, Jacob, Isaac, Abraham, Moses; the four to the right are prophets, Isaiah, Jeremiah, Ezekiel, Daniel. Just so the Rose is divided upon an historical basis into two halves, the one for those who believed in Christ *venturo*, the other for those who believed in Christ *venuto* (*Par.* XXXII, 19–27).

It does not seem to me that under the circumstances these likenesses can be dismissed as coincidental. Neither would I claim that this mosaic was specifically the source of the concept of the Rose. But I believe we may fairly conclude that it is probable that memory of this mosaic, impressed upon the mind of Dante in his most impressionable years, remained therein, more or less conscious; and that when Dante came to the devising of his Rose this memory at least confirmed, and perhaps to some extent determined, his great plan.[7]

It may be added that the caryatids of the same mosaic very possibly shared in the building of the memory which led in general to the concept of the punishment of the proud in Purgatory and in particular to the simile (*Purg.* X, 130–135):

Come per sostentar solaio o tetto,
per mensola tal volta una figura
si vede giugner le ginocchia al petto,

la qual fa del non ver vera rancura
nascere in chi la vede; così fatti
vid' io color, quando puosi ben cura.[8]

## III

Let us turn now to the upper mosaics representing the Last Judgment and the angels. Let us first review from left to right the three faces of the cupola upon which the Last Judgment is represented, and note elements of the mosaics which correspond to elements in the *Commedia*.

In the left face (Plate IV) the correspondences are not striking. The central band of the mosaic, in this and the right face as well, pictures certain of the blessed as seated in a definite order. The lower band shows a gate guarded by an angel, who is welcoming a newly arrived soul. Just to the right an angel leading a group of the blessed toward the gate bears a banner inscribed VENITE BENEDITTI PATRIS MEI POSSIDETE PREPARATUM—the summons of Dante's angel to spirits passing from Purgatory to the Earthly Paradise (*Purg.* XXVII, 58).

In the central face (Plate V), at the bottom, are six tombs, the covers raised at varying angles, with two or more figures in each tomb rising to varying heights. These tombs are the first thing the eye sees as one looks upward above the *tribuna* (see Plate I, top), and the individual variation with which they and their occupants are rendered makes them striking. They remind one of the tombs of the heretics with their raised covers (*Inf.* X, 8–9), and in particular of the tomb in which Cavalcanti kneels while Farinata stands upright (X, 52–54):

> Allor surse a la vista scoperchiata
> un' ombra lungo questa infino al mento:
> credo che s' era in ginocchie levata.

Above the two right-hand tombs stands a gigantic demon whose wings, unlike those of his neighbor to the right, are bat-wings—as are those of Dante's Satan (*Inf.* XXXIV, 49–50):

> Non avean penne, ma di vispistrello
> era lor modo.

Above the head of this demon is a tailed monster with a large head and a pair of flippers, apparently swimming in the air—reminding one slightly of Dante's Geryon.

In the lowest band of the right face (Plate VI), at the top near the left, is a demon carrying a sinner over his shoulder, as in *Inf.* XXI, 34–36:

> L' omero suo, ch' era aguto e superbo,
> carcava un peccator con ambo l' anche,
> e quei tenea de piè ghermito il nerbo.

In the mosaic, however, it is the arms that the demon is gripping. A similar but much less striking group, facing the other way, appears in the right half of the scene, a little to the right of the head of Satan.

Judas appears, hanging, with his name inscribed beside him, in the lower right corner of the mosaic.

The grotesque figure of Satan (Plate VII) has in effect three mouths—since short open-mouthed serpents project right and left from his ears. In each of the three mouths is a sinner. The sinner in the central mouth has his head within, and his body and legs hanging out. Those in the side mouths hang forward, head down. The situation is the same as in *Inf.* XXXIV, 61–67:

"Quell' anima là su c' ha maggior pena,"
disse 'l maestro, "è Giuda Scariotto,
che 'l capo ha dentro e fuor le gambe mena.
De li altri due c' hanno il capo di sotto,
quel che pende dal nero ceffo è Bruto;
vedi come si storce e non fa motto;
e l' altro è Cassio che par sì membruto."

In the central part of the scene there are several serpents of various sorts. Two sinners—the two standing to the left and right of Satan, with their heads in the mouths of the large-headed serpents on which Satan is seated—are attacked each by two serpents. These four serpents have each four very short legs, and in each case one of the two serpents stands upright and bites a sinner in the back. Two, at least, of the serpents in Dante's seventh *bolgia* have legs, specified in one case as short (*Inf.* XXV, 50, 113); and one, at least, stands upright and bites (XXV, 51 ff.). The same sinners in the mosaic are bitten, by other serpents, in the neck—as is Vanni Fucci (XXIV, 97–99):

Ed ecco a un ch' era da nostra proda,
s' avventò un serpente che 'l trafisse
là dove 'l collo a le spalle s' annoda.

The serpents on which Satan is seated hold in their open mouths, as has been said, the heads of these same sinners, and the serpent to the right presses a great tooth against the cheek of his victim—just as a serpent, attacking Agnello, puts teeth into his cheeks (XXV, 54):

poi addentò e l' una e l' altra guancia.

In the upper right-hand quarter of the scene is a sinner held feet upward with his head out of sight—reminding one slightly of Dante's simonists.

The mosaic figures representing the nine orders of the angels dominate the whole Baptistery from above. Their order, beginning at the east and reading back and forth from north to south, is Angels, Archangels, Principalities, Powers, Virtues, Dominations, Thrones, Cherubim, Seraphim. The first seven are designated by their names in large letters. The last two are not named. The order in which they appear is that followed by Dante in the *Commedia*, not that of the *Convivio.*

In the case of the mosaics of the cupola, as well as in the case of that of the *tribuna*, it seems to me impossible under the circumstances to dismiss all the likenesses as coincidental. Nor is it possible on the other hand to prove absolutely that any of the motifs of the mosaics specifically suggested any of Dante's concepts. The possibility of the existence of other plastic or pictorial suggestions now lost must be held in mind; also the possibility of invention based upon purely literary sources or upon thought alone. Yet an influence of these mosaics, even if not exclusive, may have been significant in the formation of a concept resulting from a combination of various suggestions. And it remains inherently and strongly probable that these mosaics made a deep impression upon the mind of the young Dante.

All things considered, it seems to me probable almost to the point of certainty that the striking figure of Satan in the mosaic—three-mouthed, a sinner in each mouth, legs pendent from the central mouth, heads pendent from the other two mouths—is the primary source of Dante's concept of his Satan;[9] that the biting serpents and the bitten sinners shared in the formation of the concept of the punishment of some of the thieves;[10] and that the group, to the left of Satan, of the demon carrying a sinner slung over his shoulder is the primary source of Dante's group of the demon carrying the grafter.[11]

Next in degree of probability I should place the supposition that the batwings of Dante's Satan were suggested by the bat-wings of the gigantic demon in the central face of the mosaic; and the supposition that the tombs of the mosaic shared in the formation of the concept of the tombs of the heretics.[12] If this latter supposition is valid, it becomes further probable, though I think somewhat less so, that the tombs of the mosaic were also in Dante's mind, consciously or unconsciously, when he wrote (*Inf.* VI, 94–99):

Più non si desta
di qua dal suon de l' angelica tromba,
quando verrà la nimica podesta:
ciascun rivederà la trista tomba,

ripiglierà sua carne e sua figura,
udirà quel che in etterno rimbomba

and (*Purg.* xxx, 13–15):

Quali i beati al novissimo bando
surgeran presti ognun di sua caverna,
la revestita carne alleluiando.

With regard to the other elements noted in the mosaic of the Last Judgment—the orderly seating of the blessed, the gate, the angel with the words VENITE BENEDITTI PATRIS MEI, the Geryon-like figure,[13] the presence of Judas, the sinner held feet up with head out of sight, I should claim possibility rather than probability of influence.

As to the angels, it seems to me inherently probable that their dominance in the mosaic increased Dante's interest in the angelic host in general, and in the question of the relative order of the several orders of angels in particular.

Dante's fellow townsman and contemporary, Giotto, was certainly deeply impressed by the mosaic representing hell; for, as Mr. E. F. Rothschild and I are showing in a presently forthcoming study, he repeated several of its motifs, with minor changes, in his fresco of the Last Judgment in the Arena Chapel at Padua, painted probably about 1305. Notable in particular are his repetitions of the Satan, of the demon with a sinner slung over his shoulder, and of the sinner bitten in the back by an upright reptile, and his extension of the motif of the sinner held feet up with head out of sight. He does not repeat specific motifs from the other faces of the mosaic. Dante may or may not have seen Giotto's fresco.[14] In the respects in which the fresco differs from the mosaic, Dante's concept is, except in one instance, closer to the mosaic than to the fresco. The serpents projecting left and right from the head of Giotto's Satan project so far that the effect of a three-mouthed Satan is lost; and Giotto's upright biting reptile is much less serpent-like than that of the mosaic. Giotto's increased number of figures with feet up and head out of sight reminds one, however, of the simonists more clearly than does the single figure of the mosaic.

Even if we knew that Dante saw Giotto's fresco, there would be no indication that he derived independent suggestion from it, except possibly in the case of the simonists. It is, of course, possible that sight of the motifs of the mosaic as repeated by Giotto reënforced them in Dante's memory.[15]

# Notes

1. R. Davidsohn, "Das älteste Werk der Franciscaner-Kunst," in *Repertorium für Kunstwissenschaft,* XXII (1899), 315; A. Venturi, *Storia dell' arte italiana,* III (Milan, 1904), 872; K. Frey, in his edition of Vasari's Lives, Part I, Vol. I (Munich, 1911), 328; R. van Marle, *The Development of the Italian Schools of Painting,* I (The Hague, 1923), 262.

2. A. Aubert, *Die malerische Dekoration der San Francesco Kirche in Assisi* (Leipzig, 1907), p. 68; Venturi, V (1907), pp. 217–239; van Marle, pp. 262–270. Several mosaicists took part in the work, among them, presumably, the two, Andrea Tafi and Apollonio, to whom Vasari, in his life of Tafi, ascribes it.

3. Venturi, V, 241–242; van Marle, I, 261–262, 271–275.

4. O. Siren, *Toskanische Maler im* XIII. *Jahrhundert,* Berlin, 1922.

5. The most notable other monumental representations of the Last Judgment produced in Italy before 1300 are: the fresco in Sant'Angelo in Formis, near Capua, on which see P. Jessen, *Die Darstellung des Weltgerichts bis auf Michelangelo* (Berlin, 1883), pp. 12–14, G. Voss, *Das jüngste Gericht in der bildenden Kunst des frühen Mittelalters* ( = Beiträge zur Kunstgeschichte, VIII, Leipzig, 1884), pp. 45–47, and van Marle, I, 139–140 and VI (1925), 62; the mosaic in the cathedral of Torcello, on which see Jessen, pp. 8–11, Voss, pp. 48–52, C. A. Levi, *Dante a Torcello e il musaico del giudizio universale* (Treviso, 1906; known to me only through the unsigned notice in the *Bullettino della Società Dantesca Italiana*, XX, 1913, 238) and van Marle, I, 236–239; and the fresco by Cavallini in Sta. Cecilia in Rome, on which see van Marle, I, 515–519. For other less notable representations see the references in van Marle, VI, 62; also van Marle, I, 448. There is no specific reason to think that Dante saw any of these representations. No one of them, so far as I can ascertain, possesses similarities to the *Commedia* so extensive or so striking as those pointed out in the present article. On the possibility of Dante's knowledge of Giotto's fresco of the Last Judgment at Padua, see below, p. 9. A fresco, now destroyed, containing a Satan *con più bocche* existed in Boccaccio's time on the façade of the church of San Gallo in Florence; see *Decameron*, viii, 9, and Francesco Sansovino's comment thereon in his *Dichiaratione di tutti i vocaboli . . . che nel . . . Decamerone si trovano* (Venice, 1546), reported in D. M. Manni, *Istoria del Decamerone di Giovanni Boccaccio* (Florence, 1742), pp. 515–516. In view of the general dearth of frescoes in Florence before 1300 and their multiplication soon thereafter, the chances are that the fresco was painted after Dante's exile.

6. I quote from *Le opere di Dante, testo critico della Società Dantesca Italiana*, Florence, 1921.

7. For previous suggestions as to art sources for Dante's concept of the Rose, see P. Savj-Lopez, *Il canto* XXX *del Paradiso* (*Lectura Dantis*, Florence, 1906), pp. 15–19 (Savj-Lopez does not regard as significant such suggestions as had thitherto been made); A. Gottardi, "La città di Dio e la città di Satana in una raffigurazione simbolica del secolo XII," in *Giornale dantesco*, XXIII (1915), 208–219; V. Zabughin, "Dante e la chiesa greca," in *Roma e l'Oriente*, 1915–1916 (known to me only through the notice by A. Marigo in *Bullettino della Società Dantesca Italiana,* XXVI, 1919, 85–86); F. Ermini, "La candida rosa del paradiso dantesco," in *Giornale dantesco,* XXV (1922), 306–308.

8. On the plastic precedents for the concept of the caryatids, see N. Campanini, *Il canto* X *del Purgatorio* (*Lectura Dantis*, Florence, 1901), pp. 31–33.

9. For previous suggestions as to art sources for Dante's concept of Satan, see A. Graf, *Miti, leggende e superstizioni del medio evo*, II (Turin, 1893), 92–94, 127–128; F. X. Kraus, *Dante* (Berlin, 1897), pp. 439–440; R. T. Holbrook, *Dante and the Animal Kingdom* (New York, 1902), pp. 72–76; and Gottardi, *loc. cit.*

10. For a previous suggestion as to an art source for this concept, see *La Divina Commedia . . . illustrata nei luoghi e nelle persone*, ed. by C. Ricci (Milan, 1898), pp. xxix and xxxvi.

11. So far as I can ascertain, no suggestion of an art source for this concept has previously been made.

12. This suggestion is entirely consistent with the fact that Dante's concept of the tombs of the heretics was influenced by knowledge, gained through visit or report, of the tombs at Arles (see C. Cipolla, "Sulla descrizione dantesca delle tombe di Arles," in *Giornale storico della letteratura italiana*, XXIII, 1894, 407–415) and Pola. My suggestion is to the effect that Dante gained from the mosaic a general impression of tombs as part of an image of the otherworld and the specific impression of spirits rising therein to different heights, and that knowledge of the tombs of Arles and Pola later gave breadth and definition to his concept.

13. For previous suggestions as to art sources for Dante's concept of Geryon, see A. De Vit, "Il Gerione dantesco," in *L' Alighieri*, IV (1893), 202–203; A. Venturi, "Dante e Giotto," in *Nuova Antologia*, Ser. iv, LXXXV (1900), 667; Holbrook, pp. 62–66; Gottardi, 211–213; and Zabughin.

14. The only specific basis for the supposition that Dante saw Giotto's fresco is the anecdote narrated by Benvenuto da Imola in his commentary on *Purgatorio* xi: "Accidit autem semel quod dum Giottus pingeret Paduae, adhuc satis iuvenis, unam cappellam in loco ubi fuit olim theatrum, sive harena, Dantes pervenit ad locum: quem Giottus honorifice receptum duxit ad domum suam, ubi Dantes videns plures infantulos eius summe deformes. . ." and then follows the jest as to the painter's fashioning better figures in art than in life, a jest found, as Benvenuto himself notes, in Macrobius (Benvenuto Rambaldi, *Comentum super Dantis Aldigherij Comoediam*, ed. by W. W. Vernon, III, Florence, 1887, 313). The statement of Dante's visiting Giotto appears to have been introduced as a setting for the jest. It is just such a statement as might readily have been invented, and is not confirmed by other sources. It cannot, therefore, be relied on as authentic. See A. Moschetti, *La cappella degli Scrovegni e gli affreschi di Giotto in essa dipinti* (Florence, 1904), pp. 16–17; N. Zingarelli, *Dante* (Milan, 1904), p. 215; A. Zardo, "Padova al tempo di Dante," in *Nuova antologia*, Ser. v, CXLVI (1910), 88; Holbrook, *Portraits of Dante from Giotto to Raffael* (London, 1911), pp. 128–129; A. Belloni, "Nuove osservazioni sulla dimora di Dante in Padova," in *Nuovo archivio veneto*, N. S., XLI (1921), 40–80 (Belloni argues that Benvenuto's statement is reliable: his arguments do not seem to me valid); and A. Moschetti, "Questioni cronologiche giottesche," in *Atti e memorie della R. Accademia di Scienze, Lettere ed Arti di Padova* XXXVII (1921; known to me only through the unsigned notice in *Giornale dantesco*, XXV, 1921, 80–81).

15. I am gladly indebted to my colleague Professor Rudolph Altrocchi for securing for me photographs and books used in this study. The plates are made, in accordance with permission asked and received, from photographs of the Fratelli Alinari of Florence. The photographs are, in the order of the plates, those numbered 1880, 3738, 17250, 3739, 3746, 3745, 17246.

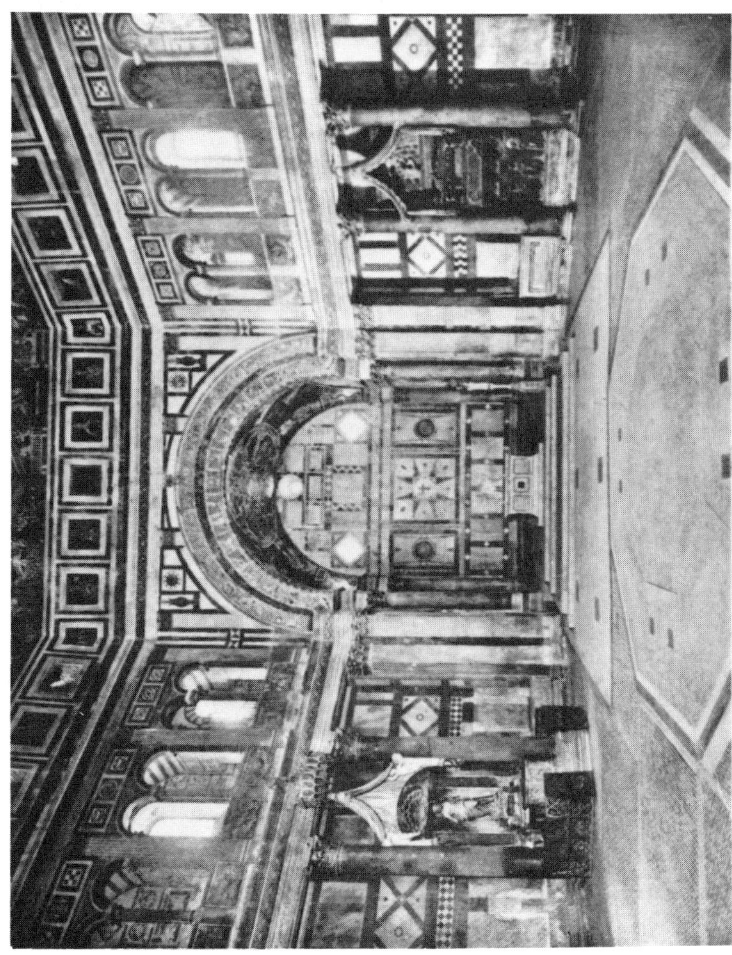

PLATE I
THE INTERIOR OF SAN GIOVANNI LOOKING TOWARD THE TRIBUNA

Plate II
The Mosaics of the Cupola

Plate III
The Mosaic of the Tribuna

PLATE IV
THE LAST JUDGMENT: LEFT FACE

Plate V
The Last Judgment: Central Face

Plate VI
The Last Judgment: Right Face

PLATE VII
THE LAST JUDGMENT: DETAIL

# Charles H. Grandgent

## The Pentateuch and the Divine Comedy

SOME SCHOLARS FIND exhilarating sport in any kind of detective work; and, be they candidates for the Doctor's degree or even professors pricked by the need of annual publicity, they harness their Sherlock-Holmes instinct to their plough. If the field they till be literary, they set themselves resolutely to the cultivation of a crop, however scant or however barren, of bookish interrelations. In other words, they make it their business relentlessly to track the literary borrower to the scene of his crime. It avails the plagiarist nothing to have been dead and forgotten these hundreds of years: his attenuated ghost, invisible to all the world beside, is marked by the nyctalopic sleuth, who eventually and inevitably brings it down with his deadly double column. To catch an author of whom nobody else has ever heard, and convict him of having borrowed something of no value whatever from another author who might just as well (except for dissertation purposes) never have been born—that is the perfect triumph.

Others there be who, indifferent to the lure of long-hidden petty larceny, are fascinated by the illusory task of tracing to its sources the inspiration of a work supremely great. To them, nothing in the environment, the biography, or the library of a man of genius can be too trivial to bear investigation. For in the reactions of the master to his material and spiritual surroundings they see the genesis of the masterpiece. Their presumptuous mysticism aspires to become one with their divinity, to enter into his mental courses, to live over again his psychic life. Interesting to them is not only what he did, but also what he did not do; his very omissions are significant. Indeed, art being primarily a process of selection, the artist is perceived both in what he takes and in what he rejects. Usually, alas! his reasons for taking or refusing escape even the most sympathetic interrogation; but in the questioning itself there lies a curious interest.

Consider, for instance, a great book which one knows to have been read carefully by a great man. To examine that book, to set it side by side with the *chef d'oeuvre* of that man, to note the incidents, the thoughts, and the phrases which he repeats, and also the striking incidents, thoughts, and phrases which he does not repeat, is in a way to read the work in his company. Yet when we try to explain the why's and wherefore's, we can do nothing but guess vaguely; we cannot even, with any certainty, measure his imagination by our own, comparing the impressions evidently made on him with those which the reading makes on us. For only a few of his reactions are recorded in his writ. Some of his intensest feelings may have been suppressed or remained unspoken, for reasons which we cannot divine—reasons artistic, moral, or philosophical. From a host of varied experiences, in life and in literature, the master chose his matter; and an experience big in reality may have contributed to his legacy only a mite. Despite these considerations, despite the peril of presumption, despite the small likelihood of conjecturing aright, such speculation offers perhaps enough satisfaction to justify the indulgence.

One might be particularly tempted to indulge such a fancy in the case of the Bible and the *Divine Comedy*. Here we have the greatest of prose books and the greatest of poems. And we know that the author of the second was a diligent student of the first; both theory and evidence tell us so. Really, he could not have escaped the study, in the course of a good Christian philosophic education. And, aside from antecedent probability, we can see its results throughout Dante's literary career: in the formation of the prose style of the *Vita Nuova*, for which he had no model in his own tongue; in the abundance of Scriptural illustration and phraseology in the *Commedia* and in all Dante's Italian and Latin prose. But here suggests itself at once the question whether he was equally acquainted with all parts of the Holy Writ. From the citations listed in Edward Moore's collection, in the First Series of his *Studies in Dante*, one may infer that our poet pretty intimately knew them all. Whether in his *Vita Nuova* days he was so thoroughly versed is another matter. A critic might perhaps make a comparative inquiry into the Biblical allusions during the different periods of Dante's life. Another investigation, and a much more rewarding one, would deal with the frequency of references to those passages of the Bible which are contained in the Church service. These, of course, were the sentences most constantly in his hearing and hence most easily recurrent to his pen. It is to be hoped that some good churchgoer will undertake this bit of research.

A vastly larger and far less definite study would have to do with the possibilities of literary suggestion in all the Bible—its vivid pictures, its dramatic incidents, its quotable verses—and the extent to which Dante has availed himself of these opportunities, either in the *Commedia* or in any of his other works. The results would of course be largely subjective, they would perhaps depend more or less on the pictorial illustrations in the family Bible of the investigator; but they might well be of interest to others. A similar inquiry, though an easier one, would take the *Aeneid* as a basis. Another might concern itself with the *Metamorphoses*. These three—the Bible, the *Aeneid*, the *Metamorphoses*—are Dante's three chief literary models, as St. Thomas and Aristotle are his great doctrinal authorities. In any quest of the kind, it must be remembered that Dante, either for the sake of universality or for love of artistic poise, was inclined to balance the profane with the sacred, the ancient with the modern. Often, no doubt, a Scriptural illustration was sacrificed to a Virgilian, or a Virgilian to a Biblical, in order to keep the proportion just. One must remember, furthermore, that, the whole Bible being to our poet the word of God, those things therein which to the literalist are merely repulsive or foolish are susceptible of a different interpretation which may render them edifying. In no literal sense, the *Commedia* tells us, are to be understood the "hand" and "foot" of God, and the six days of Creation. One must bear in mind, also, that Virgil, in Dante's opinion, wrote not without divine inspiration and veiled his disclosures in allegory. The fair and mysterious Matilda, in the Garden of Eden, declares that the ancient poets, when they wrote of the Golden Age, may have been dreaming of this happy spot. Whereupon Dante glances around at Virgil and Statius, his companions, and sees that they have greeted this suggestion with a smile (*Purg.* XXVIII, 139–147).

As a tiny earnest of what may be done, let us take a look at the five books of Moses. All of them are represented in some fashion in the *Divine Comedy*, although the share of Leviticus and Numbers, as one might expect, is pretty slim. From the former, indeed, we recognize in the *Commedia* only three passages (the Latin works furnish an additional four). The most interesting is XI, 3: "Whatsoever parteth the hoof, and is cloven footed, and cheweth the cud, among the beasts, that shall ye eat"—a passage repeated in Deut. xiv, 6. A passing reference to it, and to St. Thomas's curious allegorical interpretation, we find in *Purg.* XVI, 99, where we are told that the Pope "cheweth the cud but parteth not the hoof," meaning that he has capacity to meditate on the Scriptures but not to distinguish right from wrong in practical affairs; hence the need of an Emperor.

Le leggi son, ma chi pon mano ad esse?

Nullo; però che il pastor che procede
Ruminar può, ma non ha l'unghie fesse.

*Purg.* v, 74, contains the phrase, "the blood in which I dwelt" — a reference to the belief that the soul abides in the blood, which finds expression in Lev. xvii, 14: "for the life of all flesh is the blood thereof," or, more clearly, in the Latin, "anima enim omnis carnis in sanguine est." Wherefore the Hebrews eat no flesh that has not been drained of blood. *Par.* v, 49–51, which has to do with substitution of sacrifices, goes back to Lev. xxvii, 10–13, 28–33. What else the poet might have culled from this unexciting book is not apparent, unless he had found occasion to use a picture of the sons of Aaron burnt by fire, in punishment for taking their censers and offering "strange fire before the Lord" (Lev. x, 1–2). The way of God's retaliation — "there went out fire from the Lord" — is interesting as one of the many instances of the expression of divine indignation by fire, a mode which Dante adopted as the regular sign, in his Hell, of insult to the Divinity. By fire are punished the heretics, the Simonists, and, in the seventh circle, those who directly or indirectly did violence to God. Other visitations, such as the plagues of frogs, lice, flies, murrain, boils, hail, rain, thunder, locusts, darkness, and death of the first born (Ex. viii–xii) find no echo in the *Inferno*, although hail and rain are ingredients in one of the torments there.

Io sono al terzo cerchio, della piova
  Eterna, maledetta, fredda e greve;
  Regola e qualità mai non l'è nova.
Grandine grossa e acqua tinta e neve
  Per l'aer tenebroso si riversa;
  Pute la terra che questo riceve.

To the flood (Gen. vi–viii) we have a fleeting allusion in connection with the rainbow,

Per lo patto che Dio con Noè pose,
Del mondo, che giammai più non si allaga (*Par.* XII, 17–18),

but no description; perhaps the poet preferred Ovid's version. At any rate he neglected such fertile themes as the embarkation, the subsidence of the waters, the dove and the olive leaf (Gen. viii, 11), the drunkenness of Noah

(Gen. ix). This last incident may have impressed Dante as too vulgar, and incompatible with Noah's sacred character, just as Caesar's usurpation and tyranny were incompatible with his divinely ordained rôle as founder of the Empire. A similar feeling may have been aroused by the story of Lot and his two daughters (Gen. xix), who were left while Myrrha was taken (*Inf.* xxx, 37–41). One would like to know.

If Leviticus is poetically barren, the book of Numbers is not much better. In fact, Dante seems to have levied very few contributions on it. Possibly he got thence the epithet *obbediente* applied to Moses (*Inf.* IV, 57): "Now the man Moses was very meek" (Num. xii, 3); although the Latin, *mitissimus*, is scarcely close enough to justify such a supposition. At any rate the verse is evidently the source of our phrase, "as meek as Moses." "That people for which the sea opened was all dead ere Jordan beheld its heirs" (*Purg.* XVIII, 133–135) harks back, it would seem, to Num. xiv, 22–23, 29–30. The idea that the priesthood should hold no property, as it appears in the exclusion of Aaron and the Levites from inheritance,

> Ed or discerno perchè dal retaggio
> Li figli di Levì furono esenti (*Purg.* XVI, 131–132),

Dante may have derived from Numbers (xviii, 20, 23–24) or from Deuteronomy (x, 9; xiv, 27, 29; xviii, 1–2) or from Joshua (xiii, 14, 33; xiv, 4; xviii, 7). Can it be that the tiresome discussion of vows in *Par.* IV and V was suggested, or encouraged, by the long list of statutes on that subject in Num. xxx (cf. Deut. xxiii, 21–23)? If so, the account is squared by the magnificent description of the king in Num. xxiv, 9: "He couched, he lay down as a lion, and as a great lion"—provided, as seems likely, this figure is the model of Sordello,

> solo sguardando
> A guisa di leon, quando si posa (*Purg.* VI 65–66).

In Num. xxxiii occurs the list of the forty-two stations of the Israelites as they marched from Rameses in Egypt to the river Jordan. More than once these stations were interpreted mystically as standing for spiritual stages in the elevation of the soul to God; notable is Peter Damian's *De Quadragesima sive de Quadraginta duabus Hebraeorum Mansionibus*, which may have been known to Dante. But the attempt to derive Dante's allegory from Peter Damian's (P. Amaducci, *La fonte della Divina Commedia*, 2 vols., 1911) cannot be called successful. Other things in Numbers might have appealed to our poet, but apparently did not. The cloud which, abiding on the tabernacle, forbade journeying (Num. ix) might have been used in the *Commedia* as a symbol of law, or of divine guidance; but it was not. Divine enlightenment Dante represents by the sun; law, by the tree of knowledge of good and evil. Nor was inspiration drawn from the various episodes in which the Lord speaks out of a cloud, unless such inspiration be seen in the discourses of the guileful Guido da Montefeltro and the adventurous Ulysses from their covering of fire. "And it came to pass, as Moses entered the tabernacle, the cloudy pillar descended, and stood at the door of the tabernacle, and the Lord talked with Moses" (Ex. xxxiii, 9). Compare this with *Inf.* XXVI, 85–90, and XXVII, 7–18; there is not much resemblance. One would have thought that Dante would have longed to reproduce the picture conveyed in Ex. xxxiv, when "the skin of Moses' face shone," after his converse with the Lord. Cato's face, to be sure, on the bank of the island of Purgatory, shines "as if the sun had been in front of it" (*Purg.* I, 39); but it is bright with the reflection of the stars which stand for the four cardinal virtues, not with the direct presence of the Lord. To him, even more appropriately than to Moses, might have been said: 'Thou canst not see my face" (Ex. xxxiii, 20).

How many picturesque incidents the career of Moses affords! Dante passes them all by. He does refer to the passing of the Red Sea (Ex. xiv) in the words "e il mar fuggir quando Dio volse" (*Par.* XXII, 95); in his use of the word *idolatre* (*Inf.* XIX, 113) he does seem to have in mind the worshipers of the golden calf (Ex. xxxii); and he does paraphrase the speech of the Lord to Moses (Ex. xxxiii, 19), "I will make all my goodness pass before thee"— 'Io ti farò vedere ogni valore" (*Par.* XXVI, 42). That is all. Nothing of the command to the midwives in Egypt, under the tyrannous Pharoah, to kill all the male children (Ex. i); nothing of that favorite theme of Biblical art, Moses in the bulrushes (Ex. ii); naught of the awakening of racial indignation in the young prophet, as related in Ex. ii, 11–12: "And it came to pass in those days, when Moses was grown, that he went out unto his brethren, and looked upon their burdens: and he spied an Egyptian smiting an Hebrew, one of his brethren. And he looked this way and that way, and when he saw that there was no man, he slew the Egyptian, and hid him in the sand." That same spirit it was that moved him to help the seven daughters of the priest of Midian to draw water, when "the shepherds came and drove them away" (Ex. ii, 16–17). Of the cohesive national impulse, so mighty among the Hebrews (quarrelsome as they were), we find no mention; perhaps it fitted ill into Dante's scheme of world-empire. Neither do we find remembrance of the continual savage, ruthless butchery of tens and hundreds of thousands of men, women, and children, — the extermination of people after people by the edge of the sword, — which fills so much of the Old Testament; it seems to have been too strong for even Dante's belligerent stomach. When he has to describe a sickening scene of carnage, he picks out a battlefield in his own country (*Inf.* XXVIII, 7–21). It may be appropriate to note here that the poet, not always squeamish in his own thought or style, repeats none of the nastinesses of the Bible stories. Nor does he reproduce the old idea of a cruel, jealous, and capricious God, insistent though he be, in his *Paradiso*, on the idea of submission and predestination. One can hardly imagine Dante's God "hardening Pharaoh's heart" (Ex. iii, 13). Of the numerous God-sent plagues of high mortality ("Now they that died in the plague were fourteen thousand and seven hundred" — Num. xvi, 49) he says not a word; rather, when he would speak of a pestilence that sweeps clean a whole island, does he turn to classic fable and the island of Ægina:

> Non credo che a veder maggior tristizia
> Fosse in Egina il popol tutto infermo,
> Quando fu l'aer sì pien di malizia
> Che gli animali, infino al picciol vermo,
> Cascaron tutti . . . (*Inf.* XXIX, 58–62).

As to the primitive name of the Lord, which, as Adam informs Dante, was *I*, —

> Pria ch'io scendessi all'infernale ambascia,
> *I* s'appellava in terra il Sommo Bene
> (*Par.* XXVI, 133–134), —

one queries whether any light is thrown on that perplexing statement by Ex. iii, 13–14 and vi, 3: "And Moses said unto God, Behold, . . . they shall say unto me, what is his name? what shall I say unto them? And God said unto Moses, I AM THAT I AM: and he said, Thus shalt thou say unto the children of Israel, I AM hath sent me to you." "By my name JEHOVAH was I not known unto them." In the Vulgate I AM THAT I AM is SUM QUI SUM; I AM is QUI EST; JEHOVAH is ADONAI. It is curious that Dante, with his fondness for tracing the mysterious significance of names, should have made nothing of the change of Abram to Abraham and of Sarai to Sarah (Gen. xvii). With all his interest in dreams (witness his reference to Daniel and Nebuchadnezzar in *Par.* IV, 14), he is silent concerning Joseph's interpretation of the dreams of Pharaoh's butler and baker in prison (Gen. xl), and finally the dream of Pharaoh himself (Gen. xli), which was the starting-point of Joseph's economic career.

Returning to the history of Moses, we miss in the *Commedia* the startling scene of the burning bush, from which the Lord speaks (Ex. iii, 2, 4); we miss the "land flowing with milk and honey" (Ex. iii, 8, 17), the "spoiling" of the Egyptians (Ex. iii, 22), the making of "bricks without straw" (Ex. v); we miss the institution of the Passover (Ex. xii), the sojourn of the children of Israel in Egypt for four hundred and thirty years (Ex. xii), the beautiful picture of the pillar of cloud guiding them by day and the pillar of fire by night (Ex. xiii), the majestic descent of the Lord on Sinai while the mountain smokes (Ex. xix), the issuance of the Ten Commandments (Ex. xx), the ascent of Moses to the Lord on Mt. Sinai (Ex. xxiv), the wrath of Moses at the idolaters and his shattering of the tablets of God (Ex. xxxii). One can easily think of places where Dante, had he been so inclined, could have made use of these items. What more effective than the tale of the defeat of Amalek by Joshua, mysteriously brought about by Moses holding his hands uplifted through the fight? "But Moses' hands were heavy; and they took a stone, and put it under him, and he sat thereon; and Aaron and Hur stayed up his hands, the one on the one side, and the other on the other side; and his hands were steady until the going down of the sun." This picture, no doubt, was in the poet's mind when he spoke of Joshua's victory won by "uplifting either palm" (*Par.* IX, 122–123).

Then there are the two silver trumpets (Num. x), which might fitly have blared somewhere in the *Divine Comedy*; there is the fire in the camp, stopped at Moses' prayer (Num. xi); there is the hankering for flesh, with its gratification and its punishment, there is the weary Moses sharing his responsibility with seventy elders, there is the rain of quails and the rain of manna (Num. ix). Dante speaks of manna, both in its literal (*Par.* XXXII, 131) and in its commonly accepted spiritual sense (*Purg.* XI, 13; *Par.* XII, 84). For this latter interpretation we find warrant in Deut. viii, 3: "And fed thee with manna . . . that he might make thee know that man doth not live by bread only, but by every word that proceedeth out of the mouth of the Lord doth man live."

The sorrows of the tired and aging Moses must surely have touched Dante, but he has left us no record of his sympathy. Did not Miriam and Aaron "speak against Moses," who had married an Ethiopian; and did not Miriam, stricken by the Lord with leprosy, turn "white as snow," and was she not cured at Moses' intercession (Num. xii)? The Lord had reason to be angry at his stubborn people, whom he condemned to wander forty years and never reach the Promised Land, save only Caleb and Joshua (Num. xiv); Dante couples them with Acestes and his mates who forsook Æneas in Sicily (*Purg.* XVIII, 133–138). Rightly the earth opened and swallowed Korah and all his men (Num. xvi), although our poet puts them aside in favor of Amphiaraus, who according to Statius met a like fate (*Inf.* xx, 31–36); one phrase of the Bible story, however, "they . . . went down alive into the pit" (Num. xvi, 33), may have turned Dante's fancy to the conception of the doom of those treacherous hosts who, having massacred their guests and relatives at table (*Inf.* XXXIII, 124–147), also "go down alive," leaving devils in their stead to inhabit their bodies. Justly were the idolatrous altars destroyed (Deut. xii, 3), but without record by Dante, as was the fire which came out from the Lord and consumed the two hundred and fifty men who offered incense (Num. xvi, 35). Just, no doubt, but unsung was the wrath of Moses against the officers for saving the women of the Midianites alive (Num. xxxi). Surely the great Florentine must have grieved, as we do, that the saviour of his people was not allowed to enter the Promised Land (Deut. iii), that privilege being reserved for the extraordinary campaigner, Joshua, who had been chosen to succeed him (Num. xxvii). Moses (Deut. xxxiv, 8), like Aaron (Num. xx, 29), was mourned by the children of Israel for thirty days, thus giving a certain impressiveness to the number thirty (cf. *Purg.* III, 139).

As Siegfried in Götterdämmerung tells his life-story in his long death-song, so Moses, in the early chapters of Deuteronomy, rehearses the events of his career. Among his opponents was the giant Og. "For only Og king of Bashan remained of the remmant of giants" (Deut. iii, 11)—doubtless the race mentioned in Gen. vi, 4: "There were giants in the earth in those days." In Num. xiii, 33, we read: "And there we saw the giants . . . : and we were in our own sight as grasshoppers."

> E più con un gigante io mi convegno
> Che i giganti non fan con le sue braccia (*Inf.* XXXIV,
> 30–31).

In keeping with such inhabitants was that bunch of grapes, familiar to us all from Bible illustration (Num. xiii, 23), borne "between two on a staff." Appropriate, too, was the bedstead of Og king of Bashan, nine cubits long and four broad (Deut. iii, 11). These elements of course entered into Dante's conception of the giants with whom he surrounds the central pit of his hell

(*Inf.* XXXI); but he repeats none of them, preferring, here too, when he borrows details, to take them from the poets.

So it is, moreover, with miracles: for them, our author draws far more from pagan than from Christian sources. Yet he can hardly have been influenced by the consideration which Boileau set forth in his *Art poétique* (III, 199–200):

> De la foi d'un chrétien les mystères terribles
> D'ornements égayés ne sont point susceptibles.

Ovid's tales, to be sure, are more "égayés" than those in the Bible; but gayety was not Dante's goal when he was writing the *Inferno*. After all, it may be that the poet, regarding the *Commedia* as fiction and the *Metamorphoses* as fiction, both of them true only in a symbolical or a moral sense, while the Bible is true both literally and allegorically, conceived the idea that his own work and Ovid's belonged to one class of literature and the Holy Writ to another. He says, indeed, in the *Convivio* (II, 1) that poets and the Scripture take allegory differently. A few Biblical miracles, such as Sarah, Abraham's wife, conceiving a child at the age of ninety (Gen. xvii—xviii), might have been difficult to introduce appropriately; but most of them seem to a modern reader about as fit as the numerous supernatural incidents from the Classics. Aside from the Creation, Dante recalls four great miracles from Pentateuch: the flood (Gen. vi–ix), the confusion of tongues (Gen. xi), the destruction of Sodom and Gomorrah (Gen. xix), the parting of the Red Sea (Ex. xiv). These he merely touches incidentally. The stoppage of the Jordan, which he cites with the Red Sea prodigy, is from Joshua (iii, 13–19). These two are coupled as miracles more wonderful than the reformation of present corruption—a reformation prophesied in *Paradiso*, XXII, 94–96:

> Veramente Giordan volto retrorso
> Più fu, e il mar fuggir, quando Dio volse,
> Mirabile a veder che qui il soccorso.

Others that might have been utilized—not counting dreams, ordinary plagues, victories, the appearance and speech of God and angels—are these: the transformation of Moses' rod into a snake, while his hand becomes leprous (Ex. iv); the turning of the Egyptian waters to blood in Ex. vii, 17–25; the rods cast down change to serpents, and Aaron's rod swallows up the other rods (Ex. vii, 9–12); a tree thrown into the bitter waters of Marah makes them sweet (Ex. xv, 23–25); Moses smites a rock and water gushes forth (Ex. xvii, 5–6;

Num. xx, 2–11); of the twelve rods of the princes of Israel, Aaron's alone buds and blossoms (Num. xvii); a plague of fiery serpents is cured by a serpent of brass erected on a pole (Num. xxi). Anyone familiar with the *Divine Comedy* will quickly discover favorable spots where one and another of these scenes might have been used as imagery.

We have as yet scarcely looked at Genesis, one of the books best known and most fruitful in episodes. Here, then, let us pursue a different method, simply enumerating drily the things taken and those left. Taken, in the story of Creation, are: the earth "without form, and void" (i, 2; cf. *Inf.* XXXIV, 122–124); the six days (i) which Dante understands symbolically (*Par.* XXI, 16–30); "the Spirit of God moved upon the face of the waters" (i, 2; cf. *Par.* XXI, 21); "a garden eastward in Eden" (ii, 8; cf. *Purg.* XXVIII); "every herb . . . which is upon the face of all the earth" (i, 29; cf. *Purg.* XXVIII, 118–120); "the tree of knowledge of good and evil" (ii, 9; cf. *Purg.* XXXII, 37–48, XXXIII, 61–63); the rivers of Eden (ii, 10–14), adapted by Dante to his purpose (*Purg.* XXXIII, 112–114); the creation of man (ii, 7) and of woman (ii, 21–22), indefinitely referred to (*Par.* VII, 145–148). Later: the serpent of Gen. iii (*Purg.* VIII, 94–108; XXXII, 32); the cry of Cain, "Every one that findeth me shall slay me" (iv, 14; cf. *Purg.* XIV, 133); Adam's ripe age of 930 years (v; cf. *Par.* XXVI, 121–123); the covenant of the rainbow (ix, 11–17; cf. *Par.* XII, 16–18); Nimrod the mighty hunter (x, 8–9; cf. *Inf.* XXXI, 58–81); the tower in Shinar and the confusion of tongues (xi, 1–2, 3–9; cf. *Inf.* XXXI, 76–78, *Par.* XXVI, 124–126); the rite of circumcision (xvii; cf. *Par.* XXXII, 79–81); Sodom and Gomorrah (xix; cf. *Purg.* XXVI, 40); Esau and Jacob struggle together within their mother, offering the stock example of predestination (xxv, 22; cf. *Par.* XXXII, 67–69); Jacob's ladder (xxviii; cf *Par.* XXI, 25–42); Jacob serves twice seven years for Rachel (xxix; cf. *Inf.* IV, 59–60); the two wives Rachel and Leah, who early became types of the contemplative and the active life (xxix–xxx; cf. *Purg.* XXVII, 100–108); Potiphar's wife, whom Dante uses as an example of the liar (xxxix; cf. *Inf.* XXX, 97).

The other list, consisting of the omissions, is somewhat—though not very much—longer: the offerings of Cain and Abel, with the resulting fratricide (iv), and the never forgotten words of Cain, "Am I my brother's keeper?" (iv, 9) and "My punishment is greater than I can bear" (iv, 13); the translation of Enoch, who "walked with God" and "was not, for God took him" (v, 24); the journey of Abram to Canaan and Egypt and his prudent device—twice repeated—of passing off his wife as his sister, lest he be killed by someone who wants to take her (xii, cf. xx); the partition of land by Abram and Lot (xiii); the rescue of Lot by Abram (xiv); the pathetic and much illustrated story of Hagar, her flight from Sarai the wife of Abram (xvi) and her later exile with her son Ishmael (xxi); the scene wherein the Lord appears to Abram and Abram falls on his face (xvii); Sarah's conception at the age of ninety (xvii–xviii); the pretty picture of Lot entertaining the angels (xix); the interrupted sacrifice of Isaac (xxii); the winning of Rebekah for Isaac by Abraham's servant, with the episode of the well; the successful swindling operations of Jacob —his purchase of Esau's birthright (xxv), his theft of a blessing from Isaac (xxvii), his cattle deal with Laban (xxx); the oft-repeated tale of the barren Rachel and the fruitful Leah, and the long-delayed birth of Joseph (xxix–xxx); then Jacob's present to Esau (xxxii), his wrestle with a supernatural "man" (xxxii), and the touching encounter of the two brothers; next, the very oriental adventure of Tamaar, Judah's daughter-in-law (xxxviii); finally, the engaging figure of Joseph, familiar in every household—his coat of many colors, his interpretation of dreams, his wicked brothers who lower him into a pit and sell him into slavery (xxxvii), his success in Egypt, and his generous treatment of those who had wronged him (xlii–l), with the curious episode of Benjamin (xliv).

Out of Joseph's history, Dante takes only a reference to the false accusation brought against him by the wife of Potiphar. As to Jacob, one cannot help asking whether his dishonesty seemed to our poet out of place in a sacred patriarch; Laban, to be sure, the sorely tried son-in-law had every temptation to cheat, but for his treatment of Esau there is no excuse save predestination. Particularly surprising is the omission of the Abraham and Isaac incident, used by the theologians as an example of the only condition under which murder is justifiable, even as Samson illustrates the only permissible type of suicide—a killing performed at the direct bidding of the Lord.

Certain phrases which a modern author can with difficulty avoid citing have escaped Dante's hand, although Dante made such abundant use of Scriptural language. Hardly can such quotations have appeared hackneyed in the fourteenth century—such quotations as "Then shall ye bring down my gray hairs with sorrow to the grave" (Gen. xlii, 38; xliv, 29) and "His [Ishmael's] hand will be against every man, and every man's hand against him" (Gen. xvi, 12) and "The voice is Jacob's voice but the hands are the hands of Esau" (Gen. xxvii, 22).

One speech of Abraham's I suspect of having suggested to Dante his famous "giusti son duo" (*Inf.* VI, 73). The traveler through hell, you remember, has asked the soul of the glutton Ciacco whether any just men are left in Florence; and the reply is: "There are two just men, but no one listens to them there." Now consider Abraham's pleading for Sodom, which the Lord is minded to annihilate. "Peradventure," he says (Gen. xviii, 24), "there be fifty righteous within the city: wilt thou also destroy and not spare the place for the fifty righteous that are therein?" "And the Lord said, If I find in Sodom fifty righteous within the city, then will I spare all the place for their sakes." Thereupon Father Abraham persistently beats the Lord down to forty-five, to thirty, to twenty, to ten. This last is the lowest figure reached. "And he said, I will not destroy it for ten's sake." With this bargain in his memory, Dante seems by Ciacco's words to imply that Florence had far less righteous men than the minimum required for the pardon of Sodom.

By way of conclusion, let us look at a few phrases of Deuteronomy which may have borne fruit in the *Commedia*. As we have already seen, the idea that the soul of man resides in his blood—an idea conveyed, for instance, in Jacopo del Cassero's speech (*Purg.* v, 73–75), "the blood in which I dwelt"—has express Scriptural warrant in Lev. vii, 14: "Anima enim omnis carnis in sanguine est," as the Latin runs, the English being less precise; but it is backed both in Latin and in English by Deut. xii, 23: "Only be sure that thou eat not the blood: for the blood is the life; and thou mayest not eat the life with the flesh."

The law of retaliation, recurrent in various spots in the Bible, the *lex talionis* observed in Dante's hell, is plainly stated in Deut. xix, 21: "Life shall go for life, eye for eye, tooth for tooth, hand for hand, foot for foot."

The practice of usury was more absolutely prohibited in medieval Christian doctrine (though perhaps more generally indulged in) than under the Hebrew law, which allows some mitigation: "Thou shalt not lend upon usury to thy brother. . . . Unto a stranger thou mayest lend upon usury; but unto thy brother thou shalt not lend upon usury" (Deut. xxiii, 19–20). It is to be noted that all the usurers punished and named in Dante's hell are Italians, and all but one are Florentines.

When Alighieri is summoned by St. Peter to confess his faith, he reduces his creed to two articles, whereof the first is belief in "one God, single and eternal."

> Ed io rispondo: Io credo in uno Iddio
> Solo ed eterno, che tutto il ciel move,
> Non moto, con amore e con disio (*Par.* XXVI, 130–132).

So in Deut. vi, 4: "The Lord our God is one Lord." Called upon by St. John to declare the primary object of his love, the poet answers:

Lo Ben che fa contenta questa corte
  Alfa ed omega è di quanta scrittura
  Mi legge Amore, o lievemente o forte (*Par.* XXVI,
16–18).

"And thou shalt love the Lord thy God with all thine heart, and with all thy soul, and with all thy might," says Deut. vi, 5.

The enumeration of God's miraculous rescues of his chosen people in Deut xi, with its iteration of the words "And what he did . . ." at the beginning of verses 4, 5, and 6, finds an echo not only in the "E non pose Iddio le mani" at the close of *Convivio* II, v, but also in Justinian's account of the exploits of the Roman Eagle in *Par.* VI, with its similar recurrence of "Tu sai che fece . . ." and "E quel che fe'. . . ," with slight variations, in lines 37, 40, 43, 58, 61, 73.

Dante's favorites in dumb creation were birds. He never tired of drawing similes from them. A gentle picture of a mother bird is offered by Deut. xxxii, 11: "As an eagle stirreth up her nest, fluttereth over her young, spreadeth abroad her wings . . ." In Dante the eagle becomes a stork.

As mother stork above her nest doth stir
  In circles, when her children have been fed,
  And as the birdlet, fed, looks up at her . . .

Quale sovresso il nido si rigira
  Poi che ha pasciuti la cicogna i figli,
  E come quei ch' è pasto la rimira . . . (*Par.* XIX, 91–93).

One last guess. Can the sweet figure in Deut. xxxii, 2, "My doctrine shall drop as the rain, my speech shall distil as the dew," have had any share in that passage of Dante's *Par.* XXXIII, 61–66, so alluring to the fancy, tinkling so fairlylike in the ear?

Cotal son io; chè quasi tutta cessa
  Mia visione, ed ancor mi distilla
  Nel cuor lo dolce che nacque da essa.
Così la neve al sol si dissigilla;
  Così al vento nelle foglie lievi
  Si perdea la sentenza di Sibilla.

What is the moral of this long fable? It is this, if I mistake not. The rich artist can afford to pass in silence most of his memories, most of his reflections, most of his experience. Only the poverty-stricken needs to utilize every scrap. The great poet lets nearly all his vision slip away, and culls only the sweet residuum. He does not feel obliged to stuff into a huge volume all the thoughts, or appearances of thoughts, or minute fragments of thoughts, that breeze into his mind or can be conjured into his consciousness during the twenty-four hours of the day. No, he waits until Love inspires him; then takes note, and writes as Love dictates in his heart.

# Ezra Pound

## Hell

### A Review of *Dante's Inferno translated into English Triple Rhyme*, by Laurence Binyon.

I HAVE ALWAYS MISTRUSTED Ronsard's boast of having read the Iliad in three days, though he might have scuttered through Salel in that time. As a stunt I also might possibly have burrowed through Binyon's version in similar period had it been printed in type decently large.

I state that I have read the work, that for thirty years it never wd. have occurred to me that it wd. be possible to read a translation of the Inferno from cover to cover, and that this translation has therefore one DEMONSTRATED dimension, whatever may be left to personal taste of the reader or conjecture of acrid critics.

Fools have their uses, and had it not been for the professorial pomp of Mr. Wubb or whatever his name is, I might not have found the volume. Mr. Wubb leapt upon Binyon's opening triad of lines and managed to display such complete ignorance of the nature of Dantescan verse, and at the same time so thoroughly indicated at least one virtue of Binyon's work that I was aroused to wonder if the venerable Binyon had been able to keep on at that pace.

The venerable Binyon has I am glad to say produced the most interesting english version of Dante that I have seen or expect to see, though I remain in a considerable obscurity as to how far he knows what he has done, and how far he intended the specific results perceptible to the present examiner.

The younger generation may have forgotten Binyon's sad youth, poisoned in the cradle by the abominable dogbiscuit of Milton's rhetoric. I found our translator in 1908 among very leaden greeks, and in youthful eagerness I descended on the British Museum and perused, it now seems, in retrospect, for days the tales of . . . demme if I remember anything but a word, one name, Penthesilea, and that not from reading it, but from hearing it spoken by a precocious Binyonian offspring. MR. BINYON'S ODE, poster of, was it

The Evening Standard 'Milton Thou shoulds't', or whatever it was. 'Of Virtuous sire egregious offspring great!'

At any rate Dante has cured him. If ever demonstration be needed of the virtues of having a good model instead of a rhetorical bustuous rumpus, the life in Binyon's translation can prove it to next century's schoolboys.

Mr. B. says in preface that he wanted to produce a poem that cd. be read with pleasure in English. He has carefully preserved all the faults of his original.

This in the circumstances is the most useful thing he cd. have done. There are already 400 translations of Dante carefully presenting the English reader with a set of faults alien to the original, and therefore of no possible use to the serious reader who wants to understand Dante.

90% of the extant versions erect (as Eliot has remarked of G. Murray) 'between the reader and the original a barrier more impassable than the Greek language'.

First: Mr. Binyon has not offered us a pre-raphaelite version of Dante.

Note that even Shadwell in his delicate renderings of cantos 26 to 33 of the Purgatorio has given us something not Dante, he has given us something that might almost have started from Aucassin and Nicolette, so far as the actual feel and texture of the work is concerned. He has taken the most fragile frosting and filagree, to begin on, he started, if my memory serves me, with that particular part of the Commedia, and gradually went on to the rest, or at least first to the Purgatorio and then to the Paradiso, with great delicacy of expression.

I propose to deal with our present translator very severely. He is himself a dour man, with all the marginalia of the Commonwealth. You cd. dress him and pass him off for one of Noll's troopers, and though he be my elder in years, I am, if his preface means what I think it does, his senior in the struggle with early italian verse.

I can not imagine any serious writer being satisfied with his own work in this field, or indeed any serious writer being satisfied with his own product in this field or in any other.

If Binyon has been on this job for 12 years, I have been on it or in its environs for three and twenty or longer. 28 might be more exact. However drasticly I hack at the present translation, I warn the rash novice that I can probably make a fool of any other critic who rushes in without similar preparation.

Irritated by Binyon's writing his lines hind side before, with the verbs stuck out of place on the tail syllable, and with multiple relative clauses, I (somewhere along about Canto vi) wondered if it was worth while showing up the defects in Dante especially as it seems probable that no one since Savage Landor would have been capable of weighing them. Weighing them that is, justly, and in proportion to the specific force of the WHOLE POEM.

Heaven knows critical sense has not abounded in Italy.

## *Dante's Inferno Part One* 'Culture and Refinement'

(*Kensington Cinema billboard a.d. 1915*)

The devil of translating mediaeval poetry into English is that it is very hard to decide HOW you are to render work done with one set of criteria in a language NOW subject to different criteria.

Translate the church of St. Hilaire of Poitiers into Barocco?

You can't, as anyone knows, translate it into English of the period. The Plantagenet Kings' Provençal was Langue d'Oc.

Latin word order obeyed the laws for dynamics of inflected language, but in 1190 and in 1300, the language of the highbrows was still very greatly latin. The concept of word order in uninflected or very little inflected language had not developed to anything like 20th century straightness. Binyon makes a very courageous statement, and a sound one: 'melodious smoothness is not the characteristic of Dante's verse'.

Despite Sordello's mastery and the ingenuity of Ar. Daniel, despite Dante's Provençal studies and the melody of his own lyrics, and despite the tremendous music of the Commedia, Dante, in taking up narrative, chucked out a number of MINOR criteria, as any writer of a long poem must in favour of a main virtue, and that main virtue Binyon (willing or not meaning to) has possibly exaggerated. At any rate it is now possible to READ the 34 Canti . . . *as a continuity*.

There is no danger that the reader will be intoxicated at any one point, and lulled into delight with the sound, as he may quite well be even with the original.

Binyon is in the fortunate position of not having to introduce his poet, he doesn't have to ressurrect him, or gain attention for him. Here he is with one of the three greatest reputations in all literature. Anyone who don't know the Commedia is thereby ignoramus. It is not to be expected that I can honestly care very much how it strikes the new reader.

If, after all these years, I have read straight through the Inferno, and if, after all my previous voyages over the text, and even efforts to help the less trained, I have now a clearer conception of the Inferno *as a whole* than I had the week before last, that is a debt, and not one that I mean to be tardy in paying.

*'The love of a thing consists in the understanding of its perfections.'*
*Spinoza.*

Spinoza's statement distinctly includes knowing what they (the perfections) are NOT. Mr. Binyon has not offered a lollypop, neither did Dante. *Pensi lettor!*

The habit of a degraded criticism is to criticize all, or most books, as if all books were written with the same aim. The old teachers of dialectic knew better (Ut moveat, ut doceat ut delectet).

Dante wrote his poem to MAKE PEOPLE THINK, just as definitely as Swinburne wrote a good deal of his poetry to tear the pants of the Victorian era and to replace the Albert Memorial by Lampascus.

The style for a poem written to that end, or in translation of same, differs from the style suited to a 3000 dollar magazine story in the wake of de Maupassant.

PROSODY

I have never seen but one intelligent essay on Dante's 'metre', and that was in an out of print school-book found in a Sicilian hotel, the author cited an author who had examined Dante's actual practice and found that the 'eleven syllable' line was composed of various different syllable-groups, totalling roughly eleven syllables, and not running, so far as I can remember, to more than 17. Any pedant can verify the top limit, and it doesn't greatly matter so long as the student does not confuse the so-called 'syllabic' system with 'English pentameter', meaning a swat at syllables, 2, 4, 6, 8, 10 in each line, mitigated by 'irregularities' and 'inverted feet'.

Mr. Wubb had apparently *not* heard of the difference, at the time of his objection to Binyon. There is nothing in Binyon's own preface to indicate that he himself had it clearly in mind as a 'concept'. He does not refer to the De Volgari Eloquio. It wouldn't surprise me if he had read it and forgotten it (more or less), but a man can't be immured for forty years with Koyets' and Sotatz' without developing some sort of sensibility to outline and demarcation, and without learning to distinguish muddy from clear; neither can he go on reading Dante for 12 years with the serious intention of finding an English equivalent without perceiving at least SOME of the qualities of the SOUND of the original, whether or no he invent a 'system' or theory for explaining that sound.

SHIFT:

I remember Yeats wanting me to speak some verse aloud in the old out-of-door greek theatre at Siracusa, and being annoyed when I bellowed the

ποικιλόθρον ἀθάνατ' Αφροδίτα

and refused to spout English poesy. I don't know how far I succeeded in convincing him that English verse wasn't CUT. Yeats himself in his early work produced marvellous rhythmic effects 'legato', verse, that is, very fine to murmur and that may be understood if whispered in a drawing-room, even though the better readers may gradually pull the words out of shape (by excessive lengthening of the vowel sounds).

The musical terms 'staccato' and 'legato' apply to verse. The common verse of Britain from 1890 to 1910 was a horrible agglomerate compost, not minted, most of it not even baked, all legato, a doughy mess of third-hand Keats, Wordsworth, heaven knows what, fourth-hand Elizabethan sonority blunted, half melted, lumpy. The Elizabethan 'iambic' verse was largely made to bawl in theatres, and had considerable affinity with barocco.

Working on a decent basis, Binyon has got rid of pseudo-magniloquence, of puffed words, I don't remember a single decorative or rhetorical word in his first 10 Cantos. There are vast numbers of monosyllables, little words. Here a hint from the De Eloquio may have put him on the trail.

In the matter of rhyme, nearly everyone knows that Dante's rhymes are 'feminine', i.e. accent on the penultimate, *crucciata, aguzza, volge, maligno*. There are feminine rhymes in English, there are ENOUGH, possibly, to fill the needs of an almost literal version of the Divina Commedia, but they are of the wrong quality; *bloweth, knowing, waiteth.*

Binyon has very intelligently avoided a mere pseudo or obvious similarity, in favour of a fundamental, namely the sharp clear quality of the original SOUND as a whole. His *past, admits, checked, kings*, all masculine endings, but all leaving a residue of vowel sound in state of potential, or latent, as considered by Dante himself in his remarks on troubadour verse.

I do not expect to see another version as good as Binyon's, I can to a great extent risk being unjust to forty translators whose work I haven't seen. Few men of Binyon's position and experience have tried or will try the experiment. You can not counterfeit 40 years honest work, or get the same result by being a clever young man who prefers vanilla to orange or heliotrope to lavender perfume.

*'La sculture n'est pas pour les jeunes hommes'*

Brancusi.

A younger generation, or at least a younger American generation, has been brought up on a list of acid tests, invented to get rid of the boiled oat-meal consistency of the bad verse of 1900, and there is no doubt that many young readers seeing Binyon's inversions etc. will be likely to throw down the translation under the impression that it is incompetent.

The fact that this idiom, which was never spoken on sea or land, is NOT fit for use in the new poetry of 1933–34 does not mean that it is unfit for use in a translation of a poem finished in 1321.

Before flying to the conclusion that certain things are 'against the rules' (heaven save us, procedures are already erected into RULES!) let the neophyte consider that a man can not be in New York and Pekin at the same moment. Certain qualities are in OPPOSITION to others, water can not exist as water and as ice at the same time.

It WOULD be quite possible to conserve the natural word order, without giving up the rhymes used by Binyon, IF one used run-on instead of end-stopped verses. BUT Dante's verses are mostly end-stopped. Various alternatives are offered at every juncture, but let the neophyte try half a dozen before deciding that Binyon has sacrificed the greater virtue for the less in a given case.

He has not made such sacrifice in his refusal to bother with feminine rhyme. Specific passages must be judged line by line. And this process I propose to illustrate by particular cases before falling into general statement.

In a poem 200 pages long, or more exactly in a poem the first third of which is 200 pages long, the FIRST requirement is that the reader be able to proceed. You can't do this with Chapman's Homer. You plunge into adjectival magnificence and and get stuck. You have two or more pages of admiration, and then you wait to regather your energies, or you acquire a definite impression of Chapman's language, and very little of Ilion. There are even, and this is more pertinent, a great number of persons familiar with the Paolo and Francesca incident, and very muzzy about the Commedia as a Whole.

Literature belongs to no one man, and translations of great works ought perhaps to be made by a committee. We are cut off (by idiotic econ. system) etc. from the old habit of commentary printed WITH a text. Up to canto viii or ix I was torn between wanting Binyon to spend the next ten years revising his Inferno, and the wish he shd. go on to the end of the Commedia, and then, if he had time, turn back for revision. I now think he has earned his right to the pleasures of the Purgatorio and the third section of the poem. Some, perhaps most of the strictures made on particular passages, might better be made privately to the translator were there such opportunity or any likelihood that my opinion wd. be well received. It is nearly impossible to make the RIGHT suggestion for emending another man's work. Even if you do, he never quite thinks it remains his own. This ulcerated sense of property might disappear in an ideal republic. At most, one can put one's finger on the fault and hope the man himself will receive inspiration from the depths of his own personal Helicon.

*Dante's Inferno Part Two*
Not a Dull Moment.

*Kensington Billboard.*

If any of the following citations seem trifling or carping let the reader think how few contemporary works merit *in any degree* this sort of attention.

For most translation one wd. merely say, take it away and start again. There is nothing in the following list that couldn't be dealt with in a second or third edition.

An imaginary opponent might argue that Binyon had given us 'penny plain' for 'twopence coloured'. Sargent used to do coloured impressions of Velasquez, but so far as I know he didn't try the process on Dürer. If Binyon has given us an engraving, he has put the original in its own colour on the opposite page.

If the opponent think Binyon somewhat naîf not to try to hide the defects of Dante, this also has its use and its interest, at least as preparation for understanding subsequent Italy. At last one sees what Petrarch was trying to get away from, and why the Italians have put up with Petrarch.

Minor triumph, in 1932: I drove an Italian critic, author of a seven vol. history of Italian literature, to his last ditch, whence he finally defended Petrarch on the sole ground that 'one occasionally likes a chocolate cream'. A literary decadence can proceed not only from a bad colossal author, but from a small man's trying to avoid the defects in the work of a great man.

Returning from relative to intrinsic value: We owe Binyon a great debt for having shown (let us hope once and for all) how little Dante needs NOTES. The general lay reader has been hypnotized for centuries by the critical apparatus of the Commedia. An edition like Moore's with no notes, especially if approached by a young student, is too difficult. One was thankful in 1906 to Dent for the Temple bilingual edtn., it saved one from consulting Witte,

Toynbee, god knows whom, but at any rate from painfully digging in with a dictionary, a Dante dictionary etc. . . . and one (I believe MORE—I can not believe my experience unique) never got through to the essential fact that it is really THERE ON THE PAGE.

One got interested in the wealth of heteroclite material, incident, heteroclite anecdote, museum of mediaeval history, etc. Whenever there was an immediate difficulty one looked at a note, instead of reading on for ten lines and waiting for Dante to tell one.

Binyon's canto headings average about half a page. Up to canto XIII I can think of only one item necessary, or at least that one wanted, for the understanding of the text, which he hasn't included in his summaries.

This is really an enormous benefit, a very great work of clearance and drainage. And it ought not to pass without gratitude. It is partly due to this clearance that the version leaves one so clear headed as to the general line of the Cantico.

At the start the constant syntactical inversions annoy one. Later one gets used to the idiom and forgets to notice them. In any case there is nothing worse than Dante's own:

già mai non vada,
di là più che di qua essere aspetta.

There are however during the first dozen cantos a number of alterations from singular to plural, or vice versa, which do no good whatever.

In the main Binyon's having his eye on the word and not the thing makes for the honesty of the version, or transparency in the sense that one sees through TO the original. Later the translator gets his eye on the object without losing grip on the verbal manifestation.

MINUTIAE: Canto I *freckled* not very good for *gaetta*.

III. Not having worked into the idiom one is annoyed by inversions and extra words. Shadwell, if I remember rightly, tried an eight syllable line to get a weight equal to the Italian. I don't know that anyone has thought of attempting the poem in terza rima, but with fewer english lines than the italian. It wd. breed, probably, considerable confusion, it might cause a denseness that wd. defeat the main end: penetrability.

III. 134, *crimson* for *vermiglia*, given the context this is Binyon's worst oversight, or in strict sense *lack* of sight.

Canto V *Inspects*, good. *'I mean'* for *dico*, excellent. *Scrutinize*, excellent;

*row on row*, excellent and not literal. *Desire* and *Reason*, with caps, a little out of style; *rapt in air*, excellent.

*And comest journeying through the black air*, good. *Caina* is Cain's hell, rather than *place*.

VI, line 3, *which* (printer's error?), L. 28, faint Miltonism. *Muddy* for *tinta*, good.

*For thou wast made before I was unmade*, good.

VII, *'from class to class'*, modern and not trecento. But very interesting as lyric insertion from the translator. Certain glints or side lights, have value as comment.

IX. I don't know that it is necessary to assume that Dante's Medusa is the strictly classical female. Bunting has perhaps pierced deeper with his 'Come, we'll enamel him'. Enamel is both stone and fusing heat. Frogs don't *'run'* through water. Not quite sure re *spaldi*, it is a *gallery*; I dare say it might be a closed gallery under *battlements* (as at Assisi).

X. I don't think *'slaughterous'* helps; *nato* has gender, and wd. allow *son* as equivalent.

XI. *Of all malice*, passage, rather modern in attitude, not quite the *'odio in cielo acquista'*.

XII. Excellent example Binyon's understanding of the difference between the Dantescan line and english 'pentameter':

*'Running as in the world once they were wont'*

There is an excellent slight distortion making for greater vividness and forcing the reader to think more about the exact meaning of the original in:

*Who live by violence and on other's fear*

On the next page, a very clear example of quality of motion in the original

*che mori per la bella Deianira.*

*Figliastro*, usually *step* son (printer's error?)
XIII, *fosco*, dark, and *schietto* not so much smooth as *clean* or *straightish*; *polsi*, both *wrists* and *vigour*; *'becomes the grain'*, excellent and the kind of thing Dante liked.

XIV, *tames* for *maturi*, not so felicitous.

I, 92. Dante's metaphor (*pasto*) about all the traffic will stand, but to *seek light*, as well as to have *taste vouchedsafe* is 'uno di piu'.

XV, *avventa*? sea forced in by the wind; *nervi*, a word one cd. wrangle over; *fiera*, possibly more *proud* than *fierce*. This minor contentiousness is not impertinent if it emphasize the progressive tightening of poet's attention from Homer to Ovid, to Dante. Dürer's grasshopper in the foreground will serve for visual comparison. Dürer is about the most helpful source for optical suggestion that I can think of. One might also note the almost uninterrupted decadence of writers' attention for centuries after Dante, until the gradual struggle back toward it in Crabbe, Stendhal, Browning and Flaubert.

XVIII. Coming back again to the rhyming, not only are we without strict English feminine equivalents for terminal sounds like *ferrigno, rintoppa, argento, tronca, stagna, feruto*, but any attempt at ornamental rhyme wd. be out of place, any attempt at explosive rhyme à la Hudibras, or slick epigrammatic rhyme à la Pope or trick rhyme à la Hood, or in fact any kind of rhyming excresence or ornament wd. be out of place in the Commedia, where Dante's rhyme is but a stiffer thread in the texture, to keep the whole from sprawling and pulling out of trim shape (cf. weave of any high grade trouser material).

One advantage of having the book in penetrable idiom is that we (one, I) see more clearly the grading of Dante's values, and especially how the whole hell reeks with money. The userers are there as against nature, against the natural increase of agriculture or of any productive work.

Deep hell is reached via Geryon (fraud) of the marvellous patterned hide, and for ten cantos thereafter the damned are all of them damned for money.

The filth heaped upon Thais seems excessive, and Binyon here might have given us a note indicating the gulf between Francesca, or Rahab and the female who persuaded Alexander to burn the Palace of Persepolis. The allusive bit of conversation doesn't explain this, though I suppose it occurs in whatever account Dante knew.

Dante's morals are almost sovietic in his location of the grafters who are lower down than even the simonists. The english term barrator has been, I think, reserved for translations of Dante and occurs nowhere else outside the dictionary, the present legal sense being either different or specialized. *Baro* is a cheater at cards, in italian, and *grafter* is the exact equivalent of *barattier*, and if grafter is now a neologism, there are, despite Dante's theorizing about aulic speech, several unparliamentary and uncurial terms in this section of the Inferno. Meaning betrayer of public trust, the term is more exact than one used explicitly of appropriation of vessels at sea. The word has applied to so many members of the social register, so many multi-millionaires, american presidents, french cabinet ministers, that it will probably have social if not literary status henceforward.

XX. Whether anyone has noted the spanish sound at the end of this canto, I don't know, it is possibly a parallel for Arnaut's passage in Provençal in the Purgatorio (Sobilia, ? Sibilia, nocque, introcque).

XXV. These low circles are not for simple carnality, the damned here have always a strong stain of meanness, cheating though not, I admit, brought into strong relief: *fraudulent* homicide, Cacus for 'furto *frodolente*'. It begins with the userers in Canto XI. We have lost the mediaeval discrimination between productive and destructive investment, as we have lost the idea decay of intelligence re / ben del intelletto.

Though Dante's sense of main construction is perhaps rudimentary in comparison with Flaubert's, one might note definite parallels, or stays, tending toward general shape, apart from the diagramatic or cartographic scheme, e.g., the Spanish suggestion, Ciampolo (XXII) against the honest Romeo, Agnel in the Ovidian metamorphosis (due e nessun) vs. Bertrand (ed uno in due).

The punishment of prophets and soothsayers seems overdone, but 'wax image witchcraft' is the clue, or at any rate the link between Dante's attitude and our own, a common basis for revulsion.

> 'Fecer malie con erbe e con imago' (XX, 123).

> *Nor Ovid more of Arethusa sing,*
> *To water turned, or Cadmus to a snake.* (XXV, 97)

I give this alternative to show how easy it is to get a couple of word for word lines of smooth and liquid versification that are utterly un-Dantescan and translate much less than Binyon's contortion.

After a comparatively dull stretch canto XXV imposes Dante's adjunct. The profounder metamorphosis of the nature (soul) agglutinous fluidity, and he calls specific attention to it, and to the fact that he is adding something not in Lucan and Ovid. In fact after Guido and Dante, whatever there may have been in human mind and perception, literature does not again make any very serious attempt to enter these regions of consciousness till almost our own day, in the struggles of Henry James and of Ibsen (who has passed out of fad and not yet come back into due currency). (Even Donne and co. were engaged in something rather different.)

XXVI, moment of inattention *'winging the heavenly vault'* is nonsense, not in the original, out of place.

Re punishment of Ulysses, no one seems to note the perfectly useless, trifling unprovoked sack of the Cicones in the Odyssey. Troy was one thing, they were inveigled.

Helen's father was trying to dodge destiny by a clever combination, etc., but for the sack of the Ciconian town there was no excuse handy, it is pure devilment, and Ulysses and co. deserved all they got thereafter (not that there is any certainty that Dante had this in mind).

It gives a crime and punishment motif to the Odyssey, which is frequently overlooked, and is promptly and (?) properly snowed under by the human interest in Odysseus himself, the live man among duds. Dante definitely accents the theft of the Palladium, whereon one cd. turn out a volume of comment. It binds through from Homer to Virgil to Dante.

XXVI. Supposing this is to be the first segment the translator attempted, his later work shows very considerable progress, and a much more vigorous grasp on his matter. From here on there are one or two slack passages a matter of a line or two, there are a few extra words and there are compensations as in XXVIII, *'plow still disinters'* being more specific than *accoglie, camminata* is *corridor* rather than *chamber*, and *burella* a *pit-shaft*. One ends with gratitude for demonstration that 40 years' honest work do, after all, count for something; that some qualities of writing can not be attained simply by clever faking, young muscles or a desire to get somewhere in a hurry.

The lines move to their end, that is, draw along the eye of the reader, instead of cradling him in a hammock. The main import is not sacrificed to detail. Simple as this appears in bald statement, it takes time to learn how to achieve it.

# Theodore Silverstein

## On the Genesis of *De Monarchia*, II, v

CONVIVIO, IV, V, AND *De monarchia,* II, V, possess peculiar interest for their enthusiastic expression of Dante's view of the role of Rome in the political history of the world. The *Convivio* passage, in particular, with its numerous examples of the inspired sacrifices made by ancient Roman heroes, warmly sets forth the thesis that divine providence was directly operative in the rise and progress of the imperial city and in the deeds of its citizens.

Both chapters, as the critics have remarked, are evidently indebted to St. Augustine's *De civitate Dei,* V, xviii.[1] Of its eleven heroic instances, the *De monarchia* adduces more than half, and the *Convivio* all but three.[2] The immediate purpose of St. Augustine in offering his examples does not correspond directly to the thesis of the *Convivio,*[3] but Dante could have found sufficient suggestion for his connection of ancient heroism with divine providence, from the general setting of St. Augustine's chapter in the larger discussion of providence, virtue and glory with which most of *De civitate Dei,* V, is occupied. If the *Convivio* has, to use Vossler's phrase,[4] reversed the moral of the chapter, this might seem quite simply to be explained by general reference to Dante's admiration for ancient Rome, and by the fact that his primary source is, after all, not the *De civitate Dei*, but Anchises' stirring exposition of Roman destiny in *¢neid,* VI, 756–853, an account which lies, by more than implication, behind the words of St. Augustine also.

But such an explanation, even if it were entirely satisfactory for the general character of the *Convivio* chapter, would not do for many of its details. Nor does it clarify sufficiently the genesis of *De monarchia,* II, v. For this passage, though closely related in spirit and content to that of the *Convivio*, nevertheless diverges from it sharply in the specific nature of its argument. Here, following the demonstration in Book I of the superiority of the monarchical principle, Dante is seeking to establish the rightfulness of the assumption of the monarchy by the Romans. In Chapter v he justifies their dominion in terms of its concern for civil right (*ius*), with which he identifies the good of the republic (*bonum rei publice*). Since this good was the motivating force behind the inspired acts of the ancient Roman heroes, St. Augustine's illustrations are now, in effect, adduced as instances of a zeal for the 'goal of right' (*finis iuris*).

This represents no simple reversal of St. Augustine's 'moral.' Whatever part the *De civitate Dei* plays among its sources, Chapter v can only be fully comprehended in the light of those works intermediary between it and St. Augustine and Vergil which contributed both to the minutiae of its content and to the final form of its reasoning. What these sources are constitutes a problem of some complexity. It involves, among other things, Dante's account of the Roman heroes Brutus and Fabricius, who appear also in St. Augustine, and of Curius and Cato, who do not; Boethius, *De consolatione philosophiae* on fame and glory, together with something of the Boethian tradition; and a tractate concerning the nature of the imperial power, written by Tolomeo of Lucca.

The isolation of a chapter from its general context brings with it several dangers, which must be guarded against. It tends both to exaggerate the importance of the chapter as a separate entity and, correspondingly, to minimize dependence, in the drift of the argument, on the larger treatise of which the chapter forms but a part.[5] It may give rise, moreover, to an evaluation of the significance of particular sources in terms which, when examined against the background of the rest of the work, require considerable modification. But if these distortions be sufficiently allowed for, there is also a positive gain through isolation in the increased intensity of our view of a limited field. Only through such closely-focussed vision can we come to understand precisely the genesis of a literary work.

Let us begin with the political tractate.

At some time between 1274 and 1298, very likely in the spring or summer of 1280, Tolomeo of Lucca, a disciple of St. Thomas Aquinas, wrote a small book on the imperial power entitled *Libellus sive tractatus de iurisdictione imperii* [*Determinatio compendiosa*][6] part of which, somewhat expanded, he incorporated about the year 1300 in his continuation of Aquinas's *De regimine principum*.[7] Drawing frequently on the *Politics* and *Nicomachean Ethics* of Aristotle and St. Augustine's *De civitate Dei*, the *De regimine* maintains, among its other contentions, the superiority of monarchy as the principle of temporal rule (and this is apparently St. Thomas's own beginning[8]), shows why world dominion, which is from God, was granted to the Roman people,[9] and arranges the various grades of rule on earth according to rank, the papal power being set above all others.[10] The significance of the argument for Dante is at once plain, in both its similarity to that of the *De monarchia* and its fundamental opposition.

It is with the second point in Tolomeo's discussion, dealing with the rule of ancient Rome, that we are for the present especially concerned, for this is based on the same Chapter XVIII of *De civitate Dei,* V, which lies behind *Convivio* IV, V and *De monarchia,* II, V. It contains many of the heroic examples in St. Augustine,[11] and it also sets its argument in the thesis that Roman rule resulted from divine providence. For the rest, however, it is far closer in spirit to Dante than to St. Augustine. Its emphasis is not that of the *De civitate Dei*: that Roman sacrifice for the sake of an earthly city ought to be a source of shame to Christians, who have higher ends to serve; but the emphasis of the Second Book of the *De monarchia*: that dominion was assumed by the Romans rightfully.[12]

The Romans deserved dominion, according to Tolomeo (who is here repeating the argument from the *Determinatio compendiosa*[13]), because God inspired them to rule well. This may be proved in various ways, all of which can be included under the head of the three essential forces that moved the Roman people to power: their love of country, their zeal for justice, and their good-will towards civil society:

> Et quia inter omnes reges et principes mundi romani ad praedicta magis fuerunt solliciti, Deus illis inspiravit ad bene regendum, unde et digne meruerunt imperium, ut probat Augustinus, in libro *De Civitate Dei*, diversis causis et rationibus, quas ad praesens perstringendo, ad tres reducere possumus, aliis ut tradatur compendiosius resecatis, quarum intuitu meruerunt dominium. Una sumitur ex amore patriae, alia vero ex zelo justitiae; tertia autem ex zelo civilis benevolentiae.[14]

The book then proceeds to elaborate each of the three motivating forces separately, illustrating them with the ancient heroic examples and others.

The treatment of the first motif is particularly suggestive for *Convivio,* IV, V, especially if we look at it in the language of the *Determinatio compendiosa*. As for love of country, we read there,

> exempla veteranorum Romanorum habentur in promptu, quia tota eorum intentio erat in ipsorum regimine sive dominio ad conservan-

dam rem publicam et, ut eiusdem consuleretur profectibus. Unde Augustinus in v. de Civitate Dei c. xii. inducens verba Salustii de bello Cateline sententiam Catonis in dicto libro contentam de virtutibus veteranorum Romanorum attollit, unde et res publica divina providentia ex parva facta est magna, quia videlicet in ipsis fuit domi industria, foris iustum imperium, animus in consulendo liber neque delicto neque libidini obnoxius. Et, ut ad specialem descendamus, Augustinus in eodem libro xix. ponit exemplum de eorum zelo patriae, quia pro eius libertate quidam proprios filios occiderunt ut Brutus et Torquatus. . . .[15]

The passage continues thus, citing the sacrifices of Curtius, Regulus, Curius and Fabricius and concludes:

Propter hec igitur exempla tam digna laude Romanorum consulem concludit Augustinus in eodem libro sic dicens: *Talibus*, inquit, *dominandi potestas non datur nisi summi Dei providentia, quando res humanas iudicat talibus dominis esse dignas.*[16]

It would be difficult to avoid observing the neatness with which Tolomeo's words have in effect fashioned St. Augustine to the purpose of *Convivio*, the all but immediate suggestion in them of Dante's own treatment of the theme.

The same argument, examples, citations, appear also in the *De regimine principum* though in language perhaps less compactly suggestive for the enthusiasm of the *Convivio*. But for the *De monarchia,* II, V, on the other hand, the more diffuse treatment of the longer work is noteworthy in at least one point. This is its derivation of *amor patriae* from the first of all the virtues, *caritas,*[17] a treatment which links love of country very closely in spirit with the other two motivating forces named by Tolomeo, both of which bear a particular relationship to the *De monarchia* chapter, as we shall now see.

The zeal for justice (says the *De regimine principum*, Chapter v), which the Romans exhibited in the fairness and impartiality of their administration of the law,[18] was an important element in the rightfulness of their taking over imperial dominion. For rule is granted 'pro pace ac justitia conservanda, jurgiis ac discordiis resecandis.[19]

In quantum igitur homines virtuosi a sua probitate praepollentes pro gubernanda populi multitudine quae rege indiget et rectorem non habet, curam assumunt, et sub legibus populum dirigunt non tantum instinctu Dei moveri videntur, sed vicem Dei gerunt in terris, quia conser-

> vant hominum multitudines in civili societate, qua necessario homo indiget, cum sit animal naturaliter sociale, ut Philosophus dicit in I *Polit.* unde et in isto casu dominium videtur esse legitimum.[20]

From this statement of the social responsibility of imperial power, which lies at the heart of his consideration of justice, Tolomeo advances, after several further examples, to the climax of his discussion: the chapter on *civilis benevolentia* (Chapter VI):

> Tertia vero virtus, per quam subjugaverunt Romani mundum, et meruerunt dominium, fuit singularis pietas, ac civilis benevolentia, quia ut tradit Maximus Valerius libro quinto: 'Humanitatis dulcedo barbarorum ingenia penetrat'; et hoc experimentum habet. Unde et in Prov. VI 5, dicitur, quod *verbum dulce multiplicat amicos et mitigat inimicos*. . . . Quantum autem antiqui Romani in hac excelluerint virtute, unde exteras nationes ad suum traherent amorem, seque eisdem sponte subjicerent, exempla ipsorum deducantur in medium.[21]

We may suspend for the present the completion of this part of the discussion in order to compare with what has already been brought forward the contention of *De monarchia,* II v. Dante's entire argument for the justness of the assumption of power by the Roman people centers on their sense of civil right, of the well-being of humanity, and on their general good-will to the commonwealth:

> Quicunque preterea bonum rei publice intendit, finem iuris intendit. Quodque ita sequatur sic ostenditur: ius est realis et personalis hominis ad hominem proportio, que servata hominum servat societatem, et corrupta corrumpit. Nam illa Digestorum descriptio non dicit quod quid est iuris, sed describit illud per notitiam utendi illo. Si ergo definitio ista bene 'quid est' et 'quare' comprehendit, et cuiuslibet societatis finis est comune sociorum bonum, necesse est finem cuiusque iuris bonum comune esse; et impossibile est ius esse, bonum comune non intendens. . . . Si ergo Romani bonum rei publice intenderunt, verum erit dicere finem iuris intendisse. Quod autem Romanus populus bonum prefatum intenderit subiciendo sibi orbem terrarum, gesta sua declarant, in quibus, omni cupiditate submota que rei publice semper adversa est, et universali pace cum libertate dilecta, populus ille sanctus, pius et gloriosa propria commoda neglexisse videtur, ut publica pro salute humani generis procuraret.[22]

Stripped of its special social-legal phraseology, Dante's argument is no different from Tolomeo's. The *bonum rei publice*, the *finis iuris*, the *commune sociorum bonum*, the *salus humani generis*, are but other terms for what Tolomeo includes under the head of his three motivations, and especially under *civilis benevolentia*. Now this raises a further point of very great interest. Dante sums up his exposition of the considerate public spirit of the Romans with the striking words, 'Romanum imperium de fonte nascitur pietatis,' a phrase similar to that which he uses of Henry VII in *Epistles,* V, 3. The saying occurs, perhaps already as early as the fourth or fifth century, in the widely-known legend of St. Silvester and Constantine,[23] from some form of which Dante, who was acquainted with the legend,[24] no doubt derived it. There the story is told of the Emperor Constantine's leprosy, which can be cured only by a bath in the blood of children. Constantine has ordered the slaughter of three thousand children for the purpose but, moved by the entreaties of the mothers, he relents and cries:

> Audite me. . . , *Romani imperii dignitas de fonte nascitur pietatis*. . . . Melius est enim pro salute innocentium mori quam per interitum eorum vitam recuperare crudelem. . . . Vincat nos pietas in isto congressu. Vere enim omnium adversantium poterimus esse victores si a sola pietate vincamur; omnium enim rerum se esse dominum comprobat qui verum se servum ostenderit esse pietatis . . . dixit: Iussit pietas Romani filios suis matribus reddi. . . .[25]

In an important note on the subject, Balogh[26] has recently pointed out a similar story using the phrase in the Life of Louis VII by Suger (b. 1081), and has indicated correctly its meaning in ancient Roman political practice:

> Die Praxis römischer Realpolitik . . . hat diese *pietas* zu Staatsräson erhoben:
>
> tu regere imperio populos Romane memento—
> haec tibi erunt artes—pacique imponere morem,
> *parcere subiectis* et debellare superbos.
>
> Verg. Aen. VI, 855
>
> In jenem geheimnisvollen und nicht selten misverstandenen Satze der Monarchie hat sich vermutlich ein Stück Sentenzweisheit antiker politischer Theorie in ihrer ursprünglichen

> Formulierung erhalten. In der antiken Sentenz lebt die *antike* Idee der humanitas: die allmächtige Staatsgewalt wurzelt in der zartesten aller menschlichen Gefühle: in der 'milden, liebevollen Nachsicht des Stärkeren, der sich bezähmt.' Das ist die *pietas Romani imperii.*[27]

The later Middle Ages, which still remembered much of the original meaning of the word, knew it also in its somewhat extended sense. When, for example, in the year 1266 the English barons petitioned Henry III in the *Dictum de Kenilworth*, they appealed respectfully to his *pietas* ('ipsius pietati cum reverentia suademus').[28] It is not merely that the Roman imperial power was based on *pietas*, but that *pietas* is a characteristic princely virtue in general.[29]

All this has the closest bearing on Tolomeo's treatment of the third motivating force, which, we must not fail to recall, he names PIETAS AC *civilis benevolentia* and at once associates, by a quotation from Valerius Maximus, with the ancient Roman idea of *humanitas.*[30] He even repeats the famous lines of *Aeneid,* VI, 855–857 ("tu regere imperio populos . . .'), by way of St. Augustine,[31] and borrows from Valerius an incident in the career of Scipio as an illustration:

> Primo quidem de Scipione qui, ut refert Maximus Valerius lib. IV, cum esset in Hispania dux romani exercitus contra gentem Annibalis, ac vigesimum quartum agens annum, Carthaginem ibidem a Poenis conditam in suam redegisset potestatem, in ipsa virginem cepit eximiae venustatis, quam ut desponsatam agnovit et nobilem, ipsam inviolatam parentibus reddidit, et aurum quod in redemptionem ejus traditum fuerat, doti ejus adjecit.[32]

Valerius offers the story merely in exemplification of the virtues *continentia* and *moderatio*. At Tolomeo's hands it has become an example, suitable to be placed beside those of Louis VII and Constantine, of the imperial virtue *pietas*.

But more than this. If we turn, for a moment, to the later parts of the third book of the *De regimine*, we discover, in Chapter XVI, St. Augustine's list of ancient heroes once again. But with it now is associated a significant reference to the story of Constantine and St. Silvester:

> Si enim Regulus qui et Marcus appellatur, pro zelo suae patriae a Carthaginensibus est occisus; si Marcus Curtius in abruptum terrae hiatum se projecit ad liberationem patriae; si Brutus et Torquatus filios occiderunt

> pro justitia et disciplina militari conservandis, ut historiae tradunt, quorum zelo respublica ex parva facta est magna; . . . quare non magis Christiani reddi debent laudabiles, si se exponunt passionibus et tormentis pro zelo fidei et amore Dei, ac virtutibus variis conantur florere, ut regnum consequantur aeternum, ac Christi principatus accreseat in eorum meritis? Haec autem Augustinus *De Civ. Dei*, quasi per totum subtiliter valde ac diffuse pertractat. Propter quod et dictum librum fecit, quod et factum fuit intermedio tempore a passione Domini, usque ad tempora beati Sylvestri et Constantini, quo quidem saeculi spatio infinita populi multitudo per mortem Christo Domino suo dedicata est et conjuncta, ac suum ducem et principem est secuta. . . . Et eodem anno quo Constantinus curatus est a lepra et conversus est ad fidem, baptizati sunt circa partes romanas plusquam centum millia hominum. . . .[33]

It seems not unlikely that from the interweaving of these two chapters of Tolomeo dealing with the noble history of ancient Rome—the one extolling *pietas* in the story of Scipio, the other linked to the legend of Constantine and St. Silvester—came the hint for Dante's own summary of the justifiable motivation of Roman heroism in terms of the Emperor Constantine's striking dictum on *pietas*.

But the significance of Chapter VI of the *De regimine principum* for Dante is not yet exhausted. It completes the discussion of the rightfulness of Roman dominion with a quotation from the Fifth Book of Aristotle's *Ethics*:

> Patet igitur ex jam dicitis, quod meritum virtutis in Romanis antiquis meretur dominium . . . ex dilectione patriae, . . . ex vigore justitiae, . . . ex civili ipsorum benevolentia. . . . Pro quibus omnibus ex merito virtutum in ipsis divina bonitas consensisse videtur ad ipsorum principatum ex causis et rationibus assignatis. Sic enim quis meretur dominium, ut Philosophus in V *Ethic*. tradit, ubi dicit quod non sinimus principari hominem in quo est natura humana tantum, sed illum qui est perfectus secundum rationem. . . .[34]

Aristotle's words are διὸ οὐκ ἐῶμεν ἄρχειν ἄνθρωπον, ἀλλὰ τὸν λόγον. Since the phrase occurs in the heart of the treatment of justice by the *Ethics*, it is plain that the word λόγος, *ratio*, 'rational principle,' must here be understood in terms of this context, and that its full meaning is to be rendered, perhaps, by some such phrase as 'rational principle of civil society.' Hence Tolomeo's closing statement for the rightfulness of Roman imperial dominion, epitomizing the significance of its three-fold motivation, is essentially that it rested, not on persons, but on a regard for social principle, that is, in Dante's language, *ius*.

This has a double relationship to the *De monarchia*. Not only is it associated, as we have just suggested, with Dante's championing of the Roman cause by an insistence on the interconnection of *bonum rei publice* and *finis iuris*, but also it links the Augustinian material with that part of Aristotle from which Dante drew the definition of *ius* with which his chapter begins; 'ius est realis et personalis hominis ad hominem proportio . . .' The source of this definition has caused the critics much trouble. Whether it is Dante's own (as seems likely) or not, there can no longer be any doubt that it is primarily a formulation of Aristotle, *Ethics*, v, 3 ff., with the amplification of Aquinas and perhaps also of Albertus Magnus.[35]

We must not, however, seem to exaggerate the importance of this single point, which derives its present interest chiefly from its context. Dante had no need of special instruction by Tolomeo in the association of *imperium* and *ius*. He did not require Tolomeo's quotation to send him to the discussion of justice in Aristotle: the *De monarchia* shows other signs of having been written with an eye, as it were, on the *Ethics*. Nor, for that matter, are the separate arguments in favor of Roman rule as advanced by the *De regimine principum* exclusive with Tolomeo. They might to a degree be inferred (as they have been by Tolomeo) from the *De civitate Dei* itself. They are implicit, to some extent, in the entire 'idea of Rome' with which the Middle Ages colored Dante's thinking. And they are to be found in one form or another in the tracts on the subject which flourished in the twelfth and early thirteenth century, and which contain other elements of interest for the *De monarchia*. Lanulf (or Radulf) of Colonna, for example, in his treatise *De translatione imperii* summarizes the story of the rise of the Romans to power in these words:

> Romani enim, qui ab Aenea descenderunt, armorum exercitio, disciplina castrorum, vsu militiae, quiete libertatis, iustitiae cultu, reuerentia legum, finitimarum gentium amicitia, maturitate consiliorum, grauitate verborum & operum obtinuerunt, vt vniuersum orbem suae subiicerent ditioni. Romanus enim populus a rege Romulo in Cesarem Augustum per septingentos annos ita per vniuersum orbem virtuose & potenter arma circuntulit, ita omnia regna mundi propria virtute contriuit, vt qui eius magnifica gesta legunt, non vnius populi, sed totius humani generis facta intelligere arbitrentur. Totque laboribus, tot periculis, for-

> tunaque varia iactatus est, vt constituendo eius Imperium, contendisse simul Romana virtus & fortuna videantur.[36]

Comparable words appear in Engelbert of Admont,[37] and, some time later, in the *Tractatus de translatione imperii* of Marsilius of Padua,[38] who borrowed them, as he tells us, from Lanulf directly.[39] But one of these works brings together all the arguments in conjunction with the body of heroic instances of St. Augustine's Chapter XVIII. The union of these elements, which is the mark of Dante's and Tolomeo's peculiarity, is also the unmistakable sign of their close relationship.

That Dante could have known Tolomeo's work, there seems to be no reason to doubt. The introductory chapter of the *De monarchia*, it is true, has been held to suggest that Dante was acquainted with few, if any, contemporary treatises on the subject. But this must not be read too literally. In *Paradiso*, II, 7, he speaks of 'L'acqua ch' io prendo già mai non si corse,' in the face of the vast literature dealing with the glories of Paradise of which he was the heir.[40] Certainly the question of the temporal monarchy still awaited its Euclid, Aristotle, Cicero; and perhaps the statement that it was 'ab omnibus intemptata' is simply Dante's way of indicating the danger of pitfalls in the path of any objective treatment of so controversial a subject.

However this may be, the critics have not failed to notice the relationship between Dante and various other writers on the problem in his time. Grauert, indeed, who sought to prove that the *De monarchia* had originally been written in 1300–1301, seems to imply that it was perhaps intended as an answer to the *Determinatio compendiosa*.[41] Recently this theory of an early date has been revived with exhaustive arguments by the Dutch scholar Kocken,[42] who finds the *De monarchia* to be in part a reply to the *De regimine principum* itself, the composition of which he fixes at 1300. The date of the *De monarchia* is a vexed problem, which it is not the business of this essay to wrestle with. Whether we accept the views of Grauert and Kocken, or, following the more widely held opinion, place the book in the year 1309 or afterwards, can make but little difference. For we are interested, not primarily to establish the fact of Tolomeo's influence, which seems on other grounds virtually beyond question, but, more significantly, to determine its nature and extent within the limits of a single passage. If the result be taken to furnish, from its evidence of the closeness with which Dante parallels Tolomeo, additional support of a kind to Kocken's theory of purpose and date, this is entirely secondary to the light which it throws on the literary genesis of *De monarchia,* II, V.

But we must now turn from Dante's general argument to the smaller details of the chapter. In them traces of the *Determinatio* and the *De regimine* are still discoverable, though of quite limited importance beside the fuller influence of other books.

Dante did not draw his list of ancient heroes unchanged from Vergil and St. Augustine. In the *Convivio* he omits Cossus, Fabius, Curtius, Marcus Pulvillus, and Lucius Valerius, who appear in the two older writers, and adds Curius, who appears in neither. As to the *De monarchia*, though no persons are introduced who are missing from either *Aeneid,* VI, 817 ff., or *De civitate Dei* V, xviii, the accounts of them are amplified from various sources. For Cincinnatus, the Decii, Camillus, Brutus and Mucius, Dante refers to Livy;[43] and, in addition, for the Decii and Cincinnatus to Cicero, *De fine bonorum*, and for Cato to the *De officiis*.

Something further must be said about Cato, but it can for the moment be postponed, while we look at the passages on Brutus and Fabricius. These are of particular interest, since in them Moore[44] has seen indications of St. Augustine's special influence on the chapter. The variety of suggestions as to source made by the editors betrays the uncertainty of their conclusions.

The point of contact between St. Augustine and Dante in their accounts of Brutus, Moore observed,[45] is that both the *De civitate Dei* and the *De monarchia* quote *Aeneid,* VI, 820 ff. However, John of Salisbury (drawing on St. Augustine, it is true) makes similar use of these verses.[46] So also does Nicholas Trivet, writing in Dante's own time; and, as this occurs in a section of his Commentary on Boethius[47] which, to anticipate, bears closely in other respects on the chapters of the *De monarchia* and *Convivio,*[48] the attribution of influence to Augustine alone evidently may require qualification. Nor should the fact be neglected that Tolomeo of Lucca likewise quotes the Vergilian lines to the same effect.[49] This is, no doubt, a tenuous piece of evidence, inconclusive in itself, yet it becomes important as a possible link in a cumulative chain.

The treatment of Fabricius has more consequence. For the body of stuff which apparently went into its making, whether directly used or of value for its assimilative action only, is sufficiently rich in possibilities to enable us to learn, by close observation of its various elements, something of how complex the genesis of even a small detail may be.

Moore has alleged that there are two elements of similarity between Dante and St. Augustine: they both stress Fabricius's faithfulness to country,[50] and they associate the incident referred to 'with Pyrrhus, not with the Samnites, as in the notes of Servius on *Aen., vi*, 845, and also in Val. Max., IV. iii. §§ 5, 6.'[51] But neither of these points has any special validity as proof. Fidelity to country is a trait expressly ascribed to Fabricius in several of the ancient descriptions of his career.[52] Moreovever, Dante, nowhere definitely associates the incident with either Pyrrhus or the Samnites, but remains entirely noncommittal on the subject. The fact is that St. Augustine, when set beside other possible sources, shows little that is especially characteristic of the words of the *De monarchia*.

What Dante may have had in mind can perhaps be best observed by a direct comparison with the chief authorities, ancient and mediaeval, the passages being arranged and numbered to indicate clearly their essential traits:

*De mon.,* II, v, § 11:

Nonne Fabricius nobis dedit exemplum avaritie resistendi cum,
1) pauper existens,
2) pro fide qua rei publice tenebatur
3) auri grande pondus oblatum
4) derisit, ac derisum,
5) verbi sibi convenientia fundens
4) despexit et refutavit?

Huius autem memoriam confirmavit Poeta noster in sexto cum caneret:
1) parvoque potentem
Fabricium.

*Conv.*, IV, v, § 13:

E chi dirà che fosse sanza divina inspirazione,
3) Fabrizio infinita quasi moltitudine d'oro rifiutare,
2) per non volere abbandonare sua patria?

Aug., *De civ. Dei,* V, xviii:

3) . . . cum Fabricium didicerit tantis muneribus Pyrrhi, regis Epirotarum,
3) promissa etiam quarta parte regni
2) a Romana civitate non potuisse develli
1) ibique in sua paupertate privatum manere maluisse.

Eutropius, *Breviarium,* II, xii:

Unum ex legatis Romanorum, Fabricium, sic admiratus,
1) cum eum pauperem esse cognovisset,
3) ut quarta parte regni promissa
2) sollicitare voluerit, ut ad se [i.e. Pyrrhum] transiret,
4) contemptusque est a Fabricio.[53]

Julius Frontinus, *Strategemata,* IV, iii, § 2:

Fabricius, cum Cineas . . .

3) grande pondus auri dono ei daret,
5) non accepto eo dixit malle se habentibus id imperare, quam habere.

Aulus Gellius, *Noctes atticae,* I, xiv:

. . . legatos dicit a Samnitibus ad C. Fabricium . . . venisse et
3) obtulisse dono grandem pecuniam . . .
1) quod viderent multa ad splendorem domus atque victus defieri neque pro amplitudine dignitateque lautam paratum esse.

Tum Fabricium . . . ita respondisse:
5) dum illis omnibus membris quae attigisset obsistere atque imperare posset, numquam quicquam defuturum; propterea se pecuniam qua nihil sibi esset usus ab his quibus eam sciret usui esse non accipere.

John of Salisbury, *Prolicraticus,* v, vii:

Venerunt . . . legati Samnitum ad Gaium Fabricium, . . .
3) offerentes dono grandem pecuniam . . .
1) eo quod multa ad necessitatem uictus et splendorem domus tanto uiro deesse constaret. . . .
5) Fabricius . . . respondit: Dum omnibus his membris, quae attigi, resistere atque imperare potero, michi nichil omnino deerit, . . . Romani siquidem non curant habere aurum, sed imperare uolunt habentibus aurum . . .
3) Quid referam quod, cum ei regni medietatem Pirrus obtulisset, . . .
4) contemptus est?

Servius, *in Aen.* VI, 844:

1) FABRICIUM paupertate gloriosum.
hic est qui respondit legatis Samnitum
3) aurum sibi offerentibus,
5) Romanos non aurum habere velle, sed aurum habentibus imperare.

Valerius Maximus, *Memorabilia,* IV, iii, 3/8 6:

Idem sensit Fabricius. . . , honoribus . . . maior,
1) censu par unicuique pauperrimo.
3) Qui a Samnitibus . . . decem aeris et quinque pondo argenti et totidem seruos . . . remisit. . . .
5) quia locupletem illum faciebat non multa possidere, sed modica desiderare.

Of the passages other than Dante's here cited,[54] St. Augustine and Eutropius contain the two basic elements of the *Convivio*; no one alone could have given rise to the *De monarchia's* five, though John of Salisbury's composite account (based largely on Gellius, Frontinus, Florus, Eutropius, and Servius,[55] comes quite close. There is a partial coincidence of language in item 4 between the *De monarchia* and Aulus Gellius and John of Salisbury (*auri grande pondus—grandem pecuniam*). Between Dante and Julius Frontinus the likeness in this respect is virtually complete (*auri grande pondus—grande pondus auri*), but it is counter-balanced by the small significance of the *Strategemata* otherwise for the lines in question. As for St. Augustine, we observe that he exhibits no special similarity to Dante in language and lacks two of the chief descriptive details as well.

Tolomeo of Lucca once again comes to our aid. Though his chapters are grounded in the *De civitate Dei*, he draws on Valerius Maximus for his account of Fabricius. But it is Valerius with a difference. For it adds to the three Dantean details already found in the *Memorabilia* (i.e. 1, 3, 5) both of the other elements which Valerius himself lacks:

*De reg. princ.*, III, iv, p. 328 (cf. *Deter. comp.*, cap. XXI, p. 43):

Quam mundas etiam habuerunt manus a muneribus principes eorum,
2) pro conservanda republica. . . .
4) pecuniam . . . contempsit, ac frustratos remisit . . .
2) Continentiae suae, et zelo patriae. . . .[56]

But there is yet another approach to Fabricius. This is provided by Boethius, *De consolatione philosophiae,* II, pr. vii and m. vii, the famous lines on the evanescence of temporal fame and glory. Dante's knowledge of Boethius was intimate, and nowhere does it show itself more clearly than in precisely the two prose works with which we are dealing. Of some fifteen instances in the *Convivio* of dependence on the *De consolatione*, more than half are based on the Second Book, and five of these are from the narrow area contained between pr. v and pr. vi.[57] The *De monarchia* has fewer references, but it draws especially on m. vi and m. viii.[58] To such evidence of Dante's fondness for this part of the *Consolatio* may be added what is evidently a reminiscence of pr. vii itself in the words of *Purgatorio,* XI, 103–108, concerning the vanity of fame.[59] *Paradiso,* XXII, 151, 'L'aiuola che ci fa tanto feroci,' may owe something to m. vii.[60]

Now there is a special reason why Dante should have remembered the *De consolatione* in writing *Convivio,* IV, v, and *De monarchia,* II, v. This is that Book II, pr. vii and m. vii, represents, in effect, Boethius's treatment of the theme of *Aeneid,* VI, 817 ff., and *De civitate Dei,* V, xviii.[61] Though it is evident that to Dante, in the imperial fervor of the *De monarchia* and the Roman enthusiasm of the *Convivio*, the trend of Boethius's argument was no more immediately useful, as it stood, than St. Augustine's, nevertheless the association of passages in his mind was inescapable.

Like both Vergil and Augustine, Boethius lists a group of ancient heroes in support of his conclusions. Only three are named,[62] but they are the three with which our present interest is most engaged: Brutus, Fabricius, and Cato. The treatment of each is brief in the extreme, Brutus being merely named and the quality of the others called to mind by a single characteristic adjective: *fidelis Fabricius, rigidus Cato*. But the Middle Ages found the antidote for this brevity. From the ninth-century exposition that may be John the Scot's[63] to the Commentary of Nicholas Trivet, Dante's contemporary, it assisted the poetic economy of Boethius with ample explanation.[64]

For Fabricius the commentaries of John the Scot [?] and Remy of Auxerre,[65] and Notker's paraphrase of Boethius based on part on Remy,[66] all are apparently in debt to Servius on *Aeneid,* VI, 844, having borrowed its brief account virtually without modification. Guillaume de Conches, Nicholas Trivet, and the work ascribed to Thomas Aquinas, on the contrary, have other sources and add much that it is significant:

Conches, Paris, Bibl. nat. *MS. lat. 14380*, fol. 77, col. 2:

Iste consul Romanorum missus fuit contra Pirrum regem Epirotarum, qui,

3) oblata [*MS.* oblitta] infinita peccunia,

2) quesiuit quod proderet sibi Romanum imperium.

5) Cui ait Fabricius, 'Roma non uult aurum, sed uult imperare habentibus aurum.'

2) Et inde fidelis uocatus est.

Pseudo-Aquinas, *Comm.* (ed. Parma, 1869, XXIV, 58):

Fabritius fuit consul romanus qui cum mitteretur pugnare contra Pyrrhum regem Epirotarum,

3) rex promisit sibi partem regni sui

2) ut transiret ad ipsum:

4) quod Fabritius contempsit.

Sequenti anno Pyrrhus

3) obtulit sibi magnam pecuniam auri,

2) ut traderet sibi romanum imperium:

5) cui ait Fabritius. Roma non vult aurum, sed vult imperare habentibus aurum.

2) Propter hoc ipse dictus fuit fidelis Fabritius.

Trivet, Paris, Bibl. nat., *MS. lat. 18424*, fol. 55:

De isto Fabricio narratur in Ystoria Romanorum que dicitur Eutropii, libro secundo, quod, cum Pirrus [*MS.* emapurus] rex Epyrotarum Tarentinis uenisset[?] in subsidium contra Romanos,
1) comperto quod Fabricius pauper erat,
qui erat unus de legatis Romanorum missis ad eum,
3) optulit ei quartum partem regni,
2) ut ad se transiret.
4) Sed Fabricius eum contempsit . . .
Narratur alibi quod, cum Pirrus Fabricie
3) obtulisset aurum
2) pro prodenda ciuitate Romana,
5) respondit Fabricius, 'Roma non uult aurum, sed imperare possidentibus aurum.'
2) Propter ista fidelis appellatus est.
De cuius laude eximia loquens, Seneca ad Lucillium [*MS.* Lucillum] epistola . . .[67] 'Fabricius Pirri regis
3) aurum reppulit [*MS.* repulit],
maiusque regno iudicauit regias opes posse
4) contempnere. . . .'

It will be seen at once that only the well-documented account of Nicholas Trivet, among these commentators, parallels completely the subject-matter of the *De monarchia* passage.[68] Its inclusion of all the Dantean elements places it in character beside Tolomeo's adaptation of Valerius Maximus. A special bond exists also between Guillaume de Conches and the shorter treatment of the *Convivio.*[69] This is evident not only from the omission by both accounts of reference to Fabricius's poverty (1) and his contempt (4), but also from their remarkable similarity of language in the description of the bribe (3). If Dante's word *oro* reflects all the previous appearances of *aurum* in the Fabricius tradition, the complete term *infinita quasi moltitudine d'oro* seems to echo Guillaume's *infinita peccunia*, a phrase which I have found in no other narrative of the episode.

Just how much of the commentary tradition on Boethius was accessible to Dante is a question the solution of which awaits, among other matters, the fuller publication of that multitudinous tradition itself. The date of Trivet's work is of course a factor to be considered. But Guillaume's commentary, at least, is early enough, and its influence was probably sufficiently established in the schools of the time to have made it available to the Italian writer.[70]

But however accessible a text may be, we must not assume, without any other indication, that a small coincidence in language or a larger correspondence in content is proof positive of Dante's primary use of it. The one sure conclusion which emerges from all this laborious preoccupation with Dante's heroes is that they are based on a very broad reading in Roman history. The fullness of John of Salisbury's narrative of Fabricius and the completeness of Tolomeo's and Nicholas Trivet's are themselves the result of a composition from several sources, and this of a sort which Dante no doubt was capable of making for himself. Eutropius and Valerius Maximus, Servius and Eutropius, or, better still, Eutropius and Julius Frontinus, would easily have given the *De monarchia* account.[71] Moreover, its failure to specify Pyrrhus or the Samnites, which we have already pointed out, and the indirectness of its report of Fabricius's speech ('verbi sibi convenientia fundens') are probably to be regarded as clues to its dependence on numerous sources, the conflicting details of which it has attempted thus by vagueness to smooth over. But the very circumstance which makes both Tolomeo and Nicholas Trivet so singularly significant for the *De monarchia* is that they represent just such a composite as Dante's, set in a general context otherwise parallel with his.

One more word on Fabricius and we have done with him. His story, especially as given in Servius and its derivatives (i.e. John the Scot [?], Remy, Notker), is also told by certain other writers about his contemporary, Marcus Curius Dentatus. Cicero, *De senectute,* XVI [55], is a typical example of this treatment, which occurs likewise in *Convivio,* VI, V, 13.[72] Dante may not actually have confused the two men, though it has sometimes been suggested that he did;[73] but his recollection of them must have been difficult to keep distinct.[74] There are at least two small indications that they did in fact tend to coalesce as he recalled them, and this is a factor to be reckoned with among the multiplicity of elements which entered into the *De monarchia* passage:

(1) In Cicero's account of Curius, Curius tells the Samnite delegation that 'non enim aurum praeclarum *sibi* videri . . . sed eis qui haberent aurum imperare.' Dante's words, however, are: '*li romani cittadini* non l'oro, ma li possessori de l'oro possedere volcano.' Now in the comment on Fabricius by Guillaume de Conches, pseudo-Aquinas and Nicholas Trivet, Fabricius always begins the same statement with '*Roma* vult';[75] in Servius and the treatments based on it the phrase is, even more significantly, '*Romanos* velle.'[76] Since Servius's report of the entire speech is closer to the *Convivio*, word for word, than is Cicero, there can be no doubt about the source of the obvious influence in Dante of the Fabricius narrative on the story of Curius.[77]

(2) According to the *Convivio* the present brought to Curius is *grandissima quantità d'oro*, and this is closely matched by the *De monarchia,* II, v, 11, in the description of the bribe offered to Fabricius: *auri grande pondus*. The story of Curius, as Cicero, Valerius Maximus and Tolomeo of Lucca tell it,[78] always describes the gift as *magnum auri pondus*. Has this phrase merged in Dante's memory with the even more striking terms from the Fabricius tradition which we have already remarked,[79] the *grandem pecuniam* of Aulus Gellius and John of Salisbury, and, especially, the *grande pondus auri dono* of Julius Frontinus?

Cato of Utica was Dante's favorite hero in antiquity. Both the *Convivio* and the *De monarchia* speak of him in terms of highest praise. His appearance in the *Divina commedia* as the warder of Purgatory, whence, though both a pagan and a suicide, he is presumably to be raised to glory at the Judgment Day, has provided modern criticism with one of its most persistent problems.

The inclusion of Cato among the heroes of *Convivio,* IV, v, goes back, in the first instance, to *Aeneid,* VI, 841. Anchises' praise is brief, even ambiguous ('quis te magne Cato tacitum aut te Cosse relinquat'), and Dante accords him a hardly longer encomium, though a reference to Jerome on St. Paul is subjoined to explain the reverent intent of such silence.[80] *De monarchia,* II, v, moreover, adds to this a fuller and more significant account. Among those 'godly citizens' whose lives were shaped, in Dante as in Vergil, by Divine Providence, Cato's place is secure and high.

Now the *De civitate Dei,* V, xviii, omits all mention of Cato. For his virtue, in the Churchman's view, was irremediably tainted by the sin of suicide.[81] St. Augustine is not here damning suicide in general, however, but apparently makes a distinction between pagans and Christians in this respect. Thus he speaks of Curtius, who also killed himself:

> Si Curtius armatus equo concito in abruptum hiatum terrae se praecipitem dedit, decorum suorum oraculis serviens. . .: quid se magnum pro aeterna patria fecisse dicturus est, qui aliquem fidei suae passus inimicum non se ultro in talem mortem mittens, sed ab illo missus obierit; quando quidem a Domino suo eodemque rege patriae suae certius oraculum accepit: *Nolite timere eos, qui corpus occiderunt, animam autem non possunt occidere?*[82]

Self-destruction among the pagans is evidently sometimes to be viewed in the light of a parallel to Christian martyrdom. Cato's guilt lies, not so much in his act, as in its circumstances and motivation: his deed was performed, St. Augustine maintains, not out of greatness of spirit, but because he could not endure adversity.[83]

This judgment, as Proto has observed in what remains the most instructive treatment of the problem,[84] reflects a distinction to be found elsewhere, in both antiquity and the Latin Middle Ages. It is dealt with by Aristotle's *Nicomachean Ethics* under the heads of fortitude and justice,[85] and receives a Christian exposition in the commentary on this book by Thomas Aquinas. Of fortitude St. Thomas tells us:

> quod . . . sustinet . . . pericula, ut eveniat aliquod bonum, scilicet honestum, vel ut fugiat aliquod turpe, scilicet inhonestum. Sed quod aliquis moriatur sibi ipsi manus injiciens, vel ab alio mortem illatam libenter patiens ad fugiendum inopiam, . . . vel quicquid est aliud quod ingerit tristitiam, non pertinet ad fortem, sed magis ad timidum, duplicii ratione. Primo quidem, quia videtur esse quaedam mollities animi contraria fortitudini, quod aliquis non possit sustinere laboriosa et tristia. Secundo quia non sustinet mortem propter bonum honestum, sicut fortis, sed fugiendo malum tristabile. . . .[86]

According to Seneca, in an opinion frequently expressed in his letters to Lucillius, Cato's suicide was entirely in conformity with the dictates of this virtue:

> Vita autem honesta actionibus variis constat: in hac est . . . Catonis scissum manu sua vulnus . . .[87]
>
> Omnia ista per se non sunt honesta nec gloriosa, sed quicquid ex illis virtus adiit tractavitque, honestum et gloriosum facit . . . Mors enim illa, quae in Catone gloriosa est . . . Cato illa honestissime usus est . . .[88]
>
> Dum aliud agit, Vergilius noster descripsit virum fortem: ego certe non aliam imaginem magno viro dederim. Si mihi M. Cato exprimendus sit, inter fragores bellorum civilium impavidus . . . Cum veros vicinosque non horreat, cum contra decem legiones et Gallica auxilia et mixta barbarica arma civilibus vocem liberam mittat et rem publicam hortetur, ne pro libertate decidat sed omnia experiatur, honestius in servitutem casura quam itura. Quantum in illo vigoris ac spiritus, quantum in publica trepidatione fiducia est! Scit se unum esse, de cuius statu non agatur: non enim quaeri, an liber Cato, sed an inter liberos sit: inde periculorum gladiorumque contemptus . . . Catonis illud ultimum ac fortissimum vulnus, per quod libertas emisit animam . . .[89]

God himself, says the moral essay *De providentia*, could seek no nobler sight on earth than of this brave man, pitted against adversity, who standing amidst the ruins of the republic, found a noble alternative to submission.[90]

So stirring a picture as this of unbending though hopeless resistance must have brought Cato close home to the poet of the *Commedia*, whose own life seemed perhaps to have its bitter spiritual analogy with the ancient story.

To the extent then that the *Convivio* and *De monarchia* have the *De civitate Dei* in view, their restoration of Cato to his glory is a direct disagreement with St. Augustine, not in principle, however, but in the judgment of an individual case. Dante's defense, as the *De monarchia,* II, v, states it, is twofold: first, that the suicide was in keeping with a stern, unbending character. *De officiis,* I, xxi, §112, is quoted at length to substantiate the point, and the idea is further compactly suggested by the word *severissimi* in the phrase 'sacrificium severissimi vere libertatis auctoris Marci Catonis.' The second point is not so directly stated, but must be inferred from Dante's language. This is that Cato's deed, far from being merely a means of escape, inspired by the vice of timidity, was a supreme act of fortitude, committed in behalf of *bonum honestum*. The full quality of the argument is apprehended best in conjunction with the passage about the Decii, with which it is closely intertwined:

> Accedunt nunc ille sacratissime victime Deciorum . . .; accedit et illud inenarrabile sacrificium severissimi vere libertatis auctoris Marci Catonis: quorum alteri pro salute patrie mortis tenebras non horruerunt; alter, ut mundo libertatis amores accenderet, quanti libertas esset ostendit dum e vita liber decedere maluit quam sine libertate manere in illa.[91]

Now just before Dante's time a view of Cato similar to Seneca's had been expressed by John of Salisbury in the *Policraticus*, during an extended denunciation of divination and the false fear of death; but John's praise was vitiated in part by an echo of the traditional objection to suicide:

> Cato in Libia extremae difficultatis angustia coartatus Hamonem Iouem dedignatus est consultare, ratus sibi rationem sufficere ut persuaderet seruandam libertatem, *et non modo dominationis Cesareae iugum sed omnem notam turpitudinis fugiendam*; licet in eo errauerit quod auctoritate propria uitae munus abiecit; quod non modo fidelium institutis sed constitutionibus gentium et sapientissimorum edictis constat esse prohibitum. Veteris quidem philosophiae princeps Pitagoras et Plotinus prohibitionis huius non tam auctores sunt quam praecones, omnino illictum esse dicentes quempiam militae seruientem a praesidio et commissa sibi sta-

> tione citra ducis uel principis iussionem. Plane eleganti exemplo usi sunt, eo quod militia est uita hominis super terram.[92]

No question here, as in St. Augustine, of timidity, but rather of the desertion of duty. Yet John of Salisbury himself had elsewhere provided glowing testimony to the nobility of the motive which, in the opinion of Dante, had glorified Cato's act. It was a sacrifice, the *De monarchia* tells us, 'ut mundo libertatis amores accenderet.' Let us listen to the *Policraticus* on the subject. The eloquent significance of its words appears to have attracted the attention of few, if any, of the Dante commentators.

> Libertas ergo de singulis pro arbitrio iudicat, et quae sanis uidet moribus obuiare, reprehendere non ueretur. Nichil autem gloriosius libertate praeter uirtutem, si tamen libertas recte a uirtute seiungitur. Omnibus enim recte sapientibus liquet quia libertas uera aliunde non prouenit. Vnde, quia summum bonum in uita constat esse uirtutem et quae sola graue et odiosum seruitutis excutit iugum, pro uirtute, quae singularis uiuendi causa est, moriendum, si necessitas ingruit, philosophi censuerunt. At haec perfecte sine libertate non prouenit, libertatisque dispendium perfectam conuincit non adesse uirtutem. Ergo et pro uirtutem habitu quilibet liber est et, quatenus est liber, eatenus uirtutibus pollet; e contra uitia sola seruitutem inducunt hominemque personis et rebus indebito famulatu subiciunt; et, licet seruitus personae quandoque miserabilior pareat, uitiorum seruitus longe semper miserior est. Quid est itaque amabilius libertate? Quid fauorabilius ei qui uirtutis aliquam reuerentiam habet? Eam promouisse omnes egregios principes legimus; nec umquam calcasse libertatem nisi manifestos uirtutis hostes. Quae fauore libertatis sunt introducta nouerunt iurisperiti, et quae ob illius amorem magnifice gesta sunt historicorum testimonio percelebre est. Cato uenenum bibit, asciuit gladium, et, ne qua mora protenderet uitam ignobilem, iniecta manu dilatauit uulnus, sanguinem generosum effudit, ne regnantem uideret Cesarem.[93]

Thus conceived, Cato's deed is no desertion of duty, but a heroic and virtuous act, compatible, as Proto sees it,[94] with love of country. In this sense patriotism transcends mere military duty, whether in the Christian or in the worldly meaning of the term. In Dante's view we may even detect a reminiscence of the high Christian praise of *amor patriae* by Tolomeo of Lucca, who bases it, as we have already perceived in another connection,[95] on the first of the theological virtues, *caritas*: 'Ergo amor patriae super caeteras virtutes gradum meretur honoris.' Tolomeo, it is only fair to add, does not modify the specific judgment of the *De civitate Dei* on Cato. If he refrains from positive condemnation of the suicide, this is because, in tacit agreement with St. Augustine, he has omitted Cato entirely from the list of heroes. Dante's estimation of the suicide of Utica thus appears in oppostion to that of his Christian sources, preferring the eulogies of Cicero, Seneca and the other ancient authorities to the dispraise and silence of St. Augustine and Tolomeo and untouched by the cool scholarly reserve of John of Salisbury.

But Dante has support of a kind for his view in other Christian sources. The Boethius commentaries provided what is in many respects a similar treatment of Cato. And this is important as indicating one aspect of the history of his reputation in the Latin Middle Ages for more than five hundred years.

On the subject of Cato's virtue and stern inflexibility of character, epitomized by the *De consolatione* in the adjective *rigidus* and by the *De monarchia* with *severissimus*, the commentaries are generally no more than a minor echo of the universal chorus of praise among the ancients.[96] Unlike the others, John the Scot [?] finds in Boethius's term a reference especially to Cato's fierce appearance: 'Cato duras leges instituit et, ut seauior hostibus et cunctis appareret, capillos et barbam sibi seruauit et per hoc RIGIDVS.'[97] This is evidently a reflection of Lucan, *Pharsalia* II, 374–378:

> ut primum tolli feralia uiderat arma,
> intonsos *rigidam* in frontem descendere canos
> passus erat maestamque genis increscere barbam:
> uni quippe uacat studiis odiisque carenti
> humanum lugere genus . . .

Even if of no further present value, it suggests what the annotators of Boethius have apparently left unremarked, that the *De consolatione* may indeed originally have owed something to the passage in Lucan, and thus uncovers a possible reason why Boethius's phrase would have stirred a special response in Dante, whose portrait of Cato in *Purgatorio,* I, 34 ff., was partly drawn from the same source.

The core of the commentators' significance for the *De monarchia*, however, lies in their attitude to the suicide. 'Rigidus cato,' Notker writes,

> uuás sáment pompeio *in defensione libertatis* . uuíder iulio çesare. Únde dô iulius sígo genám . únde pompeius flíhentêr . in egypto erslágen

> uuárd . tô léita cato fóne egypto daz hére . îo cęsare nâhfárentemo . állen dén fréisigen uuég . tér dánnân gât ze utica ciuitate. Târ erslûog sih sélben cato . dáz ín cęsar negefîenge . dánnân héizet er uticensis.[98]

Both Guillaume de Conches and the pseudo-Aquinas seem to have had some scruples about what evidently gave Notker no trouble at all. For Guillaume, like St. Augustine before and Tolomeo of Lucca after him, has omitted all mention of Cato at this point;[99] and the author of the text ascribed to St. Thomas has substituted for the story of Utica an exaltation of Cato as a just man, together with a quotation of the famous words of *Pharsalia,* I, 128, anticipating in this the *De consolatione,* IV, pr. vi, 32 ff., to which he makes reference: 'et tantae justitiae fuit ut Lucanus ipsum diis compareret in judicanda causa quae fuit inter Julium Cesarem et Pompejum, dicens: Victrix causa diis placuit, sed victa Catoni. Et de hoc magis patet quarto hujus libri prosa sexta'.[100] Nicholas Trivet had no such scruples. He furnishes an account of Cato's death which, observing the distinctions made by Thomas Aquinas in his exposition of Aristotle on fortitude and suicide, and leaning heavily on Seneca, corresponds remarkably with what is evidently Dante's conception. In it the suicide is seen as an act of high virtue undertaken in behalf of *bonum honestum*, patriotic in its gesture of oppostion to the 'invader of the republic':

> Iste Cato propter zelum iustitie tante fuit auctoritatis ut in iudicanda causa que erat inter Iulium Cesarem et Pompeyum, Lucanus ipsum cum diis compararet [? ms. comprimit], id est dicens, 'Victrix causa [ms. viatrix cum] diis placuit, sid uicta Cathoni.' *Qui cum turpe iudicaret seruire inuasori rei publice*, se ipsum interfecit apud Vticam, *inhonestum* [ms. honestum] *iudicans post libertatem uero uiuere*. Vnde de eo dicit Seneca, lib. 1 ad Serenum, 'A non insipientem iniuria nec contumelia cadit [*sic!*],[101] neque enim Cato post libertatem uixit nec libertas post Catonem.'[102]

Once more we are intrigued by the question of relationship. Are *De monarchia,* II, v, 15 ff., and Trivet's account independent of one another? The commentaries of Guillaume de Conches and pseudo-Aquinas are everywhere closely connected in language and content with Nicholas Trivet, but neither contains even a hint of his peculiar treatment of Cato. Has he formed his own conception, distilling it directly from his reading in Seneca and, perhaps, the *Ethics* with its Christian expositor? Or is he merely recording from some as yet unnoticed part of the Boethius tradition a view which was abroad in his time?

Whatever the answers may be, one thing is secure. In this exposition by Nicholas Trivet of a passage from Boethius which should on every ground have affected the *De monarchia*, we have highly important contemporary corroboration of the view of Cato which modern criticism has finally come to recognize in Dante. It may lack the vivifying warmth of Dante's admiration, but it is also without John of Salisbury's qualifying doubt.

Of all the authors upon whom Dante drew in *De monarchia,* II, v, besides of course his favorite Vergil, only one is quoted directly and by name, that is, Cicero. And Cicero is used as much to indicate the special quality of the heroic acts which he describes, as merely to tell their story. One might perhaps be inclined to judge that Dante had few of his authorities immediately under his eye as he wrote. For unlike Nicholas Trivet and even John of Salisbury and Tolomeo of Lucca, he regularly gives his own brief résumé of an incident, and in one case (i.e., the account of Cincinnatus) his citation of source seems to be misleading. But some of this may be the sign of a good digestion rather than the absence of food. Throughout the chapter we detect Dante's tendency to use his reading as the basis for a fresh statement of the subject, rather than as a storehouse to be plundered. The clearest indications of this perhaps are to be found in such details as the definition of *ius* and the account of Cato, as well as in the general argument itself.

As to the reading, it was wide and many-sided indeed. Vergil, Augustine and Tolomeo of Lucca, Aristotle, Thomas Aquinas and Jacopus de Voragine, Cicero, Seneca, Livy, the numerous memorabilia and epitomes of Roman history, Boethius, perhaps, and his commentators, perhaps John of Salisbury also, and Servius on *Aeneid,* VI, 845, —all these played parts of varying importance, ranging from the well-defined and extensive to the indefinable bordering on evanescence, about which one may raise the question of source without hope of finding a certain answer.

The result is quite characteristic of Dante, rich with the fullness of its literary background, compact, and neatly shaped for contemporary effect.

# Notes

1. Moore, *Studies in Dante*, First Series (Oxford, 1896), pp. 187–189; Vossler, *Die göttliche Komödie* (2nd. ed., Heidelberg, 1925), I, 263–264; *Il convivio*, ed. G.Busnelli and G. Vandelli, II (Opere di Dante, dir. Michele Barbi, vol. V, Florence, 1937), 52, nn. 2 ff.

2. St. Augustine lists Brutus Torquatus, Camillus, Mucius, the Decii, Regulus, Cincinnatus, Fabricius, Curtius, M. Pulvillus, L. Valerius. The *Convivio* omits the last three and adds Curius, the Drusi and Cato. Besides the three missing from the *Convivio*, Torquatus and Regulus are dropped by the *De monarchia*, which replaces them only by Cato.

3. 'Proinde per illud imperium tam latum tamque diuturnum virorumque tantorum virtutibus praeclarum atque gloriosum et illorum intentioni merces quam quaerebant est reddita, et nobis proposita necessariae commotionis exempla, ut, si virtutes, quarum istae utcumque sunt similes, quas isti pro civitatis terrenae gloria tenuerunt, pro Dei gloriosissima civitate non tenuerimus, pudore pungamur; si tenuerimus, superbia non extollamur; quoniam, sicut dicit apostolus, *indignae sunt passiones huius temporis ad futuram gloriam, quae revelabitur in nobis.*' — *De civitate Dei,* V, xviii, ed. Dombart, 4th ed. rev. Kalb (Leipzig, 1928), I, 227–228.

4. *Die göttliche Komödie,* I, 264.

5. This is especially true for the *De monarchia* chapter, which is embedded in a section dealing more extensively with the sources of the Roman *imperium* and including Book II, Chapters III to VI, inclusive.

6. *Determinatio compendiosa de iurisdictione imperii auctore anonymo ut videtur Tholomeo Lucensi O. P.*, ed. M. Krammer (Hannover and Leipzig, 1909). *Determinatio compendiosa* is the abbreviation by which the work is commonly known, and I use it throughout the present article for its convenience. But M. Grabmann, 'Ein Selbstzeugnis Tolomeos von Lucca für seine Autorschaft an der Determinatio compendiosa de iurisdictione imperii,' *Neues Arhiv,* XXXVII (1911–1912), 819, calls attention to the greater correctness of the title as given above unbracketed in the text. As to date and authorship, both have been matters of question. Krammer especially (pp. vii–xxx) has given them careful consideration, and to his discussion of the Tolomean authorship Grabmann, *Neues Archiv,* XXXVII, 818–819, has added proof which seems to solve this point with finality. For date, see also H. Grauert, 'Aus der kirchenpolitischen Traktatenliteratur des 14. Jahrhunderts,' *Historisches Jahrbuch,* XXIX (1908), 498 and 536.

7. Krammer, p. xxii, sets the composition of the *De regimine* 'intra annos 1298. et 1308.,' and, p. xii, 'fortasse circa a. 1300.' Cf. Krüger, *Des Ptolomaeus Lucenis Leben und Werke* (Inaug.-Diss., Göttingen, 1874), p. 42 f. But E. J. J. Kocken, *Ter Dateering van Dante's Monarchia* (Instituut voor Middeleeuwische Geschiedenis der Keizer Karel Universiteit te Nijmegen, no. 1, 1927), pp. 93–94, offers proof that the date may be exactly fixed at 1300. For a different view, putting the work before 1282, see A. Busson, 'Die Idee des deutschen Erbreichs und die ersten Habsburger, Excurs: Die Abfassungszeit der Fortsetzung des Buches "de regimine principum" durch Ptolemäus von Lucca, *Sitzungsberichte der k. Akademie der Wissenschaften in Wien*, Phil.-Hist. Kl., LXXXVIII (1877), 723–726.

8. I, ii–vi, *Opuscula selecta* (Paris, 1881), III, 258–267. That St. Thomas was the author of even the first book and the opening chapters of Book II has, however, occasionally

been questioned; see for example, J. A. Endres, '*De regimine principum* des hl. Thomas von Aquin,' *Studien zur Geschichte der Philosophie* (Beiträge zur Gesch. d. Philos. des Mittelalters, Festgabe zum 60. Geburstag C. I. Baeumker, 1913), pp. 261–267.

9. III, i–vi especially, *Opusc. select.*, III, 321–333. Cf. *Deter. compend.*, caps. xviii–xxiii, ed. Krammer, pp. 38–46.

10. III, x ff., *Opusc. select.*, III, 341 ff. Cf. *Deter. compend.*, *passim*.

11. I.e., Curtius, Regulus, Fabricius, Brutus, Torquatus; *De reg. princ.*, III, iv–v, *Opusc. select.* III, 328, 330–331. Cf. *Deter. compend.*, cap. XXI, ed. Krammer, p. 43.

12. The significance of this transformation of St. Augustine for Dante's chapter has been briefly pointed out by Sebastiano Vento, *La filosofia politica di Dante* (Torino, 1921), p. 194–199. As for the connection between Dante's views and the work of Tolomeo and their relationship to the political theorizing of the times, see below, p. 10, nn. 41 and 42, and, especially, M. Grabmann, 'Studien über den Einfluss der aristotelischen Philosophie auf die mittelalterlichen Theorien über das Verhältnis von Kirche und Staat,' *Sitzungsberichte der bayerischen Akademie der Wissenschaften*, Phil.-Hist. Kl., 1934), pp. 91 ff. *et passim*. It should be pointed out that Tolomeo later (*De reg. princ.*, III, xvi) repeats the argument of the *De civ. Dei,* V, xviii, without modifying Augustine's emphasis. See below, p. 194–195.

13. *Deter. compend.* cap. XXI, ed. Krammer, p. 42.

14. *De reg. princ.*, III, iv, *Opusc. select.*, III, 326.

15. Cap. XXI, ed. Krammer, pp. 42–43.

16. Pp. 43–44.

17. '. . . amor patriae in radice charitatis fundatur, quae communia propriis, non propria communibus anteponit. . . . Virtus autem charitatis in merito antecedit omnem virtutem, quia meritum cujuscumque virtutis ex virtute charitatis dependet. Ergo amor patriae super caeteras virtutes gradum meretur honoris; hoc autem est dominium.'—*De reg. princ.*, III, iv, *Opusc. select.*, III, 327.

18. III, v, *Opusc. select.*, III, 329; cf. *Deter. compend.*, ed. Krammer, pp. 44–45.

19. III, v, *Opusc. select.*, III, 330.

20. *Ibid.*

21. III, vi, *Opusc. select.*, III, 331; cf. *Deter. compend.*, p. 45. That *pietas* and *civilis benevolentia* are meant to be virtually convertible terms, or at least complementary aspects of a single virtue, is clear not only from the nature of the argument which illustrates them, but also from the fact that the word *pietas* is omitted from the *Deter. compend.*, though the argument and illustrations otherwise are the same.

22. *Le opere di Dante*, Testo critico della Società dantesca italiana (1921), pp. 376–377. All references to and quotations from Dante are from this edition, unless otherwise specified.

23. See the note by F. E. Brightman in *Dantis Alagherii epistolae*, ed. Paget Toynbee (Oxford, 1920), pp. 49–51, n. 10; and (for the early date) *Deutsches Dante-Jahrbuch,* X (1928), 203. Cf. Toynbee, *Dante Studies and Researches* (London, 1902), pp. 297–298, which remarks the significance also of the Vergilian epithet 'pius Aeneas.'

24. See especially *Inferno,* XXVII, 94–95, and *De monarchia,* III, x, 1. Cf. *Inferno,* XIX, 115–117.

25. From the *Actus beati Silvestri* in the thirteenth-century Bodleian *MS. Canon. Misc. 230*, printed in Brightman's note, *Dantis Alagherii epistolae*, p. 51. Cf. Jacopus de Voragine,

*Legenda aurea*, ed. Graesse (2nd. ed., 1850), pp. 71–72.

26. Joseph Balogh, 'Romanum imperium de fonte nascitur pietatis,' *Deutsches Dante-Jahrbuch,* x (1928), 202–205. Cf. 'Rerum Dominis pietas semper amica,' *Speculum,* IV (1929), 323–324.

27. *Dante-Jahrbuch,* x, 204–205. Cf. *Digesta Justiniani,* XLVIII, ix, 5 (ed. P. Bonfante *et al.* [Milan], 1931, p. 1435): 'potestas in pietate debet, non atrocitate consistere.' In Suetonius, *Vita Domitiani*, cap. XI, the emperor appeals to the 'pietas' of the Senate. See also the phrase 'pius pauperibus' in the Merovingian epitaph of one Epaefanius, cf. E. Le Blant, *Inscriptions chrétiennes de la Gaule antérieures au* VIII$^{e}$ *siècle* (Paris, 1856–7, no. 407).

28. *Dictum de Kenilworth*, in William Stubbs, *Select Charters* (9th. ed. rev. H. W. C. Davis, Oxford, 1921), p. 408. Cf. Forcellini, *Lexicon, s.v.* Pietas, 7: 'Hinc *Pietas* est etiam titulus, quo principes atque imperatores imprimis compellantur'; and *Codex Theodosianus,* XV, i, 37 (ed. Mommsem, Berlin, 1905, I, 809), referring to the Emperors Honorius and Arcadius. Professor MacIlwain of Harvard kindly called the passage from Stubbs to my attention.

29. Balogh, in *Speculum,* IV, 323, gives another example from the *Gesta Ernesti ducis,* ed. Paul Lehmann (*Abhandlungen der bayerischen Akademie der Wissenschaften*, Phil.-Hist. Kl., XXXII, no. 5, 1927), p. 34.

30. Above, p. 191.

31. *De reg. princ.,* III, vi, *Opusc. select.,* III, 332. Cf. *Deter. compend.*, cap. XXIII, ed. Krammer, p. 45; and *De civ. Dei,* I, vi, ed. Dombart-Kalb, I, 10.

32. *De reg. princ.,* III, v, *Opusc. select.,* III, 331 *Deter. compend.,* p. 45. See Valerius Maximus, *Memorabilia,* IV, iii, 2, ed. Kempf (Leipzig, 1887), pp. 177–178.

33. *Opusc. select.,* III, 356–357. As contrasted with his earlier use of the Augustinian examples, Tolomeo has here preserved the 'moral' of the *De civ. Dei* virtually unchanged. See above, p. 189.

34. *De reg. princ.,* III, vi,*Opusc. select.,* III, 333. The quotation from Aristotle does not occur in the *Deter. compend.* See the paraphrase of Aristotle by Aquinas, *In X libros Ethicorum ad Nicomachum,*v, lect. xi, *Excerpta philosphica*, ed. P. Carbonel (Paris-Geneva, 1882), II, 841: 'non permittimus quod homines principentur, scilicet secundum voluntatem et passiones humanas, sed quod principetur homini lex quae est dictamen rationi, vel homo qui secundum rationem agat. . . .' Cf. Albertus Magnus, *Ethic.,* v, tr. iii, cap. i, 44–45, ed. Borgnet, VII, 365.

35. Thomas Aquinas, *Sum. theol.,* Secunda secundae, qu. LXI, art. 2; and *In X libros Ethicorum ad Nicomachum,* v, lect. v, *Excerpta philos.,* ed. Carbonel, II, 830 ff. Cf. Allan Gilbert, *Dante's Conception of Justice* (Durham, North Carolina, 1925), pp. 22–23. To Gilbert's remarks might be added particular reference in this connection to Aquinas, *In X lib. Eth.,* v, lect. xi, *Excerpta philos.,* II, 840–841, on political justice (Aristotle, *Eth.,* v, 6): 'Dicit ergo primo, quod justum politicum consistit in quadam communitate vitae, quae ordinatur ad hoc, quod sit per se sufficientia eorum, quae ad vitam humanam pertinent. Et talis est communitas civitatis, in qua debent omnia inveniri, quae sufficiant humanae vitae. . . . Hoc autem justum politicum, vel est secundum proportionalitatem, idest secundum aequalitatem proportionis quantum ad justitiam distributivam . . .' etc. It is directly in connection with this that the phrase quoted by Tolomeo occurs. For Albertus Magnus see *Ethic.,* v, tr. ii, especially caps. v, ix, xi, ed. Borgnet, VII, 345

ff. P. 362: 'justitia est habitus in medietate consistens quoad nos, a quo habentes hunc habitum ex electione operativi fiunt ejus quod in distributionibus et directionibus commutationum est aequale secundum proportionem: et hoc justitia reddit unicuique. Unde Plotinus, "Justitiae est servare unicuique quod suum est." Et quod in idem reddit, et Tullius in fine primae *Rethoricae*. "Justitia est habitus animi, communi utilitate servata, suam cuilibet tribuens dignitatem." Idem Tullius in libro de *Officiis*, "Justitia est virtus quae servatur in communi hominum societate, tribuendo unicuique quod suum est, aut in rerum commissarum fide".'

36. Cap. i, ed. Melchior Goldast in *Monarchia s. romani imperii* (Frankfurt, 1668), II, 89 [sig. H; pagination faulty].

37. *De ortu et fine rom. imperii* (Basel, 1553), caps. v ff., pp. 28 ff. Cf. Goldast, *Politica imperialia* (Frankfurt, 1614), pp. 756 ff.

38. Cap. i, ed. Goldast, *Monarchia,* II, 148.

39. *Ibid.*

40. The words are best understood not as denying the existence of predecessors, but as indicating how far his *Paradiso* would outstrip their work in the scope and subtlety of his intention. No doubt, this was his hope also when, somewhat earlier, he composed the *De monarchia*.

41. H. Grauert, 'Zur Dante Forschung,' *Historisches Jahrbuch,* XVI (1895), especially 542 ff.; and *Deter. compend.*, ed. Krammer, p. vi.

42. *Ter Dateering van Dante's Monarchia*. The author's views and conclusions are summed up in Chapter IV, pp. 93 ff.

43. But for Cincinnatus the History of Orosius seems in fact to have played a larger part than Livy; *Hist.,* II, 12; cf. Livy, VI, 28, 29. See *De mon.*, ed. Karl Witte (2nd ed., 1874), p. 53, n. 57.

44. *Studies in Dante*, First Series, p. 188.

45. P. 188.

46. *Policraticus*, ed. Clement C. J. Webb (Oxford, 1909), I, 273, and n. 12.

47. Paris, Bibliothèque nationale, *Cod. lat. 18424, f. 55*. See below, p. 201, n. 4.

48. Below, pp. 202–203.

49. *De reg. princ,* III, v, *Opusc. select.,* III, 330.

50. *Studies in Dante*, First Series, p. 188.

51. P. 189. Busnelli and Vandelli evidently find this view convincing, since they cite it in their edition of the *Convivio,* II, 52, nn. 2 and 3.

52. Thus Eutropius. See p. 12. Cf. Sextus Aurelius Victor, *De vir. illustr.*, cap. XXXV, 12 ff., which virtually duplicates Eutropius. In such other accounts as those by Frontinus, Aulus Gellius, John of Salisbury, Valerius Maximus, the gift offered to Fabricius is not definitely a bribe, nor expressly for the purpose of shaking his adherence to Rome. See below, pp.198–199.

53. Eutropius continues with the proposal of Pyrrhus's physician to poison his king for gold, an offer which Fabricius refuses. On hearing this, Pyrrhus cries in admiration, 'Ille est Fabricius, qui difficilius ab honestate quam sol a cursu suo averti potest.' This does not refer directly to Fabricius's faithfulness to country, but would no doubt reinforce that point in its context.

54. There are, of course, many more references in the ancient writers, but most of them (as, for example, those in Seneca, *Ep. ad Lucillium,* XX, iii, 120, ed. Hense,

pp. 582–583, and Florus, *Hist.*, I, 13 [18]), even though possibly known to Dante, have not enough detail to throw much further light on his account.

55. *Policraticus*, ed. Webb, I, 311–312 and notes, records all these sources except Servius. The influence of the Vergilian commentator appears in the phrase 'Romani siquidem non curant habere aurum, sed imperare uolunt habentibus aurum,' which Webb (p. 342, n. 18) assigns to Frontinus. But cf. the language of the quotation from Servius above, and see below, p. 203 and n. 76.

56. Valerius Maximus is also quoted in the widely known *Speculum historiale* of Vincent of Beauvais, v, ix, but without any significant modification of the original.

57. See Moore, *Studies in Dante*, First Series, pp. 376–385.

58. Moore, pp. 376–381.

59. Cf.:

> Che voce avrai tu più, se vecchia scindi
> da te la carne, che se fossi morto
> anzi che tu lasciassi il pappo e 'l dindi,
> pria che passin mill' anni? ch' è più corto
> spazio a l' etterno, ch' un muover di ciglia
> al cerchio che più tardi in cielo è torto,

and *De cons. phil.*, II, vii, 14–16 (ed. Weinberger, Corp. script. eccles. lat. [Vienna, 1934], p. 41):

Vos vero immortalitatem vobis propagare videmini cum futuri famam temporis cogitatis. Quod si ad aeternitatis infinita spatia pertractes, quid habes, quod de nominis tui diuturnitate laeteris? Unius etenim mora momenti, si decem milibus conferatur annis, quoniam utrumque spatium definitum est, minimam licet, habet tamen aliquam portionem: at hic ipse numerus annorum eiusque quamlibet multiplex ad interminabilem diuturnitatem ne comparari quidem potest.

60. I.e., to vv. 1–6:

> Quicumque solam mente praecipiti petit
> summumque credit gloriam,
> late patentes aetheris cernat plagas
> artumque terrarum situm;
> brevem replere non valentis ambitum
> pudebit aucti nominis.

This is Moore's view; *Studies in Dante*, First Series, p. 374. Others have mentioned pr. vii: 'Omnem terrae ambitum, . . . ad caeli spatium puncti constat.' See, for example, *La divina commedia*, ed. Scartazzini, 9th ed. rev. Vandelli, p. 816, n. *ad loc*. But the figure appears also in Macrobius, *In Somn. Scip.*, II, x, *init.*, and (as Toracca points out, *La divina commedia*, 6th ed., 1926, p. 846, n. *ad loc.*) a form of it was widespread in the Middle Ages through the legend of Alexander the Great. See also *Tesoro versif.*, v. 28. Among the popular Judeo-Christian visions of the otherworld, the traveller to the heavens in the fragmentary Coptic Apocalypse of Zephaniah likens the earth to a drop of water (ed. Steindorf, *Die Apokalypse des Elias* [Texte und Untersuchungen, N.F.,

II, 3a, Leipzig, 1899], p. 149, § 2; cf. M. R. James, *The Apocryphal New Testament* [Oxford, 1924], p. 530, n. 3), and the idea, though not the simile, passed thence to the Long Text of the Apocalypse of St. Paul, which was apparently known to Dante in its Latin form: 'Et respexi de celo in terra, et uidi totum mundum, et erat quasi nihil in conspectu meo. . . .' (*Visio Pauli*, ed. James, *Apocrypha anecdota,* I [Texts and Studies, II, no. 3, 1893], p. 15, § 13). See my 'Did Dante Know the Vision of St Paul?,' *Harvard Studies and Notes in Philology and Literature,* XIX (1937), 231 ff. Variations of the same theme appear elsewhere in the medieval vision-literature, for example, in the Vision of a Monk at Wenlock Abbey, reported by Boniface about the year 717 (ed. Duemmler, *Epistolae merowingici et karolini aevi,* I [*Mon. Ger. hist.*, Epistolarum tom.,III, Berlin, 1892], 252).

61. The relationship between Augustine and Boethius comes out more clearly if pr. and m. vii are considered in the light of the entire discussion of fame and glory throughout the fifth book of the *De civitate Dei*, especially Chapters XIII ff., and with a recognition of the common dependence of the two works in part on Cicero's *De republica*.

62. II, m. vii, vv. 15–16.

63. *Saeculi noni auctoris in Boetii Consolationem philosophiae commentarius*, ed. E. T. Silk (Papers and Monographs of the American Academy in Rome, vol. IX, 1935). For the authorship, see the Introduction, especially pp. xxvii–l.

64. For Brutus see above, p. 197, for Cato below, p. 204 ff. In the discussion which follows, my quotations from Guillaume de Conches and Nicholas Trivet have been from the photographic facsimiles in the Library of Congress, Washington, D. C., Modern Language Association Deposit, Nos. 99 (Guillaume) and 100 (Trivet). I wish here to thank the Association and the Library for making both of these books available to me in the Harvard University Library.

65. *Saec. non. auct. comm.*, ed. Silk, pp. 109–110; and (for Remy) H. Naumann, *Notkers Boethius* (Quellen und Forschungen, vol. CXXI, Strassburg, 1913), p. 43. Cf. *Notkers des deutschen Werke*, ed. Sehrt and Starck, Bd. I, i (Altdeutsche Textbibliothek, Halle, Saale, 1933), p. 129, n. 17. Remy varies slightly from Servius, John the Scot and Notker in referring the story, not to the Samnites, but 'Sabinorum principibus.'

66. Naumann, p. 43; Sehrt and Starck, p. 129.

67. *Ep.* XX, iii (120), *Opera*, ed. Hense (Leipzig, 1914), III, 582–583.

68. Cf. p. 198 above.

69. *Ibid.*

70. See Charles Jourdain, 'Des commentaires inédits de Guillaume de Conches et de Nicholas Triveth sur la consolation de la philosophie de Boèce,' *Excursions historiques et philosophiques à travers le moyen-âge* (Paris, 1888), p. 50 f.: 'Ainsi jusqu'au XIV$^{e}$ siècle tout au moins, Guillaume de Conches est resté, dans l'école, l'interprète en quelque sorte officiel du livre de Boèce; il a été désigné par le titre de *commentateur*, qui marquait l'estime, dont il jouissait et l'usage qu'on faisait encore de sa glosse. . . .'

71. *Il convivio*, ed. Busnelli and Vandelli, II, 52, nn. 2 and 3, mentions St. Augustine, Eutropius and Florus, but these three have no exclusive significance for the *Convivio* and, even if taken together, will not give the account in the *De monarchia*.

72. Cicero, indeed, has been named as the source of Dante's account of Curius. See, for example, Paget Toynbee, *A Dictionary of Proper Names and Notable Matters in the Works of Dante* (Oxford, 1898), art. Curio, p. 184; and Moore, *Studies in Dante*, First Series, p. 189.

73. According to Moore, p. 189.

74. Florus, as a matter of fact, has not only associated the two men as consuls against Pyrrhus, but has further linked them by dividing between them the two stories of Pyrrhus's attempted bribe and the physician's offer to kill Pyrrhus (this second, ascribed by Florus to Curius, otherwise assigned to Fabricius only): 'quid porro ipsi duces? vel in castris, cum medicum venale regis caput offerentem Curius remisit, Fabricius oblatam sibi a rege imperii partem repudiavat. . . .' (I, xiii [18], 21).

75. See above, p. 201.

76. See pp. 198–199. With this group also John of Salisbury is to be placed, whose words 'Romani siquidem . . . habentibus aurum,' are clearly influenced by the speech in Servius.

77. Julius Frontinus complicates the confusion with a procedure opposite to Dante's. Whereas the *Convivio* borrows 'li romani cittadini' from Fabricius for Curius, the *Strategemata* appropriates 'se' from Curius, as it were, and applies it to Fabricius. See above p. 12.

78. Cicero, *De senect.,* XVI, 55; Valerius, *Mem.,* IV, iii, 5; Tolomeo, *De reg. princ.,* III, iv, *Opusc. select.,* III, 328; cf. *Deter. compend.*, cap. XXI, ed. Krammer, p. 43.

79. Above, pp. 198–199.

80. Servius, *In Aen.*, n. *ad loc.*, ed. Thilo, II, i, 118, comments: 'Magne Cato Censorium dicit, qui scripsit historias, multa etiam bella confecit: nam Vticensem praesente Augusto, contra quem pater eius *Caesar* et dimicavit et Anticatones scripsit, laudare non potest.' But there is nothing in Vergil's words which need have made Dante doubt that Cato of Utica was meant.

81. *De civ. Dei.* II, xxiii.

82. *De civ. Dei,* V, xviii, ed. Dombart-Kalb, I, 225, II, 20 ff.

83. I, xxiii, ed. Dombart-Kalb, I, 38: 'De cuius facto quid potissimum dicam, nisi quod amici eius etiam docti quidam viri, qui hoc fieri prudentius dissuadebant, inbecillioris quam fortioris animi facinus esse censuerunt, quo demonstraretur non honestas turpica praecavens, sed infirmitas adversa non sustinens? Hoc et ipse Cato in suo carissimo filio iudicavit.'—Lactantius had also condemned Cato's act, but without making Augustine's distinctions. According to him Cato was the more culpable, since the real motivation for the suicide at Utica was not primarily the fear of servitude, but the desire to follow the precepts of those pagan philosophers who, in view of the immortatlity of the soul, falsely encouraged self-destruction; *Divinae institutiones,* III, xviii.

84. Enrico Proto, 'Nuove ricerche sul Catone dantesco,' *Giornale storico,* LXI (1912), 193–248.

85. Proto, p. 211.

86. *In X libros Ethicorum ad Nicomachum,* III, lect. xv, *Excerpta philosophica*, ed. Carbonel, II, 795.

87. *Ep.,* VII, v (67), ed. Hense, pp. 227–228, § 7.

88. *Ep.,* VIII–XIII, 82, ed. Hense, pp. 318–319, §§ 12–13.

89. *Ep.,* XV, iii (95), ed. Hense, pp. 457–458, §§ 69–73.

90. *Dialogi,* I, 'De providentia,' cap.II §§ 8 ff., ed. Hermes (Leipzig, 1905), I, 4 ff.

91. *De mon.,* II, v, 15, ed. Florence, 1921, pp. 378–379. Cf. *Purg.,* I, 71–75.

92. Ed. Webb, I, 159–160. Cf. I, 197 and 360. For the condemnation of suicide see *Codex Justinianus,* IX, 1, § i, 'De bonis eorum qui mortem sibi consciverunt.'

93. Ed. Webb, II, 217–218.

94. Proto, p. 213 f.

95. See above, pp. 189–190.

96. Pseudo-Aquinas, ed. Parma, XXIV, 58; and Trivet, *MS. lat. 18424*, f. 55: 'Cato autem hic rigidus dictus est propter rigorem animi qui ad nichil turpe [?] flecti potuit. De cuius rigiditate meminit Seneca in quadam epistola ad Lucillium [ms. Lucillum], que sic incipit: Aliquis uir bonus uir [*sic*], cum suasisset Lucillio [ms. Lucillo] quod aliquem uirum uirtuosum obseruaret . . . "Elige itaque Catonem. Si hic tibi nimis rigidus uidetur, elige remissioris animi uirum Lelium." ' Cf. Seneca, Ep., I, xi, ed. Hense, p. 30, 8. Cato's unbending sternness became virtually proverbial; cf. John of Salisbury on hypocrites, *Policraticus,* VII, xxi, ed. Webb, II, 191: 'Simulat et dissimulat et astutam gerit sub pectore uulpem; Stoico quouis liberior est, Catone rigidior.'

97. *Saec. non. auct. comm.*, ed. Silk, p. 110.

98. Ed. Sehrt and Starck, pp. 129–130.

99. He does, however, discuss Cato later (*MS. lat. 14380*, f. 90$^{v}$, col. 2) on Boethius, IV, pr. vi, dealing with the fallibility of human judgment.

100. Ed. Parma, XXIV, 58, col. 2. Of the way in which Lucan's line came in general to symbolize unswerving devotion to a lost cause, Otto of Freising furnishes an example which is also not without value for the history of Cato's mediaeval reputation. In the *Chronicon,* VI, xxxii, ed. A. Hofmeister (*Script. rer. germ.,* 2nd ed., Hannover and Leipzig, 1912), p. 299, Otto, recording the episode of the ousting of Gratianus (Gregory VI) from the Papacy in the year 1046, concludes: 'Hunc Gratianum Alpes transcendentem secutum fuisse tradunt Hiltibrandum, qui postmodum summus pontifex factus ob eius amorem, quia de catalogo pontificum semotus fuerat, se Gregorium VII$^{m}$ (*sic, for* VI$^{m}$) vocari voluit. Et sicut in Lucano habes: *"Victrix causa diis placuit, sed victa Catoni,"* ita et huic Hiltibrando, qui semper in ecclesiastico rigore constantissimus fuit, causa ista, in qua sententia principis et episcoporum prevaluit, semper displicuit.' For Dante's knowledge of the *Chronicon*, see Toynbee, *Dante Studies and Researches*, pp. 291 ff.

101. Seneca, *Dialogi,* II, 'De constantia sapientis,' § 2, ed. Loeb Library, p. 50: 'nullam enim sapientem nec iniuriam accipere nec contumeliam posse. . . .'

102. Trivet, Paris *MS. lat. 18424, f. 55*. Cf. Seneca, *Dialogi,* II, ed. Loeb Lib., p. 52.

# T. S. Eliot

## A Talk on Dante

May I explain first why I have chosen, not to deliver a lecture about Dante, but to talk informally about his influence upon myself?* What might appear egotism, in doing this, I present as modesty; and the modesty which it pretends to be is merely prudence. I am in no way a Dante scholar; and my general knowledge of Italian is such, that on this occasion, out of respect to the audience and to Dante himself, I shall refrain from quoting him in Italian. And I do not feel that I have anything more to contribute, on the subject of Dante's poetry, than I put, years ago, into a brief essay. As I explained in the original preface to that essay, I read Dante only with a prose translation beside the text. Forty years ago I began to puzzle out the *Divine Comedy* in this way; and when I thought I had grasped the meaning of the passage which especially delighted me, I committed it to memory; so that, for some years, I was able to recite a large part of one canto or another to myself, lying in bed or on a railway journey. Heaven knows what it would have sounded like, had I recited it aloud; but it was by this means that I steeped myself in Dante's poetry. And now it is twenty years since I set down all that my meager attainments qualified me to say about Dante. But I thought it not uninteresting to myself, and possibly to others, to try to record in what my own debt to Dante consists. I do not think I can explain everything, even to myself; but as I still, after forty years, regard his poetry as the most persistent and deepest influence upon my own verse, I should like to establish at least some of the reasons for it. Perhaps confessions by poets, of what Dante has meant to them, may even contribute something to the appreciation of Dante himself. And finally, it is the only contribution I can make.

The greatest debts are not always the most evident; at least, there are different kinds of debt. The kind of debt that I owe to Dante is the kind which goes on accumulating, the kind which is not the debt of one period or another of one's life. Of some poets I can say I learned a great deal from them at a particular stage. Of Jules Laforgue, for instance, I can say that he was the first to teach me how to speak, to teach me the poetic possibilities of my own idiom of speech. Such early influences, the influences which, so to speak, first introduce one to oneself, are, I think, due to an impression which is in one aspect, the recognition of a temperament akin to one's own, and in another aspect the discovery of a form of expression which gives a clue to the discovery of one's own form. These are not two things, but two aspects of the same thing. But the poet who can do this for a young writer, is unlikely to be one of the great masters. The latter are too exalted and too remote. They are like distant ancestors who have been almost deified; whereas the smaller poet, who has directed one's first steps, is more like an admired elder brother.

Then, among influences, there are the poets from whom one has learned some one thing, perhaps of capital importance to oneself, though not necessarily the greatest contribution these poets have made. I think that from Baudelaire I learned first, a precedent for the poetical possibilities, never developed by any poet writing in my own language, of the more sordid aspects of the modern metropolis, of the possibility of fusion between the sordidly realistic and the phantasmagoric, the possibility of the juxtaposition of the matter-of-fact and the fantastic. From him, as from Laforgue, I learned that the sort of material that I had, the sort of experience that an adolescent had had, in an industrial city in America, could be the material for poetry; and that the source of new poetry might be found in what had been regarded hitherto as the impossible, the sterile, the intractably unpoetic. That, in fact, the business of the poet was to make poetry out of the unexplored resources of the unpoetical; that the poet, in fact, was committed by his profession to turn the unpoetical into poetry. A great poet can give a younger poet everything that he has to give him, in a very few lines. It may be that I am indebted to Baudelaire chiefly for half a dozen lines out of the whole of *Fleurs du Mal*; and that his significance for me is summed up in the lines:

> Fourmillante Cité, cité pleine de rêves,
> Où le spectre en plein jour raccroche le passant.

I knew what *that* meant, because I had lived it before I knew that I wanted to turn it into verse on my own account.

I may seem to you to be very far from Dante. But I cannot give you any approximation of what Dante has done for me, without speaking of what other poets have done for me. What I have written about Baudelaire, or Dante, or any other poet who has had a capital importance in my own development, I have written *because* that poet has meant so much to me, but not about myself, but *about* that poet and his poetry. That is, the first impulse to write about a great poet is one of gratitude; but the reasons for which one is grateful may play a very small part in a critical appreciation of that poet.

One has other debts, innumerable debts, to poets, of another kind. There are poets who have been at the back of one's mind, or perhaps, consciously there, when one has had some particular problem to settle, for which something they have written suggests the method. There are those from whom one has consciously borrowed, adapting a line of verse to a different language or period or context. There are those who remain in one's mind as having set the standard for a particular poetic virtue, as Villon for honesty, and Sappho for having fixed a particular emotion in the right and the minimum number of words, once and for all. There are also the great masters, to whom one slowly grows up. When I was young I felt much more at ease with the lesser Elizabethan dramatists than with Shakespeare: the former were, so to speak, playmates nearer my own size. One test of the great masters, of whom Shakespeare is one, is that the appreciation of their poetry is a lifetime's task, because at every stage of maturing—and that should be one's whole life—you are able to understand them better. Among these are Shakespeare, Dante, Homer and Virgil.

I have ranged over some varieties of "influence" in order to approach an indication, by contrast, of what Dante has meant to me. Certainly I have borrowed lines from him, in the attempt to reproduce, or rather to arouse in the reader's mind the memory of some Dantesque scene, and thus establish a relationship between the medieval inferno and modern life. Readers of my "Waste Land" will perhaps remember that the vision of my city clerks trooping over London Bridge from the railway station to their offices evoked the reflection "I had not thought death had undone so many"; and that in another place I deliberately modified a line of Dante by altering it—"sighs, short and infrequent, were exhaled." And I gave the references in my notes, in order to make the reader who recognized the allusion, know that I meant him to recognize it, and know that he would have missed the point if he did not recognize it. Twenty years after writing "The Waste Land," I wrote, in "Little Gidding," a passage which is intended to be the nearest equivalent to a canto of the *Inferno* or the *Purgatorio*, in style as well as content, that I could achieve. The intention of course, was the same as with my allusions to Dante in "The Waste Land": to present to the mind of the reader a parallel, by means of contrast, between the *Inferno* and the *Purgatorio*, which Dante visited, and a hallucinated scene after an air-raid. But the method is different: here I was debarred from quoting or adapting at length—I borrowed and adapted freely only a few phrases—because I was *imitating*. My first problem was to find an approximation to the *terza rima* without rhyming. English is less copiously provided with rhyming words than Italian; and those rhymes we have are in a way more emphatic. The rhyming words call too much attention to themselves: Italian is the one language known to me in which exact rhyme can always achieve its effect—and what the effect of rhyme is, is for the neurologist rather than the poet to investigate—without the risk of obtruding itself. I therefore adopted, for my purpose, a simple alternation of unrhymed masculine and feminine terminations, as the nearest way of giving the light effect of the rhyme in Italian. In saying this, I am not attempting to lay down a law, but merely explaining how I was directed in a particular situation. I think that rhymed *terza rima* is probably less unsatisfactory for translations of the *Divine Comedy* than is blank verse. For, unfortunately for this purpose, a different meter is a different mode of thought; it is a different kind of *punctuation*, for the emphases and the breath pauses do not come in the same place. Dante *thought* in *terza rima*, and a poem should be translated as nearly as possible in the same thought-form as the original. So that, in a translation into blank verse, something is lost; though on the other hand, when I read a *terza rima* translation of the *Divine Comedy* and come to some passage of which I remember the original pretty closely, I am always worried in anticipation, by the inevitable shifts and twists which I know the translator will be obliged to make, in order to fit Dante's words into English rhyme. And no verse seems to demand greater literalness in translation than Dante's, because no poet convinces one more completely that the word he has used is the word he wanted, and that no other will do.

I do not know whether the substitute for rhyme that I used in the passage referred to would be tolerable for a very long original poem in English: but I do know that I myself should not find the rest of my life long enough time in which to write it. For one of the interesting things I learnt in trying to imitate Dante in English, was the extreme difficulty. This section of a poem—not the length of one canto of the *Divine Comedy*—cost me far more time and trouble and vexation than any passage of the same length that I have ever written. It was not simply that I was limited to the Dantesque type of imagery, simile and figure of speech. It was chiefly that in this very bare and austere style, in which every word has to be "functional," the slightest vagueness or imprecision is immediately noticeable. The language has to be very direct; the line, and the single word, must be completely disciplined to the purpose of the whole; and, when you are using simple words and simple phrases, any repetition of the most common idiom, or of the most frequently needed word, becomes a glaring blemish.

I am not saying that *terza rima* is to be ruled out of original English verse composition; though I believe that to the modern ear—that is, the ear trained during this century, and therefore accustomed to much greater exercise in the possibilities of unrhymed verse—a modern long poem in a set rhymed form is more likely to sound monotonous as well as artificial, than it did to the ear of a hundred years ago. But I am sure that it is only possible in a long poem, if the poet is borrowing only the form, and not attempting to remind the reader of Dante in every line and phrase. There is one poem in the 19th Century which, at moments, seems to contradict this. This is the *Triumph of Life*. I should have felt called upon today to refer to Shelley in any case, because Shelley is the English poet, more than all others, upon whom the influence of Dante was remarkable. It seems to me that Shelley confirms also my impression that the influence of Dante, where it is really powerful, is a *cumulative* influence: that is, the older you grow, the stronger the domination becomes. The *Triumph of Life*, a poem which is Shelley's greatest tribute to Dante, was the last of his great poems. I think it was also the greatest. It was left unfinished; it breaks off abruptly in the middle of a line; and one wonders whether even Shelley could have carried it to successful completion. Now the influence of Dante is observable earlier; most evident in the *Ode to the West Wind,* in which, at the very beginning, the image of the leaves whirling

Like driven ghosts from an enchanter fleeing

would have been impossible but for the *Inferno*—in which the various manifestations of *wind*, and the various sensations of *air*, are as important as are the aspects of *light* in the *Paradiso*. In *The Triumph of Life* however I do not think that Shelley was setting himself to aim at such a close approximation to the spareness of Dante as I was; he had left open for himself all of his copious resources of English poetical speech. Nevertheless, because of a natural affinity with the poetic imagination of Dante, a saturation in the poetry (and I need not remind you that Shelley knew Italian well, and had a wide and thorough knowledge of all Italian poetry up to his time) his mind is inspired to some of the greatest and most Dantesque lines in English. I must quote one passage which made an indelible impression upon me over forty-five years ago:

Struck to the heart by this sad pageantry,
Half to myself I said—"And what is this?
Whose shape is that within the car? And why—"

I would have added—"is all here amiss?"
But a voice answered—"Life!"—I turned, and knew
(O Heaven, have mercy on such wretchedness!)

That what I thought was an old root which grew
To strange distortion out of the hill side,
Was indeed one of those deluded crew,

And that the grass, which methought hung so wide
And white, was but his thin discoloured hair,
And that the holes he vainly sought to hide,

Were or had been eyes:—"If thou canst, forbear
To join the dance, which I had well forborne!"
Said the grim Feature (of my thought aware).

"I will unfold that which to this deep scorn
Led me and my companions, and relate
The progress of the pageant since the morn;

If thirst of knowledge shall not then abate,
Follow it thou even to the night, but I
Am weary."—Then like one who with the weight

Of his own words is staggered, wearily
He paused; and ere he could resume, I cried:
"First, who art thou?"—"Before thy memory,

"I feared, loved, hated, suffered, did and died,
And if the spark with which Heaven lit my spirit
Had been with purer nutriment supplied,

"Corruption would not now thus much inherit
Of what was once Rousseau,—nor this disguise
Stain that which ought to have disdained to wear it. . . ."

Well, this is better than I could do. But I quote it, as one of the supreme tributes to Dante in English, for it testifies to what Dante has done, both for the style and for the soul of a great English poet. And incidentally, a very interesting comment on Rousseau. It would be interesting, but otiose, to pursue the evidence of Shelley's debt to Dante further; it is sufficient, to those who know the source, to quote the first three of the prefatory lines to *Epipsychidion*—

My Song, I fear that thou wilt find but few
Who fitly shall conceive thy reasoning,
Of such hard matter does thou entertain.

I think I have already made clear, however, that the important debt to Dante does not lie in a poet's borrowings, or adaptations from Dante; nor is it one of those debts which are incurred only at a particular stage in another poet's development. Nor is it found in those passages in which one has taken him as a model. The important debt does not occur in relation to the number of places in one's writings to which a critic can point a finger, and say, here and there he wrote something which he could not have written unless he had Dante in mind. Nor do I wish to speak now of any debt which one may owe to the thought of Dante, to his view of life, or to the philosophy and theology which give shape and content to the *Divine Comedy*. That is another, though by no means unrelated question. Of what one learns, and goes on learning, from Dante I should like to make three points.

The first is, that of the very few poets of similar stature there is none, not even Virgil, who has been a more attentive student of the *art* of poetry, or a more scrupulous, painstaking and *conscious* practitioner of the *craft*. Certainly no English poet can be compared with him in this respect, for the more conscious craftsmen—and I am thinking primarily of Milton—have been much more limited poets, and therefore more limited in their craft also. To realize more and more what this means, through the years of one's life, is itself a moral lesson; but I draw a further lesson from it which is a moral lesson too. The whole study and practice of Dante seems to me to teach that the poet should be the servant of his language, rather than the master of it. This sense of responsibility is one of the marks of the *classical poet*, in the sense of "classical" which I have tried to define elsewhere, in speaking of Virgil. Of some great poets, and of some great English poets especially, one can say that they were privileged by their genius to *abuse* the English language, to develop an idiom so peculiar and even eccentric, that it could be of no use to later poets. Dante seems to me to have a place in Italian literature which, in this respect, only Shakespeare has in ours; that is, they give body to the soul of the language, conforming themselves, the one more and the other less consciously, to what they divined to be its possibilities. And Shakespeare himself takes liberties which only his genius justifies; liberties which Dante, with an equal genius, does not take. To pass on to posterity one's own language, more highly developed, more refined, and more precise than it was before one wrote it, that is the highest possible achievement of the poet as poet. Of course, a really supreme poet makes poetry also more difficult for his successors, by the simple fact of his supremacy, and the price a literature must pay, for having a Dante or a Shakespeare, is that it can have only *one*. Later poets must find something else to do, and be content if the things left to do are lesser things. But I am not speaking of what a supreme poet, one of those few without whom the current speech of a people with a great language would not be what it is, does for later poets, or of what he prevents them from doing, but of what he does for everybody after him who speaks that language, whose mother tongue it is, whether they are poets, philosophers, statesmen or railway porters.

That is one lesson: that the great master of a language should be the great servant of it. The second lesson of Dante—and it is one which no poet, in any language known to me, can teach—is the lesson of *width of emotional range*. Perhaps it could be best expressed under the figure of the spectrum, or of the gamut. Employing this figure, I may say that the great poet should not only perceive and distinguish more clearly than other men, the colors or sounds within the range of ordinary vision or hearing; he should perceive vibrations beyond the range of ordinary men, and be able to make men see and hear more at each end than they could ever see without his help. We have for instance in English literature great religious poets, but they are, by comparison with Dante, *specialists*. That is all they can do. And Dante, because he could do everything else, is for that reason the greatest "religious" poet, though to call him a "religious poet" would be to abate his universality. The *Divine Comedy* expresses everything in the way of emotion, between depravity's despair and the beatific vision, that man is capable of experiencing. It is therefore a constant reminder to the poet, of the obligation to explore, to find words for the inarticulate, to capture those feelings which people can hardly even feel, because they have no words for them; and at the same time, a reminder that the explorer beyond the frontiers of ordinary consciousness will only be able to return and report to his fellow-citizens, if he has all the time a firm grasp upon the realities with which they are already acquainted.

These two achievements of Dante are not to be thought of as separate or separable. The task of the poet, in making people comprehend the incomprehensible, demands immense resources of language; and in developing the language, enriching the meaning of words and showing how much words can do, he is making possible a much greater range of emotion and perception for other men, because he gives them the speech in which more can be expressed. I only suggest as an instance what Dante did for his own language—and for ours, since we have taken the word and anglicized it—by the verb *trasumanar*.

What I have been saying just now is not irrelevant to the fact—for to me it appears an incontestable fact—that Dante is, beyond all other poets of our continent, the most *European*. He is the least provincial—and yet that statement must be immediately protected by saying that he did not become the "least provincial" by ceasing to be local. No one is more local; one never forgets that there is much in Dante's poetry which escapes any reader whose native language is not Italian; but I think that the foreigner is less *aware* of any residuum that must for ever escape him, than any of us in reading any other master of a language which is not our own. The Italian of Dante is somehow *our* language from the moment we begin to try to read it; and the lessons of craft, of speech and of exploration of sensibility are lessons which any European can take to heart and try to apply in his own tongue.

* The "Talk" was delivered by Mr. Eliot at the Italian Insitute in London, and published in *Italian News*, the Journal of the Institute. It was also published in *The Adelphi*, First Quarter 1951.

# Dino Bigongiari

## The Art of the Canzone

IN THE *De Vulgari Eloquentia*, II, 9, 38[1], we read the following definition of a stanza of the *canzone*: "stantiam esse sub certo cantu et habitudine limitata carminum et sillabarum compagem." This text is given by all editors with an emendation: *limitata* is changed to *limitatam*. The emendation does not seem necessary. This definition is of considerable importance in what we might call Dante's *Ars Poetica*. For as he tells us (*ibid.*) the stanza "enfolds the entire art," "it is the structure or the enfolding of all the things that the *canzone* receives from art." We must first therefore examine the meaning which Dante gives to *art*, a term which has been variously and perhaps not accurately discussed. Reference is regularly made in this article to Marigo's work[2] not because the criticism is primarily directed against his edition of the *De Vulgari Eloquentia* but because of a certain number of interpretations below criticized which are incorporated in his text.

Dante's doctrine of art has little to do with what we might call aesthetics in the modern sense of the word. He gives us metrical schemes that are approved on the basis of the length of the lines and of their rhyming arrangements, and on their capacity to conform to a musical partition. He deals with numbers as representing sounds and with the relations existing between them, seldom if ever with significant expressions and the qualities thereof.

By "art" Dante means a set of norms and rules that tell us what to do, what not to do, and thus also indicate how much freedom is left to the poet within these prohibitions and these prescriptions. Any notion of originality or of creativeness is alien to this conception of "art." Art has to do with a routine, directed towards definite objectives; it is not genius but the proper "regulation" of genius. Something resembling our concept of inventive, creative genius Dante, in conformity with long established usage, called "ingenium," a term regularly distinguished from and contrasted with "ars." In Dante's estimate, the genuine poet is he who has a natural inventive talent ("ingenium"), which he must cultivate through long practice ("usus") in conformity with certain norms ("ars") in order that it may be able properly to express scientific thoughts laboriously acquired ("numquam sine strenuitate *ingenii* et *artis* assiduitate, *scientiarumque* habitu fieri potest," *De Vulgari Eloquentia*, II, 4, 70); of this he reminds us in *Paradiso* (10, 43): "Perch'io l'ingegno, l'arte, l'uso chiami." This distinction between *ingenium* and *ars* is frequent.[3] The combination of *ingenium, ars, usus* is ancient.[4] "Art" as a check to an otherwise uncontrolled talent is familiar.[5]

This view had been, was in Dante's time and was destined for centuries to remain a current one. In all spheres of human activity, Aristotle's definition of "ars" as "recta ratio (regula) factibilium" held. Dante tells us (*Monarchia*, I, 3, 86): "*factibilia* quae regulantur *arte*"; and again (*De Vulgari Eloquentia*, II, 4, 23): "qui magis . . . arte *regulari* poetati sunt." And Herennius had taught that "Ars est *praeceptio* quae dat certam viam *rationemque faciendi* aliquid."

In the chapter of the *De Vulgari Eloquentia* under consideration, this view of "ars" is exclusively adhered to. When Dante says (II, 9): "stantia totam artem ingremiat," he means that all the prescriptive norms governing the construction of the *canzone* as such are embodied in the structure of the stanza. And when he adds (*ibid.*): "nec licet aliquid artis sequentibus arrogare sed solam artem antecedentis induere," he informs us that no "artistic" innovation ("nec aliquid artis") is permissible in the constructing of any of the stanzas after the first one, since they must all put on ("induere") the "artistic" garment cut out for the first stanza ("artem antecedentis"). By which words surely Dante does not mean that the stanzas of a *canzone* after the first have no new poetical value. This prescriptive character of "ars" appears clearly again in *De Vulgari Eloquenita,* II, 9: "Licet enim in qualibet stantia rithimos innovare et eosdem reiterare *ad libitum*; quod, si de propria cantionis *arte* rithimus esset *minime liceret*." That is: the fact that a poet has the liberty to repeat, or not, the rhymes at pleasure, shows that the rhymes do not fall under those prescriptions which are the peculiar constituent of the "art" of the *canzone*.

If "art" then is rule, prescription or the resultant application of such norms, the next question is: what does the "art" of the *canzone* prescribe?

The stanza of the *canzone* is, like stanzas of other poems, made up of verses of different lengths (eleven, seven, five, and three syllables). Is the poet free to choose at pleasure among these different lengths? Can he place any of them at any point? Can he arrange these longer and shorter verses in any order he wants? Can any verse begin the stanza? If he breaks up his stanza into two parts and further subdivides these parts, can the resulting subsections (strophes) be made up of any verses the poet happens to like best? and in any order he feels like giving them? Can the stanza have any number of verses ad libitum? To all these questions Dante's answer is: *no*! The art of the *canzone* prescribes definite rules of construction which indeed allow the poet a certain freedom, provided it be kept within established limits.

On what grounds, we should now ask, does Dante formulate the "artistic" rules that result in the above limitations? His answer is clear. The prescriptions contained in the "art" of the stanza arise from three sources: (a) the musical pattern to which the *canzone* is to be set imposes certain metrical restrictions, (b) the fact that the different verses above enumerated have "poetical" values that are proportionate to their length (the number of syllables they contain) imposes conditions both as to the relative number of each of the said varieties of verses and as to their collocation, (c) the subject matter determines the length of the stanza. In Dante's own words (*De Vulgari Eloquentia,* II, 9): "Tota igitur ars cantionis circa tria videtur consistere: primo circa cantus divisionem, secundo circa partium habitudinem, tertio circa numerum carminum et sillabarum." In developing these three points Dante brings out those limitations which art demands and reaches conclusions that seem to be something quite different from what scholars have set forth.

(a) The musical pattern imposes several conditions to the metrical scheme. This dependence is explicitly stated by Dante and one may only deny it by perverting the meaning of the words and destroying the logical consistency of his arguments. "Omnis stantia," he says (*ibid.,* II, 10, 17), "ad quandam odam recipiendam armonizata est."[6] This can only mean that the writer in constructing his *poetical* "armonia" is bound to respect certain *musical* conditions. If we say "the room is built so as to receive a certain bed," it means that the room cannot be of any size and of any form whatsoever. It must be such as to admit the bed.

This dependence of the metrical structure on the musical function is brought out in several ways. First if the melody of the stanza is broken into two sections by the diesis,[7] the metrical structure of the stanza must also show this division. And that it is the musical partition that controls the metrical scheme and not the converse Dante clearly indicates by these words (*ibid.,* II, 10): "Quedam (stantie) vero sunt diesim *patientes*." It is the stanza that undergoes the influence; its structure is conditioned. The presence of this diesis means that the musical partition either before or after the diesis, or both before and after, must be further subdivided into two or more iterative phrases. ("Diesis esse non potest, secundum quod eam appellamus nisi reiteratio unius ode fiat, vel ante diesim, vel post, vel undique": *ibid.*) In this musical iteration is the reason why the metrical scheme is constructed with strophic repetitions capable of admitting these very musical iterations.[8] This means that the subdivision of both parts of the stanza into strophes (*pedes* and *versus*) is a *metrical* response to a *musical* demand. Any doubt about it is easily removed by referring to *De Vulgari Eloquentia,* II, 12, 81: "non aliter ingeminatio cantus fieri posset *ad quam pedes fiunt*," that is, if this adherence to the musical pattern were lacking, it would not be possible to have the reduplication of the *singing*, a situation which could not develop since it is solely that we may have this iteration of the singing that the strophic reduplications of the metrical scheme have been devised.

What this dependence of the metrical form of the stanza on the musical pattern implies we may illustrate with a few quotations from Dante, and first in connection with the strophic subdivisions. These strophes in whatever part of the stanza they may be must be made of the same varieties of lines, in the same number, in the same order. Only thus can the musical iteration rest on the proper metrical duplication: "pedes ab invicem necessario carminum[9] et sillabarum equalitatem et habitudinem accipere, quia non *aliter cantus repetitio fieri posset*. Hoc idem in versibus esse servandum astruimus" (*ibid.,* II, 11).

This dependence is further brought out in connection with the prescriptions for the use of the seven-syllable verse (*ibid.,* II, 12, 81): a three-line strophe ("pes") made up of two hendecasyllabic lines with a heptasyllabic in between, must be followed by a strophe ("pes") likewise made up of a heptasyllabic line between two that are hendecasyllabic (because otherwise the iteration of the song could not occur, "*non aliter* ingeminatio cantus fieri posset").

This same holds for the use of the pentasyllabic line. Dante would limit the number of this "inferior" verse to one. But of course if the pentasyllabic occurs in a strophic group ("pes" or "versus") there must be two, because the singing of the strophe (with its iterative phrasing) demands this duplication of the pentasyllabic, ("propter *necessitatem* qua pedibus versibusque *cantatur*") (*ibid.,* II, 12, 56). Further resultant constraints or compulsions are given in *ibid.,* II, 12, 30.

These are then conditions that limit the freedom of the poet in metrically constructing his stanza. They are external ones and come from the musical pattern.

(b) But there are others, internal ones, which are due to a canon which affirms the poetical supremacy of the eleven-syllable line (the longest admissible), after which come in order of descending excellence, the heptasyllabic, the pentasyllabic, with the trisyllabic last. (This last however is devoid of metrical substantiality and identifiable solely in connection with a rhyming arrangement.) The poet, with due regard, no doubt, for the demands of variety[10] must let himself be guided by this canon, except insofar as certain metrical features are imposed again by the *musical* structure.

The application of this canon within the framework of the limitations above mentioned results in a series of prescriptions that are enumerated in *ibid.,* II, 12: the stanza must begin with a hendecasyllabic; the number of hendecasyllabics must outweigh the other verses; the seven-syllable line should be used with moderation; the pentasyllabic only once except insofar as the musical pattern demands a metrical repetition. Instructions are given for the use of the three-syllable line.

(c) There is finally a third aspect under which the stanza must be considered, viz. the use and the arrangement of rhymes. Dante (*ibid.,* II, 13) takes up this topic, shows how extensive is the freedom allowed the poet in arranging a rhyme scheme, indicates certain beautiful effects that can regularly be produced and points out the limitations to the free choice of rhyme arrangements imposed by the musical pattern, by the demands, that is, of the *pedes* and *versus*.

With the aid of the foregoing it will be easy to rectify a certain number of what seem to be misinterpretations of Dante's text, and misapplications of his theory.

Marigo in the book above referred to, and others with him, are convinced that Dante affirms that the metrical structure of the stanza is in no way dependent upon the musical partition, but rather the reverse. He says (page 244, note 10): "La canzone è dunque concepita come forma letteraria indipendente nell'atto della composizione dalla musica"; that is the meaning which he gets out of Dante's words: "omnis stantia ad quandam odam recipiendam armonizata est" (*De Vulgari Eloquentia,* II, 10); and again (*ibid.*): "la stanza è composta in modo che possa ricevere una melodia che sì adatti all'armonica disposizione che il poeta ha dato alle sue parti," which statement at once affirms and denies the metrical independence. For if the stanza "is composed in a manner such as to enable it to receive a melody" it is obvious that the stanza must submit to certain conditions of this melody, and yet this melody must adapt itself to the metrical exigencies of the stanza, the structure of which it was supposed to control. The above interpretation of Marigo seems to fit not the text as Dante wrote it but the reverse of it, as though he had said: "Omnis oda ad quandam stantiam recipiendam armonizata est."

To support this metrical autonomy Marigo relies on a passage from the *Convivio* which, he thinks, should clinch the case. He says (*ibid.*): "Questa indipendenza è piú chiaramente affermata nel *Convivio* (II, 11, 2)." But if we look at the passage referred to we find the opposite of what Marigo's thesis demands. Dante tells us that usually other poets concluded their *canzone* with a *tornata* (an epodic stanza) the purpose of which was that when the *singing* of the *canzone* was over ("*cantata* la canzone") one might return to it by the aid of a certain part of the singing ("con certa parte del *canto*"). Dante tells us that he does not usually follow this custom, and in order that people might be aware of this departure, he (except for rare occasions) avoided a metrical structure for the *tornata* which would have placed it in the same musical order with the preceding stanzas. In other words he did not produce the metrical numbers which were *demanded* by the musical pattern of the stanza of the *canzone* ("acciò che altri se n'accorgesse, rade volte la puosi con l'ordine de la canzone quanto è a lo numero che a la nota è *necessario*"). The independence therefore here considered is not that of the stanzas from the music, but the independence of the metrical structure of the *tornata* from the *musically conditioned* metrical sequences of the other stanzas.

Equally worthless is another argument that Marigo adduces to prove his contentions. He says (page cxliv, no. 1) that according to Dante's theory the ballad did indeed have to follow a musical partition, and in that lay one difference between it and the *canzone* which was not so bound ("La ballata per l'attestazione stessa di Dante (*De Vulgari Eloquentia,* II, 3, 5) doveva communemente essere accompagnata pure al suo tempo dalla musica anche in questo distinguendosi dalla canzone"). The invoked passage of Dante tells however a different story. Dante says that the ballad was different from the *canzone* not because it was *sung* but because it was *danced* to ("indigent enim plausoribus"). He makes no mention of music as such. The argument therefore will be valid only when it can be demonstrated that dance = music.

But what does Marigo do with all the above quoted passages which show the dependence of the metrical scheme upon the musical figure? How does he deal with unmistakably musical terms such as *diesis, modulatio, cantus, sonus,*[11] *melos,* etc.? with the *cantare* in the passage of the *Convivio* just quoted? with all the references to singing? He disposes of them all by a theory of *ideal music* totally independent from the sung music, and resulting from the harmonious arrangement of words. He tells us (page cxliii): "per essa (the Italian lyrical poetry) la melodia è solo interiore e ideale misura armonica che si realizza sviluppandosi nel verso, nelle rime e nella proporzionata struttura della strofe." And again (page 249, 5): " '*habitudo* circa cantus divisionem' cioè del rapporto fra fronte e volte [*versus* in Dante's language] piedi e sirma, piedi e volte *rispetto ad un'ideale melodia.*" But this ideal melody, when we examine the text, turns out to be nothing more than the enumeration of certain numerical rapports that may exist between the constituents of a stanza which is as ideal as the enumeration of the number of feet that animals may have and of the relative size of them. There is no trace in Dante's text of this aesthetic evaluation. All he does is to provide us with a scheme and its possibilities. The poet writes verses (lines) into groups (strophes) so that these may fit into certain musical patterns or arrangements. The composer writes the score for these lines, and thus gives concrete embodiment to those general musical partitions which had determined the metrical divisions.

Dante does not tell us how to write beautiful poetry when he discusses the strophic arrangement of the stanza. He merely gives us a list of possible metrical schemes out of which we may choose if indeed the poem is to be beautiful. And he tells us that these metrical schemes have a definite relation with certain conditions of singing, of real music. This relation consists in the fact that repetitions of more or less complicated musical phrases are matched by repetitions of more or less developed metrical strophes. The question now is: is the metrical iteration there to satisfy the demands of a musical pattern or is the musical reduplication merely a response to an original metrical formation? Dante, as we have already seen, is very explicit in his answer: these metrical strophes, he says, these *pedes* are constructed to meet the demands of the musical iteration ("ad ingeminationem cantus pedes fiunt," *ibid.,* II, 12, 82). In every single instance in which this connection with the song is mentioned Dante explicitly stresses the subordination of the metrical to the musical figure. Without enumerating them, let us merely refer here to *ibid.,* II, 12, 54, where he tells us that a certain very definite *material* verse structure is demanded, or rather necessitated by the fact that it is to be musically sung in a *certain way* "propter necessitatem qua pedibus versibusque cantatur." What could be the necessity imposed by an "ideal melody"? Of course the stanza, even without being sung, when merely read or declaimed does have a "harmony" of its own. It is a harmony which results from many factors but *also* from the musical conditions above described.

We can now proceed to examine the text of Dante's definition of the stanza, which as we have seen reads as follows: "stantiam esse sub certo cantu et habitudine limitata carminum et sillabarum compagem," and ask ourselves the question: what is the meaning of *habitudo*? That will be useful not only to determine the validity of the MS reading but also to correct certain mistaken interpretations.

The word *habitudo*, used by Dante frequently in the *De Vulgari Eloquentia* but nowhere else, has a variety of meanings carried over from various currents of technical speech. It still bears in Dante's time the old classical significance of *condition, appearance, aspect,* etc., perpetuated by the *Vulgate*[12] and the early Christian writers. St. Augustine says (*De Civitate Dei*, 22, 14): "An infantes in ea sunt resurrecturi habitudine corporis quam habituri erant aetatis accessu" (will babes be resurrected in that bodily state into which they would have developed," etc.). Again he says (*In Psalmum*, 143, 9: "Quando resuscitatum mortale hoc corpus transfertur in habitudinem angelicam" (*i.e.*, is changed to the angelic condition).[13]

This meaning coincided broadly with the medical usage of the word as a translation of εὐεξία and καχεξία. In this sense it was brought close to the meaning of *habitus* (Apuleius, *Metamorphoses* 9, page 235): *habitus* and *habitudo*; and (St. Augustine, *De Diversis Quaestionibus*, 83, qu. 73. 1): "*habitum* corporis secundum quem dicimus alium alio esse validiorem, quae magis proprie *habitudo* dici debet"; and (St. Thomas, *II Sententiarum*, 24, 1, 1 ad 1): "Bernardus (who had called free will a *habitus*) large utitur nomine habitus pro habitudine quadam. Ex hoc enim liberum arbitrium in homine dicitur quod hoc modo *se habet* eius animus ut sui actus liberam potestatem *habeat*."

Another sense of the word was developed when *habitudo* came to be used as the equivalent of ἕξις or σχέσις, *i.e.*, relation. We find this in Boethius (*In Porphyrii Isagogen*, page 30, 10): "habent duas habitudines eam quae ad superiora, et eam quae est ad posteriora." This meaning became even of more current usage with mathematical writing (Euclid v): "Ratio est duarum magnitudinum eiusdem generis aliquatenus ad invicem aliqua habitudo." It is synonymous to relation: "Est enim *habitudo* vel *relatio* quaedam moventis ad motum" (St. Thomas, *Contra Gentiles,* II, 33). Dante uses it in this sense in *De Vulgari Eloquentia,* I, 6, 31, and in this sense it lived on until long after the Renaissance both in Italian and Latin technical writings. *Habitudo*, moreover, like *ordo* covered both the relationship on the basis of which an arrangement was made and the resulting arrangement itself.

The Schoolmen confronted with these many significances tried to unify them by bringing them all back to the common origin: *habere*, thence differentiating them with the aid of different syntactical relationships. In this way they gave the various related meanings a technical precision which could not be maintained, but which cannot be ignored. In this process *habitudo* followed the fortune of *habitus.*[14] The clearest account of this articulation we find in St. Thomas, *Summa*, I, 11ae, 49, 1, c. There St. Thomas strives to unify the three basic meanings of *habitus*, which are: (a) fixed disposition (first species of the accident *qualitas*); (b) possession, in opposition to privation (postpraedicament); (c) the praedicamental usage as something intermediate between the one that has and the thing which is had.[15]

In this way he was able to keep alive in the word the old classical sense, the mathematical significance, the medical and ethical meanings, and justify them by a naive application of the etymological fallacy.

The relation ("habitudo") of one triangle to another is the manner in which one *se habet* to the other. *Habitus* as the first species of *qualitas* took care of such classical meanings as we see exemplified in the Ciceronian "iustitia est habitus animi etc."[16] *Habitus* as a praedicament carried on the classical meaning of garment, attire, justified by the Aristotelian definition above given.[17] Dante uses the word in all these senses. In the *Convivio, De Monarchia, De Vulgari Eloquentia* we find "abito di scienza," "abito di arte," "habitus philosophicae veritatis," "habitus scientiarum," etc., all of which are to be interpreted by referring them to *habitus* as first species of *qualitas.*[18] In the praedicamental meaning of "attire" it is also very frequent, and we must recall this significance when we interpret *abituati* in *Purgatorio*, 29, 146; also when we encounter the phrase (*De Vulgari Eloquentia,* II, 12, 70): "qualiter tibi carminum habituando sit stantia habitudine que circa carmina consideranda videtur," for Dante had figuratively come to consider the art as the garment of the stanza: "sed solam artem antecedentis (stantiae) *induere*" (*ibid.,* II, 9, 18).

This last example shows that writers could make more than one of these various meanings converge on the word. We see this again in the *Convivio* (I, 11, 42): "dall'abito di questa luce discretiva massimamente le popolari persone sono orbate," where the privational sense of *orbate* throws upon *abito* the postpraedicamental shade of meaning (*habitus* vs. *privatio*). In *De Vulgari Eloquentia,* II, 6, 84 ("utilissimum foret ad illam [constructionem] habituandam") it is hard not to feel the pregnant or rather polysemic force of the word.[19]

We may now apply this general notion of the term to Dante's definition. As we have seen, it covers three topics or questions: first, an external relation (that which subordinates the metrical structure to the song ("sub certo cantu"); second, the question before us, viz. the *habitudo limitata*; third, the matter of the number of lines and syllables.

The first one he treats in II, 10. At the close of that chapter he explicitly states that he is through with the discussion bearing on the relation of the art of the *canzone* to singing, and that he is going on with the question of the *habitudo*.

The third one he treats in Chapter 14 (unfinished). This too is stated very explicitly: "Ex quo ⟨duoque⟩ sunt artis in cantione satis sufficienter tractavimus, nunc de tertio videtur esse tractandum, videlicet de numero carminum et sillabarum."

It is obvious therefore that in the intervening chapters (11, 12, 13) we must find the treatment of the remaining question touched upon by the definition, viz. the *habitudo limitata*, and that we are therefore authorized to draw from these chapters what we need to clarify the term under discussion.

And if we ask what this is an *habitudo* of, the answer is given by Dante (*ibid.,* II, 9) in the following passage: "tota ars cantionis circa tria videtur consistere: primo circa cantus divisionem, secundo circa *partium habitudinem*, tertio circa numerum carminum et sillabarum." The *habitudo* of the definition is then the one resulting from the arrangement of the *parts* of the stanza.

This *habitudo partium* again deals with three matters: (a) the quantitative relation of the parts of the stanza existing in virtue of the musical partition; (b) the nature of the individual lines of the stanza; (c) the rhyming connections; (*ibid.,* II, 11: "Hec etenim circa cantus divisionem atque contextum carminum et rithimorum relationem consistit").

The first of these is treated in Chapter 11, the second in Chapter 12, the third in Chapter 13. Marigo misses this arrangement entirely. He says (page 253 on XII): "Dopo l'*habitudo* della divisione melodica fondamento della ripartizione strofica si passa a spiegare l'*habitudo* delle singole parti divisibili (piedi e volte) in quanto è determinata dalla posizione reciproca che in esse hanno i versi secondo il numero e qualità," whereas Dante considers here the *habitudo* of the single, individual and indivisible lines, *not* that of the "divisible parts" (*pedes* and *versus*). This latter he has already discussed in the preceding chapter and it is mentioned here in this chapter only to indicate the *limits* it sets to the application of the canon of verse lengths. Dante in this chapter mentions the strophic groups ("piedi e volte") only in the following lines: 25–32, 55–56, 72–85; and these passages, all of them, deal exclusively with said limitations. So that Marigo's interpretation should be reversed to read as follows: "Dopo l'*habitudo* delle parti divisibili (piedi e volte) fondata sulla partizione musicale si passa a spiegare l'*habitudo* delle parti indivisibili (i singoli versi) in quanto è determinata dalla qualità (lunghezza) di essi versi e limitata dalle esigenze della partizione strofica." The phrase "carmina contexendo" (*ibid.*) does not mean, as Marigo thinks: to weave *carmina* (individual lines) into larger units ("pedes et versus"). It means to weave something so as to form with it these very *carmina*, these lines. And that "something" of course is the syllabic sequence. In fact Dante, immediately after the sentence we have quoted above, starts examining the various lines from the point of view of their syllabic length. This interpretation is demanded not only by the context but also by the meaning that Dante elsewhere gives to the word. Just a few lines before the above quoted sentence he had used the verb *contexere* in connection not with individual lines but with strophes ("quin liceat plures et pedes et versus similiter contexere," *ibid.*, II, 11, 50). There obviously Dante does not mean (nor has he ever been interpreted to mean) "it is permissible to build up something by means of the strophic *pedes* and *versus*" but rather: "to weave individual lines into these *pedes* and *versus*." And the passive construction bears out this usage: "frons tribus endecasillabis et uno eptasillabo contexta" (*ibid.*, II, 11, 24), where the texture refers to the constituent, not to the thing constituted. Likewise in *contextum carminum* (*ibid.*, II, 11, 4), *carminum* is an objective, *not* a subjective genitive.[20]

This will suffice to prove that the reasons Marigo adduces (page 253, note 12) to show how carelessly this chapter has been written by Dante are unfounded ("in nessun capitolo come in questo si accumulano gli indizi di composizione trascurata e di elaborazione non ancora ben definita della materia.") The chapter appears to be carelessly composed only if it is not correctly understood. It is not true that to the development of the topic announced only the ninth and tenth sections are devoted ("al vero soggetto del capitolo, *habitudo quedam quam carmina contexendo considerare debemus* sono dedicati in realtà solo i due 9–10," *ibid.*) *All* sections of the chapter *are* devoted to the true subject, if the subject is properly understood as Dante meant it. It is sections 9–10 instead which are *not* "in realtà" devoted to it, except in so far as they point out limitations.

A proper understanding of the other phase of the *habitudo partium*, viz. the question of the quantitative superiority or inferiority of the musically constituted subsections of the stanza, will likewise help us to correct some misunderstandings.

Within this musically determined partition, many varieties of metrical structures are possible according as in the three kinds of the subdivided stanza,[21] the superiority as to (a) number of lines, (b) number of syllables, (c) number of both lines and syllables, (d) number of strophes, passes from the section which precedes to the section that follows the diesis.

Marigo has missed the point. He says (page 251, note 31), commenting the word *numero*, "sottintendi: carminum et sillabarum," which is not correct. We must supply instead "pedum et versuum." For Dante goes on to say that in a stanza there may be three *pedes* and two *versus*, or three *versus* and two *pedes*, which clearly shows that the numerical superiority here considered is that which deals with *pedes* and *versus*, not with *carmina* et *sillabae*. This last relation is taken up later, where he says: "Et quem ad modum de victoria carminum et sillabarum diximus *inter alia*, nunc etiam inter pedes et versus dicimus," which means something quite different from what Marigo says (page 252, note 34). Dante's words have a meaning which may be paraphrased as follows: we have discussed the possible superiority (in the matter of the number of lines and syllables) that may shift from one section of the stanza to the other when the stanza is subdivided 1) in *frons* and *versus*, and 2) in *cauda* (*syrma*) and *pedes*. There remains that arrangement of the stanza which is made up of *pedes* and *versus*. In this case two things must be considered: first, the relative number of *pedes* and *versus* (and this is the statement that, as we say above, Marigo mistranslates); second, the relation of superiority and inferiority possible between the *versus* and the *pedes* as to the number of lines and syllables which constitute them, which relation exists between them in the same way that it was previously shown to exist between the other things ("inter alia"), viz. the parts of the strophe when the parts were the *frons* and *versus*, and the *syrma* and *pedes*.

In the third phase of the *habitudo* also, Marigo (and others) seem to have missed Dante's thought. This is the part that deals with the rhyming scheme. Dante informs us that he will treat of rhyme *not in itself* and *per se* but, so to speak, *per accidens*. The *per se* treatment he promises to give in a later book of the *De Vulgari Eloquentia* which has not come down to us. That this is the meaning of "Rithimorum quoque *relationi* vacemus, nihil de rithimo *secundum se* modo tractantes" (Chapter 13) is obvious. "Let us at this juncture treat," he says, "of the rhymes not *in themselves*, but only as to their relationships." Marigo, failing to see the contrast between *secundum se* and *relatio* (*perseitas* vs. accident of relativity), discovers in these words a musical doctrine totally foreign to the text. He tells us (page 263, note 1): "Parlando delle rime che sono il *segno più cospicuo per cui il verso si avvicina nella sua cadenza alla musica* si afferma che la loro disposizione consiste in una *relatio* cioè in un rapporto armonico per il quale poesia e musica hanno un comune fondamento ed anche la poesia è musica." Of this quite novel doctrine there is not a word in Dante. Nowhere does he say that rhyme is the most conspicuous sign of the similarity between poetry and music. Nor does he give evidence of an aesthetic theory that fuses into one mold the several arts. On what does this important affirmation then rest? On the meaning of the word *relatio*, we are told, provided we bear in mind the following passage from the *Convivio*(II, 13, 23) quoted by Marigo: "la quale [musica] è tutta relativa si come si vede ne le parole armonizzate e ne li canti dei quali tanto più dolce armonia resulta quanto la relazione è bella." True enough that music is "relativa," but how many thousand things besides are *relative*! and what would happen if we inferred some musicality about them all? Every schoolboy in Dante's day memorized: "relatio . . . nihil aliud est quam ordo unius ad aliud" or "relatio est secundum quam aliquae ad invicem referentur." And having memorized this, exemplified it somewhat as follows; John (who, "substantialiter," is a man) from the point of view of the accident of relativity ("ad aliquid") is the son of someone; possibly the father of somebody; the subject of a ruler or the ruler of subjects; double the weight of some person, etc. All of which exemplifies the accident of relativity in contrast to what Dante calls *perseitas*, that is when something is not considered *secundum se*. If Dante, knowing the extent of the meaning of the word *relatio*, had meant to limit it to music, could he possibly have helped to add a specifying modifier? What he means is: I will not now say what rhymes are; I will merely discuss the way in which they are arranged.

In determining the "art" of rhyming Dante stresses the great freedom that the poet enjoys. He considers the rhymeless stanza and the stanza with the same rhyme throughout. He indicates certain predilections, viz. ending a stanza with one or more rhyming couplets, and connecting the two parts of the stanza by a beautiful rhyming *concatenatio* whereby the last line of the fore part rhymes with the first line of the aft section. And he gives definite restrictions which as usual deal with the conditions to be satisfied by the strophic formations.

He also gives instructions as to the choice of rhymes from the point of view not of their arrangement, but on the basis of their quality. These remarks obviously being foreign to the declared subject of the chapter, he presents them apologetically. We give these here, he says, as an appendix to the chapter ("appendamus capitulo") because we shall not again in the course of this book touch upon the doctrine of the rhyme.[22]

These are then the three aspects of what constitutes the *habitudo partium*, and in every one of them the *habitudo* has been shown to be "limitata." The poet has a considerable range for the choice of the lines and the grouping of them but he must respect the *limits* set first by the musical divisions and secondly by the intrinsic value of the individual lines according as they are longer or shorter, the use of which in turn is again regulated by the exigencies of the strophic groups and therefore in the last analysis by the musical formation. It would seem therefore as though the MS reading could be upheld. Can the same be said of the emended text? By it Dante is made to say that the stanza is a structure of lines and syllables limited by a certain melody and a certain order. This seems to mean that a thing is *limited* by the elements that constitute it, as though we said: man is a material organism limited by sensuality and rationality. Such an expression would not seem to be tolerable. But, it may be objected, are the *cantus* and the *habitudo partium* consituents of the stanza *as vehicle of the art of the canzone?* Let us examine the text.

Dante tells us (*ibid.,* II, 10, 7) that if we want to know a thing satisfactorily we must extend our inquiry to the ultimate elements that constitute that thing ("cognitionis perfectio uniuscuiusque terminatur ad ultima elementa"). An inquiry about the stanza must therefore resolve itself into a study of its elements. But what are the "artistic" elements of the stanza? What is the art of a stanza made up of? The answer is given by Dante in II, 9, 23: "tota ars cantionis circa tria videtur *consistere*: prima circa cantus divisionem, secundo circa partium habitudinem, tertio circa numerum carminum et sillabarum." These are the three *constituent* elements of the stanza. And does he say that he will examine as elements of the stanza these constituents? Yes, in II, 1, 14: "et primo de cantu, deinde de habitudine et postmodum de carminibus et sillabis percontemur." And are not these the three things which we find in the definition of the stanza? These three therefore should be all treated as elements and no two of them as limits. The definition in question as it reads in the MSS correctly makes of the *carmina et sillabae* something like the matter of the stanza, of the other two something like formal elements. The question is: would Dante use the preposition *sub* to indicate such a relationship? We find in *De Aqua et Terra*, 18, 33: "ut materia prima . . . sit *sub* omni forma materiali"; *De Monarchia,* I, 3, 74: "ut potentia tota materiae primae semper *sub* actu sit." Though the language here is not rigorously technical, the two points of view are close enough to justify such an interpretation of *sub*. It seems therefore as though the reading of the three MSS should be maintained.

## Notes

1. The numbers of the lines are those of Moore's edition.

2. Dante Alighieri, *De Vulgari Eloquentia, ridotto a miglior lezione e commentato da Aristide Marigo*, Firenze, Le Monnier, 1938. This book is referred to in this article simply by the name of the author.

3. Cf. for Dante: *Purgatorio*, 27, 130; *Purgatorio*, 9, 125; *Paradiso*, 14, 117; *Canzoniere*, 14, 95.

4. Cf. Cicero, *Pro Balbo*, 20, 45. Victorinus made it familiar to Christian writers.

5. Cf. *Purgatorio*, 33, 141: "lo fren dell'arte."

6. Dante defines *armonizare* (*ibid.*, II, 8) as a *musical* act, thus: "cantio nil aliud esse videtur quam actio completa dictantis verb *modulationi* armonizata," where *modulatio* again is given a musical meaning as follows: "numquam modulatio dicitur cantio sed sonus, vel tonus, vel nota vel melos."

7. Diesis is a technical musical word. Dante (*ibid.*, II, 10) uses it in the uncommon sense given to it by Isidore: "diesim dicimus deductionem vergentem de una oda in aliam" ("oda" being as we have seen a musical term).

8. There are three possible models of the stanza when it is set to a melody that is partitioned by a diesis: 1. The one in which the strophic repetitions are found only in the part that precedes the *diesis*; they are then called "pedes" (Dante himself calls our attention to this unusual meaning of the word); the other part of the stanza (the posterior half) being undivided is then called *syrma* or *cauda*. 2. The one in which the strophic repetitions are found only in the part that follows the *diesis*; they are then called *versus* (again this word is used in a special meaning which does indeed survive in English, but has been dropped in Italian because of the intolerable confusion which it engenders; to avoid confusion Dante calls the individual verses [the metrical lines] *carmina*); the other part of the stanza, the anterior half, being undivided, is then called *frons*. 3. The one in which *both* parts are subdivided, the stanza then having both *pedes* and *versus*.

9. *Carmina*, as has been noticed, means *verses* (individual lines).

10. It might seem as though the best stanza would be the one consisting solely of eleven-syllable lines. But we must recall that a unison sequence, even if made up of the "best" elements, is not necessarily better than an "ordered" array of varied constituents, some of which are bound to be inferior to the "best."

11. "Dare il suono" = compose the music.

12. *Genesis*, 41, 4, and *Il Machabaeorum*, 15, 13.

13. This meaning is very frequent in St. Augustine; see *In Psalmum*, 68, 1, 4: *De Peccatorum Meritus*, I, 3, 3; *De Genesi ad Litteram*, 6, 26.

14. St. Thomas calls *sanitas* a *habitudo*: "Est velut habitudo quaedam sicut se sanitas se habet ad corpus" (in *II Sent.*, 26, 2, 4, ad 1). "Gratia ad genus qualitatis reducitur et ad primam speciem qualitatis, nec *proprie* tamen naturam habitus habet cum *non immediate ad actum ordinet* sed est velut habitudo quaedam."

15. "Unum speciale genus rerum quod dicitur praedicamentum habitus de quo dicit Philosophus ad V Metaphysicorum [c. 20, 1022 b 6] quod inter habentem indumentum, et indumentum quod habetur est *habitus* medius."

16. This is the meaning we still give the word when we say that usage "doth breed habit in a man."

17. This is the meaning we give the word when we say that "habit doth the monk display."

18. Cf. St. Thomas, *Summa,* I, 14, 1: "scientia enim habitus est"; *Summa,* I, 11$^{ae}$, 53, 1, c: "habitus conclusionum qui dicitur scientia"; *Summa,* I, 11$^{ae}$, 49, 2, c: "habitus ponitur prima species qualitatis."

19. These meanings properly grasped will help us to avoid such interpretations as we find in Marigo, p. 196, n. 44, where commenting on *scientiarum habitu* he says: "Non basta un sapere frammentario e superficiale ma occorre quello divenuto *habitus* poichè la poesia non richiede esposizione analitica di dottrina ma viva sintesi animata della fantasia e del sentimento." This no doubt brings Dante up to date, in Italian literary criticism,

but far away from the poet's meaning and the language of his times. The *habitus scientiarum* has absolutely nothing whatsoever to do with a synthesis of phantasy and what not. The most prosaic writer who knew his subject would be said by everybody in Dante's time to have the *habitus scientiae*. The only way not to have the *habitus scientiarum* is not to know them.

The proper grasp of the meaning of *habitudo* will help us to understand Dante's "pedes ab invicem necessario carminum et sillabarum equalitatem et habitudinem accipere" (*op. cit.*, II, 11) and correct Marigo's translation, which is as follows (p. 253): "i piedi ricevono l'uno dall'altro necessariamente uguaglianza e proporzionata disposizione di versi e di sillabe." Whereas Dante says that whatever number of different lines we find in one of the two *pedes*, we must find the same variety in the same number in the other *pes* ("equalitatem") and that the order in which these different lines are arranged in one of the two *pedes* must be kept in the other *pes* ("habitudo").

And again Marigo tells us (p. 245, n. 12) that the *canzoni* of Arnautz Daniel, like Dante's own *Al poco giorno*, are marked by the "assoluta mancanza di rima entro la stanza o la presenza di *rime che non costituiscono alcuna habitudo.*" But how is it possible to have a rhyming scheme without a *habitudo*? It would be like having a father and son without any relation existing between them. The very fact of a rhyme (desinential connection of several lines) sets a *habitudo*. The only way not to have a *habitudo* is to have no rhymes. And that is exactly what Dante says (*ibid.*, II, 13, 8): "Unum est stantia *sine* rithimo in qua *nulla* rithimorum habitudo actenditur."

20. This is also borne out (*ibid.*, II, 12, 13) by: "hendecasillabum propter quandam excellentiam in contextu vincendi privilegium meretur," which Marigo (p. 255) mistranslates (and finds it therefore "a fiacca espressione"). Properly rendered it is a very vigorous phrase. It does not mean as Marigo has it: "l'endecasillabo merita assolutamente il privilegio di prevalere nella testura per certa sua eccellenza"; but rather; "l'endecasillabo per la superiorità della sua testura merita il privilegio della vittoria."

21. (a) *frons* with *versus*; (b) *pedes* with *syrma*; (c) *pedes* with *versus*.

22. The third element (after *habitudo*), the one "circa numerum carminum et sillabarum," Dante treats in the fragmentary 14th chapter. It is very difficult to make sense out of it. Dante seems to say that the subject matter and the disposition of the poet have much to do with the length of the stanza. The writer may be in a mood which Dante calls *dextrum* and then his words will be "persuasive," "gratulatory" or "laudatory," or he may be in a mood that Dante calls *sinistrum* and then his words will be dissuasive, ironic, contemptuous. In the first case he should proceed leisurely to the end (write a long stanza), in the latter case, he should hurry (compose a short stanza).

This last sentence of the book has been interpreted in a way which seems unsatisfactory. Dante says: "quae circa sinistra sunt verba semper ad extremum festinent e alia decenti prolixitate *passim* veniant ad extremum . . ." Marigo translates the last clause: "le altre (parole) vi giungano *in ogni parte* con ampiezza decorosa . . ." He and others have given to the word *passim* the classical sense, which here obviously does not fit. What we need is a word meaning "slowly" in contrast to "festinent" of the first clause. And that meaning is furnished by *passim* in its current medieval sense, corresponding to "a passo" in contrast to "cursim." Says Rolandinus Pataviensis (*De Factis in Marchia Tarvis.*, XII, 18): "Tendebat ad partes illas cum gente sua, non equidem sicut *fugiens*, equis immo procedentibus *passim*." (Cf. Du Cange, *s.v.* In Glossaries we find *pedetentim* equated to *passim*.)

# Charles S. Singleton

## Dante's Allegory

In his *Convivio* Dante recognizes two kinds of allegory: an 'allegory of poets' and an 'allegory of theologians.' And in the interpretation of his own poems in that work he declares that he intends to follow the allegory of poets, for the reason that the poems were composed after that manner of allegory.

One must recall that there is an unfortunate lacuna in the text of the *Convivio* at just this most interesting point, with the result that those words which defined the literal sense as distinguished from the allegorical are missing. But no one who knows the general argument of the whole work will, I think, make serious objection to the way the editors of the accepted critical text have filled the lacuna.

The passage in question, then, patched by them, reads as follows:

> Dico che, sì come nel primo capitolo è narrato, questa sposizione conviene essere literale e allegorica. E a ciò dare a intendere, si vuol sapere che le scritture si possono intendere e deonsi esponere massimamente per quattro sensi. L'uno si chiama litterale [e questo è quello che non si stende più oltre la lettera de le parole fittizie, sì come sono le favole de li poeti. L'altro si chiama allegorico] e questo è quello che si nasconde sotto'l manto di queste favole, ed è una veritade ascosa sotto bella menzogna: sì come quando dice Ovidio che Orfeo facea con la cetera mansuete le fiere, e li arbori e le pietre a sè muovere; che vuol dire che lo savio uomo con lo strumento de la sua voce fa(r)ia mansuescere e umiliare li crudeli cuori, e fa(r)ia muovere a la sua volontade coloro che non hanno vita di scienza e d'arte: e coloro che non hanno vita ragionevole alcuna sono quasi come pietre. E perchè questo nascondimento fosse trovato per li savi, nel penultimo trattato si mosterrà. Veramente

> li teologi questo senso prendono altrimenti che li poeti; ma però che mia intenzione è qui lo modo de li poeti seguitare, prendo lo senso allegorico secondo che per li poeti è usato.[1]

Dante goes on here to distinguish the customary third and fourth senses, the moral and the anagogical. However, in illustration of these no example from 'the poets' is given. For both senses, the example in illustration is taken from Holy Scripture. It is, however, evident from the closing words of the chapter that in the exposition of the poems of the *Convivio*, the third and fourth senses will have only an incidental interest and that the poet is to concern himself mainly with the first two.[2]

It was no doubt inevitable that the conception of allegory which Dante here calls the allegory of poets should come to be identified with the allegory of the *Divine Comedy*. This, after all, is a formulation of the matter of allegory by Dante himself. It distinguishes an allegory of poets from an allegory of theologians. Now, poets create and theologians only interpret. And, if we must choose between Dante as theologian and Dante as poet, then, I suppose, we take the poet.[3] For the *Divine Comedy*, all are agreed, is the work of a poet, is a poem. Why, then, would its allegory not be allegory as the poets understood it—that is, as Dante, in the *Convivio*, says the poets understood it? Surely the allegory of the *Comedy* is the allegory of poets in which the first and literal sense is a fiction and the second or allegorical sense is the true one.[4]

Indeed, with some Dante scholars, so strong has the persuasion been that such a view of the allegory of the *Divine Comedy* is the correct one, that it has brought them to question the authorship of the famous letter to Can Grande.[5] This, in all consistency, was bound to occur. For the Letter, in pointing out the allegory of the *Commedia*, speaks in its turn of the usual four senses. But the example of allegory which it gives is not taken from Ovid nor indeed from the work of any poet. Let us consider this famous and familiar passage:

> Ad evidentiam itaque dicendorum sciendum est quod istius operis non est simplex sensus, ymo dici potest polisemos, hoc est plurium sensuum; nam primus sensus est qui habetur per litteram, alius est qui habetur per significata per litteram. Et primus dicitur litteralis, secundus vero allegoricus sive moralis sive anagogicus. Qui modus tractandi, ut melius pateat, potest considerari in hiis versibus: 'In exitu Israel de Egipto, domus Jacob de populo barbaro, facta est Iudea sanctificatio

> eius, Israel potestas eius.' Nam si ad litteram solam inspiciamus, significatur nobis exitus filiorum Israel de Egipto, tempore Moysis; si ad allegoriam, nobis significatur nostra redemptio facta per Christum; si ad moralem sensum significatur nobis conversio anime de luctu et miseria peccati ad statum gratie: si ad anagogicum, significatur exitus anime sancte ab huius corruptionis servitute ad eterne glorie libertatem. Et quanquam isti sensus mistici variis appellentur nominibus, generaliter omnes dici possunt allegorici, cum sint a litterali sive historiali diversi. Nam allegoria dicitur ab 'alleon' grece, quod in latinum dicitur 'alienum,' sive 'diversum.'[6]

and the Letter continues directly as follows:

> Hiis visis, manifestum est quod duplex oportet esse subiectum, circa quod currant alterni sensus. Et ideo videndum est de subiecto huius operis, prout ad litteram accipitur; deinde de subiecto, prout allegorice sententiatur. Est ergo subiectum totius operis, litteraliter tantum accepti, status animarum post mortem simpliciter sumptus; nam de illo et circa illum totius operis versatur processus. Si vero accipiatur opus allegorice, subiectum est homo prout merendo et demerendo per arbitrii libertatem iustitie premiandi et puniendi obnoxius est.

Now this, to return to the distinction made in the *Convivio*, is, beyond the shadow of a doubt, the 'allegory of theologians.' It is their kind of allegory not only because Holy Scripture is cited to illustrate it, but because since Scripture is cited, the first or literal sense cannot be fictive but must be true and, in this instance, historical. The effects of Orpheus' music on beasts and stones may be a poet's invention, setting forth under a veil of fiction some hidden truth, but the Exodus is no poet's invention.

All mediaevalists are familiar with the classical statement of the 'allegory of theologians' as given by St. Thomas Aquinas toward the beginning of the *Summa Theologica*:

> Respondeo. Dicendum quod auctor Sacrae Scripturae est Deus, in cuius potestate est ut non solum voces ad significandum accommodet, quod etiam homo facere potest, sed etiam res ipsas. Et ideo cum in omnibus scientiis voces significent, hoc habet proprium ista scientia, quod ipsae res significatae per voces, etiam significant aliquid. Illa ergo prima significatio, qua voces significant res, pertinet ad primum sensum, qui

> est sensus historicus vel litteralis. Illa vero significatio qua res significatae per voces, iterum res alias significant, dicitur sensus spiritualis, qui super litteralem fundatur et eum supponit.[7]

St. Thomas goes on to subdivide the second or spiritual sense into the usual three: the allegorical, the moral, and the anagogical. But in his first division into two he has made the fundamental distinction, which St. Augustine expressed in terms of one meaning which is *in verbis* and another meaning which is *in facto*.[8] And, in reading his words, we have surely recalled Dante's in the Letter to Can Grande: 'nam primus sensus est qui habetur per litteram, alius est qui habetur per significata per litteram.'

An allegory of poets and an allegory of theologians: the Letter to Can Grande does not make the distinction. The Letter is speaking of the way in which a poem is to be understood. And in choosing its example of allegory from Holy Scripture, the Letter is clearly looking to the kind of allegory which is the allegory of theologians; and is thus pointing to a poem in which the first and literal sense is to be taken as the first and literal sense of Holy Scripture is taken, namely as an historical sense.[9] The well-known jingle on the four senses began, one recalls, 'Littera *gesta* docet. . . .'

But, before going further, let us ask if this matter can have more than antiquarian interest. When we read the *Divine Comedy* today, does it matter, really whether we take its first meaning to be historical or fictive, since in either case we must enter into that willing suspension of disbelief required in the reading of any poem?

Indeed, it happens to matter very much, because with this poem it is not a question of one meaning but of two meanings; and the *nature* of the first meaning will necessarily determine the nature of the second—will say how we shall look for the second. In the case of a fictive first meaning, as in the 'allegory of poets,' interpretation will invariably speak in terms of an outer and an inner meaning, of a second meaning which is conveyed but also, in some way, deliberately concealed under the 'shell' or the 'bark' or the 'veil' of an outer fictive meaning. This allegory of the poets, as Dante presents it in the *Convivio*, is essentially an allegory of 'this *for* that,' of 'this figuration in order to give (and also to conceal) *that* meaning.' Orpheus and the effects of his music yield the meaning that a wise man can tame cruel hearts. Please note, incidentally, that here we are not speaking of allegory as expressed in a personification, but of an allegory of action, of event.

But the kind of allegory to which the example from Scriptures given in the Letter to Can Grande points is not an allegory of 'this *for* that,' but an allegory of 'this *and* that,' of this sense *plus* that sense. The verse in Scripture which says 'When Israel went out of Egypt,' has its first meaning in denoting a real historical event; and it has its second meaning because that historical event itself, having the Author that it had, can signify yet another event: our Redemption through Christ. Its first meaning is a meaning *in verbis*; its other meaning is a meaning *in facto*, in the event itself. The words have a real meaning in pointing to a real event; the event, in its turn, has meaning because events wrought by God are themselves as words yielding a meaning, a higher and spiritual sense.

But there was a further point about this kind of allegory of Scriptures: it was generally agreed that while the first literal meaning would always be there, *in verbis*,[10] the second or spiritual meaning was not always to be found in all the things and events that the words pointed to. Some events yielded the second meaning, some did not. And it is this fact which best shows that the literal historical meaning of Scriptures was not necessarily a sense *in the service of* another sense, not therefore a matter of 'this for that.' It is this that matters most in the interpretation of the *Divine Comedy*.

The crux of the matter, then, is this: If we take the allegory of the *Divine Comedy* to be the allegory of poets (as Dante understood that allegory in the *Convivio*) then we shall be taking it as a construction in which the literal sense ought always to be expected to yield another sense because the literal is only a fiction devised to express a second meaning. In this view the first meaning, if it does not give another, *true* meaning, has no excuse for being. Whereas, if we take the allegory of the *Divine Comedy* to be the allegory of theologians, we shall expect to find in the poem a first literal meaning presented as a meaning which is not fictive but true, because the words which give that meaning point to events which are seen as historically true. And we shall see these events themselves reflecting a second meaning because their author, who is God, can use events as men use words. *But*, we shall not demand at every moment that the event signified by the words be in its turn as a word, because this is not the case in Holy Scripture.

I, for one, have no difficulty in making the choice. The allegory of the *Divine Comedy* is, for me, so clearly the 'allegory of theologians' (as the Letter to Can Grande by its example says it is) that I can only continue to wonder at the efforts made to see it as the 'allegory of poets.' What indeed increases the wonder at the continued effort is that every attempt to treat the first meaning of the poem as a fiction devised to convey a true but hidden meaning has been such a clear demonstration of how a poem may be forced to meanings that it cannot possibly bear as a poem.[11]

It seems important to illustrate the matter briefly with a single and obvious example. All readers of the *Comedy*, whatever their allegorical credo, must recognize that Vergil, for instance, if he be taken statically, in isolation from the action of the poem, had and has, as the poem would see him, a real historical existence. He was a living man and he is now a soul dwelling in Limbus. Standing alone, he would have no other, no second meaning, at all. It is by having a role in the action of the poem that Vergil takes on a second meaning. And it is at this point that the view one holds of the nature of the first meaning begins to matter. For if this is the allegory of poets, then what Vergil does, like what Orpheus does, is a fiction devised to convey a hidden meaning which it ought to convey all the time, since only by conveying that other meaning is what he does justified at all. Instead, if this action is allegory as theologians take it, then this action must always have a literal sense which is historical and no fiction; and thus Vergil's deeds as part of the whole action may, in their turn, be as words signifying other things; but they do not have to do this all the time, because, being historical, those deeds exist simply in their own right.

But can we hesitate in such a choice? Is it not clear that Vergil can not and does not always speak and act as Reason, with a capital initial, and that to try to make him do this is to try to rewrite the poem according to a conception of allegory which the poem does not bear within itself?

If, then, the allegory of the *Divine Comedy* is the allegory of theologians, if it is an allegory of 'this and that,' if its allegory may be seen in terms of a first meaning which is *in verbis* and of another meaning which is *in facto*, what is the main outline of its allegorical structure?

In the simplest and briefest possible statement it is this: the journey to God of a man through three realms of the world beyond this life is what is given by the words of the poem. This meaning is *in verbis* and it is a literal and historical meaning. It points to the event. The event is that journey to God through the world beyond. 'Littera *gesta* docet.' The words of the poem have their first meaning in signifying that event, just as the verse of Psalms had its first meaning in signifying the historical event of the Exodus.

And then, just as the event of the Exodus, being wrought by God, can give in turn a meaning, namely, our Redemption through Christ; so, in the event of this journey through the world beyond (an event which, as the poem sees it, is also wrought by God) we see the reflection of other meanings. These, in the poem, are the various reflections of man's journey to his proper end, not in the life after death, but here in this life, as that journey was conceived possible in Dante's day—and not only in Dante's day. The main allegory of the *Divine Comedy* is thus an allegory of action, of event, an event given by words which in its turn reflects (*in facto*) another event. Both are journeys to God.[12]

What, then, of the *Convivio*? Does not its 'allegory of poets' contradict this 'allegory of theologians' in the later work? It does, if a poet must always use one kind of allegory and may not try one in one work and one in another. But shall we not simply face this fact? And shall we not recognize that in this sense the *Convivio* contradicts not only the *Divine Comedy* in its allegory, but also the *Vita Nuova* where there is no allegory?[13] The *Convivio* is Dante's attempt to use the 'allegory of poets.' And to have that kind of allegory and the kind of figure that could have a role in it—to have a Lady Philosophy who was an allegory of poets—he was obliged to rob the 'donna pietosa' of the *Vita Nuova* of all real existence. And in doing this he contradicted the *Vita Nuova*.

The *Convivio* is a fragment. We do not know why Dante gave up the work before it was hardly under way. We do not know. We are, therefore, free to speculate. I venture to do so, and suggest that Dante abandoned the *Convivio* because he came to see that in choosing to build this work according to the allegory of poets, he had ventured down a false way; that he came to realize that a poet could not be a poet of rectitude and work with an allegory whose first meaning was a disembodied fiction.

St. Gregory, in the Proem to his Exposition of the Song of Songs, says: 'Allegoria enim animae longe a Deo positae quasi quamdam machinam facit ut per illam levetur ad Deum'[14] and the Letter to Can Grande declares that the end of the whole *Comedy* is 'to remove those living in this life from the state of misery and lead them to the state of felicity.' A poet of rectitude is one who is interested in directing the will of men to God. But a disembodied Lady Philosophy is not a *machina* which can bear the weight of lifting man to God because, in her, man finds no part of his own weight. Lady Philosophy did not, does not, will not, exist in the flesh. As she is constructed in the *Convivio* she comes to stand for Sapientia, for *created* Sapientia standing in analogy to uncreated Sapientia Which is the Word.[15] Even so, she is word without flesh. And only the word made flesh can lift man to God. If the allegory of a Christian poet of rectitude is to support any weight, it will be grounded in the flesh, which means grounded *in history*—and will lift up from there. In short, the trouble with Lady Philosophy was the trouble which Augustine found with the Platonists: 'But that the Word was made flesh and dwelt among us I did not read there.'[16]

Dante, then, abandons Lady Philosophy and returns to Beatrice. But now the way to God must be made open to all men: he constructs an allegory, a *machina*, that is, in which an historical Vergil, an historical Beatrice, and an historical Bernard replace that lady in an action which is given, in its first sense, not as a beautiful fiction but as a real, *historical* event, an event remembered by one who was, as a verse of the poem says, the scribe of it.[17] Historical and, by a Christian standard, beautiful[18] as an allegory because bearing within it the reflection of the true way to God in this life—a way given and supported by the Word made flesh. With its first meaning as an historical meaning, the allegory of the *Divine Comedy* is grounded in the mystery of the Incarnation.[19]

In his commentary on the poem written some half century after the poet's death, Benvenuto da Imola would seem to understand the allegory of the *Divine Comedy* to be the 'allegory of theologians.' To make clear to some doubting reader the concept by which Beatrice has a second meaning, he points to Rachel in Holy Scripture:

> Nec videatur tibi indignum, lector, quod Beatrix mulier carnea accipiatur a Dante pro sacra theologia. Nonne Rachel secundum historicam veritatem fuit pulcra uxor Jacob summe amata ab eo, pro qua habenda custodivit oves per XIIII annos, et tamen anagogice figurat vitam contemplativam, quam Jacob mirabiliter amavit, sicut autor ipse scribit Paradisi XXII capitulo, ubi describit contemplationem sub figura scalae. Et si dicis: non credo quod Beatrix vel Rachel sumantur unquam spiritualiter, dicam quod contra negantes principia non est amplius disputandam. Si enim vis intelligere opus istius autoris, oportet concedere quod ipse loquatur catholice tamquam perfectus christianus, et qui semper et ubique conatur ostendere se christianum.[20]

Dr. Edward Moore once pointed, in a footnote, to these remarks by the early commentator and smiled at them as words that throw 'a curious light on the logical processes of Benvenuto's mind.'[21] But Benvenuto's words have, I think, a way of smiling back. And to make their smile more apparent to a modern reader I would transpose them so:

> Let it not seem improper to you, reader, that this journey of a living man into the world beyond is presented to you in its first sense as literally and historically true. And if you say: 'I do not believe that Dante ever went to the other world,' then I say that with those who deny what a poem asks be granted, there is no further disputing.

# Notes

1. *Convivio,* II, i, 2–4, in the standard edition with commentary by G. Busnelli and G. Vandeli (Florence, 1934). Concerning the lacuna and the reasons for filling it as this has been done (words in brackets in the passage above) see their notes to the passage, Vol. I, pp. 96–97 and 240–242. The 'penultimo trattato' where Dante promises to explain the reason for the 'allegory of poets' was, alas, never written.

2. *Convivio,* II, i, 15: 'Io adunque, per queste ragioni, tuttavia sopra ciascuna canzone ragionerò prima la litterale sentenza, e appresso di quella ragionerò la sua allegoria, cioè la nascosa veritade; e talvolta de li altri sensi toccherò incidentemente, come a luogo e tempo si converrà.'

3. One recalls, of course, that Boccaccio and many others have preferred the *theologian.* On Dante as theologian one may now see E. R. Curtius, *Europäische Literatur und lateinische Mittelalter (*Bern, Switzerland, 1948), pp. 219 ff. To see the poet as *theologian* is to see him essentially as one who constructs an 'allegory of poets,' hiding under a veil the truths of theology—a view which has a long history in Dante interpretation.

4. By no means all commentators of the poem who discuss this matter have faced the necessity of making a choice between the two kinds of allegory distinguished by Dante. More often than not, even in a discussion of the two kinds, they have preferred to leave the matter vague as regards the *Divine Comedy*. See, for example, C. H. Grandgent's remarks on Dante's allegory in his edition of the poem (revised, 1933), pp. xxxii–xxxiii, where the choice is not made and where allegory and symbolism are lumped together.

5. This, to be sure, is only *one* of the several arguments that have been adduced in contesting the authenticity of the Letter; but whenever it has been used, it has been taken to bear considerable weight. The most violent attack on the authenticity of the Letter was made by D'Ovidio in an essay entitled *L'Epistola a Cangrande*, first published in the *Rivista d'Italia* in 1899 and reprinted in his *Studi sulla Divina Commedia* (1901), in which his remarks on the particular point in question may be taken as typical (*Studi*, pp. 462–463): 'Il vero guaio è che l'Epistola soffoca la distinzione tra il senso letterale meramente fittizio, poetico velo d'un concetto allegorico e il senso letterale vero in sè, storico, da cui però o scaturisce una moralità o è raffigurato un fatto soprannaturale. Dei tre efficacissimi esempi danteschi ne dimentica due (Orfeo e i tre Apostoli), e s'attacca al solo terzo, stiracchiandolo per farlo servire anche al senso morale e all'allegorico; nè riuscendo in effetto se non a modulare in tre diverse gradazioni un unico senso niente altro che anagogico. Non è nè palinodia nè plagio: è una parodia. La quale deriva da ciò che, oltre la precisa distinzione tomistica e dantesca del senso allegorico dal morale e dall'anagogico, era in corso la dottrina agostiniana che riduceva tutto alla sola allegoria. Dante ne fa cenno, dove, terminata la definizione del senso allegorico, prosegue: "Veramente li teologi questo senso prendono altrimenti che li poeti; ma perocchè mia intenzione è qui lo modo delli poeti seguitare, prenderò il senso allegorico secondo che per li poeti è usato." Nè, si badi, avrebbe avuto motivo di mutar intenzione, se si fosse posto a chiosar il Paradiso, che, se Dio vuole, *è poesia anch'esso.*' (italics mine)

It is worth noting in this respect that Dr. Edward Moore, in an essay entitled 'The

Genuineness of the Dedicatory Epistle to Can Grande' (*Studies in Dante*, Third Series, pp. 284–369) in which he undertook a very careful refutation, point by point, of D'Ovidio's arguments, either did not attribute any importance to the particular objection quoted above or did not see how it was to be met. For a review of the whole dispute, see G. Boffito, *L'Epistola di Dante Alighieri a Cangrande della Scala* in *Memorie della R. Acad. delle scienze di Torino*, Series II, vol. 57, of the *Classe di scienze morali*, etc., pp. 5–10.

6. *Opere di Dante* (ed. Società Dantestca Italiana, 1921), Epistola XIII, 20–25, pp. 438–439.

7. *Summa Theologica*, I, i, 10.

8. *De Trinitate*, XV, ix, 15 (*PL*, XLIII, 1068): 'non in verbis sed in facto.' On the distinction of the two kinds of allegory in Holy Scripture see *Dictionnaire de théologie catholique* (Vacant, Mangenot, Amann), t. i (1923), col. 833 ff. s.v. *Allégories bibliques*. On St. Thomas' distinctions in particular, consult R. P. P. Synave, *La Doctrine de s. Thomas d'Aquin sur le sens littéral des Écritures* in *Revue Biblique*, XXXV (1926), 40–65.

9. *Literal* and *historical* as synonymous terms for the first sense are bound to be puzzling to modern minds. In the discussion of allegory by St. Thomas and others we meet it at every turn. Perhaps no passage can better help us focus our eyes on this concept as they understood it than one in Hugh of St. Victor (cited by Synave, *op. cit.*, p. 43, from ch. 3 of Hugh's *De scriptoris et scripturibus sacris*): '*Historia* dicitur a verbo graeco ἱσγορεω historeo, quod est video et narro; propterea quod apud veteres nulli licebat scribere res gestas, nisi a se visas, ne falsitas admisceretur veritati peccato scriptoris, plus aut minus, aut aliter dicentis. Secundum hoc proprie et districte dicitur historia; sed solet largius accipi ut dicatur historia sensus qui primo loco ex significatione verborum habetur ad res.'

10. It may be well to recall on this point that, in St. Thomas' view and that of others, a parable told by Christ has only *one* sense, namely that *in verbis*. This is true of the Song of Songs, also, and of other parts of Scripture. But in such passages there is no allegory, because there is no *other* meaning *in facto*, i.e., no historical facts are pointed to by the words.

11. Michele Barbi sounded a warning on this matter some years ago, but in so doing appealed to a solution (the poem as *vision*, as *apocalypse*, which needs, I think, further clarification: ' . . . Io ho un giorno, durante il positivismo che s'era insinuato nella critica dantesca, richiamato gli studiosi a non trascurare una ricerca così importante come quella del simbolismo nella Divina Commedia: oggi sento il dovere di correre alla difesa del senso letterale, svilito come azione fittizia, come bella menzogna, quasi che nell'intendimento di Dante l'importanza del suo poema non consista già in quello che egli ha rappresentato nella lettera di esso, ma debba andarsi a cercare in concetti e intendimenti nascosti sotto quella rappresentazione. Non snaturiamo per carità l'opera di Dante: è una rivelazione, non già un'allegoria da capo a fondo. La lettera non è in funzione soltanto di riposti intendimenti, non è bella menzogna: quel viaggio ch'essa descrive è un viaggio voluto da Dio perchè Dante riveli in salute degli uomini quello che ode e vede nel fatale andare.' (*Studi danteschi*, I, 12–13.) This is all very well and very much to the point. But the problem which Barbi does not deal with here and which calls for solution is how, on what *conceptual* basis, is an *allegory* given in a poem in which the first meaning is not a 'bella menzogna'—the question, in short, which the present paper is trying to answer.

12. It is essential to remember that I am concerned throughout this paper with the main allegory of the *Divine Comedy*; otherwise this can appear an oversimplification to any reader familiar with the concrete detail of the poem, and certainly many questions concerning that detail will arise which are not dealt with here. How, for example, are we to explain those passages where the poet urges the reader to look 'beneath the veil' for a hidden meaning (*Inferno,* IX, 62; *Purgatorio,* VIII, 19–21)? Do these not point to an 'allegory of poets'? I believe that the correct answer can be given in the negative. But, however that may be, we do not meet the main allegory of the poem in such passages.

Likewise, finer distinctions in the allegory of the poem will recognize that the allegory of the opening situation (*Inferno,* I, II) must be distinguished from the main allegory of the poem, and of necessity, since at the beginning the protagonist is still in this life and has not yet begun to move through the world beyond. For some considerations on this point see the author's article in *RR,* XXXIX (1948), 269–277: 'Sulla fiumana ove'l mar non ha vanto: *Inferno* II, 108.'

13. For a discussion of the absence of allegory in the *Vita Nuova* see the author's *Essay on the Vita Nuova* (Cambridge: Harvard University Press, 1948), pp. 110 ff. and *passim*.

14. *PL,* LXXIX, 473. In interpreting the Song of Songs, St. Gregory is not speaking of the kind of allegory which has an *historical* meaning as its first meaning (see n. 10 above)—which fact does not make his view of the *use* of allegory any less interesting or suggestive with respect to Dante's use of it.

15. On *created wisdom* and the distinction here see Augustine, *Confessions,* XII, XV.

16. *Confessions,* VII, 9.

17. *Paradiso,* X, 22–27:

> Or ti riman, lettor, sovra'l tuo banco,
> dietro pensando a ciò che si preliba,
> s'esser vuoi lieto assai prima che stanco.
>
> Messo t'ho innanzi: omai per te ti ciba;
> chè a sè torce tutta la mia cura
> quella matera ond'io son fatto scriba.

As every reader of the *Commedia* knows, a poet's voice speaks out frequently in the poem, and most effectively, in various contexts. But these verses may remind us that when the poet does come into the poem, he speaks as *scribe*, as one remembering and trying to give an adequate account of the event which is now past.

18. Cf. Menendez y Pelayo, *Historia de las ideas estéticas en España*, ch. V, Introduction: 'No vino a enseñar estética ni otra ciencia humana el Verbo Encarnado; pero presentò en su persona y en la union de sus dos naturalezas el protótipo más alto de la hermosura, y el objeto más adecuado del amor. . . .'

19. Those who refuse to recognize this 'mystery' in the allegory of the *Divine Comedy,*' who view it instead as the usual 'allegory of poets' in which the first meaning is a fiction, are guilty of a *reader's* error comparable in some way to the error of the Manicheans concerning the Incarnation, as set forth by St. Thomas in the *Summa contra Gentiles,* IV, XXIX: 'They pretended that whatever He did as man—for instance, that He was born, that He ate, drank, walked, suffered, and was buried—was all unreal,

though having some semblance of reality. Consequently they reduced the whole mystery of the Incarnation to a work of fiction.'

20. *Comentum* (Florence, 1887), I, 89–90.

21. *Studies in Dante* (*Second Series*, 1889), p. 86, n. 1.

# Allen Tate

## The Symbolic Imagination

### *The Mirrors of Dante*

IT IS RIGHT even if it is not quite proper to observe at the beginning of a discourse on Dante, that no writer has held in mind at one time the whole of *The Divine Comedy*: not even Dante, perhaps least of all Dante himself. If Dante and his Dantisti have not been equal to the view of the whole, a view shorter than theirs must be expected of the amateur who, as a writer of verses, vainly seeks absolution from the mortal sin of using poets for what he can get out of them. I expect to look at a single image in the *Paradiso*, and to glance at some of its configurations with other images. I mean the imagery of light, but I mean chiefly its reflections. It was scarcely necessary for Dante to have read, though he did read, the *De Anima*, to learn that sight is the king of the senses and that the human body, which like other organisms lives by *touch*, may be made actual in language only through the imitation of *sight*. And sight in language is imitated not by means of "description"—*ut pictura poesis*—but by doubling the image: our confidence in its spatial reality is won quite simply by casting the image upon a glass, or otherwise by the insinuation of space between.

I cannot undertake to examine here Dante's double imagery in all its detail, for his light alone could lead us into complexities as rich as life itself. I had almost said richer than life, if by life we mean (as we must mean) what we ourselves are able daily to see, or even what certain writers have seen, with the exception of Shakespeare, and possibly of Sophocles and Henry James. A secondary purpose that I shall have in view will be to consider the dramatic implications of the light imagery as they emerge at the resolution of the poem, in Canto XXXIII of the *Paradiso*. These implications suggest, to my mind, a radical change in the interpretation of *The Divine Comedy*, and impel me to ask again: What kind of poem is it? In asking this question I shall not be concerned with what we ordinarily consider to be literary criticism; I shall be only incidentally judging, for my main purpose is to describe.

In *Purgatorio* XXX Beatrice appears to Dante first as a voice (what she says need not detain us here), then as light; but not yet the purest light. She is the light of a pair of eyes in which is reflected the image of the gryphon, a symbol of the hypostatic union, of which she herself is a "type." But before Dante perceives this image in her eyes, he says: "A thousand desires hotter than flame held my eyes bound to the shining eyes. . . ."[1] I see no reason to suppose that Dante does not mean what he says. *Mille disiri piû che fiamma caldi* I take to be the desires, however interfused by this time with courtly and mystical associations, of a man for a woman: the desires that the boy Dante felt for the girl Beatrice in 1274 after he had passed her in a street of Florence. She is the same Beatrice, Dante the same Dante, with differences which do not reject but rather include their sameness. Three dancing girls appear: Dante's allegory, formidable as it is, intensifies rather than impoverishes the reality of the dancers as girls. Their dance is a real dance, their song, in which they make a charming request of Beatrice, is a real song. If Dante expected us to be interested in the dancers only as the Theological Virtues, I see no good reason why he made them girls at all. They are sufficiently convincing as the Three Graces, and I cannot feel in the pun a serious violation of Dante's confidence. The request of the girls is sufficiently remarkable: *Volgi, Beatrice, volgi gli occhi santi*—"Turn, Beatrice, turn those holy eyes." Let Dante see your holy eyes; look into his eyes. Is it extravagant to substitute for the image of the gryphon the image of Dante in Beatrice's eyes? I think not. *He is in her eyes*—as later, in *Paradiso* XXXIII, he will be "in" God. Then a startling second request by the dancers: "Of thy grace do us the favor that thou unveil thy mouth to him"—*disvele / a lui la bocca tua*. . . "that he may discern the second beauty which thou hidest"—*la seconda belleza che tu cele*. At this point we get one of the innumerable proofs of Dante's greatness as a poet. We are not shown *la seconda belleza*, the smiling mouth; we are shown, instead, in the first four *terzine* of the next canto, the effect on Dante. For neither Dante nor Homer *describes* his heroine. As Beatrice's mouth is revealed, all Dante's senses but the sense of sight are *tutti spenti*; and sight itself is caught in *l'antica rete*—"the ancient net"—a variation of *l'antica fiamma*—"the ancient flame"—that he had felt again when he had first seen Beatrice in the Earthly Paradise.

What the net is doing here seems now to me plain, after some ten years of obtuseness about it. The general meaning is, as Charles Williams holds, that Dante, having chosen the Way of Affirmation through the physical image, feels here in the Earthly Paradise all that he had *felt* before, along with what he now *knows*. Why did he put the worldly emotion of his youthful life into the figure of the net? It is not demanded by the moment; we should not have the sense of missing something if it were not there. If it is a simple metaphor for the obfuscation of sensuality, it is not a powerful metaphor; we must remember that Dante uses very few linguistic metaphors, as distinguished from analogical or symbolic objects; when he uses them they are simple and powerful. The net, as I see it, is not simply a metaphor for the "catching" of Dante by Beatrice in 1274, though it is partly *that* ancient net; it is also a net of even more famous antiquity, that in which Venus caught Mars; and it is thus a symbolic object. Moreover, if Beatrice's eyes are univocally divine, why do the three Theological Dancers reproach him with gazing at her "too fixedly"—*troppo fiso*—as if he or anybody else could get too much of the divine light? He is, of course, not yet ready for the full Beatific Vision. But an astonishing feature of the great scene of the divine pageant is that, as a trope, a subjective effect, the smile of Beatrice simultaneously revives his human love (Eros) and directs his will to the anticipation of the Beatific Vision (Agapé): both equally, by means of the action indicated by the blinding effect of both; he is blinded by the net and by the light, not alternately but at one instant.[2]

To bring together various meanings at a single moment of action is to exercise what I shall speak of here as the symbolic imagination; but the line of *action* must be unmistakable, we must never be in doubt about what is happening; for at a given stage of his progress the hero does one simple thing, and one only. The symbolic imagination conducts an action through analogy, of the human to the divine, of the natural to the supernatural, of the low to the high, of time to eternity. My literary generation was deeply impressed by Baudelaire's sonnet *Correspondances*, which restated the doctrines of medieval symbolism by way of Swedenborg; we were impressed because we had lost the historical perspective leading back to the original source. But the statement of a doctrine is very different from its possession as experience in poetry. Analogical symbolism need not move towards an act of imagination. It may see in active experience the qualities necessary for static symbolism; for example, the Grave of Jesus, which for the theologian may be a symbol to be expounded in the Illuminative Way, or for the mystic may be an object of contemplation in the Unitive Way. Despite the timeless orders of both rational discourse and intuitive contemplation, it is the business of the symbolic poet to return to the order of temporal sequence—to *action*. His purpose is to show men experiencing whatever they may be capable of, with as much meaning as he may be able to see in it; but the action comes first.

Shall we call this the Poetic Way? It is at any rate the way of the poet, who has got to do his work with the body of this world, whatever that body may look like to him, in his time and place—the whirling atoms, the body of a beautiful woman, or a deformed body, or the body of Christ, or even the body of this death. If the poet is able to put into this moving body, or to find in it, a coherent chain of analogies, he will inform an intuitive act with symbolism; his will be in one degree or another the symbolic imagination.

Before I try to illustrate these general reflections, I must make a digression, for my own guidance, which I am not competent to develop as searchingly as my subject demands. The symbolic imagination takes rise from a definite limitation of human rationality which was recognized in the West until the seventeenth century; in this view the intellect cannot have direct knowledge of essences. The only created mind that has this knowledge is the angelic mind.[3] If we do not believe in angels we shall have to invent them in order to explain by parable the remarkable appearance, in Europe, at about the end of the sixteenth century, of a mentality which denied man's commitment to the physical world, and set itself up in quasi-divine independence. This mind has intellect and will without feeling; and it is through feeling alone that we witness the glory of our servitude to the natural world, to St. Thomas' accidents, or, if you will, to Locke's secondary qualities; it is our tie with the world of sense. The angelic mind suffers none of the limitations of sense; it has immediate knowledge of essences; and this knowledge moves through the perfect will to divine love, with which it is at one. Imagination in an angel is thus inconceivable, for the angelic mind transcends the mediation of both image and discourse. I call that human imagination angelic which tries to disintegrate or to circumvent the image in the illusory pursuit of essence. When human beings undertake this ambitious program, divine love becomes so rarefied that it loses its human paradigm, and is dissolved in the worship of intellectual power, the surrogate of divinity that worships itself. It professes to know nature as essence at the same time that it has become alienated from nature in the rejection of its material forms.

> It was, however high the phrases, the common thing from which Dante always started, as it was certainly the greatest and most common to which he came. His images were the natural inevitable images—the girl in the street, the people he knew, the language he learned as a child. In them the great diagrams were perceived; from them the great myths open; by them he understands the final end.[4]

This is the simple secret of Dante, but it is a secret which is not necessarily available to the Christian poet today. The Catholic faith has not changed since Dante's time. But the Catholic sensibility, as we see it in modern Catholic poetry, from Thompson to Lowell, has become angelic, and is not distinguishable (doctrinal differences aside) from poetry by Anglicans, Methodists, Presbyterians, and atheists. I take it that more than doctrine, even if the doctrine be true, is necessary for a great poetry of action. Catholic poets have lost, along with their heretical friends, the power to start with the "common thing": they have lost the gift for concrete experience. The abstraction of the modern mind has obscured their way into the natural order. Nature offers to the symbolic poet clearly denotable objects in depth and in the round, which yield the analogies to the higher syntheses. The modern poet rejects the higher synthesis, or tosses it in a vacuum of abstraction.[5] If he looks at nature he spreads the clear visual image in a complex of metaphor, from one katachresis to another through Aristotle's permutations of genus and species. He cannot sustain the prolonged analogy, the second and superior kind of figure that Aristotle doubtless had in mind when he spoke of metaphor as the key to the resemblances of things, and the mark of genius.

That the gift of analogy was not Dante's alone every medievalist knows. The most striking proof of its diffusion and the most useful example for my purpose that I know, is the letter of St. Catherine of Siena to Brother Raimondo of Capua. A young Sienese, Niccolo Tuldo, had been unjustly convicted of treason and condemned to death. Catherine became his angel of mercy, giving him daily solace—the meaning of the Cross, the healing powers of the Blood; and so reconciled him to the faith that he accepted his last end. Now I have difficulty believing people who say that they live in the Blood of Christ, for I take them to mean that they have the faith and hope some day to live in it. The evidence of the Blood is one's power to produce it, the power to show it as a "common thing" and to make it real, literally, in action. For the report of the Blood is very different from its reality. St. Catherine does not report it; she recreates it, so that its analogical meaning is confirmed again in blood that she has seen. This is how she does it:

> Then [the condemned man] came, like a gentle lamb; and seeing me he began to smile, and wanted me to make the sign of the Cross. When he had received the sign, I said, "Down! To the bridal, my sweetest brother. For soon shalt thou be in the enduring life." He prostrated himself with great gentleness, and I stretched out his neck; and bowed me down, and recalled to him the Blood of the Lamb. His lips said

> naught save Jesus! and Catherine! And so saying, I received his head in my hands, closing my eyes in the divine goodness and saying, "I will."

> When he was at rest my soul rested in peace and quiet, and in so great fragrance of blood that I could not bear to remove the blood which had fallen on me from him.

It is deeply shocking, as all proximate incarnations of the Word are shocking, whether in Christ and the Saints, or in Dostoevsky, James Joyce, or Henry James. I believe it was T. S. Eliot who made accessible again to an ignorant generation a common Christian insight, when he said that people cannot bear very much reality. I take this to mean that only persons of extraordinary courage, and perhaps even genius, can face the spiritual truth in its physical body. Flaubert said that the artist, the soldier, and the priest face death every day; so do we all; yet it is perhaps nearer to them than to other men; it is their particular responsibility. When St. Catherine "rests in so great fragrance of blood," it is no doubt the Blood of the Offertory which the celebrant offers to God *cum odore suavitatis*, but with the literal odor of the species of wine, not of blood. St. Catherine had the courage of genius which permitted her to *smell* the Blood of Christ in Niccolo Tuldo's blood clotted on her dress: she smelled the two bloods *not alternately but at one instant*, in a single act compounded of spiritual insight and physical perception.

Chekhov said that a gun hanging on the wall at the beginning of a story has got to be fired off before the story ends: everything in potency awaits its completed purpose in act. If this is a metaphysical principle, it is also the prime necessity of the creative imagination. Is not St. Catherine telling us that the Blood of Christ must be perpetually recreated as a brute fact? If the gun has got to be fired, the Blood has got to be shed, if only because that is the first condition of its appearance; it must move towards the condition of human action, where we may smell it, touch it, and taste it again.

When ecclesiastical censorship of this deep insight in the laity exceeds a just critical prudence, the result is not merely obscurantism in the arts; it is perhaps a covert rejection of the daily renewal of the religious life. Twenty-five years ago the late W. B. Yeats had a controversy with the Irish bishops about the famous medieval "Cherry Tree Carol," which the hierarchy wished to suppress as blasphemous. The Blessed Virgin is resting under a cherry tree, too tired to reach up and pluck a cherry. Since Christ lives from the foundations of the world, He is omnipotent in the womb, and He commands the tree to lower a bough for His Mother's convenience; which it obligingly does, since it cannot do otherwise. Here again the gun is fired and the Blood is shed. If the modern Church has lost the historic experience of this kind of symbolism, which is more tolerable, I believe, in the Latin countries than with us, it is at least partial evidence that the Church has lost the great culture that it created, and that at intervals has created the life of the Church.

I return from this digression to repeat that Dante was the great master of the symbolism, the meaning of which I have been trying to suggest. But the symbolic "problem" of *The Divine Comedy* we must not suppose Dante to have undertaken analytically; it is our problem, not his. Dr. Flanders Dunbar has stated it with great penetration:

> As with his progress he perceives more and more of ultimate reality through the symbol [Beatrice], at the same time the symbol occupies less and less of his attention, until ultimately it takes its place among all created things on a petal of the rose, while he gazes beyond it into the full glory of the sun.[6]

The symbolic problem, then, is: How shall Dante move step by step (literally and allegorically) from the Dark Wood, the negation of light, to the "three circles, of three colors and one magnitude," God Himself, or pure light, where there are no sensible forms to reflect it? There can be no symbol for God, for that which has itself informed step by step the symbolic progress. Vision, giving us clear visual objects, through physical sight, moving steadily upward towards its anagogical transfiguration, is the first matrix of the vast analogical structure. As Dante sees more he sees less: as he sees more light the nearer he comes to its source, the less he sees of what it had previously lit up. In the Empyrean, at the climax of the Illuminative Way, Beatrice leaves Dante and takes her place in the Rose; St. Bernard now guides him into the Intuitive Way.

For the Illuminative Way is the way to knowledge through the senses, by means of aided reason, but here the "distance" between us and what we see is always the distance between a concept and its object, between the human situation in which the concept arises and the realization of its full meaning. Put otherwise, with the beginning of the *Vita Nuova* in mind, it is the distance between the knowledge of love, which resulted from the earthly love of Dante for Beatrice, and the distant "object," or God, that had made the love in the first place possible: the distance between Beatrice and the light which had made it possible for him to see her. The Kantian synthetic proposition of the entire poem, as we enter it through the symbolism of light, is: Light is Beatrice. Here the eye is still on the human image; it is still on it up to the moment when she takes her place with the other saints in the Rose, where she is only one of many who turn their eyes to the "eternal fountain." Light is Beatrice; light is her *smile*; her final smile, which Dante sees as she enters the Rose, is no longer the mere predicate of a sentence, for there is now no distance between the smile and what had lit it. Although, insofar as it is a smile at all, it is still the smile at the unveiling of the mouth, it is now the smile without the mouth, the smile of light. And thus we arrive at the converse of the proposition: Beatrice is light. Now Dante's eye is on the light itself, but he cannot see it because Beatrice, through whose image he had progressively seen more light, has disappeared; and he can see nothing. There is nothing to *see*. For that which enables sight is not an object of vision. What has been seen is, in what is surely one of the greatest passages of all poetry, "the shadowy prefaces of their truth." Illumination, or intellect guided by divine grace, powerful as it is, halts at the "prefaces." But the Unitive Way leads to the Presence, where both sight and discursive thought cease.

Whether Dante should have tried to give us an image of God, of that which is without image and invisible, is an unanswerable question. Is it possible that we have here a break in the symbolic structure, which up to the end of the poem has been committed to the visible? At the end we are with Love, whose unpredicated attribute is the entire universe. Has Dante given us, in the "three circles, of three colors and one magnitude," merely the trinitarian and doctrinal equivalent of the ultimate experience, instead of an objective symbol of the experience itself? In the terms of Dante's given structure, such a symbol was perhaps not possible; and strictly speaking it is never possible. If he was going to give us anything he doubtless had to give us just what he gave; he gave it in an act of great artistic heroism. For in the center of the circles he sees the image of man. This is the risk, magnified almost beyond conception, of St. Catherine: the return of the supra-rational and supra-sensible to the "common thing." It is the courage to see again, even in its ultimate cause, the Incarnation.

If we will look closely at the last four lines of the *Paradiso*, and double back on our tracks, I believe that we will see that there is no break in the *dramatic* structure—the structure of the action.[7] For the poem is an action: a man is acting and going somewhere, and things are happening both to him and around him; otherwise the poem would be—what I may have given the impression of its being—a symbolic machine. In the space of an essay

I cannot prepare properly the background of the suggestion that I am about to offer. For one thing, we should have to decide who "Dante" is, and where he is in the action that he has depicted—questions that nobody seems to know much about. For what it may be worth, I suggest that the poet has undertaken to involve a fictional character named Dante—at once the poet and not the poet of that name—in a certain action of the greatest possible magnitude, the issue of which is nothing less, perhaps something greater, than life or death. In this action the hero fails. He fails in the sense that he will have to start over again when he steps out of the "poem," as he surely must do if he is going to write it.

Thus I see *The Divine Comedy* as essentially dramatic and, in one of its modes, tragic. Are we to suppose that the hero actually attained to the Beatific Vision? No; for nobody who had would be so foolish as to write a poem about it, if in that spiritual perfection it could even occur to him to do so. The poem is a vast paradigm of the possibility of the Beatific Vision. No more than its possibility for the individual person, for "Dante" himself, is here entertained. What shall we make of his failure of memory, the slipping away of the final image, which he calls *tanto oltraggio*—"so great an outrage"? It would be a nice question to decide whether something had slipped away, or whether it had ever been fully there. The vision is imagined, it is *imaged*; its essence is not possessed. I confess that it is not an argument from the poem to say that had Dante claimed its possession, he would have lost that "good of the intellect" which we forfeit when we presume to angelic knowledge; and it was through the good of the intellect that he was able to write the poem. But it is an external argument that I believe cannot be entirely ignored.

The last *terzina* of the last canto tells us: *All' alta fantasia qui mancò possa*—"To the high fantasy here power failed." What power failed? The power to write the poem, or the power to possess as experience the divine essence? Is it a literary or a religious failure? It is obviously and honorably both. It makes no more sense to say Dante achieved his final vision as direct experience than to say that Sophocles married his mother and put out his own eyes; that the experience of the *Oedipus Rex* represents the personal experience of Sophocles. What Dante achieved is an *actual* insight into the great dilemma, eternal life or eternal death, but he has not hedged the dilemma like a bet to warrant himself a favorable issue. As the poem closes, he still faces it, like the rest of us. Like Oedipus, the fictional Dante learns in humility a certain discipline of the will: we may equate up to a point the dark-blindness of Oedipus and the final light-blindness of Dante; both men have succeeded through suffering in blinding themselves to knowledge-through-sense, in the submission of *hybris* to a higher will.[8] The fictional Dante at the end steps out of the frame and becomes again the historical Dante; Oedipus steps out of his frame, his fictional plot is done, he is back in the world of unformed action, blind and, like Dante, an exile. Shall Oedipus be saved? Shall Dante? We do not know, but to ask the question is to point to a primary consideration in the interpretation of *The Divine Comedy*, particularly if we are disposed, as some commentators have been, to believe that Dante the man used his poem arrogantly to predict his own salvation.

If Dante does not wholly succeed in giving us in the "three circles, of three colors and one magnitude," an image of the Godhead, I think we are ready to see that it was not necessary; it was not a part of his purpose. Such an image is not the "final cause" of the poem. The poem is an action; it is an action to the end. For the image that Dante gives us of the Godhead is not an image to be received by the reader as essential knowledge in his own "angelic" intelligence, as an absolute apart from the action. It is a dramatic image; the image is of the action and the action is Dante's. To read Canto XXXIII in any other way would be perhaps to commit the blunder that M. Gilson warns us against: the blunder of thinking that Dante was writing a super-philosophical tract, or a pious embellishment of the doctrines of Thomas Aquinas, instead of a poem. The question, then, is not what is the right anagogical symbol for God; it is rather what symbol for God will serve tropologically (that is, morally and dramatically) for the tragic insight of the poet who knows, through the stages of the Three Ways, that the Beatific Vision is possible but uncertain of realization. Dante sees himself, Man, in the Triune Circles, and he is in the Seraphic Heaven of Love. But at the end desire and will are like a "wheel moving equally"; motion imparted to it at one point turns it as a whole, but it has to be moved, as the wheel of our own deire and will must be moved, by a force outside it. The wheel is Dante's last symbol of the great failure. Since it must be moved, it is not yet at one, not yet in unity, with the divine will; it obeys it, as those other wheels, the sun and stars, moved by love, obey.

I take it that the wheel is the final geometrical projection of the *visual* matrix of analogy; it is what the eye sees, the material form, and what in its anagoge it eventually aspires to become. We must remember that Beatrice's eyes are spheres, no less than the physical universe itself, which is composed of concentric spheres. The first circles that Dante shows us are in Canto III of the *Inferno*, Charon's—"for round his eyes were wheels of flame." The last, the Triune Circles, are the anagoge of the visual circle, and are without extension; they are pure light, the abstraction or sublimation of flame. Flame burning in a circle and light lighting up in a circle, and what it encloses, are the prime sensible symbols of the poem. Only Satan, at the geometrical center of the world, occupies a point that cannot be located on any existing arc of the cosmos. This is the spherical (or circular) expression of Satan's absolute privation of light-as-love which in the Empyrean turns the will-wheel of Dante with the cosmic spheres. These are the will of God as love; and if we ignore the dramatic structure, and fail to look closely at the symbolic, we shall conclude that Dante is at one with the purpose of the universe. But, as we have seen, the symbolic structure is complicated by the action, and in the end the action prevails. That is to say, Dante is *still moving*. Everything that moves, says Dante the Thomist in his letter to Can Grande, has some imperfection in it because it is, in the inverse degree of its rate of motion, removed from the Unmoved Mover, the Triune Circles, God. By a twist of this argument, which, of course, as I shall presently indicate, is specious, Satan himself has no imperfection: he too lies immobile—except for the fanning wings that freeze the immobile damned in Giudecca—as the Still Point in the Triune Circles is immobile. If Dante's will is turning like a wheel, he is neither damned nor saved; he is morally active in the universal human predicament. His participation in the love imparted as motion to the universe draws him towards the Triune Circles and to the immobility of peace at the center, as it draws all creatures; but a defection of the will could plunge him into the other "center."

Now Dante is astonished when he sees in the Primum Mobile a reversal of the ratio of speed of the spheres as he had observed it on earth, through the senses. "But in the universe of sense," he says to Beatrice, "we may see the circlings more divine as from the center they are more removed." In the spiritual universe the circlings are more divine the nearer they are to the center. It is a matter of perspective; from the earth outward the revolutions of the spheres are increasingly rapid up to the ninth, the Primum Mobile, whose speed is just short of infinite; the Primum Mobile is trying to achieve with all points of its surface a simultaneous contact with the Still Point of the Empyrean. What he sees in the Primum Mobile is this perspective visually reversed; istead of being the outer "crust" of the universe, the Primum Mobile is actually next to the central Still Point, whirling with inconceivable speed. God, the Still Point, is a nonspatial entity which is *everywhere* and *nowhere*. The Ptolemaic cosmos, which had been Christianized by the imposition of the angelic hierarchy of Dionysius, has been, in a way not to be completely visualized, turned inside out. The spheres, which began their career as an astronomical hypothesis, are now no longer necessary; they are replaced in the ultimate reality by nine nonspatial gradations of angelic intelligence, in three triads, the last and ninth circle of "fire" being that of the simple angels, the "farthest" removed in the nonspatial continuum from the Divine Love.

Where then is the earth, with Satan at its exact center? I think we must answer: Where it has always been. But "where" that is we had better not try to say. At any rate neither Satan nor the earth is at the spiritual center. His immobility thus has no perfection. In the full spiritual reality, of which the center of the material universe becomes an outermost "rind," beyond space, Satan does not exist: he exists in the world of sense and in the human will. The darkness of hell, from the point of view of God (if I may be allowed the expression), is not an inner darkness, but an outer. So, in the progress from hell to the Empyrean, Dante has come from the inner darkness of man to the inner light of God; from the outer darkness of God to the outer light of man.

This anagogical conversion of symbol that I have been trying to follow in one of its threads is nowhere by Dante merely *asserted*; it is constantly moving, rendered moment by moment as *action*. Like most good poets, great or minor, Dante wrote better than he had meant to do; for if we took him at his word, in the letter to Can Grande, we should conclude that the *Paradiso* is a work of rhetoric calculated "to remove those living in this life from a state of misery and to guide them to a state of happiness." It seems probable that persons now enrolled among the Blessed got there without being compelled to see on the way all that Dante saw. Were we reading the poem for that kind of instruction, and knew not where else to find it, we might conclude that Dante's *luce intellectual*, with its transformations in the fourfold system of interpretation, is too great a price to pay even for salvation; or, at any rate, for most of us, the wrong price. It would perhaps be a mistake for a man to decide that he has become a Christian at the instance of Dante, unless he is prepared to see all that Dante saw—which is one thing, but always seen in at least two ways.

A clue to two of the ways is the mirror symbol. As we approach it, the kind of warning that Dante at intervals pauses to give us is not out of place. For if the way up to now has been rough, we may expect it from now on to be even rougher. The number of persons, objects, and places in *The Divine Comedy* that are reflections, replicas, or manifestations of things more remote is beyond calculation. The entire natural world is a replica *in reverse* of the supernatural world. That, I believe, we have seen so far only on the dubious authority of my own assertion. But if Dante is a poet (I agree with M. Gilson that he is) he will not be satisfied with assertion as such, even with the authority of the Church to support it. The single authority of poetry is a difficult criterion of actuality that must always remain beyond our reach. And in some sense of this actuality Dante has got to place his vast two-way analogy (heaven like the world, the world like heaven) on the scene of action, and make it move. Let us take the stance of Dante at the beginning of *Paradiso* XXVIII, and try to suggest some of the ways in which he moves it:

> as in the mirror a taper's flame, kindled behind a man, is seen by him before it be in his sight or thought,
>
> as he turns back to see whether the glass speak truth to him, and sees that it accords with it as song-words to the music;
>
> so my memory recalls that I did turn, gazing upon the lovely eyes whence love had made the noose to capture me;
>
> and when I turned, and my own eyes were struck by what appears in that orb whenever upon its circling the eye is well fixed,
>
> a point I saw which rayed forth light so keen that all the vision that it flames upon must close because of its sharp point.

(One observes in passing that even in the Primum Mobile Beatrice bears the net-noose dimension of meaning.) Beatrice's eyes are a mirror in which is reflected that "sharp point," to which Dante, still at a distance from it, now turns his direct gaze. As he looks at it he sees for the first time what its reflection in Beatrice's eyes could not convey: that it is the sensible world turned inside out. For the sensible world as well as her eyes is only a reflection of the light from the sharp point. Now he is looking at the thing-in-itself. *He has at last turned away from the mirror which is the world.* What happens when we turn away from a mirror to look directly at the object which we saw reflected? I must anticipate Beatrice's famous experiment with one of my own. If you will place upon a table a box open at one end, the open end towards a mirror, and then look into the mirror, your will see the open end. Turn from the mirror and look at the box itself. You still see the open end, and thus you see the object *reversed*. If the box were reproduced, in the sense of being continued or moved *into* the mirror, the actual box would present, when we turn to it, a closed end; for the box and its reflection would show their respectively corresponding sides in congruent projection. Quantitative visualization of the cosmic reversal is not completely possible. But through the mirror analogy Dante performs a stupendous feat of the imagination that in kind has probably not been rivalled by any other poet. And it is an analogy that has been firmly grounded in action.

In conclusion I shall try to point to its literal base; for we have seen it, in *Paradiso* XXVIII, only as a simile; and if we had not had it laid down earlier as a physical fact to which we must assent, a self-contained phenomenon of the natural order, it would no doubt lack at the end that fullness of actuality which we do not wholly understand, but which we require of poetry. The self-contained fact of the natural order is established in Canto II of the *Paradiso*, where Beatrice performs a physical experiment. Some scholars have been moved by it to admire Dante for this single ray of positivistic enlightenment feebly glowing in the mind of a medieval poet. So far as I know, our critics have not considered it necessary to be sufficiently unenlightened to see that Beatrice's experiment is merely poetry.

Before I reproduce it I shall exhibit a few more examples of the mirror symbol that appear at intervals in the five last cantos. In Canto XXIX, 25–27, form permeates matter "as in glass . . . a ray so glows that from its coming to its pervading all, there is no interval." Still in XXIX, 142–145, at the end: "See now the height and breadth of the eternal worth, since it has made itself so many mirrors in which it is reflected, remaining in itself one as before." At line 37 of Canto XXX we enter the Empyrean where Dante sees the great River of Light "issuing its living sparks"; it too is a mirror, for Beatrice explains: "The river and the topaz gems that enter and go forth, and the smiling grasses are prefaces of their truth" (i.e., of what they reflect). In Canto XXX, 85–87, Dante bends down to the waves "to make mirrors of my eyes"; and again in XXX he sees the Rose of Paradise, another mirror, in one of his great similes:

> And as a hillside reflects itself in water at its foot, as if to look upon its own adornment, when it is rich in grasses and in flowers,

so, mounting in the light, around, around, casting reflection in
more than a thousand ranks I saw all that of us have won
return up yonder.

And finally the climactic reflection, the "telic principle" and the archetype of them all, in Canto XXX, 127–132:

The circling that in thee [in the Triune God] appeared to be
conceived as a reflected light, by my eyes scanned a little,

in itself, of its own color, seemed to be painted with our effigy,
and thereat my sight was all committed to it.

Where have these mirrors, which do their poetic work, the work of making the supra-sensible visible—one of the tasks of all poetry—where have they come from? The remote frame is doubtless the circular or spherical shape of the Ptolemaic cosmos;[9] but if there is glass in the circular frame, it reflects nothing until Virgil has left Dante to Beatrice's guidance in the Earthly Paradise (*Purgatorio* XXXI); where we have already glanced at the unveiling of mouth and eyes. I suggest that Beatrice's eyes in *Purgatorio* XXXI are the first mirror. But the image is not, at this early stage of Beatrice, sufficiently developed to bear all the strain of analogical weight that Dante intends to put upon it. For that purpose the mirror must be established as a literal mirror, a plain mirror, a "common thing."

He not only begins with the common thing; he continues with it, until at the end we come by disarming stages to a scene that no man has ever looked upon before. Every detail of Paradise is a common thing; it is the cumulative combination and recombination of natural objects beyond their "natural" relations, which staggers the imagination. "Not," says Beatrice to Dante, "that such things are in themselves harsh; but on your side is the defect, in that your sight is not yet raised so high."

A mirror is an artifact of the practical intellect, and as such can be explained by natural law: but there is no natural law which explains man as a mirror reflecting the image of God. The great leap is made in the interval between Canto II and Canto XXXIII of the *Paradiso*.

Dante, in Canto II, is baffled by the spots on the moon, supposing them to be due to alternating density and rarity of matter. No, says Beatrice in effect, this would be monism, a materialistic explanation of the diffusion of the divine light. The true explanation is very different: all saved souls are equally saved, and all the heavenly spheres are equally in heaven; but the divine light reaches the remoter spheres and souls according to the spiritual gifts of which they were capable in the natural world. "This is the formal principle," Beatrice says, summing up, "which produces, in conformity to the excellence of the object, the turbid and the clear."

Meanwhile she has asked Dante to consider a physical experiment to illustrate the unequal reception of the divine substance. Take three mirrors, she says, and set two of them side by side, and a third in the middle but farther back. Place a candle behind you, and observe its image reflected in each of the three mirrors. The middle reflection will be smaller but not less bright than the two others: "smaller" stands quantitatively for unequal reception of a quality, spiritual insight; "not less bright" likewise for equality of salvation. But what concerns us is a certain value of the experiment that Dante, I surmise, with the cunning of a great poet, slyly refuses to consider: the dramatic value of the experiment.

There are *three*[10] mirrors each reflecting the *one* light. In the heart of the Empyrean, as we have seen, Dante says:

> In the profound and shining being of the deep light appeared to me *three* circles, of *three* colors and one magnitude.

In the middle is the effigy of man. The physical image of Dante had necessarily been reflected in each of the three mirrors of Canto II; but he had not seen it. I suggest that he was not then ready to see it; his dramatic (i.e., tropological) development fell short of the final self-knowledge. Self-knowledge comes to him, as an Aristotelian Recognition and Reversal, when he turns the cosmos inside out by turning away from the "real" mirrors to the one light which has cast the three separate images. For the first time he sees the "one magnitude," the candle itself. And it is all done with the simple apparatus and in conditions laid down in Canto II; he achieves the final anagoge and the dramatic recognition by turning around, as if he were still in Canto II, and by looking at the candle that has been burning all the time behind his back.

I have described some motions of the symbolic imagination in Dante, and tried to develop a larger motion in one of its narrower aspects. What I have left out of this discussion is very nearly the entire poem. In the long run the light imagery is not the body, it is what permits us to *see* the body, of the poem. The rash suggestion that *The Divine Comedy* has a tragic mode—among other modes—I shall no doubt be made to regret; I cannot defend it further here. Perhaps the symbolic imagination is tragic in sentiment, if not always in form, in the degree of its development. Its every gain beyond the simple realism of experience imposes so great a strain upon any actuality of form as to set the ultimate limit of the gain as a defeat. The high order of the poetic insight that the final insight must elude us, is dramatic in the sense that its fullest image is an action in the shapes of this world: it does not reject, it includes; it sees not only with but through the natural world, to what may lie beyond it. Its humility is witnessed by its modesty. It never begins at the top; it carries the bottom along with it, however high it may climb.

# Notes

1. Quotations in English from *The Divine Comedy* are from the translation by Carlyle, Okey, and Wicksteed, in the Temple Classics edition. Here and there I have taken the liberty of neutralizing certain Victorian poeticisms, which were already archaic in that period.

2. It seems scarcely necessary to remind the reader that I have followed in the scene of the Earthly Paradise only one thread of an immense number in a vastly complex pattern.

3. The difficulties suffered by man as angel were known at least as early as Pascal; but the doctrine of angelism, as a force in the modern mind, has been fully set forth for the first time by Jacques Maritain in *The Dream of Descartes* (New York, 1944).

4. Charles Williams, *The Figure of Beatrice* (London, 1943), p. 44.

5. Another way of putting this is to say that the modern poet, like Valéry or Crane, tries to seize directly the anagogical meaning, without going through the three preparatory stages of letter, allegory, and trope.

6. H. Flanders Dunbar, *Symbolism in Mediaeval Thought and Its Consummation in the Divine Comedy* (New Haven, 1929), p. 347.

7. By "dramatic" I mean something like *practic*, a possible adjective from *praxis*, a general movement of action as potency which it is the purpose of the poem to actualize. In the Thomist sequence, *potentia:actio:actus*, "dramatic" would roughly correspond to the middle term.

8. Oedipus does not achieve this until the end of *Oedipus at Colonus*.

9. The popular "visual" translation of Aristotle's primary Unmoved Mover producing, *through being loved*, the primary cosmic motion, which is circular. The philosophical source of this idea, Book XII, Chapter 7, of the *Metaphysics,* Dante of course knew.

10. Only two, placed at unequal distances from the candle, are strictly necessary for the experiment; but three are necessary as pointers towards the anagoge of the Trinity in the Triune Circles.

# Francis Fergusson

## The Fine Veil of Poetry

O voi, che avete gl'intelletti sani,
  mirate la dottrina, che s'asconde
  sotto il velame degli versi strani!

(O all of you whose intellects are sane,
  turn your eyes now to the knowledge hidden
  under the veil of verse, which is so strange!)
—*Inferno*, Canto IX, lines 61–63

Mr. T. S. Eliot, in his book on Dante which has done so much to lead readers of English to the *Commedia*, advises us to begin "with the poetry." He means by "poetry" the verses themselves which, even on a first reading, may give immediate pleasure. And he quotes many passages which any reader who is fairly familiar with modern lyric verse will recognize as singularly beautiful. In the last chapter I considered, not the "poetry" of the *Antipurgatorio*, but its dramatic form and its characterizations. But I believe that Mr. Eliot's advice is good. We must start to enjoy Dante by recognizing effects like those of the poetry we know, and our sense of poetry is based on the modern lyric. Moreover, Dante certainly intended to lead the reader into his complex composition through the pleasures of poetry in this sense. He expects us to start with "the Letter," by which he means the literal fiction of the journey beyond the grave; and it is the imagery and the music of his verses which give us the experience of the successive scenes which the Pilgrim enters in that spirit-world.

Mr. Eliot's advice is especially good in the reading of the *Antipurgatorio*.

I have called it a Pathos, or drama of pathetic motivation. I have also pointed out that in this realm the Pilgrim sees and feels with that directness and subtlety which we associate with childhood and its "intimations of immortality," but without intellectual understanding. This mode of awareness has been prized above all, by lyric poets, since the early romantics; they think of it as the source of poetry itself, as distinguished from philosophy, science, and all varieties of conceptual thought. When the Pilgrim is most "aware," in the *Antipurgatorio*, it is in this way that he is aware; and because he does not change or break through into new regions, he is always aware of the same "distant" or homesick scene. You may say that the *Antipurgatorio* contains a lyric of vague aspiration, very close to that of modern poetry, and that this lyric emerges from the singularly coherent imagery of the whole wandering first Day, and reaches its end in Canto VIII, the eve of change.

It is at those moments when the Pilgrim can look about him, question his deepest feeling, and sense his whole situation, that the lyric comes through most clearly. We hear it in Canto I, line 118:

> Noi andavam per lo solingo piano,
> com'uom che torna a la perduta strada,
> che infino ad essa gli par ire in vano.
>
> (We were walking along the lonely plain
> like one who turns back to the road he lost
> and, till he reach it, seems to walk in vain.)

A more suggestive variation of this image is in Canto II, line 10:

> Noi eravam lunghesso il mare ancora,
> come gente che pensa suo cammino,
> che va col core, e col corpo dimora.
>
> (We were still along the edge of the sea,
> like those who have the road ahead in mind;
> who move in spirit, and in body stay.)

A similar distance and nostalgia is expressed by Virgil (Canto III, line 25) in the terms he finds to describe his own ghostly being:

> Vespero è già colà, dov'è sepolto

lo corpo, dentro al quale io facea ombra.

(It is now evening, there where lies interred
the body, wherein I once made shadow.)

It is in the image of the flooded river, carrying the body it knows not where (Canto v), that this "lyric of aspiration" is at once most despairing and most intense, as I mentioned in the last chapter.

In Canto viii, as the Pilgrim quiets down for the evening, and lends ear to his day's experiences and their possible meanings, this lyric is epitomized and concluded. Canto viii, line 1:

Era già l'ora che volge il disio
ai naviganti, e intenerisce il core
lo dì ch'han detto ai dolci aimici addio;
e che lo nuovo peregrin d'amore
punge, se ode squilla di lontano,
che paia il giorno pianger che si more:
quand'io incomminciai a render vano
l'udire, ed a mirare una dell'alme
surta, che l'ascoltar chiedea con mano.

(It was the hour which turns back the desires
of seafarers, and makes the spirit tender
that day they told their well-loved friends good-bye;
hour when love will sting the new pilgrim
if he hear, from far away, bells ringing,
a lament, it seems, for the day's ending:
when I began to annul my sense of hearing
and gaze at one of the spirits, who arose,
and with a gesture of his hand craved listening.)

The modern reader of this passage can hardly fail to be reminded of a great deal of nineteenth-century homesickness; the far-off traveller, the evening, the distant bells, are almost too familiar. There is no doubt, I think, that Dante means to give us that "feeling" which we know so well. At the same time, the passage has the unique quality we call *Dantesque*, and that comes from the accuracy with which this inarticulate response of the inner being is defined. The literal scene with its sounds is only the signal for love (apparently from without) to pierce the Pilgrim. And he listens for it, not with the ear of the flesh, but with the whole being; he "looks" for something which is to be perceptible through the dusky scene around him. This is one of the many places in which Dante uses the shift from one physical sense to another to suggest a focus of attention which is not to be defined as sight, hearing, or any other single sense. He wants us to be poised, thus all attentive, for some clue to the meaning of the love that pierces the Pilgrim: is it frightening or comforting? Good or evil?

The clue which appears is that pair of green-feathered messengers of heaven who come winging through the evening air and alight, one on either side of the valley. It is not difficult to discover that they represent that "love" which prevails in the whole realm of purgation, the divine grace, the unearned gift, which prevents the Pilgrim from taking the wrong path until he reaches the *Paradiso Terrestre*. For the *Purgatorio* shows *one* view of human destiny, man as mysteriously capable—capable beyond what he can understand— of sane growth. The messengers' immediate errand, however, is to frighten away the snake, ancient and familiar sign of that other version of love, the human potentiality of evil, which also appears whenever darkness begins to fall and the moral will is in abeyance. The Pilgrim, poised here without will or intellectual grasp, is vaguely aware of the various meanings of his emotion and of the evening scene before him.

It is the highest point of awareness which the Pilgrim reaches in the *Antipurgatorio*, and Dante marks it by one of his author's interpolations (line 19):

> Aguzza qui, lettor, ben gli occhi al vero,
>   che il velo è ora ben tanto sottile,
>   certo, che il trapassar entro è leggiero.
>
> (Sharpen your eyes toward the truth here, reader,
>   for now what veils it is become so fine
>   that, surely, to pass through it would be easy.)

It is very much like the interpolation quoted at the head of this chapter, which also reminds the reader of the meaning behind the immediate poetic awareness, the mysterious grace which makes the whole journey possible. Its effect is to break the "veil of the verses," and thus the literal course of the narrative. We see that behind the fictive world of the dead which the verses present (what Dante in his *Letter to Can Grande* calls "the first subject") there is the meaning (which Dante calls "the second subject") that the whole poem has for human life in the actual world, as we know it here below. We are reminded that there is an analogy between some of our efforts to see meaning in our world, and the efforts of the Pilgrim to understand what he sees and feels on the evening of the first Day.

The Pilgrim himself does not have the notes of the commentators, and he does not make the deductions which the reader may make; and after the interpolated tercet, Dante returns us to the Pilgrim. For him, the valley and the evening, and even the messengers of heaven, speak only like one of Wordsworth's calm evenings; or like Baudelaire's forest of symbols, through which man passes with an odd sense of familiarity, but without quite grasping the meaning. This is one of the themes which recurs in many forms in European lyric poetry since the early romantics. Eliot uses it in many subtle variations in the *Four Quartets*. Dante himself presents the poetry of many scenes of felt but undeclared significance; the semi-transparent "veil" is always there, at the edge of whatever region we are in.

After the moment of pause with which the canto opens, the Pilgrim turns from the wide sense of his whole situation, to talk with some of the spirits who are waiting here with him. It is a movement, not of enquiry, nor of effort to pierce the veil, but of acceptance and realization. The words of Nino de' Visconti convey this acceptance with many rich overtones and echoing implications (line 67):

> Poi volto a me: "Per quel singular grado,
> che tu dei a colui, che sì nasconde
> lo suo primo perchè, che non gli è guado,
> quando sarai di là dalle larghe onde,
> di' a Giovanna mia, che per me chiami
> là dove agl'innocenti si risponde."

> (Then turning toward me: "By that special favor
> you owe to him who keeps so deeply covered
> his final purpose, that there is no way there,
> When you shall be beyond the wide water,
> tell my Giovanna to appeal for me,
> there where the innocent receive an answer.")

The passage is full of the lyric theme of "distance" in many forms: between Nino and his remembered Giovanna, between this "world" and the real world, between our counsels and the counsels of God. But the distance is patiently accepted, and accompanied by a curious tenderness of personal relationships: between Nino and his remembered daughter, and between Nino and Dante, whom he sees only briefly. These relationships, which mean so much and so little, are very much like those in Chekhov's second acts, as I have pointed out in another context. And so is the movement of the canto as a whole, from the wide but inchoate awareness of the beginning, to the descent of darkness near the end, when the stars come out. The stars—"three torches," as the Pilgrim calls them—play the role of Faith, Hope, and Charity in Dante's symbolic scheme, appearing whenever darkness makes it impossible to see ahead and move ahead. But the Pilgrim here knows them only as stars which have replaced the four he saw, near dawn, at the beginning of his day's journey.

Because the Pilgrim does not essentially change in the *Antipurgatorio*, or break through into other regions, the scene is bounded by the same lyric awareness during the whole Day, from dawn to the descent of night. And for that reason, it is the lyric effects which we hear, from time to time, throughout the eight cantos, that most directly present that childlike mode of being which Dante wished to show. But the narrative is interrupted from time to time by explanations which Virgil or one of the spirits gives, or which the author interpolates; and they remind us that this first Day is merely the prelude to a more conscious drama to follow.

Some of the explanations and comments in the *Antipurgatorio* hint at the nature of the childlike lyric awareness which bounds it, suggesting its limitations and perils. In the second canto, for example (line 112), we see the Pilgrim and the shadowy Casella caught in the enjoyment of Casella's song, a setting of Dante's own *canzone*:

> *"Amor che nella mente mi ragiona,"*
> cominciò egli allor sì dolcemente,
> che la dolcezza ancor dentro mi suona.
> Lo mio maestro ed io e quella gente
> ch'eran con lui parevan sì contenti,
> come a nessun toccasse altro la mente.

> (*"Love that in my mind discourses to me,"*
> the spirit so sweetly thereupon commenced,
> that still I hear the sweetness sound within me.
> My Master then and I and all the rest
> who were with him, showed forth such happiness
> as though our minds played upon nothing else.)

Upon which Cato scolds them for laziness and chases them away. In Canto IV, beginning with the first line, there is a very significant interpolation by the author on the psychology of *any* pleasure (or pain) which may hold the soul, depriving it of its freedom of response through the very depth of the immediate impression. And there is the explicit statement in Canto VIII which I quoted above, that the poetry is a "veil" which we must see *through* to reach the truth behind it.

Such hints and brief statements as these show that Dante regarded the childlike poetic awareness, the absorbed listening with the inner ear, as only one recurrent moment in the growth of the soul; and that he intended to get lyric effects only from time to time, even in the *Antipurgatorio*. Croce, in his reading of the *Commedia*, accurately perceived that: we hear "poetry," in the sense of the modern lyric poetry, only from time to time. Croce proceeded to reject all the rest as dead sign-language, mere allegorizing in an outworn convention. Croce's view of the *Commedia* is now, I think, generally regarded as inadequate. But because he is so consistent, pushing to its logical conclusion the attempt to read the *Commedia* according to modern notions of poetry, he reveals the perils of this method very clearly. Dante is master of a lyric style, and thoroughly understands its sources and its pleasures and insights; but in writing the *Commedia* he was limited neither by the *mystique* nor by the poetics of our modern poetry.

Because the *Antipurgatorio* is the place of vague beginnings, of hopeful responses, and of problems sensed but not solved, it should be reread in the light of the whole canticle. But the plan of these studies is to follow as closely as possible Dante's own order of exposition or interpretation. And the next step is to consider the Pilgrim's passage into Purgatory proper, the more and more conscious efforts of the second Day.

# Canto IX: The Prophetic First Night

che or sì or no s'intendon le parole.
(When now the words are clear, and now are not.)
—Canto IX, line 145.

IN CANTO IX the childlike Pilgrim of the first eight cantos goes to sleep in the last valley of the *Antipurgatorio*, dreams, and wakes in the bright sunshine of a new day in a new place: before the ancient gates of Purgatory proper. This is his first mutation, or break-through into a wider mode of awareness. Canto IX reveals this mysterious passage in many ways, foreshadowing the stages of the journey all the way to the top of the Mountain. It is a good place to pause and attempt a more careful reading, for this canto may show a great deal about the Pilgrim's half-conscious growth, and about the author's methods of composition.

The canto begins with a single smooth sentence of twelve lines, which suggests both the passage of night over our heads, and the Pilgrim's weary sinking to sleep:

La concubina di Titone antico
  già s'imbiancava al balco d'oriente,
  fuor delle braccia del suo dolce amico;
di gemme la sua fronte era lucente,
  poste in figura del freddo animale,
  che con la coda percote la gente;
e la notte de' passi, con che sale,
  fatti avea due nel loco ov'eravamo,
  e il terzo già chinava in giuso l'ale;
quand'io, che meco avea di quel d'Adamo,
  vinto dal sonno, in su l'erba inchinai
  ove già tutti e cinque sedevamo.

(The concubine of Tithonus the ancient
  was growing white on eastern parapet,
  as she came forth from her sweet friend's embraces;

her forehead was alight with shine of gems
  fixed in the figure of that cold live thing
  which with its flickering tail transfixes men;
and night, upon the stairway of her climbing,
  had mounted twice, there where we then tarried,
  and for the third her wings was down-inclining,
when I, who had in me somewhat of Adam,
  sank overcome by sleep upon the lawn,
  in that place where all five of us had rested.)

The position of the stars shows the hour. The moon's aurora is on the eastern horizon, where the constellation of Scorpio glitters as though upon a white forehead. The aurora of the moon is a false dawn, hence a "concubine." The associations are with the myths and superstitions of pagan antiquity, the hard but majestic world of unredeemed nature. The Pilgrim yields to the weight of body and to the logic and vast regularity of the movements of the heavens, like a child going to sleep in a well-ordered household. The only association with the Christian tradition in this passage is that of *Adamo*, significantly rhymed with *sedevamo*.

The whole passage is a poetic evocation of night as Sordello has predicted it in Canto VII, line 52. The darkness paralyzes the will, and therefore one cannot climb upward, though one might descend as though by gravitation back down the Mountain, toward that dead center we passed at the bottom of Hell. In all of the nights this possibility is suggested; sleep, the sign of our bodily being, our old Adam, is an image of death. But when this mortal weakness is obediently accepted, the sleeping spirit is in a sense freed for another mode of life; and that is presented in the next six lines, dawn on the Mountain and in the sleeper:

Nell'ora che comincia i tristi lai
  la rondinella presso alla mattina,
  forse a memoria de'suoi primi guai,
e che la mente nostra, peregrina
  più dalla carne e men da'pensier presa,
  alle sue vision quasi è divina:

(At the hour when begins the sad song
  which the swallow twitters near to morning,
  perhaps in memory of her first wrong,

and when our pilgrim spirit, wandering
  far from the body and the prison of thought
  is, in her visions, very near foreknowing:)

The swallow is Philomela. According to the story as Dante used it, Philomela was raped by Tereus, the husband of Procne, who was Philomela's sister. Tereus cut out Philomela's tongue, but she was able to tell Procne of her wrong by means of a tapestry she wove; and Procne then took vengeance on Tereus by serving him his son's flesh in a covered dish. When Tereus discovered what he had eaten, he pursued the sisters to kill them; but the god had pity, changing Procne into a nightingale and Philomela into a swallow. Such are the primal sufferings, the *primi guai* which we still hear in the wordless voices of the swallows when they wake near dawn.

The myth-making childhood of the race, the feel of early morning, the ancient plaint of nature in the bird-sounds, are poetically or imaginatively fused in this passage. The suggested significance of this moment and this scene is what the childlike sleeper himself might sense; and as in the night-sequence, the scene leads to the Pilgrim's state of awareness.

In the second tercet the nature of the sleeper's awareness is exactly specified: he is as free as mortals ever get from the limitations of the flesh, and also from the confinement of "thought," by which I think Dante means the concepts and the logical concatenations of the discursive reason. He is aware by means of visions, which are *almost* truly divinatory. This visionary state is akin to that "poetic awareness" which the Pilgrim had, at various moments, during the preceding day, and which we looked at in the last chapter. Here it is also associated with the poetry of the race, the heritage of myth. The whole passage is allusive, in a manner akin to the late work of Joyce, Pound, and Eliot. By means of allusion, a timeless or recurrent mode of human awareness is suggested.

But the six lines are merely introductory to the dream, which is both a dream as we know dreams, and a vision containing truth. In the latter aspect, the dream which follows is very much like the rainbow-colored shows and pageants which we shall see in the *Paradiso Terrestre*: true, but impermeable to conscious understanding. The dream follows without a break:

in sogno mi parea veder sospesa
  un'aquila nel ciel con penne d'oro
  con l'ali aperte, ed a calare intesa.
Ed esser mi parea là dove foro

abbandonati i suoi da Ganimede,
quando fu ratto al sommo consistoro.
Fra me pensava: "Forse questa fiede
pur qui per uso, e forse d'altro loco
disdegna di portarne suso in piede."

(in dream I seemed to see an eagle, taut
on his spread feathers in the sky above me,
poised there on wings of gold, intent to drop.
And I was in that place, it seemed to me,
where Ganymede abandoned his companions,
when he was snatched to the high consistory.
I thought within me: "Only in this region,
perhaps, he strikes, and elsewhere he disdains
to seize and lift one upward in his talons.")

The account of the dream, as it struck the Pilgrim, continues through line 42, when the Pilgrim wakes. The dream itself wakes the dreamer; and there is no telling how many waking minutes it occupies. The eagle swoops and lifts the Pilgrim up to the fiery sphere in which they burn together. The burning wakes the dreamer, and as he wakes his surprise is associated with that of Achilles; whose mother, the sea-nymph Thetis, lifted him up from among his enemies, while he slept, and carried him to safety. The effect of the dream-passage, as one reads it, is like that of the dreams we know: there is some sort of passage, of being carried; but the place, the people, and the purpose shift and fuse as we watch. Our sensations are ambivalent also: we are honored, terrified, reassured, and burned to the point where the whole vision breaks, we wake, and the actual world comes back.

The movement of the canto from dreaming to waking, where the dream will be explained to the Pilgrim in a certain way, does not cease. But if one stops to consider the static structure of the dream-passage, and its place in the pre-designed framework of the whole *Purgatorio*, one learns that a very extensive scale of meaning has been built into it.

At the top of this scale, beyond the understanding of Pilgrim or reader at this point, are the meanings of the Eagle in Dante's symbolic scheme. The useful notes in the Temple Classics edition refer us to the Eagle of the medieval Bestiaries, who like the Phoenix is perpetually burned and renewed, and so stands for baptismal regeneration. These notes also connect the Eagle with the Roman Empire, and so with Virgil and the pagan moral and intellectual virtues; and with the secular institutions of government that safeguard justice. Other commentators tell us confidently that the Eagle also stands for illuminating grace. The question is surrounded by erudite disputes which I am not qualified to enter. Suffice it (for my purposes) to say that the Eagle suggests secular, ecclesiastical, and divine assistance—"Grace" (the unearned gift) which may come in many ways—and which, at crucial moments, is needed for the growth of the spirit. In Dante's own plan of interpretation, these matters will be explored in many contexts farther up the Mountain, when the relations of Church and State, of tradition and individual experience, of pagan and Christian culture, are slowly sorted out by the Pilgrim and his guides.

In the center of the scale of meanings of the dream are those which the dreamer, with his non-rational but poetic and mythopoeic awareness, is groping for. He feels an analogy between what is happening to him and what happened to Ganymede, the beautiful shepherd whom Jove fell in love with and kidnapped. But as he wakes another analogy with a myth is suggested, that of Achilles borne away by his mother, not to be raped but to be saved. This analogy is closer than the first one to the literal facts of the nocturnal passage which the Pilgrim will learn when he wakes. The whole dream, near the end of the night, represents the end of a process of inner clarification. In this Dante confirms a very ancient tradition, that the dreams we have nearest the morning are the most true; and he anticipates Freud, who reaches the same conclusion. But Freud (unlike Jung) would not agree that the "truth" of morning dreams is that of a recurrent, and thus in a sense timeless mode of human experience; he sees them as revealing only the emotional state of the individual dreamer.

At the "bottom" of the dream's scale of meanings, Dante seems to be aware of the kind of truth Freud likes. The swooping bird, the ascent, and the burning-together, have erotic connotations which would have delighted Freud if he had read this passage attentively. He would have said, perhaps, that they show that the dreamer's suppressed desires were infantile, or "polymorphous-perverse," in his unpleasing phrase. I am sure Dante meant the erotic connotations, for the whole *Purgatorio* may be regarded as the epic of the transformations of love. And he also knew that the Pilgrim's love was unformed and childish at this point; the eroticism of the next dream (Canto XIX) is much more conscious, formed, and "adult." He knew that what the dreamer could grasp in his visions of this experience (itself a standard moment of psychic growth) was colored and limited by his emotional-moral state. Both mythic analogues suggest the passivity of childhood. But

Dante attaches more weight to the Pilgrim's inarticulate, visionary effort for wider understanding than he does to his emotional state at that moment; for it is partly by means of this effort (the response to what happens *to* him) that his love, or "libido," will be transformed and widened.

In the next passage (line 43) we see the Pilgrim wake from his terrible and wonderful dream:

> Da lato m'era solo il mio conforto,
> e il sole er'alto già più che due ore,
> e il viso m'era alla marina torto.

> (Only my comfort was there beside me,
> the sun already more than two hours high,
> and my gaze in the direction of the sea.)

This waking, with its mixture of relief and deflation, suggests a familiar experience. After going to sleep with an unsolved problem and spending a night of hope, fear, and half-formed insights, the daylight world comes back; but now it "looks different." The insoluble problem of the night before, whether it be one of tangled personal relationships, or an intellectual problem like those of artists, mathematicians, and scientific investigators, has been turned around during the night by some force which we do not understand. It may or may not be solved, but it appears in a new light; and now we can at least see how to work on it with the pedestrian efforts of the waking, rational mind. Modern psychology attributes this effect to the work of the subconscious; Dante believes that the Grace of God has intervened. However one may interpret it, the experience itself is undeniable; and it is the Pilgrim's experience of such a mutation which is the matter of this canto.

In the bright morning sun, which is the same and not the same as other mornings filled with work ahead, the Pilgrim learns the literal facts of his nocturnal shift: Lucia (Illuminating Grace) has carried him to this new point while he slept. Virgil, who sees by Reason, has followed; and now the Pilgrim in his turn catches up: he gets a factual and rationalized account of his mysterious translation. And though "Lucia," the crucial fact, means hardly more to him than she does to the uninstructed modern reader, at least the Pilgrim has what he needs to tackle the path immediately before him.

The rest of the canto (line 73 to the end) describes the scene before the gates of Purgatory. They are inside a narrow and inconspicuous fissure in the rocky cliff, approached by three steps, respectively white, "darker than perse," and blood red. The steps are guarded by an angel with a shining sword, who accepts the travellers when Virgil explains that it is Lucia who has brought them here. The Pilgrim, obeying Virgil, throws himself to the ground, strikes himself three times on his breast, and craves the mercy of entrance; upon which the Angel Guardian marks three P's on his forehead with his sword, and opens the gates with two keys, a silver and a gold.

This scene, like the dream, is evidently packed with unspoken meanings, some of which have been elucidated by the commentators, while others are still disputed. I refer once more to the notes in the Temple Classics edition, which give all that most readers need, and provide at least an introduction to the problems of a learned exegesis. In general it is clear that both the visible properties (sword, keys, steps, and the like) and the ritual gesture of the Guardian and the Pilgrim, are signs of that same transition to Purgation which the dream in one way, and Virgil's account of Lucia's carrying of the Pilgrim in another way, have already presented. The whole scene before the gates is like an epiphany at the end of a Greek tragedy: a tableau, or visible setpiece at the end of a completed action, showing forth its meaning in terms of its visible results.

It is the style of this passage, rather than its ultimate interpretation, that I wish to consider, for the style imitates the Pilgrim's alert but myopic mental life in the new realm, and gives the reader his clue to sympathetic understanding. The first part of the canto—night, dawn, and the dream—feels "poetic" in our sense of the word; but the scene before the gates in the bright morning light lacks the imaginative fusion, and the resonance, of the more lyric opening sections. It seems to employ an arbitrary sign-language, the kind of bald allegorizing that Croce objects to. A reader of English will probably be reminded of Bunyan's wooden personifications, which add nothing to the moral concepts they stand for. This impression, of course, is wrong, for Dante's symbols refer, not to abstract concepts, but to other objective realities, and hence there is no single key to their elucidation; one discovers that as soon as one tries, with the help of the commentators, to make a complete interpretation of this passage. But the *effect* of a sign-language which, like traffic-signals, may be blankly obeyed without full understanding or assent, is certainly intended here. Dante warns us that the style of this passage is different: speaking as author, he introduces it as follows (line 70):

Lettor, tu vedi ben com'io innalzo
  la mia materia, e però con più arte
  non ti maravigliar s'io la rincalzo.

(Reader, you clearly see how I make higher
my subject-matter; if then with greater art
I now sustain it, that is not surprising.)

Coleridge's famous distinction between the poetry of Imagination and the poetry of Fancy throws a good deal of light on the change of style, or "art," between the first part of the canto and the second. "In Imagination," Coleridge writes, "the parts of the meaning—both as regards the ways in which they are apprehended and the modes of combination of their effects in the mind—mutually modify one another." That is exactly what occurs in the poetry of night, dawn, and dream. "In Fancy," on the other hand, says Coleridge, "the parts of the meaning are apprehended as though independent of their fellow members . . . and although, of course, the parts together have a joint effect which is not what it would be if the assemblage were different, the effects of the parts remain for an interval separate, and combine or collide *later*, in so far as they do so at all." That describes very accurately the effect of the brilliant scene before the gates: each element is clear and separate, sharply actual; but they are not combined in a satisfying imaginative fusion. Because keys, sword, steps, and the rest *are* separate—a collection rather than a compound—they seem to demand some further effort on the part of reader and Pilgrim to make them combine "later."

The shift in style or art is thus away from "Poetry" as Coleridge, Croce, and many other proponents of the modern *mystique* have taught us to understand Poetry, and into a more positivistic mode of composition. For Coleridge, Fancy was an inferior style, based not upon the mode of awareness which is the source of Poetry as such, but upon the work of the discursive reason. What then does Dante mean by telling us that the daylight passage shows "greater art"? Does he mean to reject Poetry and its insights as inferior to what the waking mind can show when it is in contact with the discrete facts of its actual situation?

It is probable that Dante was proud of the rational ingenuity (or "art" in the sense of artifact) with which he devised the scene before the gates, fitting it into his whole elaborate symbolic structure. Moreover this scene is literally "higher" than the *Antipurgatorio*; it is not only the end of the night, but the basis of a new movement, an unfamiliar setting still to be explored. By breaking the texture of his narrative and speaking out as author, Dante breaks our identification with the Pilgrim, and bids us consider the development of the poem as poem. He may therefore wish us to admire not only the art of this particular passage, but the *change* of art and, in general, the extraordinary flexibility of the art of the whole canto, in which the perspectives of poetry, mythopoeia, dream, and wakeful rationality are imitated successively, each in its appropriate "art" or mode of composition.

From this more detached point of view we may divine the subject-matter of the canto as a whole: it is the Pilgrim's crucial change of heart. He tries to understand this change in various ways; but it is essentially something which happens *to* him, beyond his will and understanding, and for this reason all his ways of understanding are inadequate, and it is beyond his strength to pull them together. On the other hand, none of them is simply wrong: what Virgil tells him in the morning, what he sees at the gates, are simply other ways of understanding what he vaguely and suggestively grasped in dream. The whole sequence presents that rhythmic alternation of poetic contemplation and rational-moral effort which will be repeated in many varied figures, in many different regions, on the way up the Mountain.

But Canto IX has its own unity; it "imitates" one action of the Pilgrim, which ends. This action—his fluctuating and sharply-varied effort to grasp what is happening to him—is clearly suggested in the figure with which the canto ends. The gates open, and the Pilgrim hears singing within:

Tale imagine appunto mi rendea
  ciò ch'io udiva, qual prender si suole
  quando a cantar con organi si stea:
che or sì or no s'intendon le parole.

(Just such an image-in-the-mind was offered
  by that which I was hearing, as we are wont
  to get from people singing with an organ:
when now the words are clear, and now are not.)

# On the Dramatic Coherence Of the Canto

IN THE LAST CHAPTER I endeavored to show the poetic-dramatic coherence of Canto IX, in which the Pilgrim goes to sleep in the *Antipurgatorio*, dreams, and wakes in the morning before the gates of Purgatory proper. That canto reflects, I believe, one action (or *moto spiritale*, "movement of spirit," as Virgil will call it in Canto XVIII, line 32)—the Pilgrim's effort to understand his mysterious translation to the new realm. This action is prepared as the Pilgrim sinks to sleep, reaches its center or climax in his dream, and ends as the gates open.

The studies are all based upon this type of "dramatic" analysis of the *Purgatorio*, canto by canto. I now wish to offer a few general observations upon the purposes and methods of this approach to the poem.

It is evident that in Canto IX the imagery alone does not lead very directly to the coherence of the whole unit. The sensuous imagery is different at each stage of the developing action, as the Pilgrim grasps his experience now in one way, and now in another. Even the "art" of writing varies sharply, as Dante himself asks us to notice. The traditional symbolism of the canto—the ultimate meanings of the Eagle, Lucia, the three steps, the sword, and the rest—also does not *alone* show us what this particular canto is about. One might, with the aid of the commentators, construct a fairly consistent philosophical-theological interpretation of this canto, and its place in Dante's blueprints for his poem, by considering the meanings of those traditional symbols. But that would be to disregard the poem which Dante actually wrote; and it would, I think, do some violence to his own plan of composition, which is also a plan for the proper reading of the poem. According to this plan (as I have mentioned before) the "interpretation" is to be reached, not by looking up the answers at the back of the book, but by following "the development of the form." This developing form may be called *dramatic*, for it closely reflects, or imitates, the movements of the Pilgrim's growing and groping spirit. And each canto, for all the variety of its detail, presents the beginning, middle, and end of one such *moto spirital*.

Eliot remarks that a canto of the *Divine Comedy* corresponds to a whole play of Shakespeare's, and the *Divine Comedy* as a whole to all of Shakespeare's work. This observation is not meant to be applied literally, but it throws some light both upon Shakespeare's forms and upon Dante's. Thus, we have recently learned to see that in a play of Shakespeare's the sensuous imagery, the characters, the situation and the plot, and the "thought," are all organic parts of the composition, and cannot therefore be properly understood separately. This is also true of a canto of the *Divine Comedy*. For example, there are passages in the *Divine Comedy* in which a "thought" is presented (by Virgil or Marco Lombardo, or in an interpolation by the author) with the conceptual clarity and the logical connections which we associate with philosophy rather than poetry. One is tempted to accept such clear statements as giving the author's ultimate and full meaning—as though, after so much poetizing, he had decided suddenly to break down and tell all. But all of the philosophizing in the *Divine Comedy* is the utterance of a particular character in a particular situation. And for that reason it would be as bad a mistake to suppose that it gives the author's full meaning, as it would be to take an utterance by Othello or Gloucester as an utterance by Shakespeare. In both cases, what the characters say shows something about them, and one aspect of the situation they are describing; but it is only a part of the meaning of the poem in which it occurs. The contest is all-important—in Shakespeare, the play as a whole; in Dante, the canto as a whole.

The *Divine Comedy* is so beautifully composed that, ideally, the whole poem should be the context in which any passage is read. It is woven of many recurrent themes; at any point what has gone before and what is yet to come are implicit; and the forward movement never ceases completely until the end. The cantos form parts of larger units (like the Days on the Mount of Purgatory); they are like waves on top of a larger ground-swell. But it would be impossible to hold all of this in mind at once. It would have been impossible for Dante himself to grasp it all simultaneously, in full awareness of each vital aspect—and even more impossible for him to write it that way. He did not try to do so. He made it in units appropriate to the natural limitations both of the poet and the reader. With the beginning of each canto he takes, as it were, a new breath, for a new act of poem-making, which will closely reflect a new movement of the Pilgrim's psyche. He expects the reader, also, to take a new breath, in order to grasp the new development of the whole poem which the canto will present; and then, perhaps, to pause long enough to explore its complex and significant coherence. This coherence—the poetic-dramatic form of the canto—is the context in which the ideas, the narratives, the characters, the judgments, and the lyric passages are to be understood.

In order to grasp a canto in this way the reader must make a new effort of perception. Even between cantos which are very closely connected in matter and manner, there is a slight but crucial shift of focus, demanding the very alert attention of the reader. And if one thinks of several cantos from different parts of the poem, it is evident that they are composed, if not on different principles, at least with emphases so different as to make them in effect different kinds of poetic units.

Canto IX, for example, is difficult to grasp as a whole on first reading because its actual texture is so varied. What goes on in that canto is far below the surface—a change in the Pilgrim which he does not himself fully grasp, yet so fundamental that it adumbrates the whole purgatorial process. On the other hand, the unity of Canto XV, and the unity of Canto XVI, are evident at once because each is dominated by very consistent sensuous imagery, in Canto XV that of glaring light, in Canto XVI that of close darkness. Some cantos are dominated by a personality so strong, touching, and unique that the reader is impressed by it immediately. Canto V of the *Inferno*, for example, is Francesca's canto; for her being and destiny, as we get it in her own words, is by far the sharpest instance of the mode of being which the canto as a whole presents. Piccarda de Donati dominates her canto (*Paradiso* III) in a closely analogous way—it is even probable, I think, that Dante meant us to feel the analogy between a simple loving woman on the threshold of Hell, and a simple loving woman on the threshold of Heaven. But I do not mean to suggest, by these examples, that a canto is ever to be understood by means of its imagery or its characters alone. The emphasis on glaring light or close darkness in Cantos XV and XVI conveys a certain sharply-limited focus of the inner life, but that is presented in many other ways also in those cantos, as I shall try to show below. The emphasis on Francesca and Piccarda, in their cantos, tells us a great deal about the "new direction which love takes" at those moments; but for all the beauty of those women, it would be a bad mistake to neglect their context, the cantos in which each of them is one element only.

A single canto of the *Divine Comedy* is not the whole poem, but it is far more than a mere slice of about 140 lines. It is an *organic part* of the whole poem. It is, therefore, the smallest unit in which Dante's principles of composition may be adequately studied. And it is the smallest context we are justified in considering, if we are to understand the characters, the narratives, the lyric passages, and the philosophizing, as Dante wished them to be understood.

# Joseph A. Mazzeo

## Light Metaphysics in the Works of Dante

Dante had been interested in light speculation from the time of the *Convivio* and makes frequent reference to the doctrines. In *Convivio* III, vii, 2–3, Dante describes the manner in which the divine goodness descends upon all things, conferring and maintaining them in their existence. This goodness is at its source most simple and unified, but it is received by all things in various degrees. Citing the *Liber de causis*, he compares it to an outpouring or overflowing of the primal goodness and gives the light of the sun as an example, light which is one in its source but is received diversely by different bodies.[1] The passage he refers to from the *Liber de causis* is section 19 and is an Aristotelianized description of the Neoplatonic conception of emanation. The first cause or Good, remaining one, rules all things. Nor does its essential unity, which differentiates it from all things, prevent it from governing them. This is so because, while remaining one, it is yet able to radiate its power of life and its excellences on all things which receive its gifts to the extent that they are able. This Good which pours itself out is the first cause, and Being as well, an interesting deviation from the main stream of Neoplatonism which places the Good above Being, but in closer harmony with both Christian and Mohammedan theism. The first cause is truly active because there is no relation of continuity between it and what it makes. It is thus a true agent and governor, making things through its beauty and making their final cause a beauty which is supreme.

This inconsistent blend of Neoplatonism with Aristotelianism—which fuses emanationism with a notion of creation; which describes the Good as overflowing in one great outpouring, and yet identifies it with Being and a first cause that remains transcendent over what it produces; which makes the first cause the supremely beautiful acting as final cause through its beauty, yet describes it as the ruler of all things—is far more characteristic of medieval Platonism than any consistently worked-out position.[2]

We have already noted that this blending is best typified by Albertus Magnus among the major medieval thinkers, and, indeed, Dante follows this reference to the *Liber de causis* by a reference to Albertus' *De intellectu et intelligibile* which he cites as an authority for the parallel between the various degrees of illumination and coloring of things and their degree of immateriality. It is essentially the same doctine St. Thomas propounded in the commentary on the *De anima* but far more elaborately worked out in Albert.[3] Following Albertus, Dante makes the following classifications:

(1) There are earthly substances mixed with one of the more diaphanous elements such as air or water so that they shine in the light, for example, gold or precious stones which "multiply" the light they receive.

(2) There are completely transparent substances which transmit light and color as it does a piece of colored glass.

(3) There are completely opaque substances which can be polished to reflect light as mirrors.

(4) There are completely opaque substances almost void of a diaphanous quality, such as earth.

The brightest of these substances can even overcome the power of sight as a mirror can do.[4] Analogously the angels, men, animals, plants, and minerals share in various degrees in the divine goodness to the degree that they are diaphanous or immaterial.[5] Creatures thus share in their different degrees of the divine goodness, from the pure "luminousness" or transparency of the angels down to man, who is, metaphorically speaking, partially visible, like a man standing in water, and, further, down to the lower and more opaque orders.

This gradation or hierarchy of light, immateriality, nobility, and being proceeds not only by genus and species but by particular individuals. Within each species there is further hierarchy of individuals so that, for example, the highest of the individuals in the human species would be virtually an angel.[6] Both the sensible and the intelligible orders display this continuous gradation. Between the highest forms of animals and the lowest forms of men and between the highest forms of men and the lowest forms of angels there is really no intermediate grade, so that we see some men who are virtually nothing but beasts. Likewise we must posit a human individual so noble that he would be virtually an angel; otherwise the human species would not be continuous in both directions.[7] This best individual of the human species, virtually an angel, stands on the very pinnacle of the graded ladder of luminousness and immateriality which constitutes the universe. To use

Dante's own metaphor about man being half in the water of materiality and half in the air of materiality, such an individual would barely have his feet wet. Dante adds that Aristotle calls such people divine.[8]

The compassionate lady, the perfect individual of the human species, receives the divine virtue as an angel does,[9] and this Dante proves by the behavior of the lady in those operations of the rational soul—speaking and general deportment—proper to a rational person. This external activity is thus an expression or translation of that faculty, the rational soul, which especially receives the divine light. Her behavior, carriage, and speaking, her beauty and grace are external manifestations of the inner "light."[10] The beautiful woman is thus on the very highest point of the earthly ladder of light-immateriality-being. It is because the divine light or goodness most manifests itself in her that she is beautiful. Dante develops at some length this doctrine of external beauty as a kind of translation of the inner light.[11] Indeed, Dante means to speak of such a creature only insofar as the goodness of her soul is revealed in the beauty of her body, in sensible beauty. The soul reveals itself as color through glass—and what is smiling but a scintillation of the soul's delight, the visible outward light of the light which exists within?[12] The mouth and the eyes are the two parts through which the rational soul most fully translates this inner light into an outer light expressed in terms of sensible particulars. It is there that the rational soul is most operative in its role of beautifying its instrument, the body.[13] The most beautiful parts of the body will thus be precisely those which are closest to the soul, the eyes and lips, balconies looking out of the edifice which the soul inhabits. The soul is, as it were, a woman who inhabits a palace, the body, and the eyes and lips are her balconies. We might observe in passing that the importance of laughter or smiling was well buttressed by the authority of Aristotle, who said that man is a laughing animal.[14] Laughter is his *proprium*, a property not of his essence but one which he shares with no other animal. Hence it is not mere preference that Dante shows in emphasizing the mouth as the most "spiritual" and beautiful organ along with the eyes, all of them in the face, the most beautiful part of the body. We have already discussed the importance of the sense of sight in medieval philosophical speculation as the most spiritual and "aesthetic" of the senses, and it is only natural that the organ of this sense should share in the dignity of its function.

Dante frequently refers to other doctrines of light metaphysics in the *Convivio*. In III, xii, 6–8, he mentions the analogy between the corporeal and spiritual sun which corresponds to corporeal and intellectual light. The spiritual sun is God. God first illuminates Himself with intellectual light, then illuminates the celestial creatures and all other things in the intelligible realm. As the sun gives heat, the principle of life, and if anything is injured by it, it is not part of the sun's purpose, so God in His Goodness gives life, but if any living thing is evil, it is not part of His intention but an accident.[15]

The two kinds of light are again described, but as material and spiritual instead of corporeal and intellectual. As white is the color most filled with corporeal light, so contemplation is most filled with spiritual light of anything in this world.[16] Dante also draws the conventional distinction in light speculation between *lux, lumen, radius,* and *splendor* or the source of light and the various forms of luminosity around it. The first agent, God, colors some things by His power in the manner of a ray directly shining upon them and other things by a kind of reflected splendor. The angels receive the direct ray immediately, and other things receive it as reflected from them. *Luce* is the source of *lume*, the ray is a linear radiation from the *luce*, and the *splendor* is the light reflected from the first things which the ray emanating from the source may strike.[17]

Dante also conceives of the principle of efficacy as a divine ray. The rays of light descending from each star or planet are the means through which they exert their effects on the world below. These rays are nothing more than a light (*lume*) which comes from a source of light (*luce*). The stars emit light and therefore exert influence; the diaphanous spheres in which they are fixed, being transparent, have no influence on the world below.[18]

The Catholics, Dante tells us, place the empyrean heaven, the luminous heaven or the heaven of flame, outside of all the heavens. It is immovable because it is fully actual, that is, "it has in itself, in every part that which its matter desires." The *primum mobile* has the swiftest movement because of its intense desire to unite itself to the heaven above it, a desire so intense that it spins with enormous velocity. All motion, as in the Aristotelian universe, is a symptom of incompleteness, of the "desire" to become fully actual and to be assimilated to the Pure Act which moves the world as an object of desire. This heaven is the still and quiet light in which the Deity dwells who alone completely beholds Himself; it is the abode also of the blessed, as the Holy Church "who cannot lie" maintains.[19]

Dante continues by telling us that the divine light shines in and through the soul as it shines in the angels. The human soul possesses all the virtues of the lower forms of soul as well as the ultimate perfection of reason. By virtue of reason it participates in the divine nature as well as in the lower natures in the scale of creatures. By virtue of possessing reason the human soul is so noble and immaterial that the divine light shines on it as it does on the angels.[20] Philosophy itself is that most virtuous light whose rays make the flowers bloom, the analogy here being to the generative powers of the sun.[21]

To the two main kinds of light correspond two organs of vision, the sensible eye and the rational eye. The sensitive part of the soul has its eyes by which it discerns the difference between things according to their external coloration. Similarly, the eyes of the rational part of the soul—judgment, or discernment—estimate things according to the ends for which they were ordained. The man who lacks this faculty will follow the popular clamor whether right or wrong.[22]

It is, however, in the letter to Can Grande that the light-metaphysics doctrine is more fully worked out. Citing the *De causis*, Dante presents the chain of causality descending from God in terms of an emanation of light.

> Inasmuch as the second cause has its effect from the first, its influence on what it acts upon is like that of a body which receives and reflects a ray; since the first cause is the more effective cause. And this is stated in the book *Of Causes*, namely, that "every primary cause has influence in a greater degree on what it acts upon than any second cause." So much with regard to being.[23]

Dante continues with an exposition of the "proceeding of every essence and virtue" from the "primal one" through the mediation of the intelligences or angels. In this connection he cites both the *De causis* and Dionysius.

> Whence it is evident that every essence and every virtue proceeds from a primal one; and that the lower intelligences have their effect as it were from a radiating body, and, after the fashion of mirrors, reflect the rays of the higher to the one below them. Which matter appears to be discussed clearly enough by Dionysius in his work *On the Celestial Hierarchy*. And therefore it is stated in the book *On Causes* that "every intelligence is full of forms." Reason, then, as we have seen, demonstrates that the divine light, that is to say the divine goodness, wisdom, and virtue, shines in every part.[24]

The creation is thus derived from God in its being and in its essence, from God who is omnipresent, His glory shining throughout the universe although this omnipresence involves degrees.

> He says well, then, when he says that the divine ray, or divine glory,

> "penetrates and shines through the universe"; penetrates, as to essence; shines forth, as to being. And what he adds as to "more and less" is manifestly true, since we see that one essence exists in a more excellent degree, and another in a less; as is clearly the case with regard to heaven and the elements, the former being incorruptible, while the latter are corruptible.[25]

Thus Dante explains in the opening lines of the *Paradiso* that the glory of the First Mover shines forth in every part of the universe and why it shines forth in one part more and in another part less. Causality, being, essence, and power radiate down from the highest Reality as light, and all the universe reflects this light in varying degrees according to the capacity of its parts. The divine ray or glory penetrates everywhere as to its essence, that is to say that the light is a manifestation of God Himself, revealing what He is everywhere that it is present. It shines forth as to being because the divine light constitutes things in their being, the light conferring forms as the principle of both knowledge and being to the intelligences, who transmit them to the lower orders and control them. We may recall that the light which constitutes both the principle of knowledge and the principle of being translates the inner essence of what it constitutes. A thing is known because the same light that constitutes its being radiates out as the form or species through which it is known. The light is ultimately no more than a reflection of the glory and beauty of the Creator shining back to Him from His creation as the splendor or reflection of His light.

The radiation of the Primal Light creates a hierarchy of light, goodness, power, being, and glory; all are but splendor or reflected light of the Primal Light. The imagery here is clearly that of emanationism with all its monistic, or rather pantheistic, implications. However, like Albertus Magnus, Dante does maintain that every essence except the primary one is caused (21, l. 385—*Omnis essentia, praeter primam, est causata*). There is thus in this document an inconsistent mixture of the imagery and concepts of emanationism with Aristotelian conceptions of the transcendence of the divine and the orthodox conception of creation *ex nihilo*. Here and in the *Paradiso* Dante imagined the relation of the universe to God as one of emanation, although he never seems to have inferred any of the more heterodox implications of this conception of the universe.[26]

He continues:

> And having premised this truth, he next goes on to indicate Paradise

> by a circumlocution; and says that he was in that heaven which receives the glory of God, or his light, in most bountiful measure. As to which it must be understood that heaven is the highest heaven, which contains all the bodies of the universe, and is contained by none, within which all bodies move (itself remaining everlastingly at rest), and which receives virtue from no corporeal substance. And it is called the Empyrean, which is as much as to say, the heaven glowing with fire or heat; not that there is material fire or heat therein, but spiritual, which is holy love, or charity.[27]

The empyrean is the heaven which stands "closest to the divine light and therefore receives the most of its glory or light (*lux*)." This is glory conceived as the light itself, not as the reflected glory which shines forth or shines back. It is the supreme heaven which encloses the whole of the corporeal universe and is itself circumscribed only by the love which moves all things, itself unmoved, the love which is a spiritual fire or heat as well as a spiritual light. It is a "quiet light," everlastingly at rest.

That this empyrean receives most of the divine light can be proved in two ways: it contains all things, without itself being contained by any, and therefore stands closest, in some sense, to the Primal Light. As the containing body it stands in the same relationship to what it contains as does that which confers form to that which receives it or, in the more usual vocabulary of the schools, as does act to potency. As such it also stands in relation to what is contained as a cause to its effect, and since all causality is of the nature of a ray emanating from the first cause, and the empyrean is the highest of causes in the corporeal universe, it is clear that the empyrean must receive the most of the divine light. It thus follows from the fact that the empyrean is the most powerful of causes that it is the most luminous, for causal power or efficaciousness is a function of the light that radiates from the divine light or first cause, which is God.

> Now that this heaven receives more of the divine light than any other can be proved by two things. Firstly, by its containing all things, and being contained by none; secondly, by its state of everlasting rest or peace. As to the first the proof is as follows: The containing body stands in the same relation to the content in natural position as the formative does to the formable, as we are told in the fourth book of the *Physics*. But in the natural position of the whole universe the first heaven is the heaven which contains all things; consequently it is related to all

> things as the formative to the formable, which is to be in the relation of cause to effect. And since every causative force is in the nature of a ray emanating from the first cause, which is God, it is manifest that heaven which is in the highest degree causative receives most of the divine light.[28]

Here again we find a curious blending of Neoplatonism with Aristotelianism. There is on the one hand the distinctive light speculation of the Neoplatonic tradition, but it is coupled with the Aristotelian doctrine of natural place, the inherent source of motion or natural tendency which impels all things to seek their place in the universe. Once anything arrives in its place, assuming it had been displaced, the same nature which was the cause of motion is the cause of its quiescence.[29] When a thing is in its natural position, it is most fully actual and therefore most fully causal. At the same time it is quiescent in the sense that it does not undergo motion. Motion, in the Aristotelian universe, is a sign of lack of realization of a thing's essence. Anything which changes in the Aristotelian universe is, in a sense, very busy becoming itself, finding its place, or, finally, being resolved into its elements.

Light is thus the principle of being, efficacy, actuality, and causality. Previously (20, ll. 349 ff.) Dante had, in discussing the opening lines of the *Paradiso*, explained how by the glory of the First Mover shining forth or reflecting back in all parts of the universe in different degrees he had meant that, after the fashion of mirrors (21, l. 405), the divine light, excellence, wisdom, and virtue reglowed or shone forth everywhere (21, ll. 410 ff.). This glory, excellence, and splendor which the whole of creation reflects back on the Creator is not only beauty as light, but also perfection proceeding from the Primal Perfection as a ray. Dante argues that nothing in motion or change can be perfect. The empyrean is, however, in a state of rest. It must therefore receive most of the perfection of the light emanating from the Primal One and therefore receive more light than any other heaven.

> As to the second the proof is this: Everything which has motion moves because of something which it has not, and which is the terminus of its motion. The heaven of the moon, for instance, moves because of some part of itself which has not attained the station towards which it is moving; and because no part whatsoever of it has attained any terminus whatsoever (as indeed it never can), it moves to another station, and thus is always in motion, and is never at rest, which is what it desires. And what I say of the heaven of the moon applies to all the

> other heavens, except the first. Everything, then, which has motion is in some respect defective, and has not its whole being complete. That heaven, therefore, which is subject to no movement, in itself and in every part whatsoever of itself has whatever it is capable of having in perfect measure, so that it has no need of motion for its perfection. And since every perfection is a ray of the Primal One, inasmuch as He is perfection in the highest degree, it is manifest that the first heaven receives more than any other of the light of the Primal One, which is God. . . . Hence it is clear that when the author says "in that heaven which receives more of the light of God," he intends by a circumlocution to indicate Paradise, or the heaven of the Empyrean.[30]

He continues to strengthen this argument by citing Aristotle that the nobility or "honor" of a heaven is in direct proportion to its distance from the terrestrial. This is the heaven above the heaven to which Christ ascended that He might fill all things. It is the heaven of the delights of the Lord, the heaven from which Lucifer fell "full of wisdom and perfect in beauty."

> And in agreement with the foregoing is what the Philosopher says in the first book on Heaven, namely that "a heaven has so much the more honourable material than those below it as it is further removed from terrestrial things." In addition to which might be adduced what the Apostle says to the Ephesians of Christ: "Who ascended up far above all heavens, that He might fill all things." This is the heaven of the delights of the Lord; of which delights it is said by Ezekiel against Lucifer: "Thou, the seal of similitude, full of wisdom, beautiful in perfection, wast in the delights of the Paradise of God."[31]

Thus the hierarchies of being, truth, beauty, perfection, indeed of all value, are reduced to a hierarchy of light ascending to the very Primal Light itself, spiritual, uncreated, divine, the vision of which is the vision of all. The doctrines we have considered are the bare bones of the most important part of Dante's universe. The flesh and substance are the *Paradiso*, to which we now turn.

While the *Inferno* and *Purgatorio*, in their respective ways, are concerned with the correction of moral error, the *Paradiso* as a journey through the intelligible universe celebrates truth and involves the correction of intellectual error. Here Dante rectifies his mistakes of thought and knowledge on such questions as the ordering of the celestial hierarchy, the origin of the spots on the moon, and the language of Adam. The *Paradiso* is thus philosophical poetry, both in the obvious meaning and in the most exact sense of this term. It solves the problem of rendering a systematically ordered world of pure thought in terms of images. To the extent that the *Inferno* and *Purgatorio* deal with virtue, they bear on the ethical realm and are dramatic and psychological. Readers of the *Paradiso* are sometimes disappointed because it lacks those dramatic qualities which dominate the previous *cantiche* and which, we generally assume, are central to literature.

For Dante, however, the ethical realm and the life of conflict and choice prepare the way for a life of ideal emotional and intellectual activities. The ultimate objects of desire are not actions but states of mind and spirit—understanding, love, joy. The *Paradiso*, so to speak, evokes "a life beyond life," pure spontaneity which transcends morality and the ordinary forms of human experience. Hence comes its lyrical and evocative character, the subjective mode in which Dante describes this part of the universe. He is, in a way, the single character here, the only one still capable of surprise. What we feel about his experience at this stage of the journey we feel through the effect his various experiences have on him.

If the problem of the *Paradiso* was the reduction of objects of thought to objects of vision, how was this accomplished? First, the ladder of light constituted an ontological principle which ran through the whole of reality, from the sensible to the intelligible to God. Light metaphysics also unified and made continuous these two orders of reality, by positing light, in its various analogical forms, as the single strand running through the whole universe. To the various forms of light corresponded various forms of apperception, both sense and thought being explained by the union of "inner and outer lights." There was thus no truly sharp cleavage in light metaphysics—at least for the imagination—between the realms of matter and spirit, sense and thought. Thought was not a world of pure colorless concepts, but one of even brighter light than the world of senses. Thus the intelligible world was supersensuous both in a privative and in a positive sense. Clearly, the solution to Dante's problem lay at hand in the concepts and images of the light-metaphysics tradition. He could shape the ladder of light—the ultimate principle of all value in the universe—to render his own universal vision in terms of shapes, grades, and kinds of light.[32]

The second mode of rendering the celestial universe was to make the heavenly host *manifest* itself in space and time during the journey through the spheres. The *Paradiso*'s imagery thus functions as symbolism since it refers to a higher reality than language can formulate. Dante's images, however, far from being arbitrary are drawn from the world of knowledge and observation; they mean what they say and simultaneously point to a reality which trancends them. Dante shapes light to build the universe of the *Paradiso*, but this light has the same properties and obeys the same laws as the light of the universe according to the knowledge of his time. His universe is thus simultaneously an imaginative creation and a world about which one might ask the same questions as one asks about the real world.

The eyes whose function it is to be lured by beauty discern it through its garment of light, the latter a reflection or incarnation of the immaterial, uncreated light that is God. Luminosity in matter is simply a defective manifestation of the same power as it exists detached from matter. Thus in canto XXX a ray of immaterial light from the immaterial tenth heaven or Empyrean materializes itself at a point in the concave surface of the ninth sphere "which derives from this ray light and power." At this point time and space begin, as well as causality and natural law, for in the Empyrean "where God rules directly, natural law is of no effect." This light is the "lume" or "splendor of God" (XXX, 97–123). This power communicates existence and activity to the entire universe through the agency of the *primum mobile*, which, spinning within the Empyrean, transmits its *virtù* to all the lower spheres that it encloses and through them to all other beings. (II, 112–123). Thus the unitary power and efficacy of the heaven of light are diffracted through the stars and planets, constituting a graded ladder of light as causal power.[33]

The visible light of the stars is constantly affected by the immaterial light of the intellect that moves it—"the heaven which is beautified by so many lights takes its image from the profound mind that turns it and itself becomes the stamp of that seal." Material light reveals itself as a reflection or "copy" of the immaterial light, the "profound mind." We are thus prepared early for the assimilation of thought to light and of thinking to vision by the conception of material light as the "stamp" and image of God (II, 124–148).

God's power is therefore a function of light, distributed and differentiated through the heavenly bodies by the process of "multiplication" peculiar to light alone. Dante carefully uses the medieval term *multiplicatio* to describe the manner in which light diffuses itself (II, 137).[34] This light, the principle which beautifies the heavens, shines in various degrees in different places because "diverse power makes a diverse alliance with the precious body which it quickens" (140). As the vital principle manifests itself differently in various parts of the body, so God's power shines differently in the various parts of the heavens. Thus the physical light of the stars proceeds directly or indirectly from the immaterial qualities of the moving intellect, for "the mingled virtue shines through the body" (144). The gleam of the heavenly bodies is a reflection of God's joy in His creation, as joy in humans is evidenced by light spreading through the pupil of the eye. Recall the passages in *Convivio* III, viii, about sensible beauty as the translation of an inner immaterial quality, an external light reflecting an internal light: Dante is saying here that the sensible beauty and light of the heavens is the "translation" of the immaterial light and beauty which is God. In human beings this translation of the internal into the external light was most manifest in the eyes and the smile. Thus the stars are, metaphorically, the eyes of God: they most reveal His beauty and His joy, they gleam through a kind of rejoicing.

In *Paradiso* XIII, 52–81, light is described as the actualizing principle descending from its source, the Father, through the living Light, the Son, coequal to the source and to the Love that binds them. It shines first upon the nine subsistences that form the heavenly hierarchy, descending down to the "last potencies," and thus constitutes the ladder of actuality or being. The light from the "living Light," the Word in whose mind are archetypal forms, operates on the natural world through the agency of the light streaming from the heavenly bodies and their motions. But the potencies awaiting actualization, the "wax," and the actualizing agent, the luminous heavenly bodies, are not invariably in the most suitable relationship, so that the "idea" is not always fully realized in the matter. Thus the light of being and of beauty fails to shine through creatures in the same degree. This resistance of "matter" accounts for the inability of some individuals to embody fully the essence or idea.

Here Dante is primarily concerned with light as the principle of being; but the notion of spiritual light shining through the form which actualizes and dominates "matter" is light viewed as beauty. Note further that the relationship between the persons of the Trinity is described as a relationship between "Light," the Source, the living Light which it begets, and the Holy Spirit as the love between the two (XIII, 55–57). That Dante is simultaneously describing the ladder of beauty follows also from his personification of nature as the craftsman whose hand trembles. Nature sees the perfection of the archetypal forms but cannot perfectly produce them (76–78). Only twice did she achieve perfection, with Adam and in Christ, and then only because of the direct operation of the burning Love which is the Holy Spirit, alone capable of perfectly realizing the idea in matter (82–87).

These ideas are mere elaborations and applications of the principle announced at the very start (I, 1–6) when the luminous beauty of God was described as shining in different degrees throughout the universe. Thus light functions as the principle of actuality, being, efficacy, and beauty. The glory, power, and creativity of the Creator operate in and through light, a protean light whose ultimate source is God Himself. Intellectual vision itself is a ray of the Mind which fills all things. This ray has its origin beyond all that appears to it and is its own witness to its dependent and derivative nature. The principle of knowledge is thus described as light whose ultimate source is the divine mind (XIX, 51–56).[35]

The light which is the principle of being, beauty, efficaciousness, and knowledge emanates, we know, from the immaterial qualities of the moving intellect. This radiation of the divine power is affected by the spiritual splendor of the blessed souls and of Beatrice. This is most beautifully exemplified in Dante's and Beatrice's passage from the Moon's sphere to Mercury's (V, 94–99). Here Beatrice's joy is so great that Mercury turned brighter for it and "smiled" through its luminosity.

Let us return to the point of material light which Dante saw on the concave surface of the ninth sphere (XXX, 11) and consider some of the other functions of light. He had previously seen this point from below, a sight which so impressed him that he literally quoted a line (canto XXVIII) from Aristotle's *Metaphysics*, Book XII. The staggering significance of that point of light is best expressed by a short simple statement of philosophical truth from its discoverer. What Aristotle thought, Dante now sees: "From that point hangs heaven and all nature" (41). The point is surrounded by nine concentric circles, of which the closest circle is the *primum mobile*. It spins with maximum speed because of its great "desire," as all bodies spin faster in proportion to proximity to that point. The light emanating from here is the source of all natural things and the substantial form of the universe and, as such, is the form and nature that preserves every corporeal form and gives it power to act.

Dante next questions Beatrice about the angelic circles he sees revolving about the point. He notices that the noblest and most divine orbits, the fastest and brightest, are closest to the point, whereas in the world of sense the orbits are more divine in proportion to their increasing distance from the center. Dante, puzzled by this apparent reversal of ideal pattern and physical copy, looks to Beatrice for an answer (XXVIII, 52–57). She explains that the magnitude of the material spheres depends on the amount of power (*virtù*) diffused through their parts. Greater excellence makes greater blessedness, which in turn demands a greater body when its parts are uniformly and equally perfect. Thus the point of material light is the source of the degree of excellence and blessedness that anything possesses. The heavens and nature depend on it for their being and for their order of excellence (64–72). Dante is here elaborating the concept of light as the substantial form of the universe, one that constitutes things in their power and their being.

Beatrice concludes that Dante should interpret the spirits that appear to him as circles in relation to their power and not in terms of magnitude. Thus the outermost circle, the *primum mobile* or crystalline sphere, corresponds to the innermost circle in the "manifestation" or "appearance" of the angelic hierarchy. What the material and the angelic orbit have in common is speed of motion and intensity of light, functions of their worth and desire (73–78).[36] The relationship between the two systems of circles might also be described in terms of the scholastic doctrine of intensive and extensive quantity, the former corporeal and apparent, the latter incorporeal and unapparent.

As Dante, gazing on the point of material light in the ninth heaven, looks upon the one principle on which the whole corporeal universe depends, the light which is the substantial form of the physical order, so in the Empyrean, beyond space and time, he looks upon the "living ray" (*vivo raggio,* XXXIII, 77), that source of spiritual uncreated light which connects the categories in their transcendental being and so fuses them as to make them a "simple light" (*semplice lume*, 90). This universal form of all the categories of reality is analogous to the luminous point which, in the material order, is the source of the substantial form of the heavens and nature.

In the final vision, a purified sight penetrates more and more the ray of the "high" light which is essential truth (52–54). Here Dante insistently calls our attention not only to a new kind of sight but to an utterly different kind of light which is its object. The object is, of course, God; God is the Eternal Light (*etterno lume*, 43) as *lume* or radiated light. He is Supreme Light (*somma luce*, 67) and Eternal Light (*luce etterna*, 83 and 124) as *luce* or the source of light. The love and knowledge relating the Persons of the Trinity are a kind of circling of reflected light (127–128). As material light is the highest principle of the corporeal universe, spiritual light is the highest principle of the immaterial universe and ultimately of all reality. The one functions as the substantial form of the universe and of nature, conferring actuality, being, and excellence. The other, God as Light, is the universal form of the categories and relations which exhaust reality. Material light is seen with the eyes of the flesh; Eternal Light, with a purified vision.

The relation of multiplicity to this unitary Primal Light (*prima luce,* XXIX, 136) is one of creation and of "emanation." The higher cause remains in itself while producing that which is next below it in the order of things. It diffracts itself into many mirrors, remaining a unity nevertheless, but it also makes the mirrors into which it is broken (142–145). The mirrors in this instance are the angels, previously described as constituting a ninefold mirroring of the divine goodness (XIII, 58–59). The nine mirrors of the celestial hierarchy also constitute a hierarchy of forms of knowledge or "vision" of God.

The relation between the various orders of being including the angels is one of an "outflowing" or "downpouring"; Dante frequently describes it as a "raying" (*raggiare,* VII, 75). God pours out, without stint, His goodness, beauty, love, and light—irradiating all things and conforming them to Himself in their degree (cf. XIII, 52 ff.).[37] The pure forms of angelic intelligence, the heavenly bodies, composites of form and matter which are their instruments, and the prime matter which holds the potentiality of created things and upon which the angelic intelligences operate through the heavenly bodies—all these came into existence in the same way that light instantaneously diffuses itself through a transparent medium. The sequential creation recorded in Genesis took place after this creation, through the instrumentality of the angels (XXIX, 25–30). The primal light that irradiates (*raia*) the numberless angelic mirrors and the rest of creation is received by them—Dante calls them "splendors" or reflected lights of the primal light—in varying degrees. Hence the love which this light arouses in the angels is uneven. Note that light is defined as beauty and good, being the correlate of love (136–141).[38]

In this cosmology Dante inconsistently mingles the ideas and images of emanationism with Aristotelian doctrines as adopted and modified by Christian theism. The literature on the degree and kind of Dante's Neoplatonism tends to push him too far into either the Thomistic or Neoplatonic camp. His universe is startlingly Neoplatonic, but also colored by Aristotelianism and governed by the doctrines of Christian theism. His speculation is reminiscent of the Aristotelianized Neoplatonism of treatises like the *Liber de causis* and the *Liber de intelligentiis*. After all, Dante was a poet, not a philosopher, and the Thomistic universe was too abstract and colorless, too poor in imagery to feed the poetic imagination in any direct way. The grand and beautiful cosmic metaphors of the Neoplatonic tradition which Dante could find in the greatest of the Church fathers and in the writings of many of his contemporaries were far more stimulating. The thought and learning of this true artist were at the service of his imagination.

As we follow Dante on his journey, the spheres which increase in size, excellence, and blessedness also become more luminous. A further clue to the role of luminosity is found in cantos XIV and XXI, where we meet Solomon and Peter Damian, in this order. Solomon, the fifth and most beautiful light of his sphere, radiates light as the vesture of his love. Peter Damian shines so brightly as he comes to greet Dante that the poet says to himself: "I see well the love with which you signal to me" (45).

Solomon explains his luminosity thus: the love for God of the disembodied spirits shall radiate its vesture of light until the final resurrection of the body. The brightness of their light is in proportion to the intensity of their love, which in turn is directly proportional to the clarity and depth of each soul's vision. Finally, vision itself, or knowledge of God, is proportioned to the degree of grace each spirit receives over and above its deserts. After the resurrection, God will grant more of the light of grace which makes their vision adequate to Him. The transformed body will be even more luminous than the light the spirits now radiate; it will then possess "physical" eyes capable of direct vision of God. Even greater love will follow upon this greater vision. The physical eye and the "eye of the soul" will be fused into one organ, thought and vision will merge into one "supersense," and the very substance of the state of the resurrected saints will be a light more luminous than that which now constitutes them (XIV, 37–60).

Clearly, light is here a function and correlate of love and therefore functions as beauty—indeed, it is the principle of beauty itself. The circular operation of the triad light-love-vision, or beauty-love-knowledge, is made clearer by St. Peter Damian. A divine light centers upon him, penetrating the light of which he is made. Its power, joined to his sight, so uplifts him that he is able to see the divine essence from which it comes. This light produces the joy with which he is aflame; the clearness of the flame matches the clarity of his sight (XX, 83–90). The union of the "inner" lights of the faculties of apprehension with the "outer lights" constituting reality releases joy (*delectatio*), in the tradition of light metaphysics—a special application of the general scholastic principle that joy attends the union of a thing with that which befits it (*coniunctio convenientis cum convenienti*). Thus the wisest of men and the great contemplative expound a complementary doctrine. Increase of vision-knowledge results in an increase of love which in turn demands more and higher light. This circular process is characteristic of the ascent from heaven to heaven and ends only when the infinite eternal Light is reached.

The circularity of vision-love-light is adumbrated early (IV, 140–143) when Dante asks Beatrice whether unfulfilled vows can be compensated for by other means besides fulfillment, such as good works. Before answering, she increases in luminous beauty, a beauty which overpowers him. At the very start of canto V she explains her beauty, which blinded him, as a function of love and vision or truth. It is the flame of love, an "exterior light" which derives from the perfect and immediate vision of the Eternal Light, a vision which kindles love or, more precisely, is an amorous vision. Beatrice observes that she can already see in Dante's mind the implied "interior light," a shining of the eternal light of truth (v, 7–9).

Dante here explains the activity of the beatified consciousness partly in terms of his own, partly in terms of Beatrice's, but (witness the souls of Solomon and Peter Damian) the process also takes place in each consciousness separately. Beatrice in effect tells us that Dante now shares more fully in the eternal light and is thus prepared for the reception of the truth she is about to divulge. As Nardi demonstrated, Dante's epistemology is Augustinian and posits some form of divine illumination as the actualizing principle in the process of knowledge.[39] Beatrice concludes by explaining that the eternal light of truth is the true object of love and that any other becomes such only because the Eternal Light shines through it in its beauty (v, 1–12).

Happiness also manifests itself as light, and the brightness of a soul grows with increase of joy. Beatrice shines with greater splendor when she sees the Eternal Light of truth shining in Dante's mind (v, 7–8); Justinian glows with joy when ready to impart a new truth to Dante (130–132). As Beatrice's joy rises while she leads Dante closer and closer to ultimate reality, her beauty and luminosity increase with each ascent. But light here as everywhere in the *Paradiso* is no simple external sign of an inner state but is functional as the principle of truth, beauty, and being.

The circularity is, then, both a convenient metaphor and a structural rhythm permeating the *Paradiso*, at once the pattern of expanding consciousness and of ascent through the intelligible universe. The expanding spiral of growing awareness has a triadic structure, being constituted of moments of increasing light-beauty, followed by growth of love and knowledge and of a fresh desire which demands greater beauty. Each ascent is accompanied by an increase in knowledge and so leads toward God through the intelligible universe. We journey simultaneously through the ladder of love, the scale of being, and the hierarchy of all value rendered as light.

The virtuous triadic circularity of the *Paradiso* describes the way in which consciousness extends its range both *qualitatively* and quantitatively. It describes the progress of consciousness as the development of perception already known and as the successive introduction of new dimensions of insight not derivable from the preceding state. Each moment of Dante's "blindness" as he ascends from sphere to sphere is really the moment of superrational ecstasy which precedes conscious awareness of a new and higher level of reality; this sort of "blindness" comes from an excess of light.

But the *Paradiso* actually has a linear as well as a circular rhythm: these correspond to two simultaneous journeys, one through the sensible, the other through the intelligible, world. As the spirits of the blessed only manifest themselves in the universe of space and time but reside in the Empyrean, so the architecture of the intelligible universe is gradually revealed through its sensible analogue. Finally, with the acquisition of a new sense of vision, once the limits of the universe of space and time have been passed, all reality is simultaneously grasped in one flash. Dante's linear ascent frequently comes to life through the imagery of wings and of the arrow seeking its mark. It is interrupted as Dante, upon entering each sphere, is carried along for a time by its diurnal motion. Circularity—a "motion" proper to spiritual and incorruptible substances—manifests itself in the moment of transition from sphere to sphere primarily in Dante the pilgrim's consciousness and, upon completion of the journey, as the "motion" of his desire and will after they are "revolved by the Love that moves the sun and the other stars" (XXXIII, 145).

The state of blessedness, in the very presence of God, is not identical with the activity of consciousness on the road to God. It is rather the activity at the journey's term. This state begins with grace which rectifies and makes good the will. A good will and grace constitute merit which determines the degree of vision or "sight" of God's essence. This sight, in its own right, awakens love (XXVIII, 109–114). The circularity which Solomon and Peter Damian describe, also ultimately a gift of grace, may be said to have a fourth phase as the presupposition of its triadic movement. However, the state, as distinct from the attainment of blessedness ends with the love which follows vision, for the angels and the blessed are completely filled with beatitude, and their vision is as complete as it can be. In the process of ascent, the emphasis is placed on love's demand for more light as beauty and knowledge, since vision is not yet complete and love must therefore demand and obtain more of the light which is beauty (XII, 31–32).

This light is a reflection of the infinite, eternal light. It is divine goodness which reveals its beauty through its burning and sparkling (VII, 64 ff.) and the Primal Light irradiating the angels and eliciting their love (XXIX, 136). Every lesser good is as a light from its ray, and more than any other it moves the mind to love (XXVI, 31 ff.). It operates through all the lesser lights and beauties of creation, including Beatrice.

Beatrice's blinding supernatural beauty is but the light in which, like Peter Damian and the other saints, she is "embosomed," the light of which she is now made. Now that Beatrice has put off the corruptible body, that inner splendor shines in all its power. The incorruptible body she, along with Solomon and the other saints, will put on after the resurrection will be even more beautiful because it will have still more vision and its inner flame of love will shine yet brighter.

From the two sources of light, material and immaterial, there radiate being, actuality, excellence, blessedness, and the luminosity which is beauty itself. All, *pari passu*, constitute various hierarchical orders and are reducible to properties of the analogical forms of light. The ladders of light, being, love, knowledge, and beauty are all actually fused; this fusion permits Dante to ascend to God as poet, lover, philosopher, and mystic seer all at once. For each step in the ladder includes and transcends the qualities and perfections of the one below it until Perfection and Reality themselves are reached and found to be a "simple light," from whose virtuous radiation the entire universe is ultimately derived. The ladder of light and beauty is thus, in one way, the *scala Dei* par excellence, for if all the distinctions in reality are traceable to light, so Dante's distinctions in forms and modes of apprehension and appetition are reduced to a kind of *sui generis* unitary faculty which transcends and unifies sense and thought, love and knowledge, and is the faculty for perceiving this supersensuous immaterial light. Paradise contains no object of thought which is not at the same time an object of "sense," no object of love which is not fully an object of knowledge. To light, as the principle of All, corresponds this faculty as power of simultaneously grasping all (*totum simul*).

The light that is beauty motivates the ascent to "simple light" by engendering the desire which drives the soul to God. The light is ultimately the radiated light (*lume*) of God, His grace (I, 73–79). But light as motive power resides mediately in Beatrice's beautiful eyes which have lifted Dante from planet to planet through the heavens (XVII, 113–121). The beauty of her eyes comes into play especially as the poet mounts from sphere to sphere. The surge from the earthly paradise to the heavens begins when Beatrice fixes her eyes on the heavens and Dante fixes his own upon hers. They had previously both been looking at the sun together, she first and he imitating her.

Dante, in his reconstituted unfallen nature, can bear to contemplate the sun in all its splendor, along with Beatrice. Suddenly the sky is doubly bright, as if two suns were shining in it; Dante then fixes his eyes on Beatrice's; she, in turn, is looking heavenward (I, 49–63). Her aspect transforms, divinizes him, an indescribable experience the nature of which he suggests only by analogy with the story of Glaucus and allusion to St. Paul's experience (64–75). Only after gazing on her eyes is he transhumanized and he hears the music of the spheres. Simultaneously he sees a further increase in light which arouses his desire to know the cause of his experience (76–93).

The pattern here described repeats itself at every stage of the journey through the spheres: Beatrice looks toward a higher reality, Dante gazes into her eyes and, as light increases, reaches another sphere. At first she has to tell him that he is ascending; later, from any increase of light he gathers that he has reached a higher sphere. Such an increase of light is always accompanied by a growing desire or love and by a change in the "spiritual gravity" or natural love of the soul, which, free from sin, shoots off like a bolt of lightning toward its natural place. In the explanation which follows, Beatrice describes the doctrine of the *pondus amoris*, the internal principle of all things, corporeal and intellectual, prompting them to seek their proper place, moving to different ports over the great sea of being, each with a guiding instinct of its own (112–114). As Glaucus became a sea-god, Dante, extending the image, intimates that he has become a god in the sea of being. Beatrice concludes by explaining that his natural motion upward is no miracle. It is as natural for him to rise as it is for fire to ascend to its sphere (139–142).

The process of ascent is thus a version of the same virtuous circularity of Peter Damian's and Solomon's light-love-vision. Dante "sinks" himself in Beatrice's eyes which themselves are "sunk" in the vision of the Eternal Light. An increase of light is accompanied by an increase of love, which in turn demands more light. To clarify this process, let us examine the various moments of transition from star to star.

In ascending to the moon, Dante simply describes some aspects of the process later stated more emphatically. He fixes his eyes on Beatrice's and in an instant is carried to the lunar sphere by the "inborn and perpetual thirst for the godlike kingdom." He recalls her happiness and beauty and describes his entry into the body of the moon, still uncertain whether *he* is in his body. Weighing the possibility of the miraculous interpenetration of bodies, he likens the physical process of ascent to a ray of light passing through water without breaking it. The light of this sphere calls to mind a pearl and a diamond sparkling in the sun (II, 19–49).

Dante concludes this episode by announcing an important principle. Paradise is the direct vision of that reality which is in this world the object of thought and belief and which will not be discursively and mediately "demonstrated," but will be known with the immediacy of sight and the directness with which we know axiomatic truths (43–45). Here the theme of the developing power of vision begins, the powers of sense and thought gradually fusing until a "new sight" is acquired.

The second ascent is to the sphere of Mercury. Beatrice turns to the brightest part of the universe, the *primum mobile*. Dante, gazing upon her face, notices a changed look, and he shoots up like an arrow to the second sphere. The increase of light takes place explicitly in the planet itself and implicitly in Beatrice whose extreme joy makes the planet turn brighter, the joy and happiness of the blessed, the poet proclaims after the ascent, being signaled by their shining (v, 85–99).

Dante tells the first spirit he encounters, Justinian, that he understands his smiling because the light which constitutes him sparkles when he does so. What Dante so describes is the smile as a sparking of the soul's joy, an outer light reflecting an inner one. Here it refers to a disembodied spirit who draws the "outer light" of heaven through the eyes of the soul and whose subsequent increased love and joy it expresses through an increase of light (124–126). Finally, Justinian is so filled with joy that the light he radiates conceals his shape (133–138).

In the ascent to Venus, the increase of light and joy which accompanies every transition is depicted as an increase in Beatrice's beauty. Indeed, Dante, never aware exactly how he goes from sphere to sphere, gathers from her heightened beauty that he has arrived. The motif of her increasingly luminous beauty henceforth becomes progressively emphatic (VIII, 13–21).

In the ascent to the sun, Dante expressly emphasizes the bewildering and "unconscious" nature of the process: Beatrice, we learn, is leading him so instantaneously that the movement cannot be measured in time (x, 34–39). After Solomon's discourse on the resurrection of the body an overwhelming brightness, the "very sparkling of the Holy Ghost" (XIV, 76), blinds him. At the same time, Beatrice appears so beautiful and smiling that his memory cannot retain her beauty. The simultaneous and blinding increase of light and beauty is the "moment" of ascent to the sphere of Mars, which "smiles" with more than its accustomed brightness (76–88).

As she climbs to Jupiter, Beatrice gains more than before in beauty, especially in the luminous beauty of her eyes. Dante notes that he has ascended to Jupiter at the moment when he observes Beatrice's heightened beauty and immediately afterward senses that his circling movement in the spheres has a wider arc (XVIII, 55–69).

On the way to Saturn, the light-beauty which functions as the final cause of the ascent, turning desire into the motor power of the flight through the spheres, appears ever more strongly in Beatrice's countenance. She here explicitly mentions what we have gradually come to realize: her intensified beauty is nothing less than her "light." She increases in light-beauty as she ascends the ladder of ever-higher grades of light which lead to the uncreated light. Like Aristotle's first cause, she is the cause of Dante's motion as the object of desire. If Beatrice were to add the "second" beauty of her smile to the first beauty of her eyes, Dante would be consumed. Her "inner light" externally translated as beauty in these two regions of the "body" has become too great for him to bear (XXI, 1–18).

The ascent to the starry sphere is briefly described. Beatrice, with a sign alone, impels him up the ladder, Jacob's ladder, which leads from Saturn upward (XXII, 100–106). Ascent to the crystalline sphere, the *primum mobile*, again clarifies the process. Dante's is an enamored mind, a knowing faculty which at the same time loves. All human beauty, natural or portrayed, is a bait, serving to capture and fix the *eyes so as to possess the mind*. Beatrice's now surpasses all forms of temporal beauty; to the beauty of her eyes is added that of her smile. Dante has now the strength to bear this addition, which, at the previous ascent, Beatrice withheld lest it destroy him (XXVII, 88–99).

Human beauty, incarnate or depicted, thus has a purpose. It lures the eyes in order to possess the mind, forcing it toward a higher reality of which it is the manifestation. Through its revealing power, it initiates a process of loving and, at the same time, of knowing. The experience of beauty is self-transcending in that it arouses a love which can finally be satisified only in the Good and a desire for understanding, to be fulfilled only in Truth (X, 1–12).

The ascent to the Empyrean follows upon the vision of the angelic circles revolving around the point of immaterial light analogous to the point of material light from which nature "hangs." The increasing brightness of the central point obliterates the spinning circles, as the brightness of the rising sun outshines the stars. The blinding light and Dante's desire make him turn to Beatrice, so beautiful now that only God can see her beauty in its fulness (XXX, 7–21), a beauty no artist can describe. His whole life has been the poetic pursuit of her beauty, but now the lover-poet must be transcended and included in something higher (22–33). The task is done, and Dante is ready to see Paradise as it really is, not as it has hitherto been manifested to him (34–45).

Dante will see both the angel and the saints, the latter as they will appear at the last judgment, that is, in the resurrected flesh. He has left time and space, the "greatest body," has gone from material to immaterial light, pursuing it as beauty through the whole universe, and is now in eternity. Passing from time to eternity, the lover and poet become the saint, endowed with new sight so strong that it can bear to look upon ultimate reality. This faculty is a fusion of sense and thought, of will and intellect (46–69).

This vision of light arouses Dante's desire to know, and Beatrice, the sun of his eyes, she who, like the sun of the intelligible world, was a light for him between truth and intellect, explains that what he has seen is symbolic of ultimate reality. His new sight is not yet fully developed (70–81). Dante then "drinks" with his eyes of the river of light as a child sucks its mother's breasts; the light reveals itself as the yellow rose of Paradise. Canto xxx is filled with sensual imagery; the flowers of light intoxicate the "saintly sparks" by their odors, Dante greedily "tastes" the river of light, and the verb "to see" recurs insistently. More significantly, the senses seemed fused, for he drinks light and sees odors: mystical synesthesia which accompanies the superhuman unification of consciousness. Dante has also been reborn, having become a child once more, a conception he adumbrated by describing himself shortly before (50) as swathed in the effulgent veil of the vivid or living light (82–90).

Before this moment Dante suffered a spell of blindness, when at the end of canto xxv he was blinded by St. John's spirit prior to his examination on love. St. John, we recall, assures him that his loss of sight is temporary and that Beatrice can restore it, possessing the same power in her glance as resided in the hand of Ananias, who restored the sight of St. Paul (4–12). Dante submits, likening his eyes to doors through which passed the fire of love that Beatrice infused in him along with her image. At the moment of his examination on love, Dante points back to the beginning, the first moment of erotic possession, and begins to tell St. John all that he learned of love in his journey up the ladder: that it is both a cosmic and a supernatural principle, one which comprehends both his first experience of it with Beatrice and his last with God. When Beatrice finally restores his sight, upon this blindness, as upon all the others suffered in Paradise, there follows a higher and stronger vision.

Dante is blinded again in passing from the *primum mobile* to the empyrean; this moment of blindness precedes the acquisition of a "new sight"; indeed, it proleptically defines all its precursors. It is the blindness which prepares the candle for the flame, the moment in which the final change—qualitative and not simply one of degree—endows him with a new sight (xxx, 46–60).

Dante's previous spells of blindness had all involved the acquisition of stronger sight, but the poet, we remember, now describes a special kind of vision, not only sharper, but different. He does so by frequently repeating the word "to see," especially in a triple rhyme on *vidi* (95–99). The eaves of Dante's eyelids drink of the river of light which then becomes round in shape (85–90). There follows a description of the universe of light. The material universe is a spherical body whose outermost circumference is the *primum mobile*. A ray of divine light is projected on the sphere, conferring on it life and power, motion and efficacy. The reflection of this ray is transformed into a circular disklike shape of light which is the floor of Paradise (100–114).

The same light which swathes him and which he sees is also the light by which he sees. The splendor of God, an emanation of His light, reveals a clearer vision of the empyrean; we have returned to the same ray of immaterial light with which Dante began and which he described as materializing itself on the surface of the *primum mobile*. Above the girdle or plane of light formed by this ray there rise, tier on tier in an ever-expanding circular pattern, the souls of the blessed who constitute the petals of the heavenly rose. Beatrice's final act of "attraction" is to draw Dante into the yellow of the eternal rose (124–128).

So far we have focused our attention on Beatrice, the final cause, starting with the point at which her mission ends, considering the nature of the light to which she leads him, then going back to the beginning of the ascent and working our way forward to the goal of their joint journey. The idea of desire as the motive of the flight, a desire aroused by beauty-light and proportioned to it, finds its concrete expression in the imagery of wings, often in language so strikingly reminiscent of Plato's dialogues of love that it almost seems as if Dante had the actual texts at hand.

Let us now explicitly state the nature and function of "wings." In canto XV Beatrice is described as having made Dante grow the wings for this heavenly flight and as the person whose beauty, specifically her smile, strengthens the wings of his will or desire (49–54, 70–72). Again, in XXV, during St. James's examination of Dante on hope, Beatrice is described as the compassionate one who directs the feathers of his wings to this high flight (49–54). In the final stages of the journey, it is not desire which must strengthen Dante's wings but grace coming from the Virgin, who thus replaces Beatrice as the immediate final cause which motivates the journey. The restored original goodness of human nature which permitted Dante's wings to respond directly and immediately to the urgings of desire and to pursue Beatrice's beauty through the spheres has reached its limit. The journey so far has been natural in the sense of something possible not to fallen nature but only to restored nature—it has conformed to the cosmological principles of spiritual gravity. Henceforth the highest grace, the supreme gift of divine love, must operate, a gift which, if granted at all, is granted to prayer. As the poet and lover yield to the saint, so eros, a natural cosmological principle gives way to *agape*, a purely divine and supernatural principle (XXXII, 145–147).

Desire for the final vision is not enough. As justice and mercy were necessary for the flight from the earthly Paradise through the spheres, so supreme grace is necessary for the vision of the divine essence—"the supernatural journey." As St. Bernard says to the Virgin, whoever does not seek this grace from her is like one whose desire would fly without wings (XXXIII, 13–15). For the ultimate inexpressible vision of God even wings strengthened by Mary's intercession are not strong enough. Dante is passive, totally dependent, he is not "flying" toward his goal but is poised in the air. He need not, rather cannot, use his wings. Dante again refers to a "new sight" (*vista nova*), both the object of his apprehension and the faculty by which he apprehends it. As he seeks to understand this "strange sight" which his new unified and transcendent consciousness can see, he is struck as by a bolt of lightning, his mind is filled, and his desire is satisfied. The ambiguity of the term *vista nova*, the objective and subjective aspects of this final vision, is deliberate, for the end of the journey is union. The two aspects of the experience are now indistinguishable, and Dante is one with the love that moves the sun and the other stars. He takes on the "circular" motion of eternity (133–145). The worm has finally become the angelic butterfly (*Pur.* X, 121–126), and Dante has, at long last, realized the destiny of the human race, born to fly upward even though many fail to realize this destiny and fall back (*Pur.* XII, 95–96). Neither buffetings nor the pursuit of worldly glories stayed Dante from the attainment of his goal. The vain rationalizations by which men defend human goals, whether honorable, like law and medicine, or dishonorable, like tyranny and idleness, had no permanent effect on him (XI, 1–12), and with Beatrice's help he finally achieved his aim.

Dante was brought to Paradise called by the beauty of the heavens (*Pur.* XIV, 145 ff.), but, above all, enticed by the sight of the luminous beauty embodied in those "beautiful eyes of which love made a noose to capture me" (XXVII, 11–12). The lure of beauty for the eyes and the eyes themselves as the most beautiful of bodily parts run as a unifying thread through Dante's works from the first visions of the *Vita nuova* to the final visions of the *Paradiso*.

In the *Vita nuova* (XIV, 33–47), the vision of Beatrice at the wedding party had robbed Dante of all his senses, except sight which remained alive because love had taken possession of the eyes. This sense had its vision of beauty which captured the eyes and took possession of the mind (XXVII, 88 ff.). Like all the visions of the *Vita nuova*, it obeys a principle which Dante presents early in this work when he assigns to the image of Beatrice's beauty abiding with him continually such virtue that at no time did it allow Love to rule over him without the faithful counsel of reason in those things in which such counsel would be useful. This love then is a true eros in that it is guided by judgment. It is a superrational or an arational, not an antirational, principle, complementing reason although the counsel of reason is not always applicable to its workings.

The beauty of the lady's eyes actualizes the potentiality of love in the lover; even where it does not exist potentially she can bring it into being (*Vita nuova,* XX and XXI). Commenting on the sonnet "Negli occhi porta la mia donna amore" (XXI), Dante contends that in the first stanza he portrays the lady as reducing the potentiality for love in the lover to actuality by means of her most noble part, the eyes. In the previous sonnet, the famous "Amor e 'l cor gentil sono una cosa," the poet describes the beauty which appears in a wise lady as so pleasing *to* the eyes that it awakens in the heart a desire for the pleasing thing and thereby arouses the spirit of love (XX). These two sonnets show the dual aspect of Dante's conception of the relation of eyes or sight to beauty: the eyes themselves are lured by beauty and as the lady's most beautiful part are themselves a lure. This reciprocal relationship, analogous to that of act and potency, is also an image of the motive behind the erotic flight. The goal of this flight and its final cause Dante adumbrates in the closing sonnet of the *Vita nuova*. The lure of beauty evoking love finally leads the poet to an intuition of the world beyond space and time, an intuition not clearly understood except insofar as it involves Beatrice. After this sonnet Dante had a vision of such wondrous things that he determines to speak no more of Beatrice until he may treat of her more worthily. To this end he studies most diligently. The counsel of reason thus appears at the end of the *Vita nuova* as well as at the beginning. It is a love that both demands and seeks understanding, the full meaning of which the *Comedy* reveals to us: *Amor quaerens intellectum.*

When, in the *Purgatorio*, Dante's eyes again behold Beatrice's beauty on the summit of the mountain, they receive divine, ecstatic visions. Those same emeralds from which love once shot his darts at him (*Pur.* XXXI, 115–117) now reveal the double nature of Christ through the image of the Griffin (118–123). Again, at the very beginning of the *Paradiso*, Dante points out the importance of the eyes in the ascent. The relationship between Beatrice's eyes and those of Dante he describes as one of act and potency. A similar relationship prevails between Beatrice's eyes and the sunlight, so that the sun, Beatrice's eyes, and Dante's eyes constitute, through the light that connects them, a hierarchy of grades of actuality. The pilgrim ray of light, the actualizing principle, strengthens Dante's sight for a higher vision (I, 46–54).

The eyes are the instruments through which he gradually attains higher and higher power of vision. Beatrice's power to actualize even higher degrees of vision grows with the ascent and coincides with her increase in beauty, especially the beauty of her eyes.

Dante makes it perfectly clear that Beatrice is always the most beautiful object in the journey through the spheres. In canto XIV he seems to be rating the divine song just heard above the beauty of her eyes, but, he explains, he merely brings this accusation against himself in order to deny it, without implying that the "holy delight" of her eyes is less important than the song. In fact, in this sphere of Mars, he has not yet looked into her eyes although he precisely defines their function. His desire finds rest in them; they are the "living seals" of all beauty, and their power and beauty become stronger and purer as they rise. Dante again conceives the relationship between Beatrice's eyes and himself in terms of act and potency, Beatrice acquiring greater beauty and actualizing power as they ascend and transmitting it to Dante so that he may follow her (130–139).

Throughout the *Paradiso* the great drama is played by the eyes as they seek light and find beauty, first in the eyes of another, then everywhere. This beauty is an external light which manifests an internal splendor. It is the principle of being and knowledge, shining in sensible particulars. A beautiful woman's organs are so arranged that she reveals the qualities of the rational soul, especially through those parts closest to the soul, the eyes and mouth, "balconies" looking out upon it (*Conv.* III, ii, vi, viii). But through these two noblest parts, "portals," not only does the soul look out, but the beloved's image enters the lover's soul (*Par.* XXVI, 13–15).

By looking at the eyes we know the soul's activity and state. The smile is the "second beauty," a flash of the soul's joy, an outward light that manifests what is within. Thus in *Purgatorio* XXXI, 136–148, the theological virtues exhort Beatrice to add the second beauty of the smile to that of the eyes. The beauty of her eyes and mouth is there described as the splendor—a radiated form of light—of the eternal living light, a translation into an "outer light" of that inner light which the saints receive from their vision of the Uncreated Light Himself (142). Note that while in the mortal state the inner light is the soul and the outer light is bodily beauty, in the state of blessedness what was the inner light becomes an outer light, translating a radiation from the divine light which irradiates the heavenly host. Her beauty is light and ultimately a reflection of God's beauty and light.

The beauty of Beatrice's eyes and smile is thus affirmed throughout Dante's works with ever-greater insistence. Passing from the *Vita nuova* to the *Paradiso*, we learn more and more of what it means and how it works. This beauty possesses a revealing power and contains so much of the meaning of love that Dante often cannot fully describe it, though he knows it to be a function of that universal love which impels the soul to embellish the eyes and smile and which shines through those parts with His luminous beauty (XVIII, 7–21). This beauty, having a divine source, initiates and carries through a process of vision which ends in union with God; the primary function of both corporeal and disembodied beauty is to start and maintain this erotic flight to God. The earliest expression of this notion is found in the famous *canzone* "Donne, ch' avete intelletto d'amore" (*Vita nuova* XIX). Corporeal beauty centered in the eyes and lips functions as a superior grace established by God. The *Convivio* (esp. III, viii) more clearly expounds the idea that corporeal beauty starts the soul on its course toward God's immaterial beauty, and the clearest statement of all is found in the first lesson Beatrice gives to Dante on the summit of Purgatory.

Dante's confession, which Beatrice demands and obtains, is an admission of having turned away from her to false pleasures as soon as death had deprived him of her visible presence (*Pur.* XXXI, 34–36). But she was able to help him back to her and to salvation. Her death was thus a death of love, and her expectation had been that Dante would be attracted by a greater beauty which death bestowed. Yet he was seduced from the true course of erotic flight, and his wings were drawn downward by false "counter loves." But, we recall, Dante returned to the beautiful lures of Beatrice's eyes and lips and, by their guidance and power, climbed the ladder to God. When finally her beauty becomes so great that only God can see it (*Par.* XXX, 7 ff.), the lover and the artist have both reached their limits. As the life of moral choice leads to the eternal life of contemplation, so the finite modes of love and beauty are subsumed in their infinite source. Beatrice has finally accomplished her mission. She was the lady above who gained for him the initial grace which made the journey possible (*Pur.* XXVI, 59). But she also strengthened Dante for heaven (X, 91–93).

We have seen this strengthening in action. Her increasing light and beauty lure Dante up the ladder of love and actualize in him even higher degrees of vision and awareness, until she reaches her limit of power. In Dante's farewell to her he acknowledges her as the source of his salvation and addresses her for the first time as "tu," a sign of equality, of the complete actuality in him of all that she succeeded in actualizing (XXI, 79–84). Yet, finally, only the Virgin's light and brightness can prepare him to see Christ (XXXII, 85–87). Beatrice was able to lead him so far because she was, not simply a mortal miracle of beauty as in the *Vita nuova* (XXI, 22; XXIX, 24–41), but through her death and salvation an immortal miracle (XVIII, 61–63). If in life she gave a foretaste of the joys of Paradise, as a saint she also reflects Paradise in her eyes, for her "lights" (*luci*, 52) look in upon the Eternal Joy or Beauty which shines directly upon her. In XVIII, 4 ff., Dante describes her as the lady who is leading him to God. Unlike her, he is not in God's presence; yet both are "present" to each other. Like the rest of the souls in Paradise her true place is in God's immediate presence, in the Empyrean. She shows as much mobility as Virgil; in fact, she descended into Hell to call him, appears in Eden, and resumes her place again in the amphitheater of the rose.

To the final imageless rapture his guide is St. Bernard, who appropriately distinguished two forms of mystical contemplation. Both are forms of ecstasy. In the lower form the soul withdraws from sensation and the images which flow into us from the outer world. In higher contemplation it withdraws even from the sensuous images; this is the contemplation of the Word of God, while the less proficient contemplatives consider the saints and angels in heaven. The lower form is still an external relation to God, equivalent to the whole of the *Paradiso* up to and including the heavenly rose. The higher form is the final rapture, a direct and internal relation to God.

As in Plato's ladder of love, the beloved must be transcended, but Dante does not leave his beloved on the first rung of the ladder. Beatrice guides her lover, intercedes for him, and leads him to the penultimate rung. For Dante, the beloved is continually active, in life and death, in the work of realization and of salvation.

# Notes

1. *Conv.* III, vii, 2–3. All citations from the *Convivio* are from the *Opere di Dante*, in an extensively commented edition begun under the direction of Michele Barbi and still in progress (vols. IV and V): *Il Convivio*, ridotto a miglior lezione e commentato da G. Busnelli e G. Vandelli con introduzione di Michele Barbi (Firenze, vol. I, 1934, vol. II, 1937). Vol. I has Books I–III, and vol. II has Book IV.

2. *De causis*, 19, pp. 181–182 in Bardenhewer.

3. Busnelli and Vandelli cite appropriate passages from Albertus in Appendix III to Book III, vol. I, pp. 460–463, in their edition of the *Convivio*, esp. *De intellectu et intelligibile* i, i, tr. 3, 2 (Borgnet, vol. IX).

4. *Conv.* III, vii, 3–4.
5. *Conv.* III, vii, 5.
6. *Conv.* III, vii, 6.
7. *Conv.* III, vii, 6–7.
8. Aristotle, *Ethics,* VII, i, 2, 1145a.
9. *Conv.* III, vii, 7.
10. *Conv.* III, vii, 8.
11. *Conv.* III, viii, 3.
12. *Conv.* III, viii, 11.
13. *Conv.* III, viii, 8.
14. *Conv.* III, viii, 9. Dante cites the passage from *De partibus animalium* III, 10, 673a, in *Ep.* x, 26, and *Vita nuova* II, i.
15. *Conv.* III, xii, 6–8.
16. *Conv.* IV, xxii, 17.
17. *Conv.* III, xiv, 4–6.
18. *Conv.* II, vi, 9. Cf. III, xiv, 4.
19. *Conv.* II, iii, 8–10.
20. *Conv.* III, ii, 14.
21. *Conv.* IV, i, ii.
22. *Conv.* I, xi, 3–4.
23. *Ep.* x, i, ll. 375 ff.: Quia ex eo quod causa secunda recipit a prima, influit super causatum ad modum recipientis et repercutientis radium, propter quod causa prima est magis causa. Et hoc dicitur in libro *De Causis*, quod "omnis causa primaria plus influit super suum causatum, quam causa universalis secunda." Sed hoc quantum ad esse.

All citations and translations from the letter to Can Grande are from *Dantis Alagherii Epistolae: The Letters of Dante*, emended text with introd., trans., notes, and indexes and appendix on the *Cursus* by Paget Toynbee (Oxford, 1920).

24. *Ep.* x, 21, ll. 400 ff.: Propter quod patet quod omnis essentia et virtus procedat a prima, et intelligentiae inferiores recipiant quasi a radiante, et reddant radios superioris ad suum inferius, ad modum speculorum. Quod satis aperte videtur Dionysius de coelesti hierarchia loquens. Et propter hoc dicitur in libro *De Causis* quod "omnis intelligentia est plena formis." Patet ergo quomodo ratio manifestat divinum lumen, id est divinam bonitatem, sapientiam et virtutem, resplendere ubique.

The phrase *omnis intelligentia est plena formis* is to be understood in the light of the principle that the effect is contained eminently in the cause and that the possession of causality, of spontaneous efficacy and force, belongs pre-eminently to spiritual beings.

25. *Ep.* x, 23, ll. 428 ff.: Bene ergo dictum est, quum dicit quod divinus radius, seu divina gloria, "per universum penetrat et resplendet"; penetrat quantum ad essentiam; resplendet quantum ad esse. Quod autem subicit de magis et minus habet veritatem in manifesto, quoniam videmus in aliquo excellentiori gradu essentiam aliquam, aliquam vero in inferiori; ut patet de coelo et elementis, quorum quidem illud incorruptibile, illa vero corruptibilia sunt.
26. Cf. Geyer in Ueberweg-Heinze, *Grundriss*, 549–551.
27. *Ep.* x, 24, ll. 473 ff.: Et postquam praemisit hanc veritatem, prosequitur ab ea, circumloquens Paradisum; et dicit quod fuit in coelo illo quod de gloria Dei, sive de luce, recipit affluentius. Propter quod sciendum quod illud coelum est coelum supremum,

continens corpora universa et a nullo contentum, intra quod omnia corpora moventur (ipso in sempiterna quiete permanente), a nulla corporali substantia virtutem recipiens. Et dicitur empyreum, quod est idem quod coelum igne sive ardore flagrans; non quod in eo sit ignis vel ardor materialis sed spiritualis, qui est amor sanctus sive caritas.

28. *Ep.* x, 5, ll. 454 ff.: Quod autem de divina luce plus recipiat, potest probari per duo. Primo per suum omnia continere et a nullo contineri; secundo per sempiternam suam quietem sive pacem. Quantum ad primum probatur sic: Continens se habet ad contentum in naturali situ sicut formativum ad formabile, ut habetur in quarto *Physicorum*. Sed in naturali situ totius universi primum coelum est omnia continens; ergo se habet ad omnia sicut formativum ad formabile; quod est se habere per modum causae. Et quum omnis vis causandi sit radius quidam profluens a prima causa, quae Deus est, manifestum est quod illud coelum quod magis habet rationem causae, magis de luce divina recipit.

29. Cf. Aristotle, *De caelo,* III, 2, and IV, 3 and 4.

30. *Ep.* x, 26, ll. 471 ff.: Quantum ad secundum probatur sic: omne quod movetur, movetur propter aliquid quod non habet, quod est terminus sui motus; sicut coelum lunae movetur propter aliquam partem sui, quae non habet illud ubi ad quod movetur; et quia sui pars quaelibet non adepto quolibet ubi (quod est impossibile) movetur ad aliud, inde est quod semper movetur et nunquam quiescit, et est eius appetitus. Et quod dico de coelo lunae, intelligendum est de omnibus praeter primum. Omne ergo quod movetur, est in aliquo defectu, et non habet totum suum esse simul. Illud igitur coelum quod a nullo movetur, in se et in qualibet sui parte habet quidquid potest modo perfecto, ita quod motu non indiget ad suam perfectionem. Et quum omnis perfectio sit radius primi, quod est in summo gradu perfectionis, manifestum est quod coelum primum magis recipit de luce Primi, qui est Deus. . . . Sic ergo patet quod quum dicit "in illo coelo quod plus de luce Dei recipit," intelligit circumloqui Paradisum, sive coelum empyreum.

31. *Ep.* x, 27, ll. 510 ff.: Praemissis quoque rationibus consequenter dicit Philosophus in primo *De Coelo* quod coelum "tanto habet honorabiliorum materiam istis inferioribus, quanto magis elongatum est ab his quae hic." Adhuc etiam posset adduci quod dicit Apostolus ad Ephesios de Christo: "Qui ascendit super omnes coelos ut impleret omnis." Hoc est coelum deliciarum Domini; de quibus deliciis dicitur contra Luciferum per Ezechielem: "Tu signaculum similitudinis, sapientia plenus et perfectione decorus, in deliciis Paradisi Dei Fuisti."

32. On light metaphysics in Dante, in addition to the works of Baeumker and De Bruyne already cited, see also G. Poletto, *Amore e luce nella Divina Comedia, ragionamento critico* (Padova, 1876); G. B. Zoppi, *Il fenomeno e il concetto della luce studiati in Dante* (Rovereto, 1886); Giuseppe Tarozzi, *Luce intellectual, piena d'amore: Nota sul concetto della natura del "Paradiso" di Dante* (Torino, 1888); Stanislao Prato, "Essenza ed imagini simboliche della luce e delle tenebre confermate da vari passi della 'Divina Commedia' a specialmente del 'Paradiso,' " *Giornale dantesco,* XIII (1905), 199–236. There are two recent studies: Allan Tate, "The Symbolic Imagination: A Meditation on Dante's Three Mirrors," *Kenyon Review,* XIV, no. 2 (1952), 256–277, and G. di Pino, *La figurazione della luce nella Divina Commedia* (Firenze, 1952).

33. On light as the principle of causality in the works of Dante cf. *Conv.* II, vi, 9–10; III, vii, 1–5; III, xiv, 3–4; *Pur.* XXV, 89; *Par.* VII, 74; VIII, 2–3; XIX, 90; XXIX, 29. The *primum mobile* which divides the temporal and spatial universe from eternity is conceived as both corporeal and incorporeal, itself "surrounded" by intellectual light and love (*Par.* XXX, 38).

34. Cf. *Pur.* xv, 66, where Dante had Virgil explain how spiritual good increases by being shared. The relation of love between the eternal goodness and the blessed is likened to light reflected between mirrors. Without expressly saying so, he bases his analogy on light's reputed ability to "multiply itself" when transmitted through the diaphanum.

35. Cf. light as the principle of knowledge in *Par.* II (106–111). Beatrice says to Dante that she will fill his mind with a light so living or vivid that it will sparkle when he sees it. In line 110, I prefer the reading "verace" for "vivace," in which case she would fill his mind with a true or truth-giving light:

Or come ai colpi delli caldi rai
  della neve riman nudo il suggetto
  e dal colore e dal freddo primai,
così rimaso te nell' intelletto
  voglio informar di luce sì vivace [or "verace"]
  che ti tremolerà nel suo aspetto.

The verb "informar" is a technical term from light speculation describing light as the principle which gives form as the principle of being and, in this case, as the principle of knowledge.

36. Cf. XXVIII, 107–115, where Dante explains how the angelic hierarchy participates in various degrees in the beatific vision and love. The degree of vision (which engenders love) is proportional to merit, which in turn is proportional to grace and rectitude of will. We must deserve the "sight of Truth," and God must freely give it before we can love Him. The process here described takes place in eternity; it is not, strictly speaking, an answer to the question whether love of God precedes knowledge of Him or knowledge precedes love of Him as applied to the mortal state. The state of the blessed is one of amorous knowing or of knowing-amorous-ness, a state which presupposes the unity of will, intellect, and sense. Intellectual vision and love are therefore two moments of one function. Of course, God must in some sense be known before He can be sought; indeed, the quest for Him is a kind of knowing.

37. Dante carefully used the term *splendore* in the technical sense of some form of reflected light in XXIX, i, 15, and again in XXX, 95, where it is through the splendor of God, His reflected light, that Dante saw the kingdom of truth. So God's motive in creating the angels was to let His reflected light shine back on him from them, because His overflowing goodness led Him to create self-conscious substances as mirrors for His light. Cf. IX, 61; XIII, 58–60; XXIX, 58–60. Dante makes God the Mind which is the origin of the categories, substances, and accidents, an idea quite different from the Neoplatonizing tradition. Yet the Primal Light "materializes" itself at and pours down from the *primum mobile*. The principle of emanationism is often affirmed in terms which could have been taken from Proclus.

38. God is also the true light or light of truth (*vera luce*) in XIII, 55, and the Trinal Light (*trina luce*) in XXXI, 28–29. As eternal light cf. also XI, 20.

39. Bruno Nardi, *Nel mondo di Dante*, 218–225.

# Thomas G. Bergin

## Dante's Provençal Gallery

IN CHAPTER TWO of the second book of his *De Vulgari Eloquentia* Dante defines the "capital matters that ought to be treated supremely" by poets; they are three: "safety, love, and virtue," which are spelled out in specific language as "prowess in arms, the fire of love, and the direction of the will." He adds that "the illustrious writers have writen poetry in the vulgar tongue on these subjects exclusively, namely Bertran de Born on Arms, Arnaut Daniel on Love, Giraut de Borneil on Righteousness, Cino of Pistoja on Love, his friend on Righteousness . . . I do not find however that any Italian has as yet written poetry on the subject of arms."[1] The passage well exemplifies Dante's fondness for categories and where possible, symmetry: three subjects, three poets (at least when a gallery is complete as the Provençal is and the Italian not yet). Knowing Dante's attachment to his authorities and his cult of three, one could almost predict that if he were to write a great poem it would have three divisions and each would contain a representative of the "vulgar" tongue which had been such an inspiration to him and other writers in his own vernacular. And so, in fact, it comes out; of all Dante's triads the Provençal poets are most obviously and architectonically disposed, one for each *cantica*, each one clearly identified and prominently placed, varying only, I would say, in their degree of integration with their milieu. But before venturing any further statement on the group as a whole, I would like to pass the chosen troubadours in review.

Bertran de Born's dramatic and macabre appearance in the *bolgia* of the sowers of discord (*Inferno* XXVIII, 112 ff.) will not easily be forgotten. He appears carrying his own severed head in his hand "a guisa di lanterna." Approaching Dante, he raises his arm "con tutta la testa," a gesture of "spaventosa naturalezza";[2] the movement of the line, as Crescini remarks,[3] underlines the painful effort required. Frightful the scene is, to be sure, although the grotesque here all but verges on the comic. Where Dante got the notion of the portable head scholars have been unable to find out with any certainty: the roots are probably in folklore and myth and most American readers—of my generation at least—are prepared for the weird spectacle by the stratagem of Brom Van Brunt, in the "Legend of Sleepy Hollow." Washington Irving, as has been pointed out by various critics,[4] owed much to German folklore; probably even before Orpheus' head rolled down the Hebrus pathetically calling on Eurydice as memorialized in the Georgics, the sight that terrified Ichabod Crane was familiar to our fanciful ancestors. Joyce's Virag illustrates that the image continues to have an appeal. Cases have been cited from the old literatures, Indian, Gaelic and Icelandic, to say nothing of Gawain's odd encounter.[5] The Church too includes various *cefalofori* among its saints; St. Denis is perhaps the most famous, but the category includes also San Miniato, surely well known to Dante.

As Bertran—or so he claims—has severed the head, i.e. the father of the family, from his son, the punishment is admitted by the sinner himself to have its appropriateness. It is commonly accepted that Bertran's function here is to illustrate one subspecies of the sowers of discord; as Mohamet and Ali had created sectarian schisms and Curio and Mosca dissension in country and city, so Bertran exemplifies the same divisive role within the family, a smaller unit to be sure, but the sin as being more personal is somehow more malicious. Bertran is the last of the categories cited, as if to suggest a final grade of wickedness. Furthermore, the "discordia domestica" here exemplified had wider repercussions; since Bertran set kings at each other, his machinations had political as well as familial consequences. Bertran, standing for one category, serves also to sum up all of them.

The detached head is properly articulate and indeed even eloquent. Bertran defines his sin with a rather pretentious scriptural reference, giving it a certain dignity of tradition as it were and assigning to himself a role of importance perhaps out of proportion to historical truth. (Crescini, among others, believes that Bertran somewhat exaggerates his political importance, but Dante took him at his word—or the word of the Provençal *Vida*.)

But if Dante treats the old warrior with a certain respect, it is hardly a matter for surprise. We have noted the reference in the *De Vulgari*; in the *Convivio* (IV, ii) Dante had spoken of Bertran's generosity, and if we are to be surprised at all, it is perhaps rather to find such a fine gentleman in such an unpleasant predicament. But of course—as for Farinata, Jason, Ulysses, and others—it is precisely Bertran's stature that makes him an appropriate choice—in keeping with the suggestion laid down by Cacciaguida before Dante sat down to write his story. As for the long vexed question of "re giovane" as agaist "re Giovanni" in line 135, all modern commentators have agreed on the former reading even though it is supported by only a minority of the manuscripts and, worse, gives the line a very irregular (though not unique) metrical pattern. "Giovane" is preferred simply because critics have been unable to believe that Dante, knowing anything of Bertran at all, could fail to know of his friendship with the "young king" and of the latter's feud with his father. But along these lines something more may be said with respect to the canto we have before us.

In spite of the careful and exhaustive work of many scholars, much of Dante's acquaintance with the troubadours must remain conjectural. Santangelo argues that our poet had not studied them (although he knew about them of course) at the time of the composition of the *Vita Nuova;*[6] but when he undertook the *De Vulgari Eloquentia* (1304–05) he shows at least a superficial expertise in the field. I say at least superficial because his choice of exemplary poems seems sometimes a little capricious. The one he cites to show the virtues of Bertran, for example (*De Vulgari Eloquentia, loc. cit.*), is a rather undistinguished *sirventes* (most anthologies ignore it but the text may be found in Chaytor's *Troubadours of Dante*) and one cannot but wonder specifically what other poems were known to him. Perhaps Fraticelli is right in finding a clue in this very "re giovane."[7] For in the celebrated lament for the ill starred first born of Henry the phrase "giove re ingles" recurs in every stanza. It is Bertran's finest poem and it is not unlikely that Dante knew it and deliberately echoes the key phrase here. And if he did know it he would know too the first line, "Si tuit li dol e tuit le marrimen" or, as Ezra Pound puts it:

> If all the grief and woe and bitterness
> All dolour, ill and every evil chance
> That ever came upon this grieving world
> Were set together they would seem but light
> Against the death of the young English king.[8]

And if he knew those first lines, surely he had them in mind in his own introductory passage (lines 7–21) where he says that if all the mangled and mutilated of the many wars in Southern Italy were brought together it would be nothing compared to the sum of horrors that met his eyes in this *bolgia*. Of the modern commentators only Sapegno picks this up:[9] he cites no authority for his observation and I have not found it among any of the older editors

I have consulted, though Vossler comes close to saying as much. Yet merely to put the passages side by side seems proof sufficient; in rhythm, grammatical construction, and even their emotional element they match perfectly, although Dante's correlatives are concrete and not abstract.

Perhaps we can go a little further along this line of plausible conjecture. If Dante's bloody picture of the battle field strewn with mutilated humanity has a literary source, the most probable one is to be found in some of Bertran's other verses. Celebrated, for example, is the famous "Miei sirventes vuolh far de·ls res amdos" ("I'll make a half sirventes for two kings")—the term itself is suggestive of division as well as contempt—the ghastly imagery of which is very close to that of Dante:

> If both kings are brave and courageous we shall soon see fields strewn with quartered bodies, helmets, swords, shields, swords and saddles, and warriors cleft from bust to breeches, and we shall see many a horse roam riderless, and many a lance protruding from breast or flank. . . .

In his *sirventes* "Be·m platz lo gais temps de pascor," called by Croce a "lieto grido di battaglia,"[10] Bertran speaks of seeing, in similar fray, arms dented and pierced, soldiery with no other thought than to "split heads and limbs" and again "the dead with the blood-stained lance tips in their flanks." It is worth noting that this poem too contains the word "acesmatz" ('fixed up') which Dante italianizes in line 37 of this canto; here it is the presiding demon who "fixes up" his victims for their blood tour of the circle. Almost all commentators note that Dante's "accisma" is a Provençalism, few remark that it is the only use of the word in the Comedy. In fact it is extremely rare in Italian; Battaglia gives only one other example (from the seventeenth-century Menzini—and clearly an echo of Dante's line). The derivation of the Provençal word is uncertain (see Körting, Meyer-Lübke, Battaglia, and Hoare for a wide range of choice). The relationship to "scisma" may be phonetic rather than etymological (though Spitzer and Schiaffini postulate an *adschismare[11]) but Dante surely intended a connection. I think that whatever the etymology Dante thought of it as a Provençalism and that the word is a linguistic token of the presence of Bertran from the very beginning of the canto. His aura carries over into the next canto as well; Dante, reproached for his obsession with the gruesome sights before him, can only answer that he was fascinated by the spectacle of the lord of "Altaforte." The place name here would remind the informed reader of the siege of Hautefort and the capture of Bertran by the irate king Henry and so of all the story of intrigue and resentment surrounding the troubadour and his royal associates. But Dante's excuse, which is also a confession, is more significant on another level; he has been infected by Bertran's bloodlust (as the above-mentioned imagery shows), and—*contrapasso* within *contrapasso*—Bertran who had surveyed so many corpse-strewn battlefields with something close to delight is now the object of like contemplation—just another of the many "mortz e nafratz" and well "acesmatz" to boot.

As a character Bertran is curiously one-dimensional; far from being ashamed of his sin he thrusts himself on Dante, aparently eager to make himself known and to have his presence reported ("E perchè tu di me novella porti"), and tells with apparent complacency of his instigation of hostility between father and son. He finds a certain satisfaction, one feels, in his spiritual kinship with Achitophel and perhaps also in his knowledge of scripture; he seems in his last line to be trying to give the impression that the law of *contrapasso* has been designed for him. All the sowers of discord have something of the same characteristics; Bertran seems perhaps a little more aggressive in his self-assurance and very much aware of the effect his grotesque appearance is creating. This is in fact quite in keeping with the *autoritratto* he gives us in his own verses, which reveal a militant self-confidence and a touch of exhibitionism. He is an isolated figure too; even Mohammed has a kinsman with him and the other sinners of the *bolgia* are linked by blood or regional origin; Bertran stands alone. He is alone likewise in his associations within the Comedy. There is a faint reminiscence of his gesture in Manfred's display of his wounds in *Purgatory* III, but in the significant sense in which Farinata prepares us for Sordello or Cacciaguida recalls Brunetto there is no correspondence for Bertran, sombre, grim, and forever isolated.

So far as the role of Arnaut (the purgatorial Provençal) is concerned, it may be said to be the simplest of all of the characters under discussion here. On the terrace of lust he is not so much an actor as an exhibit; presented by the modest Guinizelli as the "miglior fabbro del parlar materno" and the one who in "Versi d'amore e prose di romanzi / soverchiò tutti" he identifies himself (in a courtly opening phrase, in substance very similar to that of Pier delle Vigne—and with a few words borrowed from Folquet de Marseille), expresses regret for his past follies, his hope for the future, and bids Dante to remember "in time" his suffering. There is no real dialogue between him and Dante and, as various commentators have noted, there is an air of detachment about him. (Momigliano is reminded of Pia.) As he steps forth from the fire he unobtrusively rounds out a poetic group almost as large as that in Limbo where Dante had been "sesto tra cotanto senno." Here he is fifth—at least in chronological order. The sequence is suggestive and in itself poetic to dwell upon: the classical Virgil, the late Latin Statius, the first of the "new poets" (see the *Vita Nuova*), Arnaut, the founder of the *dolce stil nuovo*, and Dante himself. A gallery richer in its variety and considerably more articulate (for each of the five at one point or another has his say) than that of the supreme but rather remote classical figures of *Inferno* IV.

Critics past and present have been fascinated by Dante's Arnaut, more specifically by Dante's concept of him and his place in literature. To touch first on a minor aspect of his case, the argument has raged long and loud over the meaning of lines 118–119. A first reading would justify the implication that Arnaut had written not only lyrics ("versi d'amore"), but also prose romances, and it was indeed Tasso who first ascribed to him a version of the Lancelot, which enabled later critics to make much of his association with *Inferno* V. As recently as 1952 Bowra seems willing to accept his authorship not only of a *Lancelot* but also of a Rinaldo attributed to Arnaut by Luigi Pulci. Bowra believes simply that these "prose di romanzi" are lost.[12] Gianluigi Toja however, Arnaut's most recent editor, after an exhaustive examination of the subject, rejects any such hypothesis and concludes quoting with approval Viscardi's verdict that Dante meant simply that "Arnaut was the greatest of all who had written in the vernacular, in verse or in prose."[13] And indeed with some slight manipulation of the syntax the passage may be fairly translated: "He surpassed all [who wrote either] verses of love or adventure tales in prose" which could be paraphrased: "he was best of all users of their mother tongue, whether they be the Provençal love poets or the French composers of romances in prose."

A much more provocative question is why Dante so greatly admired Arnaut. There is ample evidence, outside of Guinizelli's warm praise in this passage, that he had great esteem for him. He mentions him three times in the *De Vulgari*, and he renders him the highest tribute of all—imitation. His sestina is clearly written in rivalry of Arnaut, as is his "double sestina" as the passage in the *De Vulgari Eloquentia* indicates. All of the *Petrose* show some trace of Danielism whether it be in their *caras rimas*, their violent rhythms, or the tormented emotional atmosphere they suggest. It is not easy to understand Dante's admiration for a poet who seems very often wilfully obscure and exhibitionistic, and, in sheer substance, either incomprehensible or platitudinous. Grandgent, I think, spoke for not only his own but all modern generations when, allowing for Arnaut's virtues, he finds him, nevertheless, "one of the most laborious and tiresome of the Provençal versifiers"[14] and even Bowra, anxious to explain Dante's devotion to Arnaut, yet must admit that "great poets are not necessarily good critics" and that "we cannot read Arnaut easily for pleasure."[15] Perhaps, among the critics of our own time, it is in Ezra Pound that we may most easily find the key to Dante's estimate of Arnaut. As early as 1920, but looking ahead to a new critical school as Grandgent looks back and essentially speaks for nineteenth-century criticism—I do not mean that as a stricture—Pound writes: "And Arnaut was the best artist among the Provençals, trying the speech in new fashions, and bringing new words into writing, and making new blendings of words . . ."[16] Dante saw him as a maker of words—this was a matter of great importance to a critic who had analyzed word types in his *De Vulgari* and was to cry out for the "rime aspre e chioccie" essential for a description of lowest Hell. Del Monte has passionately defended all of Arnaut's technical tricks, finding an "aesthetic exigency" even in the *caras rimas* and affirming that even the metrical innovations are "vincolate all'originalità sentimentale e alla singolarità espressiva e non si possono quindi ridurre ad ardimenti artificiosi."[17] This is to claim more than most readers would concede, I think, but even if we cannot see the "originalità sentimentale," in a sestina for example, as clearly as Del Monte, yet we may grant that the "singolarità espressiva," the new words, the elaborate patterns are indeed the work of a remarkable *fabbro* and so may understand the admiration that Dante the "wordsmith" must have felt for a master craftsman. Grandgent speaks very properly of Dante's "gratitude" in this regard: I think it led him too far and even Pound concedes that the art of Arnaut is not literature, but the basis of it is sound enough.

As for the Provençal quoted, it may be said that even today there is considerable argument about the text; most editors are content with Vandelli's reading but Sapegno, for one, has two variations of his own. Actually even the widest variations do not change the essential meaning of the Provençal, which is remarkably clear in grammar and construction and childishly simple in vocabulary. I cannot agree with Bowra that the passage takes off Arnaut's style. It has, to be sure, a few antitheses, a commonplace of poetic rhetoric, but there are no nine lines in the work of Arnaut himself so simple in form, substance, and vocabulary. Sapegno indeed makes the comment that the "pasada folor" of which Arnaut speaks may well refer to his artificial style among other things and sees in the line "no me puesc ni vuoill a vos cobrire" an overt repudiation of the *trobar clus* where the intent was precisely to "cover oneself" against common understanding.[18] I think Sapegno is right and that two statements can be made on that basis; first, that although it be paradoxical to find Arnaut repudiating the very style which had first made Dante admire him, yet Dante's Arnaut has in fact given up both the amatory and the linguistic attitudes of the historic Arnaut. And secondly, I think it follows that his simple language may fairly be read in connection with Dante's own anti-rhetorical protestation of Canto XXIV "Io mi son un che quando" etc. If there is a message of autobiographical-critical commentary in this passage, it seems to me that Dante is telling us that he owes much to Arnaut's explorations of technique but also that he has not so much rejected as surpassed the obsession with it—as Arnaut in his new penitential illumination must also have done.

As is right and proper—and consistent as much with the less-crowded world and ampler scope of the *Paradiso* as the deference due to sainthood—Dante's celestial representative of the *gay saber* gets fuller treatment and is allowed more wordage than his colleagues in the lower realms. Folquet de Marseille, the sainted singer of the Heaven of Venus, is given in fact sixty-one lines as against thirteen for Bertran de Born and a mere eight for the self-effacing Arnaut. Further, although his own words begin with line 82, the six flattering lines which serve as Cunizza's introduction to him (describing him as a flashing jewel and assuring him of five hundred years of enduring fame) begin with line 37. He is in fact the dominant figure of his canto (Cunizza defends herself well, but has ten lines less assigned to her). His monologue covers a wide range of information and commentary. After telling Dante of his origins, his name, and his excessive devotion to love, he affirms, reinforcing Cunizza's complacent statement, that he looks back on such a life without regret, rejoicing only in the providence "ch'ordinò e provide." As another example of such Providence he calls Dante's attention to the effulgence of Rahab, his neighbor, and in the course of extolling her aid to Joshua goes on to criticize the Pope for not carrying on the Crusade to free the Holy Land. The Pontiff's negligence is in part the fault of the "accursed flower," the florin—of which Folco, son of a merchant, must have had a better understanding than his brother troubadours—greed for which has corrupted the clergy, now more intent on the lucrative study of the Decretals than on the gospels and the Annunciation. He ends by predicting that the Vatican will soon be free of this "adultery."

It is not hard to see why Dante chose Folquet for this high level of his occitanic delegation. Although he had been ruthless in his persecution of the Cathars—so much so as to seem the very Antichrist to the writer of the second part of the *Croisade contre les Albigeois*—Folquet's very zeal made him the hero of the orthodox and his conversion from poetry to the religious life must have aroused wonder and admiration in the faithful of his time. His association with the bloody crusade has marred his image for modern readers: Scartazzini quotes approvingly the phrase of Bartoli identifying Folquet as the "feroce vescovo, collegato ai crociati che andavano a distruggere la sua povera patria."[19] But quite aside from the fact that Languedoc was not the "patria" of a poet born in Marseilles of Genoese stock, it would be unfair to expect Dante in the context of his times to share our post-Reformation tenderness for the unfortunate Cathars. And in truth Stronski has assembled convincing evidence of our Bishop's good reputation even among his enemies in those trying days; he concludes: "Homme d'une intelligence supérieure et d'une activité prodigeuse . . . on le regardait généralement comme un homme de caractère honnête."[20] Add to these virtues his secure place in the troubadour tradition (Dante had already shown his awareness of it, giving laudatory mention to a canto of Folquet in *De Vulgari* II, vi.) and his election to heaven becomes predictable.

As far as his political attitudes are concerned Folquet has undergone some readjustment at Dante's hands. The crusading zeal which comes out in his reproach to the lethargic and venal papacy is authentic; aside from his own activities against the Albigensians, Folquet, in his lyric youth, had written two Crusade poems which survive: one for the Spanish struggle against the Moors, the other on behalf of the third crusade in Outremer. But into the mouth of this staunch defender of orthodoxy and the Papal right Dante puts some of the harshest words of the Comedy uttered against the conduct of the Papacy, for surely "adultery" as a description of the condition of the Church goes very far in its suggestion of illegality as well as indecency.

Benvenuto thought the term applicable particularly to Boniface VIII whose "marriage" to the Church was "adulterous" in that the true "husband" was Celestinus but, as various commentators have pointed out the link with the cognate verb "avolterate" (*Inferno* XIX, 4) may suggest a less specific application. The "crusader" Folquet, we may well believe, spoke with the same intensity but directed himself at a different target. Dante further somewhat alters the historical personage—or at least the poet as we know him—by assigning to him a greater depth of amorous commitment—a more unbriled passion—in his youth than the extant poems would seem to bear out. As compared to the sensualism of some of the verses of William of Poitou and the dedicated avowals of Bernart de Ventadorn the love verses of Folquet seem rather mild and conventional: "des réflexions laborieuses sur l'amour. . . . des tissus de motifs littéraires et de lieux communs" is Stronski's verdict.[21]

But the greatest change the troubadour suffers is in the area of his style and language. Dante had admired his *canso* "Tan m'abellis l'amoros pensamen" and indeed had exalted it as an example of the high style. He had borrowed the first three words on behalf of Arnaut Daniel but Folquet gets the better of the exchange, for in the Heaven of Venus he speaks with a language more reminiscent of Arnaut's than any of the Provençal verses chanted in the refining fire. All commentators have remarked on the baroque circumlocution with which Folquet describes the city of his birth; it takes him in fact some eleven lines to state simply "I was born in Marseilles." He goes on with references to the daughter of Belus, "the Rhodopean maid deceived by Demophoön" and Alcides, none of whom appear in his own works. Although Dante uses very sparingly the *rime riche*, no less than three examples appear in Folco's discourse (*torna, palma,* and *pianta*), and his entire speech is a web of periphrases. His rhetorical twin is Pier delle Vigne; there is no other comparison that suggests itself (certainly not the chastened Arnaut), but the Bishop is much more erudite than the Imperial Secretary. It is true that Cunizza's vocabulary with its invented *s'incinqua*, its latinisms *propinqua* and *luculenta*, and Dante's own neologisms *s'inluia, intuassi, inmii* are of the same nature. Which is to say, I think, that the whole canto is a linguistic tribute to Folquet.

I cannot help thinking (and the thought may have occurred to others although I have noted no particular reference to it) that Folquet has replaced Giuraut de Bornelh as the Provençal representative of the poetry of rectitude (*De Vulgari* II, ii). It is well known that Dante strove for consistency in his works, and once having set down his theories on the proper subjects for lofty verse there is no reason to assume that he did not continue to have them in mind and indeed to think that they could be exemplified from the Provençal (regrettably arms was still unsung by the Italians). And in fact two of his three examples mentioned in the *De Vulgari* reappear in the Comedy. But what has become of Guiraut?

When he wrote the *De Vulgari* Dante had held Guiraut in unusually high esteem. "The Limousin" is quoted four times, more often than any other troubadour, quite aside from his identification with rectitude, the highest of Dante's categories. The citations are interesting in their implications; although the first quotation is merely to illustrate the similarity of *amor* and *amore* in the two vernaculars, the second, referring to one of Guiraut's most admired *sirventes*, "Per solatz revelhar," is apparently the best example of a song of "rectitude" that Dante can think of, the third is brought in to show the majesty of the eleven syllable line and the fourth, "Ar auziretz encabalitz cantars," is held up as a model of "the most excellent degree of construction," having "flavor and grace and also elevation." In sensing a kindred spirit in Guiraut, Dante's intuition did not betray him. Chaytor finds Dante's choice of him as the poet of righteousness is "entirely justified by the high moral tone of his sirventes."[22] De Lollis pointed out that Guiraut's poetic fused most successfully "la materia amorosa e la morale,"[23] which can also be said of the "moral *canzoni*" ("Le dolci rime," "Doglia mi reca," "Tre donne intorno al cor," and "Poscia ch'amor"); Santangelo, pressing the findings of De Lollis to a logical conclusion, states that for Dante in 1305 Guiraut was the best of the troubadours, surpassing Arnaut even in amatory verse.[24]

What then has happened between 1305 and the year of *Purgatory* XXVI? Santangelo sees in the exaltation of "rectitude" over love the refuge of a poet "povero e quasi mendico, disistimato dagli uomini, non calcolato dalle donne"; later, the exile "non più vilipeso ma ben trattato e stimato" turned back to love and to the imitation of Arnaut in the *Petrose* and his exaltation in the *Purgatory*.[25] Change of spirit and attitude there must have been, but I am not sure that it is of the sort that Santangelo has in mind, springing essentially from the material condition of the poet's life or the state of his prestige. I do not see so much a turning from "rectitudo" to "amor" as the development of a different concept of "rectitudo." This would leave Arnaut unassailable as the champion of "amore," but if "rectitudo" is still to be supreme—and if it is not supreme in the Comedy then the allegory is meaningless—it is going to need another and more suitable example than Guiraut. For it seems to me that the "rectitudo" Dante had in mind in the *De Vulgari* was the kind of ethical virtue which one associates with the climate of the *Convivio* (of which the *De Vulgari* may be regarded as an interpolation or an excursus, as Dante's own remarks indicate). And without going into the *selva oscura* of *Convivio* exegesis, it may fairly be pointed out that the inspiration of that noble work is essentially philosophical; Lady Philosophy openly displaces Beatrice. The rectitude of the *Convivio* seems to have little need of Revelation. In the Comedy, on the other hand, Revelation is Dante's guide. Guiraut, at least as Dante conceived of him, could have satisfied the requirements for the *Convivio-De Vulgari* period, but for a dweller in Paradise (the only proper eternal residence for a Christian poet of rectitude) he would not quite do, and an all but canonized Bishop, happily also a singer, was evidently preferable. Although it is possibly simply an indication of a change of taste (and Dante is never more firm in his judgments than when he has had occasion to change an opinion, as he reveals in Book II of the *De Monarchia*), yet the disparagement of Guiraut in Canto XXVI of the *Purgatory* may also be meant to prepare us for his displacement from his previous high rank and so to open the way for the intrusion of Folco into the triad.

This substitution and glorification of the Bishop is underlined, it seems to me, by Dante's introduction of his new champion; not only does Cunizza introduce him in glowing terms but Dante's intense curiosity to learn of his identity is unparalleled in the Comedy—only in the case of Ulysses does he show something of the same impatience.

And it is this pointed anticipation which gives us the ultimate key and supplies the full answer to why Dante chose Folquet for his climactic love poet. For, as in the *bolgia* of the false counselors he had realized that he was among souls who shared his gifts of intellectual distinction and so could hardly wait to hear the master of many devices, so here, in Folquet, he sees a kindred spirit, a poet once consumed by love who has now put it behind him, and who, not repudiating but freely accepting his past, has yet moved on to higher concerns, still interested in the affairs of the world yet serene in his contemplation of his vision; Dante too has followed, in the brief phrase of Apollonio, "l'itinerario di Folco dalla poesia alla religione."[26] For the creator of the Comedy Folco was inevitable. And for the pilgrim too, I believe we may hazard the guess that Folco is the soul he expects to see. Cunizza's words are an indication that it must be a love poet, and her associations are with the Provençal; her phrase indicates that his five hundred years of fame have only begun—and Dante can make a shrewd guess as to who is enclosed in the jewel-like radiance. But he burns to be sure—and dramatizes his eagerness to underline the significance of his choice. The ultimate poet of love, also the poet of righteousness and not unfamiliar with arms for that matter—such is Folco. And the description would fit Dante Alighieri equally well.

With Folco the Provençal trio is complete. But there is another poet of the *Langue d'oc* who has a substantial role in the Comedy—even if his linguistic anomaly somewhat spoils the symmetry of the triangle. However, I do not think that Dante meant Sordello to "count" as a Provençal figure. I believe that, even as the poet of Goito ignores the Latinity of Virgil and sees in him only a fellow Lombard, so Dante sees in Sordello not the Provençal poet but the Italian-born patriot and judge of princes. But the language of his verse (at least as we know it today) was the *Langue d'oc*, and whether or not he is a part of the truly Provençal gallery we cannot leave him out of our considerations. Nor should we want to; his function, his aura, and his implications are well worth our study.

He is one of the important and impressive figures in the *Purgatory*. His presence takes in three cantos: in Canto VI he springs up to embrace Virgil, incidentally inspiring Dante's famous invective; in Canto VII he leads our pilgrims to the vale of the princes and points out with comment the ranking dignitaries in that crepuscular conclave, concluding with remarks on inherited virtues or rather the lack of them. In Canto VIII he calls attention to the coming of the serpent. He is a true guide (in the sense of leading our poets from one place to another), an informant, a commentator, and clearly, since his gesture touches off the aforesaid invective, an inspiration.

Obviously Dante must have had a high opinion of the warrior troubadour. But does his Sordello in fact have very much in common with the Sordello of history? Many have chosen to emphasize the differences between the lion of the mountainside and the adventurer of Goito: "Certo il Sordello di Dante non è, come oggi si ripete comunemente, il Sordello che scrisse il celebre serventese in morte di ser Blacatz . . . il Sordello ritratto da Dante non è il giudice impavido dei potenti," Gentile affirms.[27] I would be inclined to argue that he is indeed just that—yet not by any means the historical Sordello either. The facts of our troubadour's life, such as they are (and we know more about him than we do about many of his colleagues), have been summarized by his recent editor, Marco Boni, with all the up-to-date findings of scholarship at his disposal. To summarize the ninety pages dedicated to his subject's biography; we may hold it as reasonably certain that Sordello was born in Goito near Mantua, a scion of the lesser nobility, probably in the last years of the twelfth century. After a gay and carefree youth, given to the study of the troubadours' art (and somewhat to gambling) he created a scandal by eloping with Cunizza, wife of Rizzardo di San Bonifazio and sister of Ezzelino da Romano (who seems to have instigated the abduction for political reasons of his own). There is an allusion to another liaison and then (*circa* 1226) came the departure for Provence. Many years in the court of Raymond Berenguier IV followed and on the death of that lord and the marriage of his daughter to Charles of Anjou Sordello entered the latter's service. He returned to Italy with his ambitious and fortunate master, may have fought at Benevento and was rewarded by the bestowal of various fiefs including the castle of Palena (Abruzzi) with all its adjuncts. This in 1269, after which no more is heard of the poet.[28]

Essentially all this information is contained in the two Provençal *vidas* of the poet and it seems not at all unlikely that Dante was well-acquainted with such facts. Did he know more than we do? Or at least more than twentieth-century scholarship would like to guarantee? This question may be asked specifically with regard to two matters affecting the Sordello of the Mountainside; one perhaps relatively trivial, the other more important for our assessment of the troubadour. As to the first question; it is connected with the place assigned to Sordello on the mount. As we meet him he stands alone, like Saladino, as numerous commentators have pointed out. But Dante's categories are firm and permit of few unassigned casuals; we must therefore ask: are we to think of Sordello as belonging to the previous group (those who met death by violence and repented only at the last minute), or is the troubadour himself to be thought of as one of the "negligent" princes whom he later joins? Or is he—quite exceptionally—*sui generis*? If we are to assign him to the preceding group, then we must assume that he met with a violent death and that Dante was aware of this circumstance. Benvenuto is the first of the commentators to suggest any such possibility and his account has the color more of fiction than fact. Yet some scholars such as Anglade and Marigo have accepted the likelihood of Sordello's coming to a violent end, others, less certain of the fact, believe that Dante thought so; Torraca, Santangelo, and, among commentators, Casini-Barbi.[29] But I think the question can best be resolved not by refutation of Benvenuto's account but by simple examination of the text. In line 25 Dante speaks of being "free of all those souls" who are crowding on him to ask for his prayers, and so gives the clear impression of leaving that group definitely behind him. Nor does he immediately meet Sordello. In line 28 he begins with Virgil a discussion on the efficacy of prayer and this digression in the narrative takes up thirty lines; it is not until line 58 that Virgil calls his attention to the brooding Lombard poet. This, it seems to me, clearly marks Sordello off from the preceding group of souls. Furthermore, although he stands at first above them so that Dante may better study their aspects, yet he does finally join them (VIII 43–44: "Or avvalliamo omai / tra le grandi ombre . . .") "come in sua propria dimora . . . o perchè principe anch'esso . . . o almeno frequentatore di Corti, come ci è ricordato dalla storia, o meglio, qual giudice, anche in vita, di azioni e costumi principeschi."[30] As for his forming a "parte per se stesso," although this is the view of Sapegno (and, earlier, Porena), I cannot see much to be said for it; there is no case of Dante's making a category for one soul alone in all of the Comedy (even Satan has company of a sort) nor would it be easy, in Sordello's case, to say just what such a category would be. Those who remark the verbal similarity between the descriptions of him and Saladino ("E solo in una parte vidi il Saladino" / ". . . un'anima, che posta / sola soletta") might remember that Saladino too, though he stood alone, was part of a well-defined and fairly numerous category.

But the more arresting second question which has been asked in this connection is whether Dante thought of Sordello as an Italian writer and specifically whether he had knowledge of any of the poet's compositions in his native language. The mention of Sordello in the *De Vulgari* is couched in rather obscure language. In discussing the speech of Bologna and its relative excellence Dante says that its beauty may owe something to the fact that it borrows a little from neighboring towns; he goes on to say, "sicut facere quoslibet a finitimis suis conicimus, ut Sordellus de Mantua sua ostendit, Cremone, Brixie atque Verone confini; qui, tantus eloquentie vir existens, non solum in poetando, sed quomodocunque loquendo patrium vulgare deseruit" (*De Vulgari,* I, XV, 9–14). I believe the best gloss on this is Wicksteed who paraphrases the passage as follows: "The reasoning by which the relative superiority of the Bologna dialect is established is less clearly expressed than is usual with Dante. The following free paraphrase is submitted as a plausible explanation of this difficult passage. 'The peoples of every city borrow from their neighbours, and their dialects are better or worse (from the literary point of view) according to the character resulting from the mixture of the borrowed elements with the original speech. Hence the superiority of the Bologna dialect: for though the sharpness borrowed from Ferrara and Modena is bad in itself, it mixes well with the smoothness and softness borrowed from Imola. The same truth is illustrated as regards Mantua by the case of Sordello. The dialect of this place is bad, because of the badness of the elements borrowed from Cremona, Brescia, and Verona. Sordello, in fact, after some literary attempts in this dialect, found it so unsuitable that he forsook his native tongue entirely, wrote exclusively in Provençal, and became a Provençal to all intents and purposes.' "[31] Marigo, following Zingarelli, believes that the "quomodocunque loquendo" must allude to formal speeches composed in a language free from traces of dialect and only wishes some specimen of Sordello's Italian poetry were extant.[32] Bertoni in fact thought that he had found one and published it[33] and Boni, though somewhat hesitantly and only *in appendice*, prints the verses and is not entirely prepared to deny their authenticity.[34] However one may read the rather ambiguous sentence of the *De Vulgari*, the suggestion is certainly present that Dante knew of some kind of Italian work written by Sordello. Indeed, for the champion of Italian unity, for the symbol of a lofty "patriotismo dell'amore e della pace" (Gentile) I think such a hypothesis is essential.

Yet the recognizable source of Sordello's commentary on the princes is certainly the celebrated lament for Blacatz. D'Ancona notes that even the scheme of Dante's survey follows that of the *planh sirventes*; on the mountainside, as in life, Sordello, feudal spirit that he is, begins with the Emperor and works down to the lesser nobility. It has been remarked too that one prince, Henry III of England, appears in both compositions, the kind of linkage that would be, I think, characteristic of Dante. I believe too the lament is also present in another part of the Sordello episode. Dante's own invective, deploring the state of Italy and lashing out against those who are responsible for it, has similar emotional ingredients; Sapegno in fact says it is an *invettiva* which is also a *compianto*—which is merely to italianize the Provençal term *planh sirventes*.

Was Dante also familiar with Sordello's 1314 line didactic work, the *Ensenhamen*, which contained rules, ethical and social, for good conduct and correct manners—a kind of mediaeval *cortegiano* designed to teach us "de far be et de vivre gen" (line 403). If and how well Dante knew this composition would be hard to say. Torraca believed he saw an echo of some lines of the work in *Inferno* III, 34 ff.[35] and Boni seems willing to agree;[36] Guarnerio's suggestion that *Paradiso* VI, 131–132 are a like echo is a little more daring.[37] Recently Bowra has attempted to show that Dante's invective parallels the contents of the *Ensenhamen.*[38] It is true that such topics as the wickedness of the rich, the degeneration of the times, and the nobility of character as against that of birth suggest the moralizing Dante of the *Convivio*; they also suggest any number of mediaeval treatises, including some in Provençal. It would be hard to establish any real connection between the *Ensenhamen* and the contents of Cantos VI and VII. But I do think that Dante may have been familiar with the *Ensenhamen* and certainly knew that Sordello had composed such a work. For it must have been, I believe, a contributing element in building up Dante's high opinion of a figure whose presence in our poet's gallery of heroes would be otherwise hard to explain.

Sordello had not only abducted Cunizza, he had bragged, in a composition that we may hope is of his early years, of success at "lady-killing" (the phrase is his) and had issued fair warning to all husbands of his prowess in this area.[39] Italian though he was, he had spent thirty-five years of his life in the service (apparently happy) of foreign princes; he had returned to Italy in the train of the arch-enemy of Dante's empire, a fighting Guelph. It is hard to see how this record could have appealed to Dante. Flamini suggested years ago that Dante might have been acquainted with the aged Cunizza;[40] if she was in her old age willing to "indulge herself" as she was in Heaven, she may well have been willing to indulge the memory of her youthful abductor and (so they said) lover. We know that Dante thought well of Cunizza in the teeth of the "volgo," and perhaps Sordello creeps into *Purgatory* under her mantle. Perhaps too, Guelph or not, he inspired Dante's respect as the example of a poet who had also achieved success and dignity in military and political affairs—"era divenuto cavaliere nobile e austero e consigliere dei principi e gran signore," as Viscardi has it.[41] The exiled Dante would have heard something of Sordello's prominence in the courts of Northern Italy, as Boni suggests. But for the appellation "tantus eloquentie vir," something more would have been necessary; the *Ensenhamen* is precisely the kind of work that would have drawn such a comment from Dante.

I find the real puzzle lies in Dante's association of the Lombard troubadour with national patriotism. There is nothing which could be called patriotic in the *Ensenhamen* and the *planh sirventes* is, when carefully analyzed, merely the usual incitement to princes to fight for honor and their right. To be sure, the poet speaks out boldly to the great ones of the world (this too was common enough; troubadours, like jesters, were privileged characters), but his intent is clearly that of Bertran de Born's to "mesclar los baros," to stir up discord—and for the same reason; all the minor nobility and their hangers-on found in warfare their best chance for advancement and booty, and Sordello in fact did very well out of it. But of patriotism there is no trace. Here we can only say that Dante, having found in Sordello a figure to admire, a fellow poet (and some critics have seen in some of his verses a kind of adumbration of the *dolce stil nuovo*),[42] a companion of princes and a moralist—in short some one much like himself—simply made the last leap and attributed to Sordello his own passionate concern for the unity of Italy and that "patriottismo dell'amore e della pace" which burned in his own breast.

Sordello's correspondences within the Comedy are rich in implication. His personal associations are with Cunizza and Ezzelino. It is a kind of personal triumvirate with representation in all the realms somewhat similar to the Imperial trio of Frederick, Manfred, and Constance, or the Florentine clan of Piccarda, Forese, and (by 1308) Corso Donati. In his lion-like aloofness and his aggressive conversational approach he reminds us of Farinata; Gentile has noted the verbal signal in Virgil's "Vedi là" (*Inferno* X, 31 and *Purgatory* VI, 58) and quite rightly too, for they both symbolize deep political attachments; one to clan or faction ("Chi fur li maggior tui?") and the other to native country (". . . di nostro paese. . . . c'inchiese"). But his figural correspondences are even richer. The garden of the princes is the "amoenus locus" corresponding to the Limbo of the *Inferno*; Virgil's terzina (*Purg.* VII, 25–30) underlines that, lest it should escape us, even as line 20 "non per far ma per non far" indicates the "negligence" that the two groups have in common. (It is to be noted, however, that the garden here contains only political figures and lacks the poet's philosophers and scientists of the Limbo—perhaps we would expect to find such only across the *fiumicello* of eloquence and here there is no *fiumicello*.) And so some have seen him as corresponding to Virgil who leads Dante to Limbo; D'Ancona has noted the Virgilian echo in VII, 40. Looking more closely, however, the actual leading to the *castello* where the great souls are surveyed is not Virgil's work; he seems to be led himself—

or at least merely to go along as one of the group. Dante's line (*Inferno* IV, 103) "così andammo" gives no indication of who leads, but surely it must be Homer, who has first saluted Virgil and must have an accepted position of preeminence among the escorting poets. This correspondence is high honor for Sordello, but if Homer knew better than any other poet the heroes of old and their virtues, who could know better than the author of the *planh* for Blacatz the merits and weaknesses of contemporary kings? His role may in fact invite comparison with even loftier characters. Like Cato he gives topographical directions, information on the by-laws of Purgatory and some higher indoctrination as well. We may see him as a matching figure, the second warden as it were of the Ante-purgatory; Cato meets our pilgrims as they enter this realm of the tentative and Sordello sees them depart. Verbal connection may be seen in the "solo" of Cato and the "anima soletta" of Sordello. We may recall that "soletta" is also descriptive of Matelda as she confronts the emancipated Dante across Lethe. One can make too much, I think, of these verbal echoes, but since Matelda too is guide and informant for Dante and leads him, as Sordello does, to another and even more glorious assembly of great spirits, I think we may be justified in seeing an intended clue in the repetition of this word (which appears a scant four times in the Comedy). Lastly, another venerable and intercessory figure comes to mind who is to display for Dante a supreme gallery—St. Bernard. An abyss lies between them, and the gallery of princes is a poor enough prefiguring of the pillars of the church. Yet the suggestion, I think, is there and Sordello points forward to the Rose even as backward to the "bel castello" and the virtuous spirits of Limbo. The flesh and blood of the soldier-troubadour are there, in his pose, in his assurance, in his unprejudiced survey of contemporary rulers, but Dante has given him stature and significance, indeed true grandeur in what he symbolizes and what, in the context of the sacred poem, he suggests.

# Notes

1. Wicksteed's translation; see *Dante's Latin Works*, Temple Edition, p. 71.
2. A. Momigliano, *Purgatorio* (Florence, 1948), note on canto XXVIII, lines 127–129, p. 209.
3. V. Crescini, "Inferno—Canto XXVIII" in *Letture dantesche* (Florence, 1962), p. 563.
4. See, among others, H. A. Pochmann's articles: "Irving's German Sources in the Sketch Book," *SP* XXVIII (July, 1930), 477–507 and "Irving's German Tour and Its Influence on His Tales," *PMLA* XLV (Dec., 1930), 1150–87.
5. See Amanda K. Coomaraswamy, "Headless Magicians; and an Act of Truth," *Journal of the American Oriental Society*, vol. 64 (1944), 215–17.
6. S. Santangelo, *Dante e i trovatori provenzali*, 2a. ed. (Catania, 1959), chapter V.
7. In his note on Inferno XXVIII, 134, *Divina Commedia* (Florence, 1881).
8. *Personae*, New Directions, 1949 (?), p. 36.
9. In his note to XXVIII, line 7, *Inferno* (Florence, 1955).
10. See "Bertran de Born" in *Poesia antica e moderna* (Bari, 1943), p. 143.
11. André Pézard in his note in *Romania*, vol. 78 (1957), 519–524, comments on such hypotheses, adding his own for good measure.
12. See "Dante and Arnaut Daniel" in *Speculum*, XXVII (1952), 460–461.
13. *Arnaut Daniel: Canzoni* (Florence, 1960), pp. 99–106.
14. *Divine Comedy*, Revised edition (Boston, 1933) p. 561.
15. Art. cit., p. 474.
16. The essay on Arnaut Daniel may be found in *The Literary Essays of Ezra Pound* (London, 1954), pp. 109–148.
17. *Studi sulta poesia ermetica medievale* (Naples, 1953), p. 95.
18. Note on XXVI, 140, *Purgatorio* (Florence, 1956).
19. *La Divina Commedia*, 2a. ed. (Milan, 1896); note on Par. IX, lines 64–108.
20. S. Stronski, *Folquet de Marseille* (Cracow, 1910), pp. *99-*100.
21. *Ibid*, p. *66.
22. *Troubadours of Dante* (Oxford, 1902), p. 142.
23. See "Quel di Lemosi" in *A Ernesto Monaci per l'anno* XXV *del suo insegnamento* (Rome, 1901), p. 364.
24. *Op. cit.*, p. 118.
25. *Ibid.*, p. 129.
26. Mario Apollonio, *Dante: Storia della Commedia*, 2a. ed. (Milan, 1954), Vol. II, p. 810.
27. "Purgatorio—Canto VI" in *Letture dantesche* (Florence, 1962), p. 799.
28. See Marco Boni, *Sordello, le poesie* (Bologna, 1954), pp. xiii–ciii.
29. *Ibid.*, ci–ciii.
30. Alessandro D'Ancona, "Purgatorio VII" in *Letture dantesche, cit. supra*.
31. In the Temple edition of the *Latin Works*, p. 51.
32. In his edition of the *De Vulgari Eloquentia* (Florence, 1938) p. 126, n.
33. In *GSLI* XXXVIII (1901), 269 ff.
34. See *op. cit.*, 279–281 for text, cix–cx for comment.
35. See "Sul Sordello di Cesare de Lollis" in *Giornale dantesco,* IV, (1897), 42.
36. Boni, *op cit.*, p. clxxxiv.

37. In *GSLI* XXVIII (1896) 38.

38. "Dante and Sordello" in *In General and Particular* (Cleveland-New York, 1964), pp. 113–114.

39. See the *cobla* "No.m meraveil si l marit son gilos," Boni, *op cit.*, p. 195.

40. See "Nel cielo di Venere" in *Varia* (Leghorn, 1905), pp. 95–96.

41. *Letterature d'oc e d'oil*, 2a. ed. (Milan, 1955), pp. 441–442.

42. Cf. the *Cansos* "Bel m'es" and "Tant m'abellis," respectively IV and XI in Boni's edition.

# John Freccero

## *Paradiso* x: The Dance of the Stars

IN THE FOURTH CANTO OF THE *Paradiso*, Beatrice enunciates the principle upon which much of the metaphoric structure of the *cantica* depends. She tells the pilgrim that the display of souls distributed throughout the heavenly spheres is a celestial command performance in his honor a "condescension" of blessed souls from their eternal home in the Empyrean to the upper reaches of sensible reality in order that he might perceive in spatial terms the spiritual gradations of blessedness:

> Così parlar conviensi al vostro ingegno,
> però che solo da sensato apprende
> ciò che fa poscia d'intelletto degno.
>
> (*Par.* IV, 40–42)

At the same time, it is clear by the inexorable logic of the story (whose principle theme is how the story came to be written) that what applies to the dramatic action applies to the poem itself; that is, heaven's condescension to the pilgrim is matched by the poet's condescension to us. In the poem, the descent of the divine to the human is for the benefit of a pilgrim whose ultimate goal is presumably to transcend the need for any such compromise, except of course (and the whole of the poem is contained in this exception) in order to tell others of his journey. Heaven's metaphor for the state of blessedness is in fact the poet's metaphor for a spiritual experience that transcends the human, an *exemplum* of what it means to *trasumanare*: "l'essemplo basti / a cui esperienza grazia serba" (*Par.* I, 70).

The extraordinary poetic implication of Beatrice's words is that, unlike any other part of the poem, the *Paradiso* at this point can claim no more than a purely *ad hoc* reality. When the pilgrim's ascent to the celestial rose is completed, the blessed return to their seats in the heavenly amphitheater and the heavenly bodies are left to travel in their respective spheres unaccompanied by the family of the elect—no Farinata strikes an attitude here for all eternity. This amounts to saying that the representation points to no reality, however fictive, beyond itself. The structure of the *cantica* depends, not upon a principle of *mimesis*, but rather upon metaphor: the creation of a totally new reality out of elements so disparate as to seem contradictory by any logic other than that of poetry. What is more, some of the elements represent fragments of world systems long since abandoned by Dante's time and fused together only long enough to attempt a rendering in images of what cannot be imagined. The concession of a command performance to the pilgrim within the fiction of the story stands for a poetic *tour de force* whereby Dante reconciles Christian images of heaven with a neoplatonic cosmic vision in a synthesis which, for all of its reputedly "medieval" flavor, seems almost baroque in its daring and fragility. It is the poignancy of the *Paradiso*, as it is of baroque poetry, that the synthesis is dissipated by the poem's ending:

> Così la neve al sol si disigilla,
> così al vento ne le foglie levi
> si perdea la sentenza di Sibilla.
>
> (*Par.* XXXIII, 64–66)

Whether the reader is left, like Dante, with an ineffable sweetness in his heart, or with what a baroque theorist called "the taste of ashes"[1] is a question that transcends the limits of poetry.

We can, however, set out to identify the various elements that go to make up the kaleidoscopic structure of the *Paradiso* with a view to understanding not only how they fit together, but also their metaphoric relationship to the spiritual reality they were chosen to represent. It is my intention in this paper to examine a very small portion of the *Paradiso* with these ends in view. Specifically, I should like to identify some of the elements of symbolic cosmology contained in Dante's description of the Heaven of the Sun and to discuss some of the themes that make possible in these cantos the translation of beatitude into astronomical terms.

Before proceeding, however, it would be well to identify, in Dante's terms, the process whereby he pieces together his spatial metaphor for beatitude. It is characteristic of the poet that at the moment of his striking *tour de force* he should invoke the authority of the Bible for his accommodation of spiritual reality to human faculties. Immediately after telling Dante about the descent of the blessed to the planetary spheres, Beatrice says:

Per questo la Scrittura condescende
  a vostra facultate, e piedi e mano
  attribuisce a Dio, ed altro intende . . .

(*Par.* IV, 43–45)

We have already noted that the accommodation of heaven to the senses of the pilgrim stands for the accommodation of the poet's experience *per verba* to us, but the pattern for all such accommodation was established by the Bible, the eternal witness of God's accommodation—his Word—to man. Thus, at precisely the point in the *Paradiso* where Dante seems to depart most radically from the Christian tradition, he implies that his accomplishment is essentially an imitation of the Bible. This passage might well serve as confirmation (if confirmation were still required) of Charles Singleton's thesis[2] that Dante consciously chose to write an allegory which *he* took to be Biblical even in those passages where *we* are inclined to see more of Plato, Servius, and Macrobius than of the Holy Spirit.

Nevertheless, the Christian mystery underlying Dante's representation seems to be clothed in Platonic myth. Beatrice's words in the fourth canto are occasioned by what the pilgrim assumes to be a resemblance of the *Paradiso* to Plato's *Timaeus*, inasmuch as the blessed souls seem to dwell eternally in the stars, "secondo la sentenza di Platone" (v. 24). If Plato's text means what it says, Beatrice denies that the resemblance can be real. If, on the other hand,

. . . sua sentenza è d'altra guisa
che la voce non suona, . . . esser puote
con intenzion da non esser derisa.

(*Par.* IV, 55–57)

The implication is that if Plato intends his account to be read as myth, then it may be taken to bear a resemblance to the representation of the *Paradiso*. Whatever this implied resemblance suggests for the interpretation of Plato, it certainly seems to reinforce the suggestion that the descent of the blessed to the heavenly spheres is in fact a dramatization of the process of mythmaking and, as such, is an extended figure for what the poet is himself doing as he writes his poem. The relationship of the true home of the blessed in the Empyrean to the temporary positions they occupy in the celestial spheres is exactly the relationship between Plato's presumed meaning and his mythical account of it in the *Timaeus*. Paradoxically then, in this most theological of *cantiche*, Dante seems to fashion his representation according to what might be called the allegory of poets (for Plato is surely a poet in this respect); yet the paradox is compounded and thus, perhaps, resolved by the suggestion that, while the technique and the terms of the figure may be Platonic, the inspiration is essentially Biblical. The Biblical representation of Divine Reality in anthropomorphic terms would seem to be the exemplar of all such verbal accommodations, in which the letter says one thing "ed altro intende."

It should be noted in passing that Beatrice's theory about the possible meaning of the Platonic myth concerning the stellar origin and the stellar destiny of the human soul may indirectly shed some light on the question of how extensive was Dante's knowledge of the *Timaeus* tradition.[3] She suggests that the myth really refers to the doctrine of stellar influences:

S'elli intende tornare a queste rote
  l'onore de la influenza e 'l biasmo, forse
  in alcun vero suo arco percuote.
Questo principio, male inteso, torse
  già tutto il mondo quasi, sì che Giove,
  Mercurio e Marte a nominar trascorse.

(*Par.* IV, 58–63)

It happens that this explanation of the myth as an "integumentum"[4] for describing stellar influence occurs in twelfth-century apologetics for Plato associated with the School of Chartres.[5] In particular, Guillaume de Conches, in his glosses on the *Timaeus*, not only ascribes this kind of meaning to Plato, but immediately follows his interpretation with a qualification, lest he be accused of an heretical astrological determinism.[6] Similarly, in his glosses on the meter of Boethius which alludes to the Platonic myth, he puts forward the same interpretation and a similar qualification:

> Deus disposuit animas super stellas, idest ejus nature fecit animas, quod effectu stellarum, habent suum esse in corporibus. Ex stellis enim est calor, sine quo est nulla vita, nec anima esse potest; non quod dicunt omnia que contingunt, ex stellis venire homini, sed quedam, ut calores et frigora, quedam infirmitates et similia. Si vero aliquis dicat: Nonne ista a Deo fuerunt? Responsio: Fiunt, sed per effectum stellarum.[7]

It would seem, then, that Beatrice's similar interpretation of the passage from the *Timaeus*, with its corresponding qualification about the limits of astrological influence, reflects a knowledge on the part of the poet that is more than casual of both the text and the interpretation which made the theme acceptable to Christian philosophers.

It is quite clear that Beatrice's suggested philosophical interpretation of the Platonic myth cannot provide us with a literary explanation of why Dante chose to structure his *ad hoc* poetical representation so as to resemble it. We have seen that the extended metaphor of the *Paradiso*, established by the command performance of the elect for the benefit of the pilgrim, is in fact a poetic reconciliation of the Platonic myth of the stellar souls with the Christian conception of Heaven.[8] We have also observed that in constructing his representation, Dante seemed to be imitating the technique of both Plato and the Bible. I should now like to discuss other facets of the significance attributed to the Platonic myth in the Middle Ages, not mentioned by Beatrice, but nonetheless crucial for understanding how this theme from the *Timaeus* functions within the extended metaphor of the paradisiac representation. This will lead us directly into an examination of the Heaven of the Sun, our example of metaphoric structure in the *Paradiso*.

In a series of previous studies I have tried to show that the tradition established by the *Timaeus* according to which the spiritual development of the soul was represented by corporeal movement is the ultimate (although not necessarily proximate) source of Dante's own allegorical journey in the poem.[9] For Plato, the most perfect of all corporeal motion was that exemplified by the regular, diurnal circulation of the stars. It follows, at least according to the logic of myth, that the most perfect movement of the mind, the microcosmic equivalent of the universe, could best be represented by the movement of the stars.[10] The stars, that is, perfect rationality, represent at once the soul's birthright and its destiny; education is the process whereby the star-soul, fallen to earth, struggles to regain its celestial home. So in Dante's poem, the stars represent the goal of the itinerary of the mind: a goal barely glimpsed at the end of the *Inferno*, within reach by the end of the *Purgatorio* and achieved at journey's end.[11]

This allegorical significance of stellar movement is probably implicit in the somewhat obscure etymology of the latin word *consideratio* (*cum * siderare*, to move with the stars?) which was given technical force in the mystical theology of St. Bernard. Such a resonance seems to come very close to the surface in the verse that Dante uses to describe the soul of Richard of St. Victor, "che a considerar fu più che viro" (*Par.* X, 132). Given the profusion of comparisons of the "spiriti sapienti" to the stars and the fact these blessed souls represent most particularly the intellectual perfection for which the pilgrim strives, it does not seem too much to suppose that Dante intended to give the word a Platonic force whether or not that force is demonstrably part of the semantic tradition.[12] At any rate, it is clear to the most casual reader of the *Paradiso* that the souls of the Heaven of the Sun, as well as those of Mars, Jupiter and Saturn are repeatedly compared to the fixed stars.

On the face of it, this comparison of the souls to stars would seem to create a poetic difficulty somewhat analogous to the difficulty of reconciling the immaterial Christian Paradise with the Platonic heavenly spheres, at least as far as the representation of the Heaven of the Sun is concerned. Put most simply, that representation raises the question of what stars are doing in the sphere of the Sun. The blessed souls have achieved the spiritual perfection toward which the pilgrim strives by degrees; the fiction of their temporary descent to the heavenly spheres makes it possible for the pilgrim to see and talk with them while he is still short of his goal. In imagistic terms, the perfection toward which he strives and which they have achieved is expressed in terms of the fixed stars. Under what circumstances can stars be said to "descend" to the Sun? The rules of physics or of logic admittedly do not apply to poetic representations; once having accepted the fact that Dante's representation is not meant to represent any recognizable material reality, we are inclined to accept without question a *stellar* display, the souls of the "spiriti sapienti," in the sphere of the *Sun*, especially since we do not believe in a *sphere* of the Sun and are inclined to take a post-Galilean view of astronomical imagery anyway. However, a contemporary of the poet with an equal amount of astronomical learning would not have failed to see that there is in the Heaven of the Sun an image mediating between the solar and stellar elements of the poet's metaphor and therefore binding them together into the kind of coherence that one would expect of a metaphor that seeks to establish a new reality.

The poet sets forth the controlling image of his representation by beginning the canto with one of his most imperious and most famous addresses to the reader, inviting him to look up, neither to the stars nor to the sun, but to a point on the Zodiac, the Sun's apparent path through the stars:

Leva dunque, lettor, a l'alte ruote
  meco la vista dritto a quella parte
  dove l'un moto e l'altro si percuote;
e lì comincia a vagheggiar ne l'arte
  di quel maestro che dentro a sè l'ama

tanto che mai da lei l'occhio non parte.
(*Par.* x, 7–12)

We shall have occasion to discuss the significance of these verses later in this paper. For the moment, however, I should like to show that this mention of the Zodiac, which may at first seem somewhat irrelevant, in fact invites the reader to consider that part of the heavens which, because of traditional associations, probably suggested to the poet the scene that he describes in the rest of the canto.

Were it any other poet, a similar scene might strike us as bizarre or at least as undignified. The twelve spirits form a circle around the poet and his guide and begin their dance:

Poi sì cantando quelli ardenti soli
si fuor girati intorno a noi tre volte,
come stelle vicine a' fermi poli,
donne mi parver—non da ballo sciolte,
ma che s'arrestin tacite, ascoltando
fin che le nove note hanno ricolte.
(*Par.* x, 76–81)

The consummate artistry of these lines temporarily suppresses the astonishment that one experiences in retrospect when one realizes that these twelve stars are among the greatest heroes of Christian philosophy and theology. The masterstroke of the second terzina, the pause before the continuation of the dance, both sets the scene dramatically for the speech that is to follow and allows the reader the time to comtemplate the *tour de force*; it is in fact a subtle underscoring of what I have been referring to as the "command performance" quality of the *cantica*—in the normal course of things, the circumpolar dance of the stars awaits no man.[13] In spite of the reader's sense of novelty in reading these lines, however, it happens that they depend in part upon a very precise tradition, an examination of which may help us to see that the dance is in fact zodiacal.

The origins of the theme of what I shall call the "zodiacal dance" of wisemen are doubtless lost in antiquity and are at any rate not immediately relevant. For our purposes, the earliest and best text I am able to offer is Gnostic in origin, was known to St. Augustine[14] and was transmitted in apocryphal Acts of John. On close inspection, it seems to reveal many of the elements present in the Dantesque scene. After recounting several incidents of his discipleship, the pseudo-John tells us that the Saviour one day called the apostles together and commanded them to form a ring around him and to sing and dance:

> So He commanded us to make as it were a ring, holding one another's hands and Himself standing in the middle. He said, "Respond 'Amen' to me." He began, then, to sing a hymn and to say: "Glory to Thee, Father!" And we, going about in a ring, said: "Amen"
>
> Glory to Thee, Word! Glory to Thee, Grace!
> Amen . . .
> I would wash myself and I would wash. Amen.
> Grace is dancing.
> I would pipe, dance all of you! Amen.
> I would mourn, lament all of you! Amen.
> An Ogdoad is singing with us! Amen.
> The Twelfth number is dancing above. Amen.
> And the Whole that can dance. Amen . . .[15]

Nowhere is the astronomical imagery explicit in this hymn, but without it, the last three lines are incomprehensible. The "Ogdoad" is the number eight, the favorite of the Gnostics, standing for, among other things, the eight celestial spheres.[16] "The Whole" that can dance seems in fact to be a reference to the cosmos, whose rotation is the eternal dance to the "harmony of the spheres." Finally, the "twelfth number" that dances above, the emblem of these twelve disciples who dance below (and the ancestor of the twelve spirits who dance in the Heaven of the Sun), is the Zodiac, whose twelve constellations were represented, in a tradition that goes as far back as the Chaldeans,[17] surrounding the most important of all heavenly bodies (see illustration).[18] In short, the hymn depends upon one of the most ancient of Christian mysteries: Christ is the Sun.[19] As the twelve constellations surround what Dante calls the "sole sensibile," so the twelve disciples turn about Christ, Whom Dante calls the "Sole de li Angeli" (*Par.* x, 53). It is one of the ironies of intellectual history that the cult of the Sun, adapted eventually to the exigencies of Christian symbolism, should have reached its highest point within a Ptolomeic world-view, when its centrality was regarded as purely symbolic.[20]

The comparison of the twelve disciples to the twelve signs of the Zodiac is not simply an inference from an isolated text. The theme has been care-

Sketch of part of the pavement of the Baptistery of Florence
(See footnote 18).

fully documented by Jean Daniélou,[21] who has traced it from Judaeo-Hellenic antiquity (the comparison of the twelve tribes to the Zodiac) to fourth-century Christianity, although he does not mention the hymn quoted above. The persistence of the theme throughout the Middle Ages had been previously traced by F. Piper in the nineteenth century.[22] To sum up their findings, we may say that the association arose because of the importance of the number twelve in both the astronomical (twelve hours in the day, twelve months in the year, twelve signs of the Zodiac) and the Biblical (twelve tribes of Israel, twelve gates of the temple, twelve apostles, etc.) traditions. Indeed, some historians of comparative religion trace the rise of the latter to the former.[23] The exegetical tradition centered the association on those Biblical passages which seemed to identify Christ as the "Day of the Lord" (Ps. 117, 24) and as the "Year of the Lord" (Is. 61, 2).

It may seem like forcing the text to invoke this tradition for an explanation of the scene in the *Paradiso*. If twelve theologians and philosophers are easily assimilable to twelve Apostles, can the same be said for the signifiers of the respective comparisons? That is, could Dante have assimilated a whole Zodiacal sign or a whole constellation with a single star? A Biblical passage which has little relevance for Daniélou's exposition but which is central to ours enables us to answer in the affirmative. In a passage from the Apocalypse which is probably of some importance for understanding the imagery of *Paradiso* XXIII (and such an understanding does seem to be required for all but the Crocean reading of the poem), there appear to be twelve stars which the exegetical tradition assimilated to the theme under discussion: "And there appeared a great wonder in heaven; a woman clothed with sun, and the moon under her feet, and upon her head a crown of twelve stars" (Apoc. 12, 1). The Sun in this portrait was invariably glossed as a reference to Christ and the twelve stars as his disciples.[24] The motif of the crown of stars is explicitly recalled in the tradition studied by Daniélou (Ps. 64, 12: "Benedices coronae anni benignitatis tuae") as it is by Dante (*Par.* X, 65; *Par.* X, 92); *Par.* XIII, 13–15). The passage from the Apocalypse seems to supply the complement to the Zodiacal theme required for an account of Dante's representation.

There is another passage in *Paradiso* X which, when interpreted in the light of this central theme, gains considerably in coherence. It is not in itself obscure, yet it seems difficult to understand its presence in the poem until we consider the central astronomical figure which binds it to the rest of the canto—an organizing principle, as it were, at the imagistic level. I refer to the exquisite image of the mechanical clock at the end of the canto. For all of its familiarity to us, it must have startled contemporaries, most of whom had undoubtedly never seen any such device.[25] It serves as an example of how radically juxtaposed elements, in this case the most ancient ideas of astronomic speculation and the most modern of mechanical inventions, are fused together in Dante's synthesis, much as Solomon and Siger of Brabant[26] both find a place in his cast of characters:

> Indi come orologio che ne chiami
>   ne l'ora che la sposa di Dio surge
>   a mattinar lo sposo perchè l'ami
> che l'una parte l'altra tira e urge,
>   "tin tin" sonando . . .
>
> (*Par.* x, 139 ff.)

Of the many themes alluded to in this dense and beautiful passage—the sun and the liturgy,[27] the Church and Christ as Bride and Bridegroom, the dawn song of lovers[28]—I should like to single out just one: the aptness of comparing the "spiriti sapienti" to an instrument for measuring the diurnal course of the Sun. We have seen from the discussion of Daniélou's work that solar imagery applied to Christ in both of his symbolic roles, as both the Day and the Year of the Lord. Because the Sun measures both the day and the year (it is for this reason "lo ministro maggior de la natura"—*Par.* x, 28), its path, the Zodiac, may be said to mark both the hours and the months. The manifestation of the number twelve would seem to serve to compress universal history—the span of history represented by the "spiriti sapienti," the hours and the years—into the eternal *now* of the "dance" in the Empyrean of which this is a foreshadowing. A text from St. Ambrose will serve as an example of the tradition:

> If the whole duration of the world is like a single day, its hours mark off centuries: in other words, the centuries are its hours. Now there are twelve hours in the day. Therefore, in the mystic sense, the Day is indeed Christ. He has his twelve Apostles, who shone with the light of heaven, in which Grace has its distinct phases.[29]

So in Dante's *Paradiso*, the souls of the blessed take in all of history by gazing into history's center: ". . . mirando il Punto / a cui tutti li tempi son presenti" (*Par.* xvii, 17–18).[30]

The fact that this is a foreshadowing of the movement of the blessed souls in the Empyrean may serve to explain why the center of this circular dance is not occupied by the *Sol salutis,*[31] but simply by the pilgrim and his guide. Beatrice clearly contrasts this representation with the paradisiac original when she contrasts this material sun with the "Sole di li Angeli." There is, however, one comparison that suggests Beatrice's role in the representation, her position in the center of the circular dance, is very much like that of a heavenly body—not the Sun, but the Moon:

> Io vidi più fulgor vivi e vincenti
> far di noi centro e di sè far corona,
> più dolci in voce che in vista lucenti.
> Così cinger la figlia di Latona
> vedem talvolta, quando l'aere è pregno
> sì che ritenga il fil che fa la zona.
>
> (*Par.* x, 64–69)

This passage cannot be dismissed as merely decorative or merely metaphoric, for the comparison it suggests between Beatrice and the pilgrim on one hand and the Moon on the other has been rigorously prepared by the verses which immediately precede it. Beatrice tells the pilgrim to thank God, Whom she refers to as the Sun, for having given him the grace to ascend to the sphere of the material Sun. He does so with such concentration that he forgets Beatrice for the moment: "E sì tutto il mio amore in lui si mise / che Beatrice eclissò ne l'oblio" (*Par.* x, 59–60). The word "eclipse" here refers, not to a darkening, but rather to a blotting out by a greater light, as Benvenuto da Imola observed: "[Beatrix] eclipsata est, idest, nubilata in luce."[32] It is a commonplace of symbolic astronomy that the Moon regularly endures such an "eclipse" as it approaches the light of the Sun, which for this reason is thought of as a lover embracing his beloved.[33] This submerged significance of Beatrice's "eclipse" by God comes to the surface in the lines immediately following, when she is indirectly compared to the Moon.

The phenomenon of the halo around the moon (sometimes referred to in the Middle Ages as *Iris*, like the rainbow to which Dante later compares the spirits [*Par.* xii, 10 ff.])[34] is a substitute for an astronomical spectacle, the Sun surrounded by the stars, which no mortal eye can ever see. We may presume, then, that it stands to the Sun as the human to the divine or, to use Dante's own language, as the "essemplo" to the "essemplare" (*Par.* xxviii, 55–56). It is abundantly clear that the Sun is here a symbol for divinity and that Beatrice is associated with the moon; it remains for us to establish the sense in which she may be said to substitute for the referent of the solar image whose history we have discussed. It will come as no surprise, given what we know of what Hugo Rahner[35] has called the "Christian Mystery" of the Sun and Moon, if we suggest that Beatrice's role here is meant to be emblematic of the Church guiding the faithful. Put most simply, we may say that if the twelve Apostles are the Zodiac of *Sol Christi*, then the twelve philosophers and theologians are the "corona" of *Luna Ecclesiae*.

From the earliest days of Christianity, as Rahner has shown, "it is as though Helios and Selene were only created in order—to quote Origen—'to carry out their stately dance for the salvation of the world.' "[36] The ancient world had already established the relationship between Sun and Moon as that of lovers; it remained only to apply the teaching of Paul about the Heavenly Bridegroom and His Bride to that ancient image-complex in order to see in the *mysterium Lunae* the whole drama of the Church. The waxing and waning of the Moon, the derivation of its light from the Sun, its illumination in darkness and its fading in the light of day all seemed perfect allegories of the relationship of Christ to the Church. The woman "clothed with the Sun" of Apoc. 12 (quoted above) became the *locus classicus* for discussions of this kind which, according to Rahner, were perfected in the writings of Augustine. Rahner ends his discussion by citing *Paradiso* XXIII, Dante's direct treatment of the theme:

> Quale nei plenilunii sereni
> Trivia ride tra le ninfe etterne
> che dipingon lo ciel per tutti i seni,
> vidi, sopra migliaia di lucerne,
> un Sol che tutte quante l'accendea,
> come fa il nostro le viste superne
>
> (*Par.* XXIII, 25–30)

If, as a recent critic has suggested, the function of this metaphor is "purely emotional,"[37] then it must be said that the emotion is that of all of Christendom, occasioned by the fulfillment of universal history. This moment in the poem marks the shift in the metaphor we have been discussing and in many others as well—perhaps of all of the astronomical metaphors of the *Paradiso* up to this point. The contrast is still between the "Sole de li Angeli" ("Un Sole . . .") and the "Sole sensibile" ("il nostro") but this time their functions are reversed: for the first time in the poem, the *Sol Christi* may be beheld by the pilgrim, while the material sun is simply a memory of the sphere and the world below. If that transcendent Sun is compared to the moon (Diana—Trivia) and the stars (*ninfe*) here in our world, it is because the *mysterium Lunae*, the Church, is all we have on this side of the frontiers of material reality to foreshadow the Triumph of Christ, a contingent, provisional image, like those of *Paradiso* x, until the break of the eternal Day.

I have tried to show that the traditional image of the Apostles and the Zodiac may be taken as the background for the controlling theme of *Paradiso* x and that the shift from Apostles to theologians and philosphers finds its counterpart in a shifting of the center from the Sun to Beatrice and the pilgrim or, according to one of the comparisons, the Moon. There are two additional reasons that can be adduced to support the hypothesis that this shift is implicitly from Christ to a traditional image for the Church. The first of these is that the comparison to the Moon surrounded by water vapor (expressed in terms subtly suggestive of generation and maternity: *cingere, pregno, zona*), like the faint suggestion of flowers and fields noticed by Aldo Scaglione in the *Trivia* image ("le ninfe etterne / che dipingon lo ciel . . ." Cf. "le piante [di] questa ghirlanda," *Par.* x, 91)[38] underscores precisely the elements of moon imagery which enabled early exegetes to identify the heavenly body with the Church. Rahner makes the point:

> What causes the Sun's light to grow more mild is that Selene mingles the fire of Helios with the water of her own being, and I might as well at this stage tell you more about the rioting fancies of Greek thought on the subject of "heavenly moonwater." Poets and nature mystics produced an abundance of ideas about it, ideas which lingered on for a thousand years. . . . Selene becomes a giver of water, dew is created which she causes to drip down;. . . it is a begetter of life upon the earth; it brings about the growth of the grass and the growth of beasts and makes it possible for human mothers to bear their children. . . . In view of what has been said, it is not surprising that in seeking to give expression to his own beliefs the Christian should have made use of this lunar imagery with which the whole Hellenistic world was familiar.[39]

He then goes on to demonstrate how this imagery seemed perfect for conveying ideas about spiritual rebirth and the water of Baptism associated with the Church. The virgin goddess Diana (or "Trivia," to use Dante's name for her), in her role as moon mother, was transformed by Christianity into the image of Divine Matriarchy on earth: *Mater Ecclesia*.

The second, much more obvious reason for thinking that the triumph of the theologians and philosophers is a Triumph of the Church foreshadowing the Triumph of *Sol Christi* has already been mentioned, although in passing. It is simply this: the harmonic song produced by the dance of the philosophers and theologians is compared by the poet at the culminating point of the canto to the liturgical song of the Church, the eternal present marked by the hours of the day.[40] By referring to this song in erotic terms (". . . la sposa di Dio surge / a mattinar lo sposo perchè l'ami . . ." [*Par.* x, 140–141)] the poet binds into a single stunning unity not only Christ and His Church, Sun and Moon, Apostles and theologians, but also his own longing relationship to God, through the mediation of Beatrice. It would be foolhardy to generalize this mediation into an identification. We may say only that the mediation on the personal level, this man's salvation, finds its counterpart in human society in the role of the Church and for this reason Dante chose to use the traditional imagery of mediation to describe her. It is in this sense, as the relationship of incarnate reality to salvation history, that Beatrice may be said in this canto to be a *figura Ecclesiae.*

The ending of the narrative and therefore of the canto calls our attention to Christ, the Second Person of the Trinity and the exemplar of all Wisdom—*Somma Sapienza*. The propriety of such an ending in the canto of the "spiriti sapienti" is too obvious to require extensive commentary. What is equally obvious, however, is that the beginning of the canto seems to have little to do with this ending, for all of the didactic insistence of the involved address to the reader. The opening lines of the canto hint at some of the most complicated of all problems of medieval thought: the inner life of the Trinity, its role in the creation, the relationship of the heavens to generation and corruption on earth and, finally, the relationship of all these problems to the moral life. After touching upon all of these themes, the poet somewhat impatiently dismisses his reader:

> Or ti riman, lettor, sovra 'l tuo banco,
> dietro pensando a ciò che si preliba,
> s'esser vuoi lieto assai prima che stanco.
> Messo t'ho innanzi: omai per te ti ciba!
> chè a sè torce tutta la mia cura
> quella materia ond'io son fatto scriba.
>
> (*Par.* x, 22–27)

It would take more than a lifetime to complete the task set for us in these lines and certainly more than this article to sketch out how this doctrinal passage serves to introduce not only the tenth canto, but the next four as well. To conclude this paper, however, I should like simply to point to a few elements of the opening verses that relate to my subject, the translation of beatitude into astronomical terms. This will require first of all a return to our discussion of the relevance of the Platonic tradition to the canto's theme.

The theme of the circular dance of the stars is a familiar one in the *Timaeus*. The phrase "choreae stellarum" used in the translation of Chalcidius is already a figurative application of the word meaning "choral dance" to the exigencies of astronomical description. In the commentary of Guillaume de Conches a definition is offered of the movement of the starry spheres that might equally well describe the dance of the "spiriti sapienti": "Et est chorea circularis motus cum concordi sono. Inde dicunt philosophi stellas facere choream quia circulariter moventur et ex motu concordem reddunt sonum."[41] Elsewhere, he identifies the music specifically as *cantus*.[42] The song produced by the stellar dance is of course the music of the spheres, the music produced by the varying movements of the heavenly bodies, inaudible to mortal ears.[43] The music of the Heaven of the Sun, "voce a voce in tempra," seems to have the same transcendent quality, for the poet twice insists that it cannot be heard here below (*Par.* x, 75 and 146). Of more importance for the association of these ancient, admittedly generic themes with the tenth canto is the fact that it is the Sun, according to the *Timaeus*, that sets the standard of motion for all of the heavens by measuring time:

> And in order that there might be a conspicuous measure for the relative speed and slowness with which they moved in their eight revolutions [*chorea*], the god kindled a light in the . . . Sun—in order that he might fill the whole heaven with his shining and that all living things for whom it was meet might possess number, learning it from the revolution of the same and uniform. Thus and for these reasons day night came into being, the period of the single and most intelligent revolution.[44]

It should be observed that the Sun has an equally regulatory function in Dante's metaphoric universe even down to the detail of the motion which it induces in the "spiriti sapienti." When their rank is doubled and the poet asks us to imagine two garlands circling about a center, the description he gives us of their motion, as if "l'uno andasse al prima e l'altro al poi" (*Par.* XIII, 18), is part of the defintion of time: "numero di movimento [celestiale] secondo prima e poi."[45] Time may have its roots in the *Primum Mobile*, but its measure in hours and years is determined by the Sun.

The centrality of the Sun and its essential role in the cosmos led very early, possibly with the Stoics, to the idea that it represented the location of the World Soul, the *Anima Mundi*, whose varied history in the Middle Ages, including identification with the Holy Spirit and then finally with the Goddess Natura, has been traced by Tullio Gregory.[46] By Dante's time, of course, no Aristotelian could take the idea of a World Soul seriously, but a poet was perfectly free to do so and I have attempted in a previous study to outline what I take to be survivals of the idea in Dante's poem.[47] In the present context, I should like simply to point out a poetic survival, not explicitly stated, in the form of an associative principle that binds together the introduction of the tenth canto with the narrative contained within it and relates both to the moral imperative of the journey. That associative principle finds its expression precisely in the address to the reader; when Dante asks the reader to look up at that critical point in the Zodiac he is in fact asking us to contemplate not only the image which underlies the narrative of the canto, as we have seen, but also the complex of themes traditionally associated with the Zodiac in the tradition of symbolic cosmology.[48] The Zodiac was traditionally believed to be the emblem of the Creator's mark on the world and the seal of rationality both on man and on the heavens. So in the tenth canto, it is the sign of "quanto per mente e per loco si gira" (v. 4).

The text that first associated the circular movement of rationality (*per mente*) and of the heavens (*per loco*) with the circularity of divinity was Plato's *Timaeus*. In his myth concerning the World Soul he tells how the Demiurge formed it by cutting a strip of "soul-stuff" in two and then crossed the two pieces in order to form the letter "X". He then bent up the two ends in order to form two hoops, one inside the other, setting them circling in opposite directions. After he was finished, he fashioned the soul of man in precisely the same manner. It was perfectly clear to subsequent commentators on Plato's text that the motions of the World Soul, for all of their apparently mythical character, were in fact derived from the two motions observable in the heavens: the diurnal circling of the Sun from East to West, marking the hours of the day, and the annual circling of the Sun in the opposite direction along the Zodiac, marking the months of the year. When the Sun crossed the equator at its point of intersection with the ecliptic, "dove l'un moto e l'altro si percuote," it was thought to occupy the central point of the Platonic "X" and thus to mark the spot where the Demiurge had set into motion both the soul of the world and the soul of man.[49] Boethius' *Consolation of Philosophy* (III, m. 9) provided the Middle Ages with a most concise statement of the manner in which the universe bears the image of the *Anima Mundi*:

> You release the World Soul throughout the harmonious parts of the universe . . . to give motion to all things. That soul, thus divided, pursues its revolving course in two circles, and, returning to itself, embraces the profound mind and *transforms heaven to its own image.*[50]

It remained only to identify the Demiurge with the Father, the profound mind with the Son and the World Soul with the Holy Spirit in order for Christians to see in both the heavens and the human mind the image of the Trinity.[51]

The history of the assimilation of the three Persons of the Trinity to Their Platonic counterparts is of course a substantial part of the history of Christian philosophy in the Middle Ages and especially in the twelfth century.[52] What is of more concern to us here, however, is the assimilation of Platonic imagery to the Christian revelation. It happens that, from the earliest days of Christianity, the Platonic emblem of the Demiurge's creative act, the letter "chi" corresponding to the intersection of celestial movement that Dante asks his reader to contemplate, was associated with the emblem of Christ and of His redemptive act: the cross. The history of that association has been traced by W. Bousset.[52a] Among the passages he cites, one is of particular interest to us, for it brings together the theme of Wisdom in the person of Christ and the theme of celestial harmony. The passage comes from the apocryphal Acts of John, quoted above in relation to the dance of the disciples. The Lord appears to John and shows him a celestial "cross of light" specifically distinguished from the true cross:

> This cross of light . . . is the marking off of all things and the uplifting and the foundation of those things that are fixed and were unsettled, and the harmony of the wisdom—and indeed the wisdom of the harmony. . . . This, then, is the cross which fixed all things apart by the Word, and marked off the things from birth and below it, and then compacted all into one.[54]

In his commentary, Bousset has shown that this passage reflects a blending of the cosmological theme from the *Timaeus* with elements of the Gospel and of the Sapiential books of the Old Testament. He goes on to document the diffusion of the idea throughout the Patristic era and we may add to his findings that it survived well into the Middle Ages, for the association of the Platonic "X" with the cross reappears in the works of Peter Abaelard.[55] The general relevance of these Christian accommodations of Plato's text to a reading of the *Paradiso* is probably considerable—the cross of light in the Acts of John, for example, seems particularly suggestive for an interpretation of Dante's representation in the heaven of Mars. In the present context, however, the relevance is simply this: the history traced by Bousset provides an analogue to the opening verses of the tenth canto, wherein a glance up at the celestial "X" (the intersection of the equator and the ecliptic on the Zodiac) also serves to evoke the central mysteries of Christianity, through the mediation of Platonic myth.

If both the movement of mind (*per mente*: the "spiriti sapienti") and the vital principle of the universe (the heavens and the "mondo che li chiama"—v. 15) can be encompassed by the same astronomical motif (the Sun and the Zodiac), it is by virtue of the Christianization of the Platonic theme of the *Anima Mundi*. The Platonic theme and its Christian elaboration, together with a glance up at the Zodiac which exemplifies the concepts they represent, provide us with a sufficient background for interpreting the entire introduction to the canto.

The opening of the canto sets forth the two-fold movement of the three-fold Deity:

> Guardando nel Suo Figlio con l'Amore
> che l'uno e l'altro etternamente spira,
> lo primo ed ineffabile Valore,
> quanto per mente o per loco si gira,
> con tant'ordine fè, ch'esser non puote
> sanza gustar di lui chi ciò rimira.
>
> (*Par.* x, 1–6)

Were it not for the standard Christian effort to re-establish equality in the hierarchical relationship of the One, Mind and Soul in a neoplatonic system, this opening might well be a paraphrase of Macrobius.[56] At any rate, Dante intends here to set forth the two motions of the Trinity or, as he puts it in v. 51, "mostrando come *spira* e come *figlia*." These two motions, intellectual generation and the spiration of Love, volition, are the two motions in the Trinity which find their counterpart in the cosmos, "dove l'un moto e l'altro si percuote," insofar as the cosmos can reflect the inner life of the Trinity. Because of the way in which these two motions along the Zodiac affect all of creation, they are the instruments of God's Providence in the world (*Par.* x, 13–21).[57] More than that, however, because of the parallelism previously mentioned, the motions are the exemplar of all created mind as well: whatever rotates *per mente* or *per loco*. It is for this reason that all mind and all of the heavens offer a foretaste of the Trinity.

This, I take it, is the force of the word "dunque" in the address to the reader: "Leva *dunque*, Lettor, a l'alte ruote / meco la vista" (vv. 7–8). The call to look up at the heavens to contemplate the wonders of the creation is of course a familiar religious theme,[58] but it is also a Platonic theme that fits in very well with the microcosmic-macrocosmic context of the opening lines. It is exactly in the context of the passage in Macrobius referred to above, reminiscent of the poet's Trinitarian opening, that the significance of the motif is clearly enunciated:

> Human bodies . . . were found to be capable of sustaining, with difficulty, a small part of it [the divinity of Mind], and only they, since they alone seemed to be erect—reaching toward heaven and shunning earth, as it were—and since only the erect can always gaze with ease at the heavens; furthermore they alone have in their heads a likeness of a sphere . . . the only one capable of containing mind.[59]

The glance up at the heavens is in this sense the fulfillment of human rationality.

Finally, in order to end this paper and at the same time point to the ways in which its findings may be generalized to extend to the entire representation of the Heaven of the Sun, I should like for the last time to mention the circular dance of the star-souls. There are of course two motions described when all of the "spiriti sapienti" finally appear. We have discussed the two-fold motion of the Trinity, whereby it *figlia* and *spira*, with intellect and volition. We have suggested its analogies with the two-fold motion of the Sun along the Zodiac. It seems reasonable to assume that the Trinity is also the exemplar upon which the movement of the heavenly garlands[60] is based. The repeatedly parallel syntax used to describe each pair of motions

> l'Amore
> che l'uno a l'altro etternamente spira (*Par.* x, 1–2)
> dove l'un moto e l'altro si percuote (*Par.* x, 9)
> e l'un ne l'altro aver li raggi suoi (*Par.* xiii, 16)

leads one to suspect that the poet intends to associate the movement of the "spiriti sapienti" with the two-fold movement of the Trinity, comparing both to the two movements of the Zodiac. The suspicion is confirmed by the descriptions of the two wheels. The two movements of the Trinity (the generation of the Word and the spiration of Love) represent respectively an act of intelligence and an act of will. However else one divides the cast of characters in the Heaven of the Sun, there seems general agreement that the first circle represents intellectuals who shone with "cherubic splendor" and the second represents lovers who burned with "Seraphic ardor,"[61] exemplifying respectively intelligence and will.

The evidence of the zodiacal nature of the imagery beyond the tenth canto is equally clear, although perhaps not as widely recognized. First of all, as soon as the second circle appears, Dante describes the movement as that of a "mola" (*Par.* XII, 3), a mill-stone, the same word that he used in the *Convivio* in order specifically to distinguish zodiacal motion from generically circular motion.[62] Again, he refers to the song of the souls as more beautiful than that of "nostre muse, / nostre serene" (*Par.* XII, 7–8), the mythological goddesses who presided over the turning of the spheres.[63] We have seen that the phrase "l'uno andasse al prima e l'altro al poi" (*Par.* XIII, 18) recalls the measurement of time by celestial motion. Most convincing of all, perhaps, is the fact that the two accounts of the lives of the saints, obviously constructed in parallel, make reference to the course of the Sun at precisely the same verse—the "rising" of Francis is associated with the rising of the Sun, while the "rising" of Dominic is associated with its setting. At verse 51 of the *Paradiso* XI, Dante describes Francis' birth as a sun coming to the world, "come fa questo tal volta di Gange." At verse 51 of *Paradiso* XII, he describes the birth of Dominic as taking place near where "lo sol tal volta ad ogni uom si nasconde." This evidence would seem to indicate that the two-fold zodiacal motion constitutes the pattern even of the narrative portions of the succeeding cantos.

When the third light appears above the other two, the "vero sfavillar del Santo Spiro" (*Par.* XIV, 76), we, like the pilgrim, are unable to make it out precisely. As the light appears, the poet's comparison is to twilight:

> E sì come al salir di prima sera
> comincian per lo ciel nove parvenze,
> sì che la vista pare e non pare vera . . .
>
> (*Par.* XIV, 70–72)

The pilgrim ascends almost immediately to the next heaven, as if he were not quite ready to see this celestial, but not yet Paradisiac triune light. In this metaphoric area that is Dante's own creation, somewhere between the daylight of earth and the daylight of eternity, the Sun with his two motions sets the scene for the revelation that is to follow. It is clear here, as it was in the *Convivio*, what that revelation will be, for, as Dante put it, "Nullo sensibile in tutto lo mondo è più degno di farsi essemplo di Dio che 'l sole."[64]

# Notes

1. Emanuele Tesauro, *Il Cannocchiale Aristotelico* (Venezia, 1655), p. 493, quoted by Eugenio Donato, "Tesauro's Poetics: Through the Looking Glass," *MLN,* LXXVII, No. 1 (Jan. 1963), p. 19: "Reduced to this level of reality, the concepts expressed by the metaphor are nothing but 'argomenti urbanamente fallaci,' because 'ad udirle sorprendono l'intelletto, parendo concludenti di primo incontro, ma esaminate, si risolvono in una vana fallacia: come le mele nel Mar Negro, di veduta son belle e colorite, ma se le mordi, ti lasciano le fauci piene di cenere e di fumo.' "

2. Charles Singleton, *Dante Studies 1. Commedia: Elements of Structure* (Cambridge, Mass.: Harvard University Press, 1957), chapter I: Allegory. For the various figurative modes of the *literal* level of Scripture, see P. Synave, "La Doctrine de St. Thomas d'Aquin sur le sens littéral des Ecritures," *Revue biblique,* XXXV (1926), p. 40 ff.

3. G. Fraccaroli (trans.), *Il Timeo* (Torino: Bocca, 1906): Appendix: "Dante e il Timeo," pp. 391–424. Fraccaroli seems to think it certain that Dante knew the text in the translation of Chalcidius and possibly a commentary. For a more recent view of the diffusion of the *Timaeus* in Dante's time, see Guillaume de Conches, *Glosae super Platonem*, ed. E. Jeauneau (Textes Philosophiques du Moyen Age, XIII Paris: Vrin, 1965), pp. 29–31. Jeauneau utilized, among others, a thirteenth-century ms. from Ss. Annunziata in his collation.

4. See E. Jeauneau, "L'usage de la notion d' 'integumentum' à travers les glosses de Guillaume de Conches," *Archives d'histoire doctrinale et littéraire du moyen âge,* XXIV (Paris, 1957), pp. 35–100. Cf. Guillaume de Conches, *Glosae*, p. 19.

5. *Ibid.*, pp. 24–25 and bibliography.

6. *Ibid.*, 210–211.

7. Guillaume de Conches, *Commentary on Boethius,* III, m. 9. Ms. Troyes 1381, fol. 57, published in part by C. Jourdain, "Des Commentaires inédits," *Notices et Extraits de la Bibliothèque Impériale,* XX (Paris, 1865) pp. 77–78. The selection from the manuscript published by Jourdain concerning William's explanation of the myth of Orpheus is extremely suggestive for a reading of Canto IX, *Inferno*. William sees in the story of Eurydice an echo of Luke 9, 62, a passage frequently related to the story of Lot's wife turned to salt. According to J. Hatinguais ("En marge d'un poème de Boèce: l'interprétation allégorique du mythe d'Orphée par Guillaume de Conches," *Congrès de Tours et Poitiers: Actes* [Paris: "Belles Lettres," 1954], p. 285 ff.) the allegorical descent into Hell by Orpheus faces a "tentation du passé." So does the pilgrim when he comes upon Medusa.

The echoes of the *rime petrose* in the rhyme words of *Inf.* IX, 50, 52, 54 (*alto, smalto, assalto*, cf. *Rime,* C, v. 58 ff.) suggest a "tentation du passé" that might well be glossed as William glosses the story of Orpheus.

8. The difficulty with any philosophical reconciliation stems from the fact that the Platonic myth suggests a *decadence* to the world of matter and hence a metaphysical dualism incompatible with Christianity. For the problem, see my "Dante's 'per sé' Angel: The Middle Ground in Nature and in Grace," *Studi danteschi,* XXXIX (1962), 5–38 (p. 13 ff.).

9. "Dante's Pilgrim in a Gyre," PMLA, LXXVI, No. 3 (1961), 168–181; "The Final Image," MLN, LXXIX, No. 1 (1964), pp. 14–27.

10. Freccero, "Final Image," pp. 20–22.

11. *Inf.* XXXIV, 139: "a riveder le stelle;" *Purg.* XXXIII, 145: "a salire a le stelle;" *Par.* XXXIII, 145: "il sole e l'altre stelle."

12. Ernout and Meillet, in the *Dictionnaire Etymologique de la langue latine* (Paris: Klincksieck, 1951) *s.v.* acknowledge that "A *sidus* les anciens rattachaient déjà *considerare, desiderare*," cf. Paulus Festus, 66, 7: "desiderare et considerare a sideribus dici certum est." But they then conclude "Ce sont sans doute d'anciens termes de la langue augurale." The Pythagorean idea of the intellectual quality of sidereal movement as enunciated by Timaeus (*Timaeus* 40A ff.) seems to me a more plausible hypothesis, indicating a familiar *moral* distinction: *desiderare* = a fall to *temporalia* (Ernout and Meillet: "cesser de voir"). The moral force of *consideratio* seems to survive in the Middle Ages. See, for example, Johannes Sacrobosco, *Sphaera* II: "motus rationalis . . . id est . . . quando fit *consideratio* a creatore per creaturas in creatorem ibi sistendo," referring to the movement of the stars. Lynn Thorndike, *The "Sphere" of Sacrobosco* (Chicago: University of Chicago Press, 1949), p. 86. At any rate, there can scarcely be any doubt of the celestial associations in antiquity. Franz Boll's essay on the astronomical origins of the theme of contemplation ("Vita Contemplativa," *Kleine Schriften zur Sternkunde des Altertums*, ed. V. Stegemann [Leipzig: Koehler & Amelang, 1950], pp. 303–331) has gathered together many texts suggesting the astronomical force of *contemplatio* (see below, note 56), some of which illustrate a similar force for *consideratio*: see, for example, Cicero, *Acad.* II, 127: "Est enim animorum ingeniorumque naturale quoddam quasi pabulum *consideratio contemplatioque* naturae: erigimur, altiores fieri videmur, humana despicimus cogitantesque supera atque caelestia haec nostra ut exigua et minima contemnimus," Boll, p. 323. St. Bernard's treatise, *De consideratione (Patrologia Latina* 182, 727), gave the word the technical force that it surely has, resonances apart, in Dante's description of Richard of St.-Victor, for whom, however, the key word was *contemplatio*. See Richard of Saint-Victor, *Selected Writings on Contemplation*, trans. C. Kirchberger (London: Faber & Faber, 1957), 269 ff.

13. Sapegno describes the mediaeval "ballata" upon which this description is based. See *La Divina Commedia*, ed. N. Sapegno (La Letteratura italiana: Storia e testi, 4; Milano-Napoli: Ricciardi, 1957), *ad. loc.,* with bibliography. See also A. H. Lograsso, "From the *Ballata* of the *Vita Nuova* to the Carols of the *Paradiso* . . ." in *83rd Annual Report of the Dante Society* (1965), 23–48, and Bruno Nardi, "Il canto decimo del Paradiso," Convivium, XXIV (1956), p. 650 ff.

14. Augustine, Letter to Ceretius (*Patrologia Latina* 33, col. 1034 ff.), referred to by Theodor Zahn, *Acta Joannis* (Erlangen: Deichert, 1880), p. 220.

15. *Acta Joannis*, ed. Zahn, p. 220, trans. B. Pick, *The Apocryphal Acts of Paul, Peter, John, Andrew and Thomas* (Chicago: Open Court, 1909), p. 181. For the Gnostic sources,

see R. A. Lipsius, *Die Apokryphen Apostelgeschichten und Apostellegenden* (Braunschweig: Schwetschke, 1883), I, 520. For similar dances in antiquity, see Lipsius' notes as well as Erwin Rohde, *Psyché*, trans. A. Reymond (Paris: Payot, 1928), p. 270 ff. and Robert Eisler, *Weltenmantel und Himmelszeit* (München: Beck, 1910), pp. 462 and 472, where "star-dances" of antiquity are cited.

16. For the number 8, its significance and its sources, see H. Rahner, who quotes the saying "all things are eight," *Greek Myths and Christian Mystery*, trans. B. Battershaw (London: Burns and Oates, 1957), p. 74 ff. and bibliography.

17. Almost all of the standard works on the history of astrology attempt to trace the origins of the idea, beginning with the fundamental A. Bouché-Leclercq, *L'Astrologie Grecque* (Paris: Leroux, 1899), *s.v.* and Franz Boll, *Sternglaube und Sterndeutung* (Leipzig-Berlin: Teubner, 1919), *s.v.* and subsequent editions. I have found W. Gundel, *Dekane und Dekansternbilder* (Studien der Bibliothek Warburg; Hamburg: Augustin, 1936) *s.v.* particularly useful. For a fuller bibliography, see J. Baltrusaitis, "L'Image du monde céleste du IX$^{e}$ au XII$^{e}$ siècle," *Gazette des Beaux-Arts,* XX, No. 6 (1938), p. 138 n. 1.

18. The illustration is reproduced after a sketch of the pavement of the baptistry published by G. B. Befani, *Memorie Storiche di San Giovanni Battista di Firenze* (Firenze: Pia Casa di Patronato, 1884), frontispiece, first brought to my attention by Rev. Ernest Kaulbach, whom I should like to thank. I should like to point out the palindrome encircling the solar disc: EN GIRO TORTE SOL CICLOS ET ROTOR IGNE. The fact that the phrase can be read in both directions is an ingenious way of conveying the two-fold motion of the Sun. For further details, see Befani, p. 38. For the prevalence of such schemata, see J. Baltrusaitis, *art. cit.*

19. The wealth of citations from the Old and New Testaments, classical and Gnostic sources are brought together in Franz Dölger's *Sol Salutis* (Munster: Aschendorff, 1925), 445 ff., as well as "Sonne und Sonnenstrahl als Gleichnis in der Logostheologie des Christlichen Altertums," *Antike und Christentum,* I (1929), p. 271.

20. For the importance of solar mysticism at the time of the Copernican revolution, see E. Garin, *Studi sul Platonismo medievale* (Firenze: Le Monnier, 1958), p. 190 ff.: "La Letteratura 'solare' e l'orazione al Sole di Giuliano" and bibliography cited there.

21. "Les Douze Apôtres et le zodiaque," *Vigliae Christianae,* XIII (1959), p. 14 ff. One of the key texts cited by Daniélou to document the transference of the number 12 from the Jewish to the Christian tradition is from Clement of Alexandria: "The twelve gems [of the grand priest] arranged in groups of four on his chest describe the zodiac with the four changes of the seasons. One may also discern there . . . the prophets who denote the just men of each of the alliances. We will not be deceived if we say that in fact the Apostles are both prophets and just men" (*Stromata* V, 6, 38; quoted by Daniélou, p. 21).

22. *Mythologie und Symbolik der christlichen Kunst* (Weimar: Landes-industrie-comptoir, 1847–1851), II, p. 292 ff. See in particular his tables on pp. 305 and 306, listing the transformation of the significances of the various signs of the zodiac.

23. See Eisler, *Weltenmantel, cit.,* p. 264 ff., where "twelves" from Greek, Jewish, Etruscan, Roman and Germanic traditions are cited as possible examples of astrological survivals.

24. For the zodiacal origins of these verses, see Franz Boll, *Aus der Offenbarung Johannes* (Leipzig: Teubner, 1914), p. 39. For a typical gloss, see Hugo de S. Caro, *Commen-*

*tum in Apocalypsim* (Lugduni, 1669), *ad loc.*: "Hae sunt duodecim Apostoli, qui dicuntur *corona* quia quodammodo Christus per ipsos devicit mundum," f. 400v.

25. For the invention of the mechanical clock, see Lynn Thorndike, "Invention of the Mechanical Clock about 1271 A.D.," *Speculum,* XVI, No. 2 (1941), p. 242.

26. It is not my intention in this paper to discuss the propriety or the rationale of the ordering or selection of the characters in this representation. The classic discussion concerning the presence of Siger is Etienne Gilson, *Dante and Philosophy*, trans. D. Moore (New York: Harper, 1963), p. 275.

27. For the liturgical day, see Odon Casel, *Le Mystère du culte* (Paris: Editions du Cerf, 1946), chap. V: "Le mystère du jour liturgique" and Dölger, *Sol Salutis, cit.,* chap. 22: 'Sol Salutis: Christus als Sonne im Morgenhymnus."

28. See Sapegno, *ad loc.*

29. *In Lucam* VII, 222, Sources Chrétiennes, p. 92, quoted by Daniélou, pp. 14–15.

30. For the theme, see G. Poulet, "The Metamorphoses of the Circle" in *Dante*, ed. J. Freccero (20th Century Views; Englewood Cliffs, N. J.: Prentice-Hall, 1965), p. 151 ff.

31. Dölger, *cit.*

32. Benevenuti de Rambaldis de Imola, *Comentum super Dantis Aldigherij Comoediam*, ed. Lacaita (Firenze: Barbera, 1887), Vol. V, *ad loc.*

33. See Rahner, *cit.,* p. 158.

34. For a typical comment see Guillaume de Conches, *De Mundi Constitutione*: "De iride: sunt aliquando etiam duo arcus, quia luna similiter arcum facti, plenum tamen, quia non est ipsa Iris, et solet esse imminentibus ventis aut pluviis." In Bede, *Opera dubia et spuria, Patrologia Latina* 90, col. 888. Dante alludes to the two types of "rainbows" in *Purg.* XXIX, 78 in a context which suggests the heavenly couple: "onde fa l'arco il Sole e Delia il cinto."

35. Rahner, chap. IV: "The Christian Mystery of Sun and Moon."

36. *Ibid.*, p. 111, quoting Origen *On Prayer*, 7.

37. Aldo Scaglione, "Imagery and Thematic Patterns in *Paradiso* XXIII," *From Time to Eternity*, ed. T. Bergin (New Haven: Yale University Press, 1967), p. 163.

38. *Ibid.*, pp. 156–157.

39. *Op. cit.,* p. 160.

40. See above, n. 27.

41. *Timaeus a Calcidio translatus*, ed J. H. Waszink (Plato Latinus, IV; Leyden: Brill, 1962), p. 33, *Timaeus* 40C; Guillaume de Conches, *Glosae, ed. cit.,* p. 197.

42. *Glosae*, p. 186.

43. On the theme of harmony, see Leo Spitzer, *Classical and Christian Ideas of World Harmony*, ed. A. G. Hatcher (Baltimore: Johns Hopkins University Press, 1963).

44. *Timaeus* 39B. Francis Cornford, *Plato's Cosmology* (New York: Liberal Arts Press, 1957), p. 115.

45. See *La Divina Commedia*, commentata da Isidoro del Lungo (Firenze: Le Monnier, 1931), III, p. 763: "l'una al 'prima' e l'altra al 'poi,' secondo il concetto e il linguaggio aristotelico (cf. *Convivio* IV, ii, 5–6), che 'il tempo è numero di movimento secondo *prima e poi*.' " See the notes of G. Busnelli and G. Vandelli, *Convivio* (Firenze: Le Monnier, 1954), Vol. II, p. 16.

46. Tullio Gregory, *Anima Mundi* (Firenze: Sansoni, 1955), esp. chapter III: "L'Anima del mondo e l'anima individuale," p. 123.

47. "Pilgrim in a Gyre," *cit.*

48. For an outline of the apparent movement of the Sun along the Zodiac, see M. A. Orr, *Dante and the Early Astronomers*, 2nd ed. (London: Wingate, 1956), pp. 172–181.

49. *Timaeus* 36B ff. and Cornford's notes *ad loc.*

50. Boethius, *Consolation of Philosophy* (New York: Liberal Arts Press, 1962), p. 72.

51. These identifications are commonplace in the commentaries. I chose for an example the commentary published by E. T. Silk, *Saeculi nonis Auctoris in Boetii Consolationem Philosophiae Commentarius* (Rome: American Academy, 1935): for the association of Mind with the Son, see p. 175: "Dicit Boetius mundum PERPETUA RATIONE regi, quia intellexit illum per *sapientiam* Dei, id est per Filium Dei, non tantum factum esse sed etiam gubernari." For the various arguments in the controversy concerning the identification of *Anima* with the Holy Spirit, see Gregory, p. 146 ff.

52. Z. Hayes, *The General Doctrine of Creation in the Thirteenth Century* (München: Schöningh, 1964), p. 88.

53. "Platons Weltseele und das Kreuz Christi," *Zeitschrift für die Neutestamentliche Wissenschaft,* XIV (1913), p. 273.

54. Pick, *op. cit.*, p. 184.

55. *Theologia Christiana* in Petri Abaelardi *Opera*, ed. V. Cousin (Paris: Durand, 1859), Vol. II, p. 406–407.

56. Macrobius (I, 14) is a *locus classicus* for a résumé of the neoplatonic doctrine of emanation and creation. See Macrobius, *Commentary on the Dream of Scipio*, trans. W. H. Stahl (New York: Columbia University Press, 1952), p. 142 ff. and Stahl's notes.

57. For the astronomical details of zodiacal inclinations, its effects and its sources, see the parallel discussions in the *Convivio* III, v, 23 ff. and Busnelli-Vandelli notes *ad loc*. See also below, note 56.

58. For the religious theme of the glance up at the sun, see Dölger, *Sol Salutis, cit.*, especially chapter 18: "*Sursum corda* und der Aufblick zum Himmel."

59. Macrobius I, 14; Stahl, p. 144. It is in this chapter that Macrobius derives *contemplatio* from "the temple of God." See Stahl, p. 142 and notes. Dante echoes the tradition in *Par.* XXVIII, 53: "questo miro e angelico templo." The poet seems to blend elements of both the Platonic and religious traditions when he describes the divine providence of the two-fold motion: "O ineffabile sapienza che così ordinasti . . . ! E voi a cui utilitade e diletto io scrivo, in quanta cechitade vivete, non levando li occhi suso a queste cose, tenendoli fissi nel fango de la vostra stoltezza!" (*Convivio* III, v, 22).

60. The circular movement of a "corona" (Ariadne's garland—*corona borealis, Par.* XIII, 14–15) is identified as the movement of the Zodiac by Remi d'Auxerre's commentary of Martianus Capella (I, 30.14): "per coronam, zodiacus . . . in modum coronae spheram caelestem quasi Iovis verticem cingit." *Commentum in Maritanum Capellam*, ed. Cora Lutz (Leiden: Brill, 1962), p. 121.

61. *Par.* XI, 37–39:

> L'un fu tutto serafico in ardore;
> l'altro per sapienza in terra fue
> di cherubica luce uno splendore.

The source of the exhortation to conform human conduct to the angelic hierarchies is

Gregory the Great, *In Evangel. sermo* xxxiv (*Patrologia Latina* 76, 1252). Alanus ab Insulis identifies the Seraphim with "viri contemplativi qui divino amori omnino sunt dediti, ut viri claustrales," while the Cherubim are the "magistri in sacra pagina," *Hierarchia Alani*, Alain de Lille, *Textes inédits*, ed. M. T. d'Alverny (Etudes de Philosophie Médiévale, LII; Paris: Vrin, 1965), pp. 230–231. See d'Alverny's comments, p. 107. The importance of the comparison is not only doctrinal but poetic as well, for the angels are in fact the archetype for the circular movement of the blessed in the Empyrean, see Freccero, *Final Image, cit.* Furthermore, they are in fact the movers of the Primum Mobile and the sphere of the fixed stars respectively, i.e., the intelligences which cause the celestial movement which is the counterpart of this movement in the physical world.

62. "[Conviene] esso sole girar lo mondo intorno giù a la terra . . . come una mola de la quale non paia più che mezzo lo corpo suo." *Convivio* III, v, 14, ed. Busnelli-Vandelli, I, 313.

63. For the assimilation of the muses to the "Sirens of the Spheres" in the *Republic* (x, 617B), see Pierre Boyancé, "Les Muses et l'harmonie des sphères," *Mélanges dédiés à la mémoire de Félix Grat* (Paris: Pecqueur-Grat, 1946), p. 3 ff.

64. *Convivio* III, xii, 6; Busnelli-Vandelli, I, p. 399; see H. Gmelin (ed.) *Die Göttliche Komödie, Kommentar,* III Teil: *Das Paradies* (Stuttgart: Klett, 1957), *ad loc.* For the importance of the Sun in Aries as an *essemplo* of Christ, see Rahner, p. 109 ff.

# Robert Hollander

## *Vita Nuova*: Dante's Perceptions of Beatrice

If one were asked to guess how many times Beatrice appears to Dante in the *Vita Nuova* one might, in view of Dante's fondness for the number, very well guess nine times. Since that is probably the correct answer it is at least a little surprising that no *dantista*—at least none known to this writer—has even made any effective attempt at a count.[1] There are various objects of various kinds of "seeing" in the *Vita Nuova*, as will be described below. This discussion will be dominantly concerned with the appearances of Beatrice. An "appearance of Beatrice" is defined simply as what is recorded of a single particular awareness of Beatrice as actually being in Dante's presence, whether this awareness come from actual encounter, dream, or fantastic imagining. It is likely that from Dante's point of view one of the most important subjects of the *Vita Nuova* is its record of Beatrice's appearances. For this reason it does not matter whether a single event is described once or twice (i.e., in prose *and* in verse). What we wish to determine, first of all, is the number of her appearances to Dante. It may then be fruitful to study the qualities of these appearances. In order that the following survey be complete and clear, it will include specific apparitions of others to Dante as well as specific "non-apparitions" of Beatrice—occasions on which Dante expects or hopes to see her but does not.

1. Beatrice appears to Dante (they are both in their ninth year) dressed in crimson (II, 3).

2. Nine years to the day later, dressed in white, between two *gentili donne*, she appears to Dante and grants him her salutation (III, 1).

3. That same day Dante, while sleeping, has a *maravigliosa visione* of Beatrice

held in the arms of Amore, a vision which is the subject of the first poem of the *Vita Nuova* (III, 3–7, 10–12).

4. In church Dante sees Beatrice but is thought to be admiring the lady who sits in his line of sight; she will serve as his *schermo de la veritade* (V, 1).
   4a. Dante sees the corpse of *una donna giovane e di gentile aspetto molto* whom he had seen several times in the company of Beatrice (VIII, 1–2).
   4b. Amore appears in Dante's imagination and announces the name of a second "screen lady," as is recounted in the following sonnet (IX, 3–6, 9–12).

5. Beatrice, "passando per alcuna parte," denies Dante her *dolcissimo salutare* because of the gossip concerning Dante's infatuation with the second "screen lady" (X,2).
   [5a. We are told that whenever Beatrice appeared Dante was filled with charity; here no specific occasion is alluded to (XI, 1).]
   5b. Amore appears in Dante's sleep, as he had done many times before, and urges Dante to justify himself against slanderous gossip by means of verse addressed to Beatrice (XII, 3–9).

6. A friend takes Dante along to a marriage feast where he sees Beatrice among the ladies (XIV, 4).
   6a. Dante, finding himself in the company of certain ladies, is relieved not to find Beatrice among them so that he can discuss the nature of his love with them (XVIII, 2).
   6b. Dante goes to the funeral of Beatrice's father; he overhears departing ladies describe Beatrice's grief, but does not see or hear her himself (XXII, 3–5).

7. Dante, ill in his room, has wild imaginings of Beatrice's death and ascent to Heaven; his *erronea fantasia* is so strong that he even sees women covering Beatrice's head with a white veil and the last rites being administered to her; the central *canzone* recounts these imaginings (XXIII, 4–10, 17–28).

8. Dante sees Beatrice preceded by Guido's Giovanna after imagining that Amore had appeared to cheer him; the two episodes are united when they are recounted in a sonnet (XXIV, 2, 3–5, 7–9).
   8a. A year after her death, Dante, sketching an angel, has a thought of Beatrice which he records in the "anniversary poem" (XXXIV, 1–3).

8b. Dante sees a *gentile donna* looking compassionately at him (xxxv, 2).
8c. He sees her several more times (xxxvi, 2).

9. In his imagination Dante seems to see Beatrice, as young as she was at their first encounter, and, as then, dressed in crimson; he repents his desire for a new love (xxxix, 1–2).
   9a. In a sonnet Dante describes the heavenly voyage of his *pensero/sospiro*; it ascends to Beatrice, and though Dante's earthbound intelligence cannot understand what his heavenly thought comprehends of Beatrice's miraculous being, he does know that it is fully occupied with Beatrice alone, since he frequently hears it say her name (xli, 3–7, 10–13).

The final vision of chapter xlii will be discussed later.[2]

In the prose of the *Vita Nuova* Dante makes use of three different modes of seeing:

1)actual seeing
2)seeing in dream
3)imaginary or fantasized seeing.

For each of these modes of seeing there is a specialized vocabulary of vision and/or appearance. There are no observable inconsistencies in Dante's use of these three vocabularies. None, at least, if we confine our investigation to their use in the prose of the work. As will be pointed out later, there are a number of inconsistencies between various interjoined *prose* and *poesie*. Since it is the prose, written as a self-conscious unit, which gives us our best clues as to Dante's intentions in the *Vita Nuova*, it is only logical that it should here receive the major share of our attention.

Let us begin by examining Nicolò Mineo's assertion that Dante uses the terms *visione, imaginazione*, and *fantasia* without apparent distinction.[3] *Imaginazione* and *fantasia* are in fact used almost interchangeably to denote the third mode of seeing. In describing things seen *imaginazione* is used a total of seventeen times,[4] *fantasia,*[5] eight. The appearances of Beatrice to which they refer are items 7 and 9 in the preceding list; the appearances of Amore to which they refer are 4b and 8. In all four cases Dante explicitly informs his reader that the scene he describes occurred in his own mind and nowhere else—that it is a fantasy, an imagining, something limited to his own consciousness. *Visione*, on the other hand, *pace* Mineo, has two uses, neither of which is to be confused with the uses of *fantasia* and *imaginazione* in our third mode. The word is used only seven times in the *libello*, and only thrice after the initial cluster of four which describes Dante's dream of Beatrice in the arms of Amore (item 3).[6] In this first case the word joins with another, *sonno*, to make the nature of the *visione* clear: it is a seeing in dream. The next time the word is used (item 5b), it describes Amore's appearance in a dream. Again it is accompanied by *sonno.*[7] Items 3 and 5b are, strictly speaking, the only two dreams recorded in the *Vita Nuova*. One kind of *visione*, then, is that which occurs in dream. Our examination of the second kind lies ahead of us.

Thus far we have accounted for two kinds, or modes, of seeing in the *Vita Nuova*. But as our initial catalogue of Beatrice's appearances to Dante makes clear, a third kind of seeing has the lion's share: actual seeing. Six of Beatrice's appearances to Dante are of this nature: items 1, 2, 4, 5, 6, and 8. Is there a characteristic vocabulary at work here too? It is again simpler to proceed by means of a catalogue.

(1) Beatrice's first appearance to Dante: *apparire* is used five times, *vedere* once.[8]

(2) Beatrice's second appearance: again *apparire.*[9]

(4) Dante sees Beatrice in church: *vedere.*[10]

(5) When Beatrice denies Dante her *salutare* her actions are described directly, and there is no verb of appearance or perception used, simply direct narrative description.

(6) Dante sees Beatrice at the wedding feast: *vedere.*[11]

(8) Dante sees Giovanna followed by Beatrice: *vedere* is used for both sightings.[12]

From this description it is evident that in the *Vita Nuova* even common words like *vedere* and *apparire* are also used "technically" in a vocabulary of appearance and vision that is impressively careful.[13] To summarize these findings as briefly as possible: the *Vita Nuova* yields the following schema of modes of appearance and seeing (this table refers only to appearances of Beatrice to Dante):

| KINDS OF SEEING | DESIGNATIVE TERMS | MODAL TERMS |
|---|---|---|
| 1) in actuality (1,2,4,5,6,8) | ——————[14] | *apparire* or *vedere* |
| 2) in dream (3) | *sonno* and *visione* | *parere, parea vedere,*[15] *apparire* |
| 3) in fantasy (7,9) | *imaginazione* and *fantasia* | " " " " |

Discussion of Dante's final vision will return to this schema.

We set out to investigate the number and quality of Beatrice's appearances to Dante. She appears to him nine times in three different modes. Each of these modes has its own vocabulary of appearance and vision. Dante most likely limited his reports of her "formal" appearances to nine consciously—

Beatrice *is* a nine.[16] And for this reason, it might be argued, the references to his having seen her on other occasions or generic references to the fact that he has seen her are limited to being just that—references—they are not formally "appearances of Beatrice."[17] Similarly, apparitions of Amore and of the *gentile donna*, though they variously share the modes of appearance and seeing in which Dante perceives Beatrice, are not to be considered as having as significant a function in the work as the apparitions of Beatrice. Their function is that of a supportive scaffolding for Dante's major purpose, which is to be *scriba Beatricis*—not of what she says, of what she is. Yet Dante's treatment of Amore deserves closer attention. For it too reveals the consistency of Dante's distinction-making process in the *Vita Nuova*.

Caught between the conventions of thirteenth-century love poetry (as represented by his early lyrics) and the requirements of his own new poetic life (as represented by the prose of the *Vita Nuova*), Dante is forced to a somewhat ungainly compromise. Until we reach the twenty-fifth chapter of the work we must be prepared to encounter Amore in one of two guises: either as an actual "character" or as an internalized agency of Dante's being.[18] Descriptions of his external behaviors occur in only four places in the prose. The following description proceeds in the order of Dante's composition, that is, from the earlier poems to the accompanying prose.

1. (3) In the first sonnet of the *Vita Nuova* Amore appears to Dante holding Beatrice in his arms. The verbs used to describe his appearance and Dante's beholding are *apparire*[19] and *vedere* (III, 11, 12). In short, without the accompanying prose[20] the action of the sonnet might be taken by a reader as either being or pretending to be the recounting of actual events. Dante's prose description of these events, however, makes it clear that the whole experience occurred during his sleep. The words used to describe the appearance of Amore ("uno segnore di pauroso aspetto"[21]) and Beatrice, as well as Dante's perceptions of them, carefully separate seeing in dream and appearance in dream from actual seeing and actual appearance.[22]

1a. [(4a) In the sonnet "Piangete, amanti, poi che piange Amore" (VIII, 4–6) Dante sees Amore weeping ("ch'io 'l vidi lamentare in forma vera"—v. 10) over the dead form of the *donna giovane e di gentile aspetto molto*. In the prose (VIII, 1–3) Amore is not mentioned at all. He has momentarily been excused from the fiction.]

2. (4b) In the sonnet "Cavalcando l'altr'ier per un cammino" (IX, 9–12) Dante

finds Amore on the road ("trovai Amore in mezzo de la via"—v. 3). Once again in the sonnet Amore performs as an actual "character." In the prose (IX, 1–7) he is again described periphrastically and appears only in Dante's imagination.[23]

3. (5b) The *ballata* which follows Dante's second and last dream in the *Vita Nuova* (XII, 3–9) does not involve Amore as a "character" who interacts with Dante. In the prose, where he does appear, he is once more not called by name, and once again (as in item 3) is presented as having been seen in dream.[24]

4. (8) In the sonnet "Io mi senti' svegliar dentro a lo core" (XXIV, 7–9) Dante sees Amore coming toward him ("e poi vidi venir da lungi Amore"—v. 3). Though in the sonnet he appears as an actual "character," in the accompanying prose he is described as being instead "una imaginazione d'Amore" (XXIV, 2). His appearance is thus sharply contrasted with those of Giovanna and Beatrice, who are *seen*, since they are actually present, both in the sonnet (XXIV, 8) and in the prose (XXIV, 3).

What emerges from this summary is a perhaps surprising fact: not once in the prose of the *Vita Nuova* is Amore treated as having actual existence; he is allowed this only in four of the sonnets, which had been previously composed. One of the aesthetic and rational problems of the *Vita Nuova* is Dante's rather confusing treatment of Amore.[25] It is a problem which he himself partly acknowledges in the brilliant if self-serving twenty-fifth chapter of the work, one of the most brilliant passages of literary criticism written between the time of Servius and Macrobius and the close of the thirteenth century. The proximate cause of Dante's examination of poetic license in this passage is the contradiction raised by Amore's actualistic behavior in the sonnet of XXIV after what Dante has said of him in the preceding prose. Amore as internalized mechanism of Love runs the length of the *Vita Nuova*. He first appears in Chapter II and he is heard of for the last time in the final sonnet (XLI, 10). As a "character" he is essentially taken off after his appearance in the last dream recorded in the work (XII, 3–9). One can sense Dante's growing embarrassment with his presence as "character" in several passages.[26] The only time after XII that he is treated as "character" is in the sonnet (XXIV, 7–9) that is the cause of his final dismissal as "character." It is as though his re-appearance in the *monna Vanna / monna Bice* sonnet were the last straw. And if we study his first appearance, which is conjoined with that of Beatrice, we can see that the author of the prose *Vita Nuova* never wanted him to be taken literally: the Amore who takes control of Dante's soul does so "per la vertù che li dava la mia imaginazione" (II, 7). This is the first use of the word *imaginazione* in the work, and it sharply contrasts with the four uses of *apparire* and the use of *vedere* which describe the appearance of Beatrice. It is of some use to understand that the Dante of the *Vita Nuova* was as careful in keeping distinctions between fiction modeled on "history" and fiction that is "fabula"—the *bella menzogna* of *Convivio*—as was the author of the *Commedia.*[27]

Fiction that is modeled on history—medieval *argumentum*—is the basic fictive mode both of the *Vita Nuova* and of the *Commedia*. This does not necessarily mean that either Dante (or the present writer) believed that the actions recorded in either work actually occurred in history, but only that this is their fictional convention. Dante did not labor under the delusion that he had actually visited the afterworld. The question of his sense of the historicity of Beatrice is more complicated. While there may be almost enough documentation to suggest that the *Vita Nuova* records historical events in a historical relationship, whether or not Beatrice was Bice Portinari, whether or not she existed at all, is not terribly important. The next step taken by critics who take that first step is, however, generally the wrong one: if she is not "real," she must be "allegorical." While questions concerning her actual existence are not terribly important, what is centrally important is to grasp the significance of Dante's treatment of her as actual. The same remark may be applied (and with some force) to the *Divina Commedia*. Dante was ahead of his contemporaries in this too, for he realized the aesthetic and intellectual superiority of a convention of fiction that is mimetic in nature, partly because he was a Thomist on this point, at least, and understood the implications for a poet of the priority of knowledge held through the senses and partly because he was the kind of man and poet who could not think without reference to the senses, for whom *nomina sunt consequentia rerum* (XIII, 4).

There are many apparitions or sightings in the *Vita Nuova*. It is at least likely that the numerologically inclined Dante gave some of these a numerological structure. It is also likely that such a structure would involve Beatrice (rather than anyone else), and that its number would be a nine.[28] However, if agreement can be reached that Dante records nine appearances of Beatrice in the *Vita Nuova* (six in actuality, two in fantasy, one in dream[29]), it is also true that this accountancy does not include his most important vision of Beatrice, the *mirabile visione* that concludes the *libello*. This vision is unlike all the previous nine sightings in many respects. One of the more important of these is that it is undescribed. In the preceding chapter Dante tells us that his thought ("il mio pensero"—XLI, 3) flew up beyond the *primo mobile* (and thus into the Empyrean), saw a *donna* honored there (it can only have been Beatrice), but that what it had seen is beyond the capacity of Dante's intellect and that his thought spoke wholly of his lady (XLI, 3–7). The sonnet, the last poem of the work, is in basic accord with the prose[30] and makes the identity of Beatrice specific (XLI, 13). This chapter does not technically record a sighting of Beatrice by Dante. The point it makes is that he was then incapable of seeing with heavenly vision. But if Dante is unable to understand, within the fiction, the implications of what his *pensero* returns from heaven with, his readers have perhaps received enough training at this stage in the work to understand what the character cannot. The play is taken out of our hands before we have time to give the problem much thought, for, suddenly, in chapter XLII, Dante has been able to follow his thought to Heaven. His intellect, as though trained by the near-vision of "Oltre la spera che più larga gira," has finally been granted what has always been the goal of the pilgrimage in love that is the *Vita Nuova*. To put this another way, his intellect has finally achieved comprehension of the new life.

The language with which Dante describes the fact of the vision is interesting: "Appresso questo sonetto *apparve* a me una mirabile *visione*, ne la quale io *vidi* cose che mi fecero proporre di non dire più di questa benedetta infino a tanto che io potesse più degnamente *trattare* di lei" (XLII, 1—italics added). As has been previously noted, up to this moment in the *Vita Nuova* Dante has distinguished three vocabularies of appearance and vision.[31] Now he brings together his vocabularies of seeing in dream (*visione*) and of actual seeing (*vedere*). (Since *apparire* has been assimilated by each of these two categories before, it is not clear at first which one it joins here.) Is the *mirabile visione* to be understood as dream seeing, or as actual seeing? The correct answer is probably neither, though more the latter than the former. On two previous occasions, when he recorded dreams, Dante has clearly told us they were dreams.[32] Since he does not do so now, we have no reason to suppose that the vision is a dream. With regard to actual seeing in the *Vita Nuova*, it is limited, naturally enough, to perceiving the things apparent on this earth, which is to see through a glass darkly. And while the ability to discern what is actually before the eyes of the earthly beholder is essentially the same ability which enables the organs of sight to see face to face, the objects seen in the mystical vision, even when they are presented to mortal sight, are unrecognizable unless the beholder has undergone that change which Paul was believed to have referred to in 1 Corinthians 13:12.[33] Dante's *mirabile visione* is not a vision in a dream, a Macrobian veiled presentation of the truth, as were the first two dreams; nor is it to be confounded with perception of earthly reality (the preceding sonnet makes that absolutely clear); it should most likely be taken as the result of a *raptus*,[34] of a sudden seeing *in gloria*, with heavenly sight. The words *apparire, visione*, and *vedere* have gained an exalted context and new meanings.

*Visione* has a biblical counterpart—there are many fewer than one might think to choose from in the New Testament—that might well have been in Dante's mind. In all of St. Paul's works the word *visio* occurs only once: "Si gloriari oportet (non expedit quidem), veniam autem ad visiones et revelationes Domini" (2 Cor. 12:1). It is this passage which leads into the description of his *raptus*: "Scio hominem in Christo ante annos quattuordecim, sive in corpore nescio sive extra corpus nescio, Deus scit, raptum huiusmodi usque ad tertium caelum" (12:2). All one can claim is that if the experience recorded in *Vita Nuova* XLII is to be thought of as Pauline *raptus*, the word *visione* is likely to come from the same source. This does not seem an unlikely hypothesis, especially since Paul, in possession of knowledge it is not lawful to utter, continues as follows: "Nam, etsi voluero gloriari, non ero insipiens, veritatem enim dicam; parco autem, ne quis me existimet supra id quod videt in me aut aliquid audit ex me" (12:6). His disclaimers are at least likely to be behind those of Dante, who intends "di non dire più di questa benedetta infino a tanto che io potesse più degnamente trattare di lei" (XLII, 1).[35]

The verb *trattare* may also have a Pauline context here. Paul's use of the verb is indeed its single occurrence in the New Testament. He urges Timothy to show himself to God as an "operarium inconfusibilem, recte tractantem verbum veritatis" (2 Tim. 2:15). The last four words describe Dante's desire in Chapter XLII rather well. *Trattare*, however, has a more immediate context in the *Vita Nuova* that should not be overlooked. It is used a total of fourteen times.[36] Its first use has reference to writing about Beatrice (V, 3) as an earthly being, and does not seem to have any unusual overtone. The second *trattare* of the *Vita Nuova* is used in a technical sense to describe the middle three stanzas of the *canzone* "Donne ch'avete intelletto d'amore." The subject of these three stanzas is the desire of the angels in Heaven to have Beatrice in their midst. Their request is spoken to by no less a being than God Himself, in His only speaking part in the *Vita Nuova* (the influence of Guinizelli's "Al cor gentil" is probably felt here). It seems possible that Dante's use of the word might reflect not only his technical sense of the division of a *canzone*, but the subject treated in that part of the *canzone*—things heavenly.

The next occurrence of the word (two uses in XX and one, retrospectively, in XXI) is entirely without such overtones. Here Dante, in the most overtly Guinizellian poem of the collection ("Amore e 'l cor gentil sono una cosa"), treats "philosophically" (and not "theologically") the nature of Amore. The next use (XXV, 3), in a discussion of love poetry as written by vernacular and "lettered" poets, seems to have the same meaning—a "philosophical" treatment of a subject in verse. Then, however, *trattare* enters the work for the penultimate time in a highly charged cluster (used six times in ten lines—XXVIII, 2). Beatrice is dead and Dante will not "treat" her death.[37] For the purposes of this investigation it is important to see that again the subject—though it is *not* treated—is "theological." The next chapter explains that Beatrice was a nine, or miracle (XXIX, 3). And in this chapter the second reason Dante gives for not treating Beatrice's death looks strangely familiar if it is seen in the perspective of chapter XLII: "ancora non sarebbe sufficiente a trattare come si converrebbe di ciò" (XXVIII, 2)—"infino a tanto che io potesse più degnamente trattare di lei" (XLII, 1). To treat of Beatrice is to treat of high things indeed. Of the fourteen uses of *trattare* in the *Vita Nuova* nine (and here no further numerological point is intended) indicate the treatment of celestial *materia*. Three elements are involved in this heightened use of *trattare*: a thought of Beatrice desired in Heaven, the fact of Beatrice's death (and thus her implied presence in Heaven), and the final vision of Beatrice in Heaven. In the *Vita Nuova* the only "treatment" we are allowed to read is the first. The second is refused and the third only promised.

After the many purely technical and "philosophical" uses of *trattare* in the *Convivio*, the verb—now with "theological" overtones—reappears (like so much else in the *Vita Nuova*) in the *Commedia: Inferno* I, 8; *Paradiso* IV, 27; *Paradiso* XXV, 95. While all three uses are to the point here, the last one is particularly interesting. Dante's final response to St. James is to say that his Hope is based on scriptures in both Testaments (Isaiah 61:7, 10 and Revelation 7:9–17). Both these passages tell of the souls of the blessed sitting in Glory. Dante refers to the second of the two as follows: "là dove tratta de le bianche stole" (cf. Rev. 7:14: "Hi sunt qui venerunt de tribulatione magna et laverunt stolas suas et dealbaverunt eas in sanguine Agni"). Is not this precisely where and how we may presume Dante saw Beatrice in the *mirabile visione*? Seated in the presence of God in the sure and certain hope of the resurrection. At least one may now advance this fairly common view of Beatrice's heavenly situation with a particular text in view: Revelation 7:9–17. For where Paul does not recount his "visiones et revelationes Domini," John explicitly describes what Paul must have seen. In a sense it is he who offers one like Dante, who wanted to know what Paul saw, the only canonical description available. If Dante had previously thought of the form of his experience of the final vision in terms of a *raptus Pauli*, its content could come only from John's Apocalypse.[38]

It is not until *Paradiso* XXXI, 70–93, that Dante will actually see Beatrice sit in Glory. That is very likely what his *pensero / sospiro* saw in the thirty-first and final poem of the *Vita Nuova*.[39] And what she is said to gaze upon in the last line of the *Vita Nuova*, "la faccia di colui *qui est per omnia secula benedictus*," is what she gazes upon now: "sorrise e riguardommi; / poi si tornò a l'etterna fontana" (*Par.* XXXI, 92–93).[40] Dante coming closer to seeing God by seeing Beatrice see God is a common element in both passages.[41]

And so, if Dante ostensibly maintains a Pauline official silence about the content of the *mirabile visione* at the conclusion of the *Vita Nuova*, he also conspires, overtly as well as tacitly, to let all but *li più semplici* of the *Vita Nuova's* readers have a fairly sure idea of what his memory retained of the vision, both its form (Pauline) and its content (Johannine). If we had nothing else, the two little verbs that tell us Beatrice's condition and activity in Paradise—she knows and she gazes—are really enough to let the major fact about her be a most salient one. "E di venire a ciò io studio quanto posso, sì com'ella *sae* veracemente . . . quella benedetta Beatrice, la quale gloriosamente *mira* ne la faccia di colui *qui est per omnia secula benedictus*." In the first twenty-seven chapters of the *Vita Nuova* Beatrice is described in the "historical past," that is, by the past absolute. In the next fourteen chapters Dante looks back to the dead Beatrice in the same tense. After the *mirabile visione* a small grammatical miracle not only resurrects her from the dead, it even stands as a rebuke to the backward-looking intention of the entire *libello: "Incipit vita nuova.* Sotto la quale rubrica io trovo scritte le parole le quali è mio intendimento d'assemplare in questo libello." The liver of the new life must not be content to be the historian of his first awakening. As long as Dante is only able to live in his memory of past events he cannot live the new life. His new life may be said to be truly undertaken once he can speak of Beatrice in the present, as the living soul *in Gloria* who will draw him on up. The *incipit* of the *Vita Nuova* is the unvoiced *explicit* as well.

For these reasons it seems proper to look upon Dante's final vision of Beatrice as the first one, as an experience of such different order from that of her previous nine appearances that it should be set aside from these in our minds (as it certainly seems to have been in Dante's) as a kind of epilogue that transcends the rest of the work and which serves, as many have said before, as prologue to the great poem.[42]

# Notes

1. Nicolò Mineo, in his remarkable book, *Profetismo e Apocalittica in Dante* (Catania: Università di Catania, Pubblicazioni della Falcoltà di Lettere e Filosofia, 24, 1968), claims that there are "otto casi di visioni del Dante protagonista" (p. 104). His *visioni* are not limited to those Dante has of Beatrice. Cf. note 2, below.

2. Mineo's procedures of accountancy are as follows (p. 104): The "vision" are, according to him, what are here numbered as 3, 4b, 5b, 7, 8, 9, 9a, as well as the final vision of chapter XLII. It is not difficult to perceive the common denominator of this list: actual sightings of Beatrice do not count, only more traditionally (if loosely) defined *visioni* of her and of Amore. Thus Amore has a large place in this list (alone in 4b, 5b; accompanying Beatrice in 3 and 8), while Beatrice alone is the object of visions in 7, 9, 9a, and the final vision. Mineo, it should be added, claims there are *twelve* visions in all: four described twice (in prose and in the accompanying verse— 3, 4b, 7, 8), equalling *eight; three* described once (5b, 9, 9a); *one* (the *mirabile visione* of XLII) not described.

3. *Ibid.*, p. 104n. While the following discussion owes little to Mineo, and while it disagrees strongly with some of his findings, it should be pointed out that Mineo is the first writer, at least the first writer known to this reader, to make a significant effort to develop a systematic account of the relationships among various kinds of vision in the *Vita Nuova* (pp. 133–141, esp. pp. 139–141). His book is a mine of new insights into the *Commedia* and the *epistole "politiche"* as well, whether or not one accepts his basic stance. For valuable surveys of all Dante's uses of these elements of his vocabulary of vision, cf. the apposite entries in the *Enciclopedia Dantesca* (Roma: Instituto della Enciclopedia Italiana, 1970–78). Charles S. Singleton, *An Essay on the Vita Nuova* (Cambridge, Mass.: Harvard University Press, 1949), pp. 14–15, makes some distinction among dreams, daydreams, and fantasies in the *Vita Nuova* in his discussion of the visions of the work. His basic opposition is between *visioni* and *imaginazioni*. What is here referred to as item 9 (*V.N.* XXXIX) is unaccountably not included among the latter.

4. Including the verbal form *imaginare* (seven times): IX, 3, 7; XXIII, 4, 6 (twice), 7, 9, 10, 15, 22, 23, 26, 31 (twice); XXIV, 1, 2; XXXIX, 1. In this and the other surveys that follow, the usages studied only include those involving seeing or apparition; e.g., with reference to *parere* (cf. note 12, below): the English "there *seemed* no point in going" would not be included, while "she *seemed* to be calling my name" would, since a visual appearance is implied. The distinction is not always easily made, as in the second example.

Commentators and editors of the *Vita Nuova* consulted during the preparation of this study are as follows:

K. Witte (Leipzig: Brockhaus, 1876)
A. D'Ancona (Pisa: Libreria Galileo, 1884)
T. Casini (Firenze: Sansoni, 1905)
M. Barbi (Milano: Hoepli, 1907)
G. Melodia (Milano: Vallardi, 1911)
G. L. Passerini (Palermo: Sandron, 1919)
K. McKenzie (Boston: D. C. Heath, 1922)
L. Di Benedetto (Torino: Unione tip. edit. Torinese, 1929)

M. Scherillo, 3rd ed. (Milano: Hoepli, 1930)
N. Sapegno (Firenze: Vallecchi, 1931)
D. Mattalia (Torino: Paravia, 1938)
A. Pézard (Paris: Gallimard, 1965).
The text of the *Vita Nuova* used here is that of the Società Dantesca Italiana, 2a ed. (Firenze: Nella Sede della Società, 1960), as reprinted in F. Chiapelli, *Tutte le opere* (Milano: Mursia, 1965).

5. Used only for Dante's sick-bed imaginings of Beatrice's death: XXIII, 4, 5, 6, 8, 13, 18, 29, 30. Thus *fantasia*, though closely related, seems an even stronger form of *imaginazione*. An interesting collateral use occurs at XVI, 2: "quando la mia memoria movesse la fantasia ad imaginare quale Amore mi facea." Here the relationship, colloquially expressed in the terms of our day, might be that of unconscious to subconscious. Whatever their precise meanings for Dante, they do seem closely related.

6. The first grouping occurs at III, 3, 8, 9; IV, 1; the second at XII, 9; XIII, 1. XLII, 1, contains the final use; which will be discussed below.

7. *Sonno* and its "cognates" are used only to describe these two dream apparitions. The vision of Beatrice in the arms of Amore is achieved in sleep (III, 3, 9). In III, 15, Dante explicitly informs his reader that the vision recorded in the first poem of the *Vita Nuova* is a dream (*sogno*). In the second case Amore appears to Dante "nel mezzo de lo mio dormire" XII, 3; Dante recognizes Amore's speech because he has heard it before "ne li miei sonni" (XII, 4); when Amore "disparve, lo mio sonno fue rotto" (XII, 9). Nowhere else in the work does Dante present what he sees as seen in dream. Lest we become confused in XXIII, 12, the wild fantasy of Beatrice's death, Dante explicitly points to the fact that he was *not* dreaming by having his sister [?] think he is asleep and dreaming ("credendo che io sognasse") when he is not.

8. Including its Latin form, *apparuit*, and the substantive *apparimento*, which looks back to the event from the following chapter: II, 1, 2, 3, 5; III, 1. At II, 2, *vedere* is conjoined as follows: "apparve a me, ed io la vidi." At XXXIX, which also looks back to this first appearance, *apparire* is again used.

9. III, 1.

10. "vedea la mia beatitudine"—V, 1.

11. "vidi tra loro la gentilissima Beatrice"—XIV, 4.

12. XXIV, 3, 8, 10. It is perhaps useful to observe that in the following sentence Dante imagines Amore speaking within him. We can watch him move from literal description to less literal rendering: "Queste donne andaro presso di me così l'una appresso l'altra, e *parve* che Amore mi *parlasse* nel cuore. . . . Ed anche mi *parve* che mi *dicesse* . . ." (XXIV, 4–5; italics added). *Parere* (we speak here only of its use to denote appearance and vision) is elsewhere used some thirty-six times (see cautionary note 4, above) in the prose of the *Vita Nuova*, sometimes in conjunction with *vedere* in the formulaic *mi parea vedere*, and always to describe the way things appeared either in dream or in fantasy, that is, *never* to describe actions directly observed. An interesting example of Dante's use of *parere* in a poem and *vedere* in the accompanying prose occurs at XXVI, 1 and 5. "Tanto gentile e tanto onesta *pare*/la mia donna. . . ." In the prose those to whom she "appears" in the poem "correano per *vedere* lei." Two excellent recent discussions of this sonnet and of the sense of things seen *in the poems* of the *Vita Nuova* pay little or no attention to the questions addressed in this paper—and *vice versa*: Gianfranco Contini, "Esercizio d'inter-

pretazione sopra un sonetto di Dante," in *L'immagine,* v (1957), 291–295, reprinted in his *Varianti e altra linguistica* (Torino: Einaudi, 1970), pp. 161–168; Domenico De Robertis, "Lo stilo de la loda," in his *Il libro della "Vita Nuova"* (Firenze: Sansoni, 1970), pp. 129–156, esp. pp. 141–156.

*Apparire* is used in both senses. It may refer to the beholding of objects in either fantasy or dream, where it tends to be used as a synonym for *parere*; then it is always found in the company of *imaginazione/fantasia* or *visione/sonno* (ten times: III, 8, 9, 11; IX, 3, 7; XII, 9 [twice]; XXIII, 4 [twice]; XXIV, 10). Or it may refer to "actual seeing," where it receives a certain primacy from not being conjoined with any other term of perception (nine times: II, 1, 2, 3, 5; III, 1; III, 3; III, 12; XI, 1; XXXIX, 1). Its only other use occurs in XLII, of which there will be discussion below.

13. In the subsidiary items 5a, 4a, 6a, 6b, 8b, 8c, 9a, all of which scenes describe actual seeing, the verbs of appearance or perception are, respectively, *apparire* (XI, 1) and *vedere* (VIII, 1, 2; XVIII, 2; XXII, 3; XXXV, 2, 5; XXXVI, 2; XXXVII, 1; XXXVIII, 1; XLI, 5, 6, 11, 12). However, when Dante uses *vedere* in conjunction with *parere* (e.g., *mi parea vedere*) it is always in describing things seen in dream (3 and 5b) or fantasy (4b, 7, 8, 9)—and there is at least one such usage in each of these six cases. Cf. note 12, above. The relative brevity, incompleteness, and unsystematic nature of earlier discussions of some of the terms discussed above do not preclude the presence of some helpful and suggestive analyses. A few examples follow: B. Terracini, "Analisi dei toni narrativi nella 'Vita Nuova'," in his *Pagine e appunti di linguistica storica* (Firenze: Le Monnier, 1957), pp. 264–272. Comparing three uses of *vedere* (XIV, 4 vs. the "actual seeing" of XXXV, 2, and one other), Terracini says, "La realtà è che la forma interna di Dante riduce questi polisindeti narrativi a una precisa visione di qualche cosa che gli si presenta come un' apparizione" (p. 265). Aldo Rossi devotes four pages (69–73) to a study of Dante's anaphoric use of *mi parea* (in III, 3–8; IX, 3–7; XII, 3–9; XXIII, 4–10; *Purg.* IX, 19–33; *Inf.* XXXIII, 28–37) in his "Dante nella prospettiva del Boccaccio," in *Studi Danteschi,* XXXVIII (1960), 63–139. His conclusion: "Ma ormai bisogna ammettere che ci troviamo di fronte ad uno stile istituzionalizzato, propriamente allo *stile visionario*, il cui distintivo consiste nel marcare ogni membro rilevante della narrazione con l'avvertimento che di visione si parla (verbo *parere*), e nel fissare, come estremi non sottintesi, l'inizio col sonno propiziatorio (o stato affine) e *l'explicit* con la rottura di quello" (p. 72). He has perhaps enlarged upon remarks made by Alfredo Schiaffini, "La tecnica della 'Vita Nuova'," in his *Tradizione e poesia*, 2nd ed. (Roma: Edizioni di "Storia e Letteratura," 1943), pp. 95–106, which briefly (pp. 96–97) discuss the anaphoric use of *apparire* in II as it meets the equally anaphoric *mi parea vedere* in III. Cf. also Aldo Vallone, *La prosa della "Vita Nuova"* (Firenze: Le Monnier, 1963). For a more general treatment of actuality and vision cf. Pino Da Prati, *Realtà e allegoria nella "Vita Nuova" di Dante* (Sanremo: Edizioni "Grafiche Bracco," 1963), esp. the chapters "Fantasia, energia spirituale e lirica in Vita Nuova" (pp. 59–74) and "Discontinuità narrativa in Vita Nuova" (pp. 89–94). And cf. Michele Rak's article, "imaginazione," in *Enciclopedia Dantesca*, Vol. III, pp. 369b–370b.

14. While there is a total absence of "designative terms" in scenes described as being actually seen, the narrative technique, one modeled on historical narrative, itself functions as "designative" in all cases.

15. In 3 (III, 9) there is a single example of *vedere* used in this sense but without *parere*: "scrissi a loro ciò che io avea nel mio sonno veduto." Here the "cognate" is *in sonno*,

and the result is the same; dream seeing (like seeing in fantasy) is kept distinct from actual seeing.

16. "ella era uno nove, cioè uno miracolo, la cui radice, cioè del miracolo, è solamente la mirabile Trinitade" (XXIX, 3). That Dante sees this "nine" nine times and in three modes is at least suggestive.

17. Cf. 5a (XI, 1) and XV and XVI for generic reflections of Beatrice rather than specific appearances.

18. Traces of this second aspect continue through the last sonnet of the work (XLI, 10), but the first ends at XXIV, 7.

19. Here clearly used to describe actual seeing. Cf. note 12, above.

20. The concluding description of the poem forthrightly states that the vision is a dream (III, 15).

21. It is a fact that Amore, when he is described in the various prose accounts of his actions—under discussion are only passages in which he is treated as an actual "character"—is not once referred to by that name, but only by periphrasis.

22. III, 3–9. The words are *apparire* (here used to describe what is perceived in dream—cf. notes 12 and 15, above), which occurs thrice; *visione*, four times (including its retrospective use at IV, 1); *sonno*, twice; *parere* and the formulaic *mi parea vedere*, eight times.

23. "Lo dolcissimo segnore . . . ne la mia imaginazione apparve" (IX, 3). When he departs, "disparve questa mia imaginazione" (IX, 7).

24. He appears as "uno giovane vestito di bianchissime vestimenta" (XII, 3). The terms of vision and appearance in XII, 3–9, are *apparire* (used twice to describe what is perceived in dream); *visione*, used twice (including its retrospective use at XIII, 1); *sonno*, twice; *parere* and the formulaic *me parve vedere*, five times.

25. Still one of the most interesting treatments of Amore's "disappearance" (whether he "becomes Beatrice," as some have it, or the loving agency within Dante, or a combination of these) is J. E. Shaw, *"Ego tanquam centrum circuli,"* in his *Essays on the Vita Nuova* (Princeton: Princeton University Press, 1929), pp. 77–108. More recently cf. Armand Caraccio, "Note sur le mythe d'Eros et sur l'apparition d''Amour' en tant qu'allégorie extérieure à Dante dans la *Vita Nuova*," in *Revue des études italiennes*, XI (1965), 30–39. Hesitations about this study are expressed by N. Mineo, who offers more interesting hypotheses (*op. cit.*, pp. 130–132, with bibliography).

26. Perhaps none is as illustrative as that found at XV. Here "uno pensamento forte" has a speaking part that has previously been reserved to Amore. In fact, in the accompanying sonnet it is Amore who speaks.

27. For a brief presentation of the medieval distinctions among three kinds of narrative (*fabula, historia, agrumentum*) cf. R. Hollander, *Allegory in Dante's Commedia* (Princeton, New Jersey: Princeton University Press, 1969), pp. 257n–258n. For Dante's suggestion that the *Vita Nuova* is not to be taken as *parlare fabuloso*, cf. II, 10. For a treatment of the distinction *historia/fabula* in *Convivio* IV, XXV, 6; XXVI, 9; XXX, 4, see G. R. Sarolli, *Prolegomena alla "Divina Commedia"* (Firenze: Olschki, 1971), p. 140n.

28. For a similar appreciation of another use of "nine" by Dante, cf. "The Invocations of the *Commedia*" in R. Hollander, *Studies in Dante* (Ravenna: Longo, 1980), pp. 31–38.

29. That the fantastic and dream sightings are perhaps even more important than the actual ones is attested to by their association with the "best" numbers: dream, 3; fantasy, 7 and 9.

30. The sonnet calls *sospiro* what the prose calls *pensero*. It is perhaps suggestive that nine plus one, which expresses the relationship between Beatrice's nine appearances to Dante and his final vision of her, is also the relationship in Dante's cosmology between the nine celestial spheres and the Empyrean.

31. To review: In one category, that of things actually seen, we find *apparire* (roughly half its uses) and *vedere*; in a second, that of dream seeing, we find *apparire* (five uses—one quarter of all uses) and *parere/mi parea vedere* used in a similar sense, conjoined with the designative terms *sonno* and *visione*; in a third, that of fantasy, we find *apparire* (five uses) and *parere/mi parea vedere* used in a similar sense, conjoined with the designative terms *imaginazione* and *fantasia*.

32. This practice is rigorously maintained in the *Commedia* as well, *sileant* those *dantisti* who, since the fourteenth century, have wished to regard the poem as a dream vision. See Mineo's instructive comments, *op. cit.*, pp. 195–201, concerning the nature of vision in the opening *canti* of the *Commedia*.

33. As St. Thomas believed. Cf. Grandgent's excellent headnote to *Paradiso* XXX (*La Divina Commedia*, rev. C. S. Singleton [Cambridge, Mass.: Harvard University Press, 1972], p. 894. Cf. also Mineo, *ibid., "De raptu,"* pp. 44–51; and Joseph A. Mazzeo's important discussion, "Dante and the Pauline Modes of Vision," Chapter Four of *Structure and Thought in the Paradiso* (Ithaca: Cornell University Press, 1958), pp. 84–110.

34. N. Mineo, *ibid.*, p. 108: "siamo quindi dinanzi ad una vera e propria visione di tipo paolino, a un *raptus*," following G. Salvadori and A. Marigo against the objections of M. Barbi and E. G. Parodi. The argument that Dante is thinking in terms of Pauline vision is probably given further support by the concluding Latin phrase of the *Vita Nuova*. Various commentators (many give no ascription at all) are understandably content with pointing to the Bible as a generic source of *qui est per omnia secula benedictus*—forms of *benedico* and *saeculum* occur frequently in conjunction in both Testaments. A few scholars are more specific, among whom: E. Moore, *Studies in Dante*, First Series (Oxford: Clarendon Press, 1896), p. 376; Romans 9:5; M. Scherillo (Milano: Hoepli, 1930), p. 305: Psalms 71:17–19; 88:53; 112:2; Romans 1:25, 9:5; 2 Cor. 11:31; A. Pézard (Paris: Gallimard, 1965), p. 83: Psalms 80:16, 112:2; Romans 1:25, 9:5; 2 Cor. 11:31. Among these favored candidates only two are within one word of forming a nearly precise quotation, as may be seen from the following list:

*Vita Nuova* XLII, 3: "qui est per omnia secula benedictus"
Psalm 71:17: "Sit nomen eius benedictum in saecula"
Psalm 80:16: "et erit tempus eorum [inimicorum Domini] in saecula"
Psalm 88:53: "Benedictus dominus in aeternum"
Psalm 112:2: "Sit nomen Domini benedictum ex hoc nunc et usque ad saecula"
Romans 1:25: "qui est benedictus in saecula. Amen."
Romans 9:5: "qui est super omnia Deus benedictus in saecula. Amen."
2 Cor. 11:31: "qui est benedictus in saecula."

If Dante meant to cite a particular passage in Scripture, it seems likely that he had in mind either Romans 1:25 or 2 Cor. 11:31. Either context is highly appropriate. The passage in Romans condemns lust (1:24) and those who served the creature more than the Creator (it is a passage that is remembered at *Purg.* XVII, 91), "qui est benedictus. . . ." That in 2 Corinthians asserts that God, "qui est benedictus . . .," knows that Paul is not a liar. The following chapter (12:2–4) describes his *raptus*: "raptus est in Paradisum et audivit arcana verba, quae non licet homini loqui" (12:4). While this second passage would seem to offer the best context for the close of the *Vita Nuova*, and while it will be remembered in *Par.* I, 73–75, one must admit that it is impossible to do any more than assert that it is the one Dante had in mind.

35. For the relationship of 2 Cor. 12 to *V. N.* XXIX (in particular Dante's third reason for not describing the death of Beatrice) cf. C. H. Grandgent, "Dante and St. Paul," in *Romania,* XXX (1902), 14–27. While Dante's final vision is referred to in the article, Grandgent does not specifically relate Paul's *raptus* to it. J. E. Shaw, *Essays on the Vita Nuova*, p. 157, takes issue with Grandgent's finding in terms of its appropriateness to *V.N.* XXIX. While his discussion also includes reference to chapter XLII, Shaw also fails to think of the likely relationship between the final vision and Paul's. Yet either of their discussions would be likely to have just that effect.

36. V, 3; XIX, 15, 17; XX, 2 (twice); XXI, 1; XXV, 3; XXVIII, 2 (six times); XLII, 1. Paget Toynbee, "Dante's Uses of the Word "trattato" in the *Convivio* and *Vita Nuova*," in his *Dante Studies* (Oxford: Clarendon Press, 1921), pp. 29–35, deals with four technical senses of the word as it appears in Dante. The most important is that in which it indicates the narrative or didactic portion of a *canzone* as distinct from its *proemio*. E. R. Curtius, *European Literature and the Latin Middle Ages*, tr. W. R. Trask (New York: Harper Torchbooks, 1963), p. 222, as part of his brilliant exposition of the *forma tractandi* of the ninth paragraph of the Letter to Can Grande, defines the verb as meaning "to treat philosophically," which works well for the many uses in *Convivio*, but is perhaps too general for the use in *V.N.* XLII and those in the *Commedia* (Curtius cites only *Inf.* I, 8).

37. It is a vexed passage. For some possible reasons for Dante's not doing so, cf. J. E. Shaw, "*Non è del presente proposito*," in his *Essays on the Vita Nuova*, pp. 143–159.

38. Barbara Nolan, "The *Vita Nuova*: Dante's Book of Revelation," *Dante Studies,* LXXXVIII (1970), 51–77, is more suggestive than explicit in her remarks about the relationship between the two books. She adduces John's eating of the book held by the angel (Rev. 10:8–11)—as well as Ezekiel's eating of the roll, or scroll (the model for John's passage: Ezekiel 3:3)—for Beatrice's eating of Dante's heart in the dream of III, 6, 12 (p. 59)—but cf. the earlier and firmer discussion of J. A. Scott, "Notes on Religion and the *Vita Nuova*," in *Italian Studies,* XX (1965), p. 19. Also adduced is Rev. 21:4 (in a rather general way) for Dante's *imaginazione* (incorrectly referred to as a "dream") of Beatrice smiling [!] at the "vision of the fountainhead of peace" (p. 72). Mark Musa's translation of *V.N.* XXIII, 8–9, yields the likely source of the error (as his translation of "la forte fantasia" of XXIII, 13, rendered "my realistic dream," may account for the previous mistake): ". . . and it seemed to me that her face *was so filled with joyous acceptance* that it said to me: 'I am contemplating the fountainhead of peace' " (Dante: ". . . e pareami che la sua faccia *avesse tanto aspetto d'umilitade*, che parea che dicesse: 'Io sono a vedere lo principio de la pace'.")—italics added; also brought to bear (p. 76) are "the forty-two months of waiting before the Last Judgment" (which is not to count the intervention of several other events, much less the Millenium) as being correspondent to the forty-two chapters of the *Vita Nuova*; it was E. Proto, reviewing the first edition of M. Scherillo's commentary (1911) in *Rassegna critica della letteratura italiana*, XVII (1912), p. 247, who first suggested the forty-two mansions of the Israelites in the desert (Numbers

33) and/or the forty-two months of the affliction of the Church in Revelation 13:5. He did not mention another medieval exegete's delight, the forty-two generations of Jesus in Matthew 1.

39. Here one may wonder whether the numerical identity is not, in fact, intentional.

40. Aristide Marigo, *Mistica e scienza nella Vita Nuova di Dante* (Padova: Drucker, 1914), p. 70, takes basically the same position, but adduces other *loci* in the Empyrean as parallels: "Il sommo della visione era vedere Iddio, per la 'chiarezza' della sua donna gloriosa, come la chiarezza di Maria 'sola . . . può disporre a veder Cristo' (*Par.* XXXII, 87); era infine un congiungere 'l'aspetto col Valore infinito' (*Par.* XXXIII, 81) . . . Ed il nucleo e la finalità della *Commedia*, la visione *per essentiam* della divinità . . . è pure la finalità della *Vita Nuova*." J. A. Scott, "Notes on Religion and the *Vita Nuova*," in *Italian Studies*, XX (1965), 17–25, takes Marigo as his starting point for an examination of religio-mystical aspects of the *V.N.*

41. In the last visionary moment of the *Commedia* he will look momentarily at the cause of her beatitude and momentarily he will share the ultimate vision (*Par.* XXXIII, 124–132). If what was ineffable in the *Vita Nuova* had there to remain unexpressed, and was expressed in the *Commedia*, the final vision of the *Commedia* is in its turn ineffable.

42. The rather useless argument as to whether or not Dante had the *Commedia* in mind when he wrote *V.N.* XLII that so exercised nineteenth- and early twentieth-century commentators of the *V.N.* is not joined here. Whether or not Dante had the *Commedia* in mind is beyond knowledge. But when he wrote the *Commedia* he knew very well what promise he was fulfilling.

# Robert Fitzgerald

## Mirroring the *Commedia*
## An Appreciation of Laurence Binyon's Version

### I

ONE BRILLIANT EPISODE of "the Pound era" has fallen into such obscurity as to remain unregistered in Hugh Kenner's book of that title, marvel of registration though the book is. In telling of Ezra Pound's life in London between 1908 and 1920, Kenner refers once or twice to his friendship with Laurence Binyon, poet and Deputy Keeper of Prints and Drawings in the British Museum. But he says nothing of Pound's interest, years later, in Binyon's translation of *The Divine Comedy*. Now, from early in 1934 to late in 1939, this interest animated a great deal of correspondence between the two men and ended with quite remarkable enthusiasm on the part of Pound. In fact, he all but took a hand in the translation. It would be fair to say that he gave as much time and attention to Binyon's work as he had in other years—in another way—to that of James Joyce, and for the same reason: that he thought the work supremely good. Pound could be wildly wrong about some things but not, I think, about a rendering of Dante in English verse. If anyone's ear and judgment had authority in such matters, his did.

Not only has this whole episode been lost to view, but the translation itself is generally and peculiarly disregarded. Teachers of Dante appear to be only dimly aware of it. And yet the rendering of the *Commedia* that most nearly reproduces the total quality of the original poem is surely Laurence Binyon's. Why is it not likely to be supplied to the student, or the serious reader of English, either at the University or elsewhere? After puzzling over this state of affairs for some time, I have learned enough to realize that it, too—this relative neglect—is a masterpiece in its way, a *capolavoro* composed by the sheer accidents of history, the fortunes of war and peace.

Here, then, is a story.

## II

At Oxford in 1890, Laurence Binyon won the Newdigate Prize with a poem entitled "Persephone." The year and the title combine to bring us the essential fragrance of a period and to suggest the poetic and scholarly tradition that Binyon inherited. Confining to the sensibility though it had certainly become, that tradition had its points, as Binyon's life would demonstrate. He was a studious poet and a sober man. After Oxford he went to work in the print division of the British Museum, where he was to become a pioneer interpreter of the art of the East to the West, author of *Painting in the Far East* (1908) and later a friend of Charles Freer and Langdon Warner. In 1913 Binyon became Deputy Keeper of Prints and Drawings at the Museum. He and young Ezra Pound met one another from time to time and were notably unaffected by each other's work. Binyon's poems , after all, were in the tradition that Pound proposed to shake. One of them became extremely well known: "To the Fallen," first printed in the London *Times* in September, 1914. This turned out to be so memorable in the English-speaking world that after 1918 many war memorials throughout Britain and the Commonwealth bore a Simonidean stanza from it, cut in stone: "They shall not grow old, as we who are left grow old, etc."

It is worth remembering that in the Print Division Binyon's eye received an education from the masters of line in East and West. He did a great deal of work on Blake. To an eye so educated, no poetry, probably, could match Dante's in visual fascination. Binyon was not an Italian scholar, but as an amateur, early in the '20s, with the advice and encouragement of his friend Mario Praz, he began translating *The Divine Comedy*. In 1933 *Inferno* was ready, and late in the year MacMillan published it in one volume with the Italian text on facing pages. The book was dedicated to Praz and carried a brief preface.

The modesty of Binyon's prefatory remarks may have veiled the special nature and ambition of this poem. He had tried, he said, to communicate not only the sense of the words but something of Dante's tone and of the rhythm through which that tone was conveyed. This was not merely a matter of matching, with "triple rhyme," Dante's *terza rima*. It involved a more intimate correspondence. So far as English would permit, and in the decasyllabic line native to English, he had imitated the Dantean hendecasyllable, scanning by syllables rather than feet, but through systematic elisions achieving flexibility in syllable count. The result was a regular but very subtle refreshment and quickening of rhythm, e.g., in *Inferno* IV, 49–50:

"Did ever any of those herein immured
By his own or other's merit to bliss get free?"

But this was not all, either. By using fine distributions of weight and accent, he had contrived to avoid the beat of pentameters and to even out his stresses on the Italian model. For one conspicuous instance of this he prepared the reader, noting how he had occasionally rhymed on an unaccented syllable (*Inferno* I, 2, "That I had strayed into a dark forest," rhyming with "oppressed")—not intending an abnormal pronunciation, but as "the placing of a heavy or emphatic syllable before the final word seems to have the effect of mitigating the accent on that word, so that it is rather balanced between the two syllables than placed with all its weight on one. Such elasticity of stress seems congenial to Dante's verse. . . ." No doubt Binyon learned the possibility of this, and the advantage of it, from Dante Gabriel Rossetti, who had resorted to it here and there in his translations of Dante' sonnets and *canzoni* in the *Vita Nuova*.

But Binyon went far beyond Rossetti, as he had to, in working out a style adequate to the *Commedia*—a style versatile but consistent, firm, but well-wrought, and swift. Drawing on the English of earlier centuries, he would admit old forms and words, but with a selective and measuring ear, so that his archaicisms generally gave body and life to his verses, not quaintness. The diction, thus slightly expanded and elevated, was an accomplishment in itself. It stood, in fact to twentieth century English very much as Dante's living Tuscan does to twentieth century Italian. One brief example may suffice (*Inferno* xxv, 64–66):

As runneth up before the burning flame
On paper, a brown colour, not yet black,
And the white dieth, such their hues became....

Binyon's *Inferno* was published, as I have said, late in 1933. The editor of *The Criterion* in London, at Ezra Pound's request, sent this book to Pound for review. Pound was then living in Rapallo; he had left London thirteen years before, and he had not spent the interval extolling the English literary establishment, to which Binyon in a quiet way belonged. But a foolish note on Binyon's translation had fallen under his eye and aroused his curiosity. The editor of *The Criterion* must have awaited Pound's review with several kinds of interest. The review appeared in April, 1934.

> I state, [wrote Pound], that I have read the work, that for thirty years it never would have occurred to me that it would be possible to read a translation of the *Inferno* from cover to cover, and that this translation has therefore one DEMONSTRATED dimension. . . . The venerable Binyon has, I am glad to say, produced the most interesting English version of Dante that I have seen or expect to see. . . .
>
> The younger generation may have forgotten Binyon's sad youth, poisoned in the cradle by the abominable dogbiscuit of Milton's rhetoric. . . . At any rate, Dante has cured him. If ever demonstration be needed of the virtues of having a good model instead of a rhetorical bustuous rumpus, the life in Binyon's translation can prove it to next century's schoolboys. . . . He has carefully preserved all the faults of his original. This in the circumstances is the most useful thing he could have done.

What these faults were, the reviewer did not expressly say, but it became clear that he meant inversions of word order. Unspeakable syntax had been a *bête noire* to Pound since the days of Imagism, and he now found himself irritated by "Binyon's writing his lines hind side before." But on reflection he had come round to seeing that some of this was appropriate.

> The devil of translating medieval poetry into English is that it is very hard to decide HOW you are to render work done with one set of criteria in a language NOW subject to different criteria. . . . The concept of word order in uninflected or very little inflected language had not developed to anything like twentieth century straightness.

When the reviewer got down to cases, his technical observations were as acute as might have been expected.

> Working on decent basis, Binyon has got rid of magniloquence, of puffed words, I don't remember a single decorative or rhetorical word in his first ten cantos. There are vast numbers of monosyllables, little words. Here a hint from the *De Eloquio* may have put him on the trail. In the matter of rhyme, nearly everyone knows that Dante's rhymes are 'feminine,' i.e. accent on the penultimate, *crucciata, aguzza, volge, maligno*. There are feminine rhymes in English, there are ENOUGH, possibly, to fill the needs of an almost literal version of the *Divina Commedia*, but they are of the wrong quality; *bloweth, knowing, wasteth*. Bin-

yon has very intelligently avoided a mere pseudo or obvious similarity, in favour of a fundamental, namely the sharp clear quality of the original SOUND as a whole. His *past, admits, checked, kings*, [are] all masculine endings, but all having a residue of vowel sound in state of potential, or latent, as considered by Dante himself in his remarks on troubadour verse.

The fact that this idiom, which was never spoken on sea or land, is NOT fit for use in the new poetry of 1933–34 does not mean that it is unfit for use in a translation of a poem produced in 1321. . . . Coming back to the rhyming, not only are we without strict English equivalents for terminal sounds like *ferrigno*, *rintoppa*, *argento*, *tronca*, *stagna*, *feruto*, but any attempt at ornamental rhyme à la Hudibras, or slick epigrammatic rhyme à la Pope or trick rhyme à la Hood, or in fact any kind of rhyming excrescence or ornament would be out of place in the *Commedia*. . . .

One ends with gratitude for [the] demonstration that forty years' honest work do, after all, count for something; that some qualities of writing cannot be attained simply by clever faking, young muscles or a desire to get somewhere in a hurry. The lines move to their end, that is, draw along the eye of the reader, instead of cradling him in a hammock. The main import is not sacrificed to detail. Simple as this appears in bald statement it takes time to learn how to achieve it.[1]

These remarks seem to be valuable above all in that they cast a shrewd—and unique—craftsman's light on the art of *The Divine Comedy* and the task of translating it. Pound obviously felt enticed by the challenge that Binyon had taken up—so much so that he could not stay on the sidelines. In the course of preparing his review, he wrote to Binyon on January 21st, 1934.

My dear Laurence Binyon, [he said], "If any residuum of annoyance remain in yr. mind because of the extremely active nature of the undersigned (it is very difficult for a man to believe anything hard enough for it to matter a damn *what* he believes, without causing annoyance to others)—anyhow. . . . I hope you will forget it long enough to permit me to express my very solid appreciation of yr. translation of the *Inferno*. *Criterion* has asked me for a thousand words by the end of next week, but I am holding out for more space [he got six thousand] which will probably delay publication for heaven knows how long. When and if the review appears and if it strikes you as sufficiently intelligent,

> I shd. be glad thereafter to send you the rest of the notes I have made. Minutiae, too trifling to print. But at any rate I have gone through the book, I shd. think, syllable by syllable. And as Bridges and Leaf are no longer on the scene, the number of readers possessed of any criteria (however heretical) for the writing of English verse and at the same time knowing the difference between Dante and Dunhill is limited. . . . I was irritated by the inversions during the first 8 to 10 cantos, but having finished the book, I think you have in every (almost every) case chosen the lesser evil in dilemma. For 40 pages I wanted you to revise, after that I wanted you to go on with the Purgatorio and Paradiso before turning back to the black air. And I hope you will. I hope you are surviving the New England winter. . . .[2]

Binyon was surviving it very well. At sixty-five he had retired from his job at the British Museum and had gone to Cambridge, Massachusetts, for the academic year to give the Norton Lectures—he followed Eliot in that chair—lecturing not on poetry but on Oriental art. He replied from the Commander Hotel on February 18th:

> My dear Ezra Pound, I was very glad to hear from you, and to learn that you had read my Inferno version with so much interest. The difficulties are so immense—often I was in absolute despair—that after surmounting them in a way that didn't seem too bad one was inclined to rate the feat too highly: now, when I turn the pages again a lot of it seems terribly inadequate. (Of course *all of it* is inadequate; that goes without saying; but some passages read well, I think, at any rate apart from the Italian.) When you say 'inversions,' do you mean grammatical inversions or inversions of accent? I shall see when your review appears, if it does appear, as I hope. I shall certainly be very glad of your notes, as I know one can go on improving forever in the matter of details. Shall I go on with the Purgatory and Paradise? I don't know. It takes a devilish amount of time and hard work, but I have done I think 8 cantos of Purgatory so hope to finish that some day. We are having the severest winter on record in the States, but are surviving without any frostbitten members so far. The bright sun is welcome after grey London, which I have now left for good. . . .[3]

So ran the first exchange—friendly if a trifle wary on the part of both men (I hear a reticent gesture of *rapprochement* in Binyon's last remark about London). This led to four or five other exchanges in the course of 1934. Pound's letters were copious and high-spirited, Binyon's briefer and plainer; every now and then he would patiently maintain a point. He enjoyed the *Criterion* review which he found waiting for him in June on his return to England and to his retired farmhouse in Berkshire. He wrote to say that he felt encouraged and grateful, and venerable though he might be he had lots of energy left and hoped to go on. Pound reported in June: "Yeats rumbled in last week / also agreed that you had done a damn good job (my phrase, not his) . . . he assented with noble dignity."[4] As he had promised, Pound sent Binyon his review copy of the book with marginal notations, which Binyon recorded gratefully before returning the book in July. "Of course," he wrote, "in many places you pounce on [things] I should vastly have preferred to be quite plain and direct, but it is devilish hard to get the rhyme, at the same time—as you know. In fact, sometimes impossible. However, you have noted a number of lines wh. I shall try to improve."

In August Binyon wrote to thank Pound for sending him a copy of the Cavalcanti *Rime* in Pound's edition. He said: "I quite see that the having music in view was a gain to the lyric of Campion, etc., necessitating clearness, lightness, a clear contour. But it seems to me that you couldn't go on forever within those limits: and I don't see that the alternative is necessarily rhetorical declamation. Poetry to me is a kind of heavenly speech. . . ." As though by tacit agreement, neither man ever mentioned what each knew the other had in mind: the poetry of Milton. In November Binyon sent Pound versions of the first cantos of the *Purgatorio*. At the end of January, 1935, he added a few more and said that at Eliot's request he had sent the Sordello canto (V) to the *The Criterion*. Then he went off to Egypt to lecture. Pound continued to think the work over. On the 29th of April he concluded a letter (the last in this series):

> When you get the *Paradiso* done the edition shd. go into use in all university Dante study; at least in America. I don't know WHAT study is committed in England . . . possibly Dante is still considered an exotic. Temple edtn/ was used in my undergrad/ time, but yours sheds so infinitely much more light. . . . And as translation, I don't mean merely of Dante, but in proportion to any translation I can think of, I don't know of any that is more transparent in sense that reader sees the original through it. A translation that really has a critical value, i.e. enlightens one as to the nature of the original. That is rarissima. I don't think my own DO. I have emphasized or dragged into light

> certain things that matter (to me at any rate) but it is not the same thing. . . . I shall probably do a note on the Purg in Broletto [a new monthly magazine published at Como].[5]

After this there was a long hiatus in correspondence. It was nearly 3 years later, February 25th, 1938, when Binyon wrote again. "I imagine you will be thinking me extinct," he said. "I have at last finished the Purgatorio, and it has gone to the printer. I didn't want to bother you with bits at casual intervals but I wonder if you would care to look through proofs of the whole?" Pound agreed at once. Late in April the proofs were sent. Pound's letters with detailed comments now came thick and fast, more than half a dozen long letters on batches of cantos between April 22nd and May 12th.

Binyon had cautioned him: "But don't take *too* much trouble *now*; because, as my Inferno was a complete failure from the sales point of view and MacMillan lost over 200 over it, I can't expect them to pay for a heavy lot of corrections, nor can I afford to pay myself." This had not the slightest effect on Pound. Typical of Poundian comments gratefully received and acted on were his remarks on XI, 86–87, *gran disio del eccellenza*. as to which he wrote: " 'desire of excelling or beating someone else' is the meaning, not the 'desire of perfection,' Our 'excellence' is almost a synonym with 'goodness,' As the whole poem is one of fine moral distinctions, this dissociation is worth making."[6]

Wrote Binyon on April 27th: "What I have aimed at above all is getting something like Dante's 'tone of voice,' and my Italian critics and Italian friends all think this is the chief merit of my version. It is the first thing they say. (The English ones say terza rima is un-English, etc.)" Pound's enthusiasm mounted as he read. After Canto XVII he wrote: "MAGNIFICENT FINISH! Utterly confounds the apes who told you terza rima isn't English. . . . The beauty here would *only* have been got by using terza rima. Lascia dir gli stolti who don't see it and who have been for two centuries content that *technique* went out of English *metric* with Campion and Waller . . ." At Canto XXI he exclaimed, "Banzai, my dear BinBin. . . ." and at XXVIII, "Bravo, Bravo, Bravo. . . ."

We might listen to a passage from that Canto, XXVIII: the narrator's account of his meeting with Matilda in the *paradiso terrestre*:

> Already my slow steps had borne me on
> So far within that immemorial wood
> That I could no more see whence I had gone;
> And lo! a stream that stopped me where I stood;

And at the left the ripple in its train
  Moved on the bank the grasses where it flowed.
All waters here that are most pure from stain
  Would qualified with some immixture seem
  Compared with this, which veils not the least grain,
Altho' so dark, dark goes the gliding stream
  Under the eternal shadow, that hides fast
  Forever there the sun's and the moon's beam.
With my feet halting, with my eyes I passed
  That brook, for the regaling of my sight
  With the fresh blossoms in their full contrast,
And then appeared (as in a sudden light
  Something appears which from astonishment
  Puts suddenly all other thoughts to flight)
A lady who all alone and singing went,
  And as she sang plucked flowers that numberless
  All round about her path their colours blent.
'I pray thee, O lovely Lady, if, as I guess,
  Thou warm'st thee at the radiance of Love's fire,—
  For looks are wont to be the heart's witness,—
I pray thee toward this water to draw near
  So far,' said I to her, 'while thou dost sing,
  That with my understanding I may hear.
Thou puttest me in remembrance of what thing
  Proserpine was, and where, when by mischance
  Her mother lost her, and she lost the spring.'

The reader of severe contemporary taste and habituated to contemporary style may find this idiom—one, as Pound put it, "never spoken on sea or land"—at first glance an exercise in the antiquarian. But he will be aware of its clearness and fluency, and as he reads on he will, I believe, begin to feel, as Pound did, the distinction of its fashioning as a medium for the great medieval poem. This cumulative effect cannot be conveyed by quotation, but from the quoted passage the reader may gain an inkling of the means employed. One may notice, for example, in the third tercet the limpid monosyllables of the enclosing lines and the cunning "immixture" of polysyllables in the line enclosed. The fourth tercet is a good one in which to sense the evenness that Binyon achieved in weight of syllables, like musical notes, an effect twice assisted on this page by a flattening-out of the rhyme-word ("contrast" and "witness"). In the final tercet one may hearken not only to subdued alliteration ("puttest," "Proserpine," "mischance," "mother") but to covert internal rhyming ("hear," "where," "her"). Every one of these refinements is a resemblance to the Italian. So controlled and sustained is Binyon's artifice, and so free of any kind of flashiness, that it acquires a life of its own, and this life in the end seems very nearly the life of the original.

In Canto XXXII Pound came upon what he called "the *only* line of really *bad* poetry I have found. . . . 'But when she rolled on me her lustful eye' might be Gilbert and Sullivan. Positively the only line that is out of the sober idiom of the whole of your translation. Like Omerus he SLEPT. Moderate verb and adjective wanted." (Binyon toned it down.) At the end Pound wrote: "Once again my thanks for the translation. And there are damned few pieces of writing that I am thankful for. . . . Nobody has had such a good time of this kind since Landor did his notes on Catullus. . . . And now, Boss, you get RIGHT ALONG with that Paradiso as soon as you've stacked up the dinner dishes. . . ."

Binyon's *Purgatorio* was published in September, with an acknowledgement of Pound's assistance. As he had promised to do three years before, Pound wrote a notice of the book in Italian for *Broletto*. It appeared in Number 34, for October, 1938. This article has to my knowledge never been translated and has remained forgotten or unknown. Yet it expressed a serious and long meditated judgment, without reserve. It was headed: "BINYON: we greet a most valuable translation of the Divine Comedy," and it proceeded (my translation):

> I can repeat all the praises published in *The Criterion* when the translation of the *Inferno* appeared; but I must add still others. Constantly developing his technique, Binyon in his description of the Terrestrial Paradise reaches a true splendor and clarity never achieved before. It seems to me that this can be said not only in comparison with the other translations of Dante, but perhaps also in comparison with the whole body of translations into English of any author whatever . . .

What about Golding's Ovid and Douglas's *Aeneid*, old favorites of Pound? These were, he observed, works of poetry that had no need of the originals and served not as interpretations of the originals but as "comment" of a special kind.

> Binyon [he said], triumphs in another way, he triumphs through an honesty that from time to time amounts to genius. His version of Dante

gives me a clearer sense of the original. It is like a window with glass so polished that one is not aware of it, one has the impression of the open air. . . .

My generation in America suffered from the assumption that to understand Dante it was necessary to suffocate in a pile of commentary. I, at least, at seventeen was distracted by the abundance of comments and notes and sometimes lost the continuity of the poem. With a prose 'argument' of half a page or less for each Canto, Binyon has very clearly shown the falsity of this assumption. . . .

As for *terza rima*, Binyon achieves beauties that he could never have attained except by making the effort to employ this form, in which he gets a very English flavor with words like *coppices*, or *highlander* for *montanaro*. . . .

The defects of his version are superficial. I see none except in little inversions, which could easily disappear in a revision which the translator already intends to make as soon as he has finished the whole version of the poem. Some defects have already disappeared between the first proofs and those passed for the printer. . . .

But undoubtedly Binyon has already made us a triple gift. First true poetry, in his most felicitous pages. Second: a sense of the continuity and comprehensibility of the poem. Third: an assistance to students. . . . every class for the study of Italian poetry in any foreign university ought to make use of this version to facilitate the comprehension of the *Commedia*.

A decadence begins when attention turns to the ornamental element and is detached little by little from the meaning. In Dante (and in Guido) the meaning is extremely precise; if you doubt it, look at Canto XVIII of the *Purgatorio*. The idiom of Binyon's version is the idiom suitable for translating a poet to whom meaning was far more important than ornament. The defects are like nutshells on the table after a magnificent meal.[7]

## III

I digress from my story a little, but I'll return to it. The grace of God came to Dante in many forms but in none happier for his poem than the *terza rima*. It was a miraculous formal invention or *trouvaille*. As the formulaic hexameter buoyed and carried the Homeric singer, so the *terza rima* collaborated (it is not too much to say) in the making of the *Commedia*. It gave Dante what he needed for his narrative, a flexible unit beyond the line, capacious enough for description and figure, argument and speech, capable of endless varieties of internal organization, and yet so compact as to make for the famous concision; above all, through the ever-developing rhyme scheme, it gave him continuous movement forward. *Terza rima* is a formal paradigm of Aristotelian Becoming—the latent or "virtual" thing constantly coming into actuality, as each new tercet fulfils with enclosing rhyme the rhyme enclosed in the preceding one. The lyric tercet, moreover, conduced to the design of the poem in cantos or songs of lyric length (the average length in fact nearly conforms to Poe's limit for lyric, reckoned five hundred years after Dante). For these reasons and others, the life of the *Commedia* is inseparable from its form, and a prose rendering alters the nature of the animal even more drastically than usual. Implicit acknowledgment of this is made in the Temple Classics version where the Carlyle-Okey-Wicksteed prose is printed in units or versicles corresponding to Dante's tercets.

The "transparency" valued by Pound in Binyon's version was therefore a formal achievement: Binyon had emulated and matched in English the labor of the original poet in Italian, so that the reader could see through the movement of the English poem the movement of the original composer's invention, working in verse and in verse of just this kind. Of just this kind? Yes, insofar as the Italian hendecasyllable can be mached by decasyllabic lines in English. And in fact the one is closer to the other than may superficially appear. It is close historically, because Chaucer wrote his heroic line with continental syllabic verse, in particular Dante's Italian, in his ear (he was Dante's first translator), and easily every third line in Chaucer is hendecasyllabic because of the nature of Middle English. It is close rhythmically, by virtue of the phenomenon noted by Pound: that in many a "masculine" ending in English the terminal consonant will carry a latent following vowel sound similar at least to the semi-syllable of "e muet" if not to the Italian full vowel. The poet and scholar, F. T. Prince, has been able to argue that it was from the Italian hendecasyllable that Milton derived his line in *Paradise Lost*,[8] and Binyon in turn derived his system of elision from Milton as analysed by Robert Bridges. By the device he pointed out in his Preface and by other subtle means, he gave his lines the metrical character of the lightly running Italian.

Now twenty years of work on Binyon's part and nearly six years of attentive participation by Erza Pound led up to nothing less than the miseries and oblivions of the Second Great War. After sending drafts of the first *Paradiso* cantos to Pound and writing to him on December 29th, 1939, Laurence Binyon never heard again from his friend in Rapallo. The correspondence they had already had remained in their respective files. No English translation of Pound's *Broletto* article appeared, or was to appear until this writing. Binyon kept his pad on his knee in the wartime evenings; he finished his *Paradiso*. MacMillan published it in 1943. On March 10th of that year Laurence Binyon died in a nursing home in Reading, and his obituary appeared next day in the London *Times*. Along with it appeared news of the Russian armies defending Kharkov and the latest R.A.F. raid on Germany—five hundred tons on Munich. It was not a good year for Italian studies. If MacMillan had lost money on Binyon's *Inferno*, it certainly did not make any on his *Purgatorio* and *Paradiso*. In the event, indeed, all three volumes were allowed to go out of print for long periods and have almost never been in print at the same time.

So matters stood when the war ended in 1945. What trouble had come upon Ezra Pound it is hardly necessary to recall; few people knew or would know for years of his admiration for Binyon's Dante or the reason for it. Some Dantisti remained aware of the Binyon translation. When Paolo Milano edited a *Portable Dante* for Viking in 1947, MacMillan, for a "courtesy fee," allowed him to include Binyon's entire *Divine Comedy*. "Binyon," wrote Milano, "never distorts the original style; he never takes us beyond the range of Dante's own voice." But Binyon's preface, with its clues as to how this great virtue had been worked for, did not appear, nor was it quoted, in the Viking Portable.

W. H. Auden reviewed this book briefly but appreciatively in the New York *Times*; so did Louise Bogan in *The New Yorker*. In the United States the portable sold moderately for a while (bringing nothing, courtesy of MacMillan, to the Binyon heirs), and moderately, again, in a paperback edition (1955), but there was no counterpart in England during the '40s. In those years, however, Penguin Books began to bring out, as "Penguin Classics" under the general editorship of E. V. Rieu, paperback translations, like Rieu's *Odyssey*, priced within range of the railway bookstall trade. For the Penguin Dante, the translator selected was Dorothy Leigh Sayers, and her *Hell* was published in 1949.

It was a formidable work. She, too, had done the poem in English *terza rima*. She quoted Binyon's friend Maurice Hewlett as saying that for the translator of Dante it was "*terza rima* or nothing." With Anglo-Catholic ardor and intellectual bounce, the author of *Gaudy Night* and *The Nine Tailors* provided a long introduction, extremely full notes, and a glossary. In her time Dorothy Sayers had won a first in medieval literature at Somerville College, Oxford, and she wrote with professional skill. Her *Hell* caught on and has been reprinted practically every year. She followed it with a Penguin *Purgatory* in 1955, and after her death in 1957 her friend Barbara Reynolds, General Editor of the *Cambridge Italian Dictionary*, added the concluding dozen or so cantos of *Paradise* for publication in 1962. *Purgatory* and *Paradise* have been reprinted many times. All are to be found in university book stores in the United States.

One result of these estimable works, however, was not fortunate. If MacMillan had ever intended in the fullness of time to venture a new printing of Binyon's *Divine Comedy*, in the edition with Italian and English on facing pages, the currency of the Sayers version in inexpensive Penguins must have made such a venture seem quixotic. In 1965, in fact, when the question arose, MacMillan pondered a new printing and decided against it. One further development has probably ruled out the possibility forever. In 1972, Chatto and Windus brought out the Viking *Portable Dante* in England, re-titled *Dante: The Selected Works*. Remarkably enough, Binyon's name appears neither on the cover nor on the title page of this book, but his version of *The Divine Comedy* is now in print in this form (again minus the preface) in the United Kingdom. Neither there nor in the United States can you buy the bilingual edition that Pound thought should supplant the Temple Classics edition for the undergraduate study of Dante, and the chances are heavily against undergraduates or anyone else ever having it.

This being the case, and admitting the seriousness and utility of Dorothy Sayers' presentation, the quality of her translation, which has already represented the poetry of Dante to several generations of students, invites a little study. When she undertook her work, she was apparently unaware of Pound's *Criterion* review of Binyon's *Inferno*, nor could she have known of the Pound-Binyon correspondence, since none of it appeared in print until eight of Pound's letters were published by D. D. Paige in *The Letters of Ezra Pound* in 1950. If thereafter she became aware of this material, she gave no indication of it in her *Purgatory* or *Paradise*. This may or may not have been to her advantage. Consider the question of feminine rhyming in imitation of the Italian Hendecasyllabic line.

"I have used a liberal admixture of feminine rhyme," she wrote in her first introduction. "This is the usual English custom, and I do not know why Dante's translators for the most part fight shy of it." It was perhaps an understandable perplexity, but it had already been resolved by Binyon and Pound. Even without benefit of that solution, the translator might have reflected that a *liberal* admixture of lines that differ in termination from the norm is not like Dante's practice. His *versi tronchi* (accent on the ultima) and *versi sdruccioli* (accent on the antepenult) are rare and exceptional. But once her decision was taken, Sayers went vigorously ahead and allowed herself a good deal of the rhyming "excrescence" that Pound thought out of place in the *Commedia*. At the opening of *Inferno* XXII, for example, she composed four successive tercets with nothing but feminine rhymes and in the fifth added a flourish of the *sdrucciolo* type. It is true that in the Italian of this passage there are subtle irregularities of accent, but the effect of the Sayers English is to carry these to the point of burlesque—and what is true of this passage is true of all too many others.

One might argue that variety of this kind, not only in meter and rhyming but in diction as well (she did the Provençal of Arnaut in *Purgatorio* XXVI in Border Scots) make the Sayers translation more readable and save it from monotony. That may be true in this sense: clearheaded and ingenious as she was, but endowed with limited gifts as an English poet or stylist, Dorothy Sayers did well to conceive her work in a way that would utilize her strengths. Her translation is not often dull and is almost always clear—at times clearer than Binyon's. Let one example suffice, *Paradiso* VIII, 49–51:

Così fatta, mi disse: 'Il modo m'ebbe
giù poco tempo; e se più fosse stato,
molto sarà di mal, che non sarebbe. . . .'

Binyon: Transfigured thus, it spoke: 'The world below
Held me not long; and much would not have happed,
Had it been longer, that now comes in woe. . . .'

Sayers: And shining thus he said: "The earthly scene
Held me not long: had more time been allowed
Much ill that now shall happen had not been. . . ."

With her command of workmanlike English and her chosen latitude in rendering, she managed often enough, as in this case, to avoid the "faults of the original"—and of Binyon—in the matter of inverted word order. Without reference to the Italian, as an extended work converting Dante tercet by tercet into English verse, her *Comedy* is a considerable achievement.

Binyon's is simply an achievement of a higher order. His taste is finer. He does not indulge those bright ideas that confuse everything. His style is distinguished and steady, as for all its resouces of idiom and invention one feels Dante's style to be. He had indeed caught Dante's "tone of voice." His or any English must be more humid than the dry burning Italian, more muted in sonority, less Latinate and closely-knit. But line by line he represents his original with that honesty amounting to genius that Pound remarked. In order fairly to support this judgment, let me examine in both versions a passage of some length, at a point in the poem where each translator after much practice may be supposed capable of his best—the opening of the *Paradiso*.

La gloria di colui che tutto move
per l'universo penetra e risplende
in una parte più e meno altrove.

Sayers: The glory of Him who moves all things soe'er
Impenetrates the universe, and bright
The splendour burns, more here and lesser there.

Occurring at the end of the first line, "soe'er" could not be a more noticeable archaism. It is also an addition to what the Italian says, and it concludes the line with a double sibilance following the plural "things." No less conspicuous in another way is "impenetrates" in line 2, an uncommon word that seems tautological rather than intensive; in fact, as it adds nothing to the idea of penetration, it seems forced. In line 3, the verb "burns" goes beyond the Italian, and does so emphatically through the position of the verb at the point of caesura.

Binyon: The glory of Him who moveth all that is
Pervades the universe, and glows more bright
In the one region, and in another less.

Here there is archaism in the old form, "moveth," but the word occurs mid-line and is compact, not fluttery. It serves to avoid sibilance, and it reproduces the dissylabic Italian *move*. "All that is" preserves the singular of the Italian *tutto*. In line 2, "pervades" is the right word to render penetration by light, and the three syllables of "glows more bright," follow the contour of *risplende*. Getting in the comparative in this line not only accords with English idiom but makes it easy for the next line to retain the chiastic order of the Italian, "more . . . in the one region . . . in another . . . less." Moreover, the word *parte* is translated here, as it is not by Sayers.

Nel ciel che più della sua luce prende
fu'io, e vidi cose che ridire
ne sa ne può chi di la su discende;

Sayers: Within that heav'n which most receives His light
Was I, and saw such things as man nor knows
Nor skills to tell, returning from that height:

"Most" in line 1 is adverbial with "receives" and barely suggests the partitive genitive of *più della sua luce*. The verb "receives" connotes more passivity than *prende*. In line 2, "was I" closely renders the past definite *fu'io*, as "saw" does *vidi*, but vagueness begins with "as man nor knows/ nor skills to tell." First of all, this adds a good deal to the Italian by making the subject generic. The implication that this is an experience of mankind in general befogs the precision of the singular (though indefinite) subject understood and the singular pronoun of the Italian. Secondly, by pressure of English idiom (we cannot say that one "knows to tell"), as by the line division here, the alternatives suggested are knowing on the one hand and having skill to tell on the other, which misrepresents the original.

Binyon: In that heaven which partakes most of His light
I have been, and have beheld such things as who
Comes down thence has no wit nor power to write;

"Partakes most of His light" renders the active force of the Italian verb and partitive expression. "I have been," the English perfect, though a looser rendering of *fu'io*, is not only allowable but suitable to the tone of the passage as expressing a more contemplative and less purely narrative time sense. There is concision in "comes down thence," and "has no wit nor power" not only renders the alternatives correctly but unfolds what is latent in the two Italian verbs.

perchè appressando se al suo disire,
nostro intelletto si profonda tanto,
che dietro la memoria non può ire.

Sayers: For when our intellect is drawing close
To its desire, its paths are so profound
That memory cannot follow where it goes.

The first line and a half closely render the Italian, but the next clause expands the metaphor with an image, "paths," that raises two questions: first, why the plural? and second, why such a degree of concreteness as to make that question arise? In line 3, *dietro ire* is presumed to mean "follow," implying a relationship between intellect and memory that is only superficially plausible.

Binyon: Such depth our understanding deepens to
When it draws near unto its longing's home
That memory cannot backward with it go.

Here line 1 subtly embodies equivalences to the quality of the Italian: a four-syllable word, "understanding," to match and even chime with the participle *appressando*, and alliteration of four "ds" to match the"s's" and "ds" of the original. In line 3 the Italian is interpreted more precisely than in the Sayers version; here it is not that memory cannot "follow" the intellect but that it cannot return with it, taking *dietro* to mean "back," or indeed "back again," rather than "behind."

Are such points as these mere niggling? Before us on the open page is the philosophical poem of Christendom. It was written, as Ezra Pound once said, to make people think. In every line it exemplifies that activity. The translator's first job is to render Dante's meaning exactly and with delicacy. His second but no less crucial job is to render what he can—and again, with delicacy—of the verbal and metrical form in which the poet did his thinking. It sees that in both respects, again and again, one translation surpasses the other—not a bad one, either—bearing out what Pound said in *Broletto* about Binyon's idiom. But let us continue.

Veramente quant'io de regno santo
nella mia mente potei far tesoro,
sarà ora matera del mio canto.

Sayers: Yet now, of the blest realm whate'er is found
Here in my mind still treaseured and possessed
Must set the strain for all my song to sound.

"Whate'er" in line 1 rarefies the solid *quanto*. The agent *io* and the past action of treasuring up are transposed to a present passive construction. In the monysllabic line 3, there is insensitive alliteration of four "s's," and the businesslike *sarà ora matera* becomes a tired poeticality, "must set the strain."

Binyon: Nevertheless what of the blest kingdom
Could in my memory, for its treasure, stay
Shall now the matter of my song become.

The echo of the Latin *verumtamen* in *Veramente* has been perceived and carried into the rendering. *Quanto* is, curtly, "what," and is first the subject of a past action as in the Italian it was the object of one, then the subject of a future statement exactly, and in exactly the same terms, as in the Italian.

O buono Apollo, all' ultimo lavoro
fammi del tuo valor si fatto vaso,
come dimandi a dar l'amato alloro.

Sayers: Gracious Apollo! in this crowning test
Make me the conduit that thy power runs through!
Fit me to wear those bays thou lovest best!

Here several displacements have occurred, from *buono* to "gracious" for Apollo, from *ultimo lavoro* to something quite different, a "crowning test," and most interesting of all, from *vaso* to a "conduit" through which the god's power is conceived to run. For the covert and intricate alliterative pattern of the third Italian line (*me . . . man . . . ma* . . . and *di . . . di . . . da*) we have "bays . . . best". In this final phrase a small ambiguity appears: do we understand that bays in general are what the god loves best, or that there are certain ("those") bays that among all bays he loves best?

Binyon: For the last labour, good Apollo, I pray,
Make me so apt a vessel of thy power
As is required for gift of thy loved bay.

Here lines 1 and 2, without obscurity or difficulty, adhere to the vocabulary of the Italian including "vessel" for *vaso,* not less felicitious for not narrowing the conception to an open channel or pipe. The last line lacks any such obvious alliteration as that of the Sayers version, but the closing consonants of "gift" are quietly echoed by those of "loved," and the vowel sound of "required" is echoed by "thy."

## IV

Though Binyon finished his *Paradiso* without benefit of Pound's criticism, he undoubtedly brought to bear on it what he had absorbed from Pound's notes on the other two *cantiche*. As to the *Inferno,* in recording Pound's marginal notations in 1934 he said he intended some day to bring out a revised edition, and this in fact became a serious undertaking. Using an extra set of clean page proofs of the poem, he went through it canto by canto, making in pen revisions of lines or passages that either he or Pound had found improveable. It is uncertain when most of this work was done; whether he did indeed wait until he had finished the *Paradiso* before returning to the "black air," as Pound suggested, or whether he began at once in 1934 and gave occasional hours to revision over the next eight or nine years. When he died he left among his papers a full set of page proofs of all thirty-four cantos, each bearing a number of revisions, in all more than 500, in almost all cases clear improvements.

The value of this concluding labor was clear to Binyon's widow, who typed out all the revisions and intended to have them incorporated in a new MacMillan printing. This has never taken place. The revisions remained among Binyon's papers until the late '60s when Binyon's daughter, Nicolete (Mrs. Basil Gray), contrived to get them incorporated in the *Viking Portable* text, in a new edition dated 1969. The very first of these revisions may stand as representative of them all. Canto I, line 1 of the *Inferno* in 1934:

> Midway the journey of this life I was 'ware . . .

In the new edition:

> Midway life's journey I was made aware . . .

The first version announced to the ear at once Binyon's system of elisions (journey of) and his deliberate allowance of a quota of archaism in style ('ware). Evidently to his later judgment, certainly influenced by Pound, these features were not enough to justify such a finicky line. He replaced it with what Pound called "straightness."

# Notes

1. Ezra Pound, "Hell," *Literary Essays of Ezra Pound*, ed. with an introduction by T. S. Eliot (London, 1954), 201.

2. Ezra Pound, *The Letters of Ezra Pound*, ed. D. D. Paige (New York, 1950), 251.

3. This and other letters of Laurence Binyon are quoted by kind permission of Nicolete Gray and The British Society of Authors. I am very grateful to Mrs. Gray for her consideration in placing these and other papers of her father at my disposal.

4. Quoted from letters in the possession of Nicolete Gray. For permission to use these letters I am grateful to the Literary Executors of Ezra Pound.

5. From a letter in the possession of Nicolete Gray.

6. Ezra Pound, *The Letters of Ezra Pound*, 310.

7. Ezra Pound, "Binyon," *Broletto, Periodico della Città di Como*, 3 (October, 1938), 14. For the opportunity of consulting this periodical and copying portions of Pound's article, I am indebted to the kindness of Professor Louis Martz, in 1975 Director of the Beinecke Rare Book Library of Yale University.

8. F. T. Prince, *The Italian Element in Milton's Verse* (Oxford, 1954), rev. 1962.

# Bibliographical Sources


Bergin, Thomas G. "Dante's Provençal Gallery." *Speculum* 40 (1965): 15–30. Published by the Medieval Academy of America and reprinted here with their permission.

Bigongiari, Dino. "The Art of the Canzone," from "Notes on the Text of Dante," *The Romanic Review* 41 (1950): 81–95. Reprinted by permission. This essay has been reprinted more recently as "Appendix: The Art of the Canzone," in *Essays on Dante and Medieval Culture*. Florence: Leo S. Olschki, 1964.

Da Ponte, Lorenzo. "Critique on Certain Passages in Dante." *The New York Review and Atheneum Magazine* 1 (1825): 156–58, 241–42, 325–27.

Eliot, T. S. "A Talk on Dante." An address delivered at the Italian Institute in London, and published as "What Dante Means to Me" in *To Criticize the Critic* by T. S. Eliot. Copyright 1965 by Valerie Eliot. Reprinted by permission of Farrar, Straus and Giroux, Inc.

Fergusson, Francis. "The Fine Veil of Poetry," "The Prophetic First Night," and "On the Dramatic Coherence of the Canto," in Francis Fergusson, *Dante's Drama of the Mind: A Modern Reading of the Purgatorio*. Princeton: Princeton University Press, 1953. Reprinted by permission of Princeton University Press.

Fitzgerald, Robert Stuart. "Mirroring the *Commedia*: An Appreciation of Laurence Binyon's Version." *Paideuma* 10 (Winter 1981): 489–508. Reprinted with permission from *Paideuma*, vol. 10–3; copyright 1981 by the National Poetry Foundation, Univ. of Maine, Orono, Me.

Freccero, John. "*Paradiso X*: The Dance of the Stars." *Dante Studies* 86 (1968): 85–111. Reprinted with permission of the Dante Society of America.

Grandgent, Charles H. "The Pentateuch and the Divine Comedy." *Dante Society of America Annual Reports* 47–48 (1929–30): 1–17. Reprinted with permission of the Dante Society of America.

Gray, John Chipman. Review of 1813 edition of *La Divina Commedia di Dante Allighieri*. *North American Review* 8 (1819): 322–47.

Harris, W. T. "The Spiritual Sense of Dante's *Divina Commedia*." *The Journal of Speculative Philosophy* 21 (1887): 349–63, 424–25, 436–51.

Hollander, Robert. " 'Vita Nuova': Dante's Perceptions of Beatrice." *Dante Studies* 92 (1974): 1–18. Reprinted with permission of the Dante Society of America.

Longfellow, Henry Wadsworth. Review of "*A History of the Italian Language and Dialects: Saggi di Prose e Poesie de' piu celebri scrittori d'ogni secolo*, vol. 6, selected by L. Nardini and S. Buonauti. London, 1798." *North American Review* 35 (October 1832): 288–99.

Longfellow, Henry Wadsworth. *Poets and Poetry of Europe*. Cambridge: Metcalf & Co., 1845.

Lowell, James Russell. "Dante." *Among My Books* (2nd series). Boston: J. R. Osgood & Co., 1876.

Mazzeo, Joseph. *Medieval Cultural Tradition in Dante's "Comedy."* Ithaca: Cornell University Press, 1960. Used by permission of the publisher, Cornell University Press.

Norton, Charles Eliot. " 'The New Life' of Dante." *The Atlantic Monthly* 3 (March 1859): 330–39. Reprinted with permission of The Atlantic Monthly Company, Boston, Mass.

Pound, Ezra. "Hell," review of *Dante's Inferno translated into English Triple Rhyme*, by Laurence Binyon. *The Criterion* 13 (April 1934): 382–96; repr. in *The Literary Essays of Ezra Pound*, ed. T. S. Eliot, London: Faber and Faber, 1954. Copyright 1934 by Ezra Pound. Reprinted by permission of New Directions.

Rand, Edward Kennard. "Dante and Servius." *Dante Society of America Annual Reports* 33 (1914): 1–11. Reprinted with permission of the Dante Society of America.

Santayana, George. "Dante." *Three Philosophical Poets*. Cambridge: Harvard University Press, 1910. Copyright 1938 by George Santayana. Reprinted with permission of Harvard University.

Silverstein, Theodore. "On the Genesis of *De Monarchia*, II, v." *Speculum* 13 (1938): 326–49. Published by the Medieval Academy of America and reprinted with their permission.

Singleton, Charles S. "Dante's Allegory," *Speculum* 25 (1950): 78–86. Published by the Medieval Academy of America and reprinted with their permission.

Tate, Allen. "The Symbolic Imagination: The Mirrors of Dante." *Essays of Four Decades*. Chicago: Swallow Press, Inc., 1968. Reprinted with permission of Ohio University Press.

Wilkins, Ernest Hatch. "Dante and the Mosaics of his 'Bel San Giovanni.' " *Speculum* 2 (1927): 1–10. Published by the Medieval Academy of America and reprinted here with their permission.

**Dante in America: The First Two Centuries** brings together significant essays on Dante from John Chipman Gray's review (1813), which established Cambridge as a center of Dante studies, to Robert Fitzgerald's sensitive essay on Lawrence Binyon's translation of the *Comedy*. Selections from Longfellow, Norton, and Lowell display their important contributions to Dante studies; W. T. Harris explores philosophical aspects, as does Santayana. C. H. Grandgent writes on the *Comedy* and the Pentateuch; E. K. Rand provides a classical viewpoint. Theodore Silverstein studies *De Monarchia*; Bigongiari writes on the *canzone*; Singleton, on Dante's allegory, and Bergin, on Dante and Provençal. Generous selections are included from the work of Lorenzo da Ponte, E. H. Wilkins, Francis Fergusson, Allen Tate, Joseph Mazzeo, Robert Hollander and John Freccero. The collection also includes lesser-known pieces by Ezra Pound and T. S. Eliot, embodying the continuing conversation between English and American *dantisti*.

The volume demonstrates broadly the impact that Dante has had on American letters and thought, and is not confined solely to literary criticism. Included are representative essays from people either born in America, or born abroad but educated here, from as early as possible in America's history to the present, and from a variety of perspectives. Beneath the literary, philosophical, and cultural comment on Dante, one can hear the constant exchange of English and American voices as our culture seeks to find the voice truly appropriate to Dante. Like so much else in American intellectual and cultural history, the response to Dante has been an exercise in translation.

**A. Bartlett Giamatti** is president of Yale University and a scholar of both Renaissance and medieval literature, with emphasis on Dante and Provençal poetry. He is also the author or editor of numerous books and articles on Renaissance epic. He held the first John Hay Whitney professorship, has received the honorary title of Commander in the Order of Merit of the Italian Republic (1979), and was elected a Fellow of the American Academy of Arts and Sciences in 1980.

# mrts

**medieval & renaissance texts & studies**
is the publishing program of the
Center for Medieval & Early Renaissance Studies
at the State University of New York at Binghamton.

**mrts** emphasizes books that are needed —
texts, translations, and major research tools.

**mrts** aims to publish the highest quality scholarship
in attractive and durable format at modest cost.